An Etienne Gilson Tribute

Photo by Ashley & Crippen, Toronto

An
Etienne Gilson
Tribute

Presented by his North American Students
with a Response *by Etienne Gilson*

CHARLES J. O'NEIL, *Editor*

THE MARQUETTE UNIVERSITY PRESS · MILWAUKEE

ᏅᎣ Foreword

✿ ✿ ✿ ✿ ✿ ✿ ✿ ✿ ✿ ✿ ✿ ✿ ✿ ✿

TRIBUTE is an old word with a long history. We who use it here do not use it in its more primitive sense of answer to an imposed obligation. Indeed, we could not. For the man we honor is now actively completing his thirteenth year as Director of Studies in the Pontifical Institute of Mediaeval Studies, Toronto. As he completes these three decades he also completes his own seventy-fifth year. It is already a long career well marked with honors and distinctions, but not with the imposition of obligation; for it is marked most distinctively by a free and generous devotion not only to the loving pursuit of wisdom but marked also by sharing with his students and colleagues the fruits and methods of his scholarship. Tribute, then, we are using in its later sense of honor, praise, meed, acclaim. To be sure, for the honorable and praiseworthy any occasion is suitable for honor. Which is no doubt the reason why Etienne Gilson has received so many marks of honor.[1] But since—as Aristotle and his proverb have it—"friendship is in sharing," all who have shared in the preparation of this volume are themselves deeply honored. For Etienne Gilson has joined them in this volume; and thus it is not only a tribute to him, but a tribute to them and through them a tribute to his students everywhere. *Amicus amicis. Amici amico.*

To be sure, if all the students and colleagues, who are ready, willing and able to pay honor to Gilson were included this

[1] For a list up to the date of its publication see Maritain, Forest, Gouhier et al. *Étienne Gilson: Philosophie de la Chrétienté.* (Paris: Editions du Cerf, 1949). Among others since that publication have been the Aquinas Medal of the American Catholic Philosophical Association, 1952; the Mellon Lectures, 1951; and the three testimonial volumes of 1959 of which this volume is but one. Like the list of his honors Gilson's bibliography is not yet at an end but for a recent statement see A. C. Pegis, *A Gilson Reader* (New York: Doubleday, 1957), especially pp. 347-53.

modest volume would run to quite a number. Hence the conviction of the Board of Editors that those who do appear are but delegates for many, many more. Spatially those who have united in the preparation of this volume span the whole of the North American continent; temporally they reach over the whole of Gilson's thirty years at Toronto. Our tribute marks a date in a career and a life, but a continually and continuously active career and life. *Ad multos annos.*

The unity of this volume has deeper sources than temporal and geographical grouping. These brief prefatory remarks can indicate only two. Our authors are united in freedom and independence of scholarship. History shows that philosophers sometimes have produced only commentator-disciples. The teacher's ambition is greater: to produce students characterized by freedom and independence of worthwhile scholarly judgment. The authors herein present their own philosophical and historical judgment on the topics with which they deal. To their freedom and independence the best testimony that can be given is a simple historical fact. When there was question of grouping these studies topically the only thing the editor, Board, and authors could be brought to agree on was the alphabet. Clearly Gilson has the honor of having contributed to the formation of independent scholars. For a teacher there is hardly a tribute higher than this.

A second profound tribute and deep source of unity lies in respect for the notion and possibility of Christian philosophy. But even within this framework there is little or no dogmatic or methodic unity. What happens is rather this. In these pages some of the authors are doing the work of Christian philosophy. But what they have in common with their teacher and friend, the "philosophe de la Chrétienté" is neither a dogmatic content nor a methodological unity. Rather it appears to be a sharing with him in a unity which is the serenity of the Faith. Even this remark should not be taken as exclusive or "divisive." For anyone who has read Gilson or meditated with him ever so little on *fides quaerens intellectum* or *intellectus quaerens fidem* knows that there is nothing merely parochial about his pursuit of the truth. This is a faith seeking the reason to make it more reasonable, and a reason seeking the faith to perfect its rationality. Consequently, those who love or have loved wisdom in any age are or have been his colleagues, and faith and reason alike make dear to him in love the assurance that "the truth shall make you free." To such a man a volume in testimony to the triumph of belief within deepened rationality and the crowning of rationality by a serene faith is a fitting tribute.

In brief, we of the Board of Editors feel that this volume presents a timely tribute of honor and thanks from all of Etienne Gilson's North American students and colleagues. But special thanks are also due to those who have made the published volume itself possible.[2] To the Pontifical Institute of Mediaeval Studies, to St. Louis University, to the American Catholic Philosophical Association (in particular to the late Right Reverend Monsignor Charles A. Hart), and to Marquette University the Board of Editors is grateful for special financial assistance.

CHARLES J. O'NEIL

---

[2] In every study the references are those of the author of the study. But the editor wishes here to express his personal thanks to the authors for their singular patience and affability; to Mr. Patrick Coffey, his graduate assistant in Marquette University for invaluable help with references and proofs; and to the library staffs of Marquette University, Northwestern University, and the University of Chicago.

ß✍ Contents

☆ ☆ ☆ ☆ ☆ ☆ ☆ ☆ ☆ ☆ ☆ ☆ ☆ ☆

৯৯ Is God's Knowledge Scientific? A Study in Thomism

by James F. Anderson

The setting of the question

WHEN ONE ENTERS into the question of predicating the "scientific" of God's knowledge, certain landmarks of Thomistic metaphysics appear. When one views God's knowledge in the perspective given by such landmarks, both divine and human "science" are evaluated afresh. In approaching the "scientific" character of God's knowledge, therefore, we will first direct our attention to a few of these landmarks. We will then consider the difficulties or objections which may be raised against predicating the "scientific" of God's knowledge. And when we have noted the metaphysical considerations which arise, we will be in a position to dispose of these objections.

First, then, names expressing "pure" or intrinsically unlimited perfections signify God Himself. Although they are predicated substantially of Him, they do fall short in infinite degree of representing Him as He is; God immeasurably exceeds the whole of that creation from which our scant knowledge of Him is wholly gleaned.[1]

Man, in this life, cannot know the essence of God in its own being, but only its shadowing forth in the perfections of finite things. Thus do human words speak of Him.[2] And properly so with respect to the divine reality which they adumbrate, though not at all so far as their mode of signification is concerned, which

---

[1] *Summa Theologiae* I, q. 13, a. 2, with *Summa Contra Gentiles* I, 51; *Quaestiones disputatae: De potentia Dei* q. 7, aa. 2, 4, 5.

[2] *Sum. Theol.* I, q. 13, a. 2, ad 3m.

must needs be either "concrete," as befits only composite things, or "abstract," and therefore incompatible save w i t h the non-sub-sistent.[3]

Next, let us note that although such names designate the simple substance of God, their significance varies. For while the divers created actualities grounding all our ideas flow from a unique Source, are one in It and with It, they nonetheless exist in our thoughts not as one, but as many. Man's multifarious conceptions of God have all a common point of reference: a single incomplex principle. Accordingly, the names he applies to God signify the selfsame divine Reality in many different ways through notions dimly reflecting some facets of His infinite nature.[4]

This is also fundamental: that it is upon identity in essence that univocal predication is properly grounded. And since God and creatures are infinitely diverse in essence, nothing can be said of them univocally. Perfections present in creatures are distinct from one another and from the essence of the thing possessing them. The creature is thus said to have them but not to be them, whereas God is His perfections. And because all that a creature has and is, is limited, a name which is applied to a particular creature's perfection and is thought of as a property of its essence does "in a manner circumscribe and comprehend the thing signified";[5] but this is by no means true of the same name said of God.

The difficulties

The statement of these basic positions does not, of course, sweep away the special difficulties of predicating science or scientific of God. And these difficulties we ought now to gather together from St. Thomas' various statements of them.

There is the argument, for example, that science shares the lot of all intellectual knowledges in the accidentality of its being; whereas God is without accidents.

Moreover, since science is the fruit of a certain process from principles to conclusions,[6] it necessarily signifies something caused.

---

[3] *Ibid.*, 2, 3 with a. 1, ad 2m: cf. *S. G. G.* I, 30; *Scripta super libros Sententiarum* I d. 22, q. 1, a. 1; d. 8, q. 4, a. 3; *De potentia Dei* q. 7, a. 4, ad 6m.

[4] *Sum. Theol.* I, q. 13, a. 4, with *S. C. G.* I, 5, and *De potentia Dei* q. 7, a. 4.

[5] *Sum. Theol.* I, q. 13, a. 5, c.

[6] This formula is properly interpretable as embracing every genuine work of rational inquiry, for all variously seek in common true knowledge of what is.

And one asks whether an effect can befit the nature of that which is uncaused.

Then, too, every science is either universal or particular. Now if it is universal, it is abstract and consequently non-subsistent; if it is particular, it is limited. Nothing qualified in either way can be said of God. And it does no good to object that God's knowledge is universal in the sense of extending to all things, for even so it would have to be abstractively universal in its mode; the singular is never a direct and proper object of intellect.

One observes, moreover, the inherent imperfection of all abstractive knowledge; it is only in their individual being that things are known as they really are; any general understanding of them must needs remain comparatively defective. Individuality and commonness are incompossible.

Furthermore, even if it could be shown that God's knowledge of Himself is "scientific," His knowledge of created, i.e., contingent, things could not be so; science is of the necessary.[7]

Consider, also, that "science, unlike wisdom," signifies knowledge through secondary, not simply ultimate causes.[8] Now God knows only through the loftiest principle — Himself. He therefore enjoys wisdom, but not science.

Then there is the reminder that while God's simplicity precludes all manyness, he who speaks of "science" invokes the plurality of knower, knowable, and known. Nor is this all.

For if "science" signified the divine substance — God himself — how could any other perfection possibly exist in Him? Indeed what remains in the human substance unexpressed by the word "man"? But clearly science does not mean goodness, nor love, justice or mercy, nor even wisdom. Would not one therefore monstrously assert its substantial identification with God? And yet denial of this claim is admission of its improper ascription to Him.

Lastly, one hears the Aristotelian dictum: science concerns conclusions, intellect, principles;[9] the knowledge that is science is terminal, not inceptive. God, however, knows nothing after the fashion of a conclusion derived from any kind of premises; process, inquiry, research, discourse—all are alien to His way of knowing.

---

[7] Aristotle, *Posterior Analytics* i. 2. 71b 15.

[8] *Cf. Sum. Theol.* I-II, q. 57, a. 2.

[9] Cf. Aristotle, *Nichomachaean Ethics* vi. 6. 1140b 31.

In short, God understands, but He is without *science*.[10]

Now it is a fact that St. Thomas Aquinas often uses the word *scientia* in speaking of God's knowledge.[11] Is he really implying that God properly possesses science, or has he only in mind a sweeping notion entitling any sound and certain knowledge to that name?[12]

The analogical consideration of scientia

The Aristotelian concept of science, supposedly well known, contains a value frequently missed or ignored. For Aristotle the unqualifiedly scientific mode of cognition (ἐπίστασθαι) consists in knowing the proper cause, precisely as such, upon which an effect depends, grasping likewise the ontological necessity involved.[13] In this what presently interests us is an implication that St. Thomas sees.

He comments that we are said to know a thing simply or unqualifiedly through apprehending it "in itself"; to know it in another is to have but a relative or qualified understanding. Several possibilities present themselves. One can know a thing in its subject, either as a part in a whole (e.g. knowing a house by perceiving its wall), or as an accident in a subject (e.g. knowing a man by observing him approaching), or as an effect in a cause (e.g. knowing a conclusion or an effect by having foreknowledge of it in its premises or causes), or, he adds, in any similar manner.[14] This includes every case of understanding a thing otherwise than "in itself."

Now the question immediately arises whether the statement that absolute scientific knowledge consists in knowing a thing in itself, is reconcilable with the celebrated *certa cognitio per causas?*

According to St. Thomas the act of "science" (*scire*) is a "perfect" way of knowing: "*scire aliquid est perfecte cognoscere ipsum.*" He says not "comprehensive," "exhaustive," nor even "complete." *Scire* means to know a thing in its achieved being (*per-factum*);

[10] The preceding arguments have numerous loci, explicit and implicit, in St. Thomas' writings. For example, see *Sum. Theol.* I, q. 14, aa. 1, 6; I-II, q. 57, a. 2; II-II, q. 9, a. 2; *In I Sent.* d. 35, q. 1; *Quaestiones Disputatae: De veritate* q. 2, a. 1.

[11] *E.g.,* in *Sum. Theol.* I, q. 14, a. 3; *In I Sent.* d. 35. q. 1; *S. C. G.* I, 44; *De potentia Dei* q. 7, a. 5.

[12] *Cf.* Aristotle, *Post. Anal.* i. 3. 72b 18.

[13] *Post. Anal.* i. 2. 71b 8.

[14] ". . . aliquid dicimur scire simpliciter quando scimus illud in seipso. Dicimur scire aliquid secundum quid, quando scimus illud in alio. . . . Et hoc est scire per accidens." *In Post Anal.* i. cap. 2, lect. 4, no. 4.

nothing else, nothing more, nor less, is implied. We are here asked to entertain the proposition that "science" is knowledge of a thing as it is, which means grasping the truth of it, for the principles of a thing's being and its truth are the same.[15] Bear in mind that this conception admits and requires the full breadth of analogical interpretation in the light of the unrestricted transcendentality of all these terms — "thing," "actually," "is," "truth."

Here, in the simplest affirmative language, is the doctrine that to know a thing *scientifically* is to know it in itself; that to know it in itself is to know it in its truth; that if the thing is an effect, then to know it in its truth is to know it in relation to its cause, (since it is and truly is only as caused); that were the effect known as caused but not precisely as the effect of its cause, there would be no unqualified scientific knowledge of it.[16] Such knowledge, moreover, is by essence "certain," i.e., simply determinate or exclusive of relativity.[17]

Indeed, it is true that the act of science or scientific knowing is for St. Thomas brought about by judging with certainty respecting the truth of something: "Man attains to certainty of judgment concerning truth through a discursive process of reasoning, and thus human science is acquired from the demonstrative reason."[18]

Reiterated for centuries, this doctrine nevertheless contains the insufficiently noticed point that the accomplished act of scientific cognition is intuitive or intellective, the discourse being but a means to it, however essential in the ordinary acquisition of such knowledge; in other words, that this demonstrative scientific way of knowing is not ratiocinative save procedurally; that when conclusions are *seen* in the light of principles, then alone is science achieved, the rational movement having found fulfillment in un-

---

[15] ". . . scire aliquid est perfecte cognoscere ipsum, hoc autem est perfecte apprehendere veritatem ipsius: eadem enim sunt principia esse rei et veritatis ipsius . . ." In *Post Anal.* i. cap. 2, lect. 4, no. 5.

[16] St. Thomas, *ibid.*

[17] "Certitudo nihil aliud est quam determinatio intellectus ad unum . . ." *In III Sent.* d. 23, q. 2, a. 2, sol. 3, c. *Cf. De veritate* q. 6, a. 3, c.; *Sum. Theol.* II-II, q. 4, a. 8, c.; also my study, "The Notion of Certitude," *The Thomist*, XVIII, (Oct., 1955), p. 526.

[18] "Homo consequitur certum judicium de veritate per discursum rationis; et ideo scientia humana ex ratione demonstrativa acquiritur." *Sum. Theol.* II-II, q. 9, a. 1, ad 1m.

derstanding (*intellectus*),[19] through a terminal act, moreover, that is judgmental.[20]

True enough, man comes into possession of certitude of judgment by discursive means. But God has it immediately through simple intuition.[21]

Consider why discourse is foreign to God's knowledge.[22] Comparing our knowledge to His,[23] we see that ours entails a double discursus: mere psychic succession from knowledge of one thing to that of another, but also a properly logical procedure through causal connections, understanding of principles or premises initiating a movement toward the attainment of conclusions caused by them. Of course neither process is possible in the cognitive act of a being without potency; God sees all things together in one Thing, Himself: "*Deus effectus suos in seipso videat sicut in causa.*"[24]

Does this last phrase mean that God's knowledge is not merely *cognitio* but also *scientia?* An affirmative answer may develop in succeeding pages but not without some preparations.

Note first, then, that St. Thomas has said not that God knows His effects *per causam,* but *in causa.* The prior formulation could imply movement from a cause previously known toward the knowledge of effects yet unknown; clearly, not so does God understand "through the cause." He rather sees the effect — every created and finite thing—*in* the cause, namely *Himself;* comprehended simultaneously is the cause (God Himself) and the effect (every creature).[25]

---

[19] "Alio modo potest considerari intellectus noster secundum ordinem ad rationem quae ad intellectum terminatur, dum resolvendo conclusiones in principia per se nota, earum certitudinem efficit: et hoc est assensus scientiae." *In III Sent.* d. 23, q. 2, a. 2, sol. 1. c. This does not mean that intellect and reason are diverse powers in man. (*Cf. Sum. Theol.* I, q. 79, a. 8; *De veritate* q. 15, a. 1; q. 16, a. 1.) These terms refer rather to diverse acts of the same power: "intellect" to the immediate, intuitive act of knowledge; "reason" to the cognitive process or movement involved; and the one is compared to the other as rest to motion, or as the act of possessing to that of coming into possession.

[20] "Nomen scientiae importat quamdam certitudinem judicii . . ." *Sum. Theol.* II-II, q. 9, a. 2, c.

[21] ". . . in Deo est certum judicium veritatis absque omni discursu per simplicem intuitum . . .; et ideo divina scientia non est discursiva vel ratiocinativa, sed absoluta et simplex." *Sum. Theol.* II-II, q. 9, a. 1, ad 1m.

[22] *E.g.,* in *Sum. Theol.* I, q. 14, a. 7; *S. C. G.* I, 55-57; *De potentia Dei* q. 9, a. 2, ad 10m; *Quaestiones de Quolibet* q. 11, a. 2, ad 2m.

[23] *Cf. Sum. Theol.* I, q. 14, a. 7.

[24] *Sum. Theol.* I, q. 14, a. 7, c.

[25] "Deus non cognoscit per causam, quasi prius cognitum, effectus incognitos; sed eos cognoscit in causa." *Sum Theol.* I, q. 14, a. 7, ad 2m.

Secondly, observe the implication of the argument that God is universally perfect because perfection is commensurate with existence in act, and He is pure act.[26] For in that case He lacks no perfection found in any genus or order of things, and therefore understanding befits Him. Moreover, since whatever is in God is God, it follows that His understanding is Himself, the pure act of being which He is — simple, eternal, invariable, utterly devoid of potency.

Thirdly, if it be asked what the medium of this understanding is, one must reply: nothing other than God Himself. For since knowledge is actuated through its mediating principle, God's power of knowing and His act of knowing, if distinct, would be mutually related as potency to act. But God is in potency to nothing.

Furthermore, an intellective medium distinct from the mind in which it resides has an accidental mode of being — something wholly incompatible with the divine actuality.

And finally, light upon this same point may come from one's asking the universal question: what is that which is known primarily and essentially? For the universal answer is: that thing through whose intelligible form the intellect understands.

Now in God's case this "form" or "species" is nothing other than Himself. It is because He is completely devoid of potentiality that His intellect and its object must be utterly the same. Neither is He without the intelligible species, as our intellect is when it understands potentially, nor is the intelligible species other than the very substance of His intellect, as ours is even when we understand actually. On the contrary, the mediating principle of the divine knowledge is itself the divine intellect: ". . . *seipsum per seipsum intelligit.*"[27]

What, then, is the correct reply to the question whether this divine self-knowledge is scientific? It is "no" — if "science" be taken to mean knowledge of an effect through its cause. But we shall understand that this "no" does not close the question if only we recall that the accomplished act of scientific knowing consists *essentially* in the judgmental understanding of truth, i.e., in knowing a thing in its true being, or as it truly is.

To be sure, "science," in the Aristotelian conception, bears upon conclusions, "understanding" upon principles.[28] Though this mode

26 "Si aliquid est cui competit tota virtus essendi, ei nulla nobilitatum deesse potest quae alicui rei conveniat." *S. C. G.* I, 28.

27 *Sum. Theol.* I, q. 14, a. 2, c.

28 *Cf.* Aristotle, *Nic. Eth.* vi. 6. 1140b 31; *Post Anal.* i. 3. 72b 20.

of scientific cognition is foreign to God, as involving inquiry, never-theless St. Thomas would have us keep firmly in mind the in-separability of the concept of science from that of truth. And so we are frequently reminded,[29] in the Anselmian vocabulary he loved to use in this connection, that truth is a certain "rectitude" or straightness — an undeviating conformity to the thing known.

In this perspective it is possible to see the scientific character of God's self-knowledge — not, however, His knowledge of Himself as essence, but as being (*esse*). This indeed is a crucial distinction for the Thomistic conception of science in general and of the divine science in particular.

For the object of such knowledge is truth, which primarily con-cerns the-act-of-being (*esse*) and not essence, because it is by virtue of this act alone that any possible object of knowledge *is*. And it is because science is universally conclusive and judgmental in charac-ter that God's self-cognition could be denied the name of "science" only on pain of evacuating its very notion. That is why God's act of knowing, though one and identical with Himself, is said to be "scientific" in attaining His being (*esse*) and "intellective" as it concerns His nature or essence.[30] Nor is the significance of this dis-tinction for us in any way diminished by the fact of God's utter simplicity.

Philosophy slumbers in a mind that closes itself to the meaning of a term in its ultimate reach. And to stay awake, one must some-times move an infinite distance. In this case the infinity must be at-tempted by our saying that the concept of science as certain judg-ment of truth is verified of God's knowledge of Himself as the divine being (*esse*), understanding that the act of knowing, the principle of knowing, and the thing known are here in reality one, namely God Himself.

Do such considerations as these warrant the inference that the word "science" is to be understood in terms of *judging things in their true being* rather than simply in terms of *cognitive certitude*

---

[29] Cf. *De veritate* q. 1, a. 1; *In I Sent.* d. 35, q. 1, a. 1, ad 5m.

[30] ". . . ea quae dicuntur de Deo, semper intelligenda sunt per eminentiam, ablato omni ex eo quod imperfectionis esse potest. Unde a scientia, secundum quod in Deo est, oportet auferre discursum rationis inquirentis, et retinere rectitudinem circa rem scitam. Sed quia scientia proprie complexorum est, et intelligere proprie est quiddi-tatis rei, ideo Deus dicitur *sciens* inquantum cognoscit *esse* suum, et dicitur *intel-ligens,* inquantum cognoscit *naturam* suam, quae tamen non est aliud quam suum esse, nec magic simplex. Et ideo in Deo non est aliud intelligere quam scire, nisi secundum rationem. *In I Sent.* d. 35, q. 1, a. 1, ad 5m; (italics added).

through causal connection? I think not. Far from implying a disjunction, these formulae are co-implicative, though the first one is
more radically metaphysical than the second, although it must remain somewhat less a defining formula. Designating the completed
act of scientific knowing, the first formula is expressly existential.
The second, understood to envisage the type or mode of knowledge
constituting science, has a definitory and quidditative character,
being secondary to the first, moreover, in signifying the "means" of
the act's accomplishment.

That second formula is therefore clearly inapplicable to God's
self-knowledge if the term "cause" be understood to involve dependency in being and real otherness. But in place of this notion
let us suppose the substitution of the concept of "principle" as signifying a true source devoid of any such necessary implication. Then
we shall see that the formula eminently fits the case; God knows
Himself scientifically through that principle which He is.

Beyond question this is Thomistic doctrine. For in St. Thomas
the term "cause" suffers some restriction in comparison with the
term "principle" when the latter, unlike the former, has a proper
sense without needing to imply dependency in being or even actual
distinctness.[31] It is, however, precisely from the viewpoint of the
completed act of scientific knowing that God's self-cognition as
divine being *(esse)* is scientific in the most radically metaphysical
mode. This conclusive act of attaining *esse* is what makes science
to be science. And the nature and condition of the means or principles through which it is accomplished, while not unessential, are
metaphysically secondary. Science is *defined* in terms of cognition
through a cause, but is *fulfilled* in judgment of *vere esse*. To express adverbially a common analogy, not every such judgment is
"scientific" formally, but it is so materially.

One may still feel inclined to insist: "Is there, yes or no, a proper
sense in which God's knowledge is formally and definitely scientific
according to the usual Aristotelian lexicon?" With St. Thomas I
answer: clearly if God is through His very own essence the cause
of all else, then in knowing Himself He knows everything besides
as caused by Himself. The divine causality attains to being as being.
Nothing escapes it.[32] Now of course God's causal action — the giv-

---

[31] *Cf. Sum. Theol.* I, q. 33, a. 1, c.

[32] *Sum. Theol.* I, q. 45, a. 1, c.; q. 65, a. 3, c.; *S. C. G.* I, 22; *Cf.* J. F. Anderson, *The Cause of Being* (St. Louis: Herder, 1952), pp. 30, 144.

ing of being — is continuous and not intermittent, so that in knowing Himself, God knows whatever proceeds from Him, namely each
finite thing. And He knows the latter *qua* being; that is to say,
perfectly: ". . . What is known only in a general way is not perfectly
known', for one does not yet know what is most important in that
thing, namely the ultimate perfections, by which its proper being
is completed; so that by such a knowledge a thing is known potentially rather than actually. Since, then, by knowing His own
essence God knows everything in a universal way, He must also
have a proper knowledge of things."[33] God knows things not only
in their natures but also in their existences, comprehensively just
as they are. And he knows them in Himself as effects of Himself,
the proper cause of their being as such.

That is the ultimate verification, undreamed of by Aristotle, of
the Aristotelian concept of scientific knowledge. And that is why
St. Thomas Aquinas can remark that God is said properly to know
scientifically according as He knows Himself and other things:
*"Unde proprie Deus . . . dicitur . . . sciens secundum quod se et
alia cognoscit."*[34]

But God's knowledge is not only scientific by virtue of His necessarily knowing Himself as proper cause of the being of His effects;
it is scientific also in that, through knowing Himself and all else
in Himself, He necessarily knows all the relationships between all
secondary causes and their particular effects. It is thus manifest
that in a *proper* sense there is science in God: *"Manifestum est quod
in ipso proprie scientia est."*[35] And yet this properly scientific
knowledge is a matter of simple vision, comprehensive, immediate.[36]

St. Thomas does, however, distinguish God's "science of simple
intelligence" from His "science of vision" on the ground that the
former envisages things that neither are, nor were, nor will be, the
latter existents.[37] This distinction concerns only the mode of being
enjoyed by the finite things which God knows; it implies no diversity in the manner of His knowing them. The selfsame intuitive

[33] *S. C. G.* I, 50, no. 5 (trans. A. C. Pegis, in: St. Thomas Aquinas, *On the Truth
of the Catholic Faith: Summa Contra Gentiles,* [New York: Image Books, 1955], Book
I, p. 183.)

[34] *In I Sent.* d. 35, q. 1, a. 1, ad 5m.

[35] *S. C. G.* I, 94.

[36] "Non tamen sit [sc. scientia divina] per ratiocinationem causata, sicut scientia
nostra ex demonstratione causata." *Ibid.*

[37] *Sum. Theol.* I, q. 14, a. 9; *S. C. G.* I, 66, *in fine; De veritate* q. 20, a. 4, ad 1m.

act of God's knowing is called "intelligence" on the analogy of the human act of apprehending essences or quiddities in the state of pure possibility. It is said to be "simple" in order to exclude everything extraneous to the knowledge-to-known relationship, whereas "science of vision" adds a reference to the proper existence of things, while the phrase "science of approbation" imports order to the divine will.[38]

Now God's "science of vision" attains not only things presently in act but also whatever will be or was.[39] For His act of understanding, which is His Being, is measured by eternity, which, enduring successionlessly, embraces all time, so that He knows all things existing in any time.

We commonly apply the word "seen" to things for two reasons — their presence to the seer, and their distinct existence outside him. Hence the propriety of the expression, "science of vision." The phrase, "science of simple intelligence," is similarly appropriate, since it formally envisages no relationship to the proper existence that merely possible entities could enjoy.

To the question whether the word "science" is even analogously fitting in this connection, I think one may reply affirmatively, inasmuch as "pure possibility" here implies atemporal existence in God; things possible, which neither are, nor were, nor will be, are presently existing in the power of God, their cause and *raison d'être;* and this suffices to make the knowledge of them "scientific." As for God's science of vision, it is in a sense even more "scientific"; at least it is so with respect to humanly commensurate ways of knowing and the creature's mode of being. For "science of vision" concerns creatures according to the manner in which they properly exist, and likewise the mode wherein they are scientifically knowable to us.

Perhaps it would be well to consider for a moment just how it is that God possesses "science," properly speaking, without reasoning or demonstration, through simple intuitive cognition.

In John of St. Thomas we find a remarkably lucid explanation of this point.[40] God enjoys "science," he says, in the strict and proper sense of the term—*"scientiam proprie et stricte sumptam"* — because by His act of cognition, single and simple though it is,

[38] *Cf. De veritate* q. 3, a. 3, ad 6m.
[39] *Cf.* Cardinal Cajetan, *In I Sum. Theol.,* q. 14, a. 9 (in St. Thomas Aquinas, *Opera Omnia,* [ed. Leonine; Rome: Leonine Commission, 1888], IV, 182).
[40] *Cursus Theologicus,* II, disp. 16, art. 3.

the thing is known truly and properly through its cause. Thus we
are enabled to see that the essential concept and definition of
"science" includes no requirement of a plurality of cognitive acts;
which indeed only argues imperfection in the knower. For "science" formally means knowledge through the essential cause on
whose account a thing is or is such and such; the number of cognitive acts involved is purely accidental. In fact, it is a mark of the
eminence and perfection of scientific knowledge to be accomplished
through one cognitive act. The necessity of many such acts but
demonstrates the knower's imperfection and limitation, his relative lack of penetration and perspicacity. God, however, enjoys
the perfection of scientific knowledge, free of the imperfections,
as in human science, of cognitional plurality.

   But against this notion of "science" in God there is a certain
objection, expressible in the form of questions, that merits our
close attention.[41]

   Is it not true of every mode of intellectual knowledge, including science, that everything known is attained through something
more known? Has not a cause greater intelligibility in itself than
an effect; is not the prior, as such, more knowable than the posterior,
just because it is prior? But is it not absurd to speak of a "more
and less" in God's knowledge — which is Himself? Then how can
He possibly be said to have "science" of anything, save perhaps of
Himself alone?

   The objection, St. Thomas points out,[42] is by no means for-
midable if we but bear in mind a simple distinction: gradation
in things does not argue gradation in knowledge. And even
though there is gradation in all creaturely knowledge, none exists
in the divine: because God is simple He sees all things together
in one and the same intuitive act; the act by which He knows Himself and therein all other things remains incomplex and invariable,
in perfect oneness with Himself. Of the things that God knows,
however, some are more knowable in themselves, others less. And
because this divine knowledge is eminently causal, it is eminently
scientific: *"salvatur in Deo ratio scientiae"; "Ipse enim praecipue
omnia per causam cognoscit."*[43]

   Now if God truly enjoys science, what kind of science is it?

[41] *Cf. De veritate* q. 2, a. 1, obj. 5.
[42] *Ibid.*, ad 5m.
[43] *Ibid.*

The distinctions "speculative" and "practical" have a threefold basis: subject-matter, manner of knowing, and end. And in this connection it is well to note that the natural congruence of subject-matter with end (the *finis operis* alone is meant) requires that the subject-matter of any practical science or discipline be operable in nature; that of the speculative non-operable, i.e. unproducible by any action or work.[44] It is then easy to see that God's science of Himself is simply and solely speculative; for He is non-operable. Of all else, however, God has both practical and speculative science. Always speculative in its mode — since He is concerned not with the *how*[45] but the *is* — God's science is practical in respect of its end as well as its subject as regards the creatures He actually made, makes, or will make. His science of things that He can make, but neither has made, nor does, nor will, is not actually practical in its end, being unordered to any actual production, yet it is practical in point of the nature of its subject: the operable.[46]

Also, let us bear in mind the fact that within creatures God knows causally all the relations and connections of one entity with another; such knowledge is *science.* Then, too, of course, He knows Himself as the cause of the being of all finite things, since the whole of their being depends on participation in His.[47] Accordingly: *"per reductionem ad se plenissimam de his omnibus scientiam habet."*[48]

There is no difficulty in seeing that this notion of science is non-univocal in respect of the creaturely and the divine mode. For, indeed, the creature possesses nothing in common with God according to the selfsame concept. And yet perhaps it is not so easy to understand how this notion then retains any actual unity of meaning. For how can terms infinitely distant be really compared? The fact of the real and most intimate bond between creature and God is the foundation of the solution to this problem. In default of such a relationship, God would not in knowing His own essence know creatures, nor indeed would they be at all. And man would be completely barred from attaining any knowledge of God whatever from the only natural starting-points available to him, namely,

---

[44] *Cf.* St. Thomas, *Expositio super librum Boethii De Trinitate,* q. 5, a. 1.

[45] Namely, the application of form to matter. God knows things as they are, and in knowing them makes them to be as they are; He needs and has no "know-how."

[46] *Cf.* St. Thomas, *loc. cit.*

[47] *Cf. Sum. Theol.* I, q. 14, aa. 5, 6.

[48] John of St. Thomas, *op. cit.,* II, disp. 16, a. 3 *(ed. cit.,* p. 451, no. 6).

created things. Nor, among all the names derived from our contact with such things, would any one of them befit God more than
another. Pure equivocation, simple notional otherness, marks the
triumph of irrelevancy; anything goes and nothing makes sense.

The only escape from absurdity lies in the admission that a name
like "science," said of God's science and ours, is not purely equivocal
and still less, flatly univocal, but analogical or proportional, not as
implying any finite commensuration between the terms, but a
composite and purely proportional commensurate one. This proportionality, as St. Thomas puts it, involves no determinate relationship whatever between its terms, so that a mutual likeness of
two proportions is obtained, the common analogous term (in this
case "science") implying in its essential meaning no shadow of
defect or potency.[49]

The difficulties removed

We are now in a position to answer, in the order in which they
were raised above, the difficulties or objections that St. Thomas
saw and that others have seen since, both independently and in his
company, of predicating "science" of the very being of God and of
predicating "scientific" of the knowledge of God.

Of course, scientific knowledge at the creaturely level is a quality existing in a mind and is not simply identical with it. But if
the name "science" refers essentially to a perfect way of knowing
whereby a thing is grasped conclusively in its true being, then what
would prevent its ascription to God? Considered in itself purely
and simply, would this idea imply potency or limitation? Indeed it
would not; "science," as designating a pure perfection, is no quality
in God, but the pure act and substance that He is.[50]

As to the allegation regarding the discursive and caused character of scientific knowledge, let it be said first of all that because God
is self-subsisting being, all being, mixed and multiple and caused in
creatures, enjoys simple existence in oneness with Him.[51] Words

---

[49] To my knowledge the best and fullest Thomistic text on this subject is found
in the *Disputed Questions on Truth* (q. 2, a. 11, c.; ed. Spiazzi, p. 51).

[50] See, for example, *Sum. Theol.* I, q. 14, a. 1, ad 1m; q. 4, aa. 1, 2; *S. C. G.* I, 28;
De veritate q. 2, aa. 3, 13.

[51] "Cum Deus sit ipsum esse subsistens, nihil de perfectione essendi potest ei
deesse. Omnium autem perfectiones pertinent ad perfectionem essendi. Secundum
hoc enim aliqua perfecta sunt, quod aliquo modo esse habent. Unde sequitur quod
nullius rei perfectio Deo desit." *Sum. Theol.* I, q. 4, a. 2, c.

signifying the various modes of human knowledge reflect the relative deficiency of everything finite. Thus, while man's cognition of principles, as such, bears the Thomistic name of "intelligence,"[52] the term "science" is restricted formally to his knowledge of conclusions, "wisdom," "counsel," and "prudence" naming other modes. And so on, the point being that God's oneness and simplicity guarantee and require that all these knowledges coincide in Him with His own self-identical act of understanding.[53] And, therefore, to this uncaused act all these names are applicable in such fashion that no imperfection or limitation, no potency whatever, qualifies their meaning. That is why "science," said of God, precludes all discourse.

In this connection one may mention the denial[54] that God has scientific knowledge of His attributes and of things pertaining to Himself, on the ground that not only is there nothing caused in God, but not even a distinction of reason, based on any distinctness in Him, can be found or formed, whereas the very notion of "science" demands at least a notional diversity among the terms.

Recall, however, that knowledge can be genuinely scientific if it attains with certitude the essential and necessary reason or cause of something.[55] For this is the case with God's knowledge of His attributes or perfections; e.g., He sees the necessary connection between His immutability and His eternity; He sees that He is eternal *because* He is immutable.[56] While of course there is in the ordinary sense no cause-effect relationship here, nevertheless, the one is the essential and necessary reason of the other. And so with His knowledge of the connections between all the other divine and unrestrictedly transcendental perfections. This cognition, therefore, is properly scientific.

---

[52] The Thomistic sense of this *"intelligentia"* is but loosely expressed by the usual word "understanding." For *intelligentia* here signifies precisely the intuitive act of knowing "premises," and, by analogical extension, principles within any realm of meaning.

[53] "Unde simplex Dei cognitio omnibus istis nominibus nominari potest; ita tamen quod ab unoquoque eorum, secundum quod in divinam praedicationem venit, secludatur quidquid imperfectionis est, et retineatur quidquid perfectionis est." *Sum. Theol.*, I, q. 14, a. 1, ad. 2m.

[54] *E.g.*, by Sylvester of Ferrara, *In I S. C. G.*, 24 (in St. Thomas Aquinas, *Opera Omnia*, [ed. Leonine; Rome: Leonine Commission, 1918], XIII, 77).

[55] "Propter quid scire est per causam scire." St. Thomas, *In Post. Anal.* I, lect. 14, no. 7.

[56] "Cum Deus sit maxime immutabilis, sibi maxime competit esse aeternum." *Sum. Theol.* I, q. 10, a. 2, c.

In fact, even *our* knowledge of these things is scientific to the extent that it demonstrates such "reasons"; e.g., although unity is indeed not the "effect" of being in the sense of depending upon it as something other, even so we do possess true science in knowing that unity is convertible with being *because* every being, in so far as it is, is undivided in its being (*esse*).[57]

Likewise, we truly demonstrate one divine perfection through another — God is infinite because He is self-subsisting being; He loves all things because He wills good to all;[58] and so on. Since God is omniscient[59] He sees the eminent, though purely virtual, distinction between His own attributes, as well as their interconnectedness.[60] And such distinction suffices for scientific knowledge in so far as the essential reason (*ratio propter quid*) of it is demonstrated or shown forth.

As to the seeming dilemma that every science must be either universal or particular, this disappears in the light of the principle that if God's knowledge is truly scientific, then, unlike everything created, no least element of imperfection or potency can possibly qualify it. So that of necessity science in God would be subsistent, unbounded, all-perfect—one with that pure act which He is.[61]

Let it be quickly admitted, moreover, that the human notion of scientific knowledge includes the plurality of knower, knowable, and known. And yet does it follow that these three must differ in reality? It does not. For to understand that the intellect in act of knowing is one with what is actually being known is to see that there is no plurality of knower and known in the very act of knowing. What then prevents the possibility of an intellect that is in potency in no respect and to nothing, but rather totally in act? In fact the ground of such a possibility can be recognized in the very essential meaning of knowing. No potentiality qualifies the nature of the act of knowing as such. The proper and proportionate object of an intellect wholly in act would be something likewise whol-

---

[57] St. Thomas, *Sum. Theol.* I, q. 11, a. 1, c.

[58] *Sum. Theol.*, I, q. 7, a. 1, c.; q. 20, a. 2, c.

[59] *Sum. Theol.* I, q. 14, a. 7, c.

[60] For not only do the perfections of all things pre-exist in Him eminently (*ibid.*, q. 4, a. 2, c.), He knows Himself and everything else comprehensively and perfectly, and this includes the mode of science. (Cf. *ibid.*, q. 14, a. 3, c.; S. C. G. I, 3; *De veritate* q. 2, a. 2, ad 5m).

[61] For, God *is* His *intelligere* (*Sum. Theol.* I, q. 14, a. 4, c.), and "in Deo non est aliud intelligere quam scire, nisi secundum rationem" (*In I Sent.* d. 35, q. 1, a. 1, ad 5m).

ly in act, namely itself, knower and known thus being simply and always identical. There exists no knowable object distinct from knower and known; for a knower thus in act is actually knowing all that there is.[62]

Then, too, the contention that God cannot know created things scientifically because of their very contingency, is set aside by the consideration that He knows them, not in themselves, but in Himself.[63] In knowing contingent things through that necessary cause which is Himself, God enjoys true scientific knowledge of them. As John of St. Thomas so aptly remarks, the fact that creatures have an infallible cause in God suffices to make the knowledge of them truly scientific.[64]

Let us note, furthermore, that if "science" be taken to mean knowledge through inferior causes in opposition disjunctively to "wisdom," understood as knowledge through the highest causes, then God is unpossessed of science apart from wisdom. But these terms, though not convertible, are for St. Thomas congruent and continuous: "every wisdom is a science, though not vice versa, since that science alone is wisdom which considers the highest causes."[65] Thus, if the word "science" be used in connection with God's knowledge through secondary or inferior causes, bear in mind that "science," for St. Thomas, signifies a "perfect way of knowing," of which "wisdom" is a mode — indeed the loftiest one.[66]

Consider also that while it is perfectly true that "science," said of God, signifies God Himself, it does not follow that such an attribution would bar the co-existence in Him of any other perfection. On the contrary, names of pure perfections said of God signify the divine substance itself by simple and total identification, God in His attributes, and conversely.[67] That is why these perfec-

---

[62] All these points are most lucidly explained by St. Thomas: *ibid.*, ad 3m.

[63] *Sum. Theol.* I, q. 14, a. 5.

[64] ". . . sic habent [creaturae] causam infallibilem in Deo, quod sufficit ad veram rationem scientiae." *Cursus Theologicus*, II, disp. 16, a. 3 (ed. Reiser, p. 452, no. 7).

[65] "Sapientia vero non ponit in numerum cum scientia et intellectus; quia omnis sapientia scientia est, sed non convertitur: quia illa scientia sola sapientia est, quae causas altissimas considerat . . ." *In I Sent.* d. 35, q. 1, a. 1, ad 5m.

[66] "Sapientia non est qualitercumque scientia, sed scientia rerum honorabilissimarum ac divinarum, ac si ipsa habeat rationem capitis inter omnes scientias." *In decem libros Ethicorum expositio VI*, lect. 6 (Pirotta, 1184); (ed. Vivès; Paris, 1875, p. 498).

[67] Cf. *Sum. Theol.* I, q. 13, a. 2; *De potentia Dei* q. 7, aa. 4, 5; *In I Sent.* d. 2, a. 2; *S. C. G.* I, 51.

tions signify Him indefinitively.[68] Essential definition is the encompassment of a nature by a univocal concept. And this is possible only with an essence that is not *esse,* namely a created and finite thing. Since God is no such thing, He cannot be defined or enwrappèd in univocal conception. Accordingly: *impossible est aliquid praedicari de Deo et creaturis univoce.*[69] In a word, the objection we have been dealing with implies that names properly said of God signify the divine substance univocally, in definitory and circumscriptive fashion, even as the word "man" designates the human substance. But since God assuredly is not an essence — a limitable thing — He cannot be circumscribed or defined.

To the last objection, that science ill becomes God in bearing upon conclusions reached through some process from principles, St. Thomas' reply is particularly illuminating. First, he points out that the same actuality which in God is unlimitedly perfect, of necessity suffers some deficiency in the creatures possessing it; since no creature is pure act, it owns nothing purely in act. The creature imitates God only in respect of that which is perfect in it. Now the perfection of human science lies in its certainty; *"quod scitur, certitudinaliter cognoscitur."* Its imperfection is manifested in the discursive factor — the movement — involved. Knowledge in process of being achieved is as such potentially scientific, and it remains so, in ever decreasing degrees, until the process is concluded.[70]

Science in act emerges at that moment when the result is known with that precise certitude which the real state of affairs demands and allows. The essential note in this aspect of scientific knowledge is certitude — nothing else.[71] "Science" is said of God's knowledge

68 *Sum. Theol.* I, q. 13, a. 5; etc.
69 *Sum. Theol.* I, q. 13, a. 5, c. Cf. *S.C.G.* I, 32, 34; *De potentia Dei* q. 7, a. 6.
70 ". . . scientia quae in nobis invenitur, habet aliquid perfectionis, et aliquid imperfectionis.
"Ad perfectionem ejus pertinet certitudo ipsius, quia quod scitur, certitudinaliter cognoscitur; sed ad imperfectionem pertinet discursus intellectus a principiis in conclusiones, quarum est scientia; hic enim discursus non contingit nisi secundum quod intellectus cognoscens principia, cognoscit in potentia tantum conclusiones; si enim actu cognosceret, non esset ibi discursus: cum motus non sit nisi exitus de potentia ad actum.
"Dicitur ergo in Deo scientia ratione certitudinis de rebus cognitis, non autem ratione discursus praedicti, qui nec etiam in angelis invenitur . . ." *De veritate* q. 2, a. 1, ad 4m.
71 Thus, as John of St. Thomas neatly puts it: "de ratione scientiae non est evidentia, sed solum certitudo." *Cursus Theologicus,* I, disp. 2, a. 3 (*ed. cit.,* p. 451, no. 6). For, he explains (*ibid.*), the habitus of science is quite compatible with utter absence of natural rational attainment of its principles, as in dogmatic theology, which pro-

precisely because of and with respect to the certitude He has of the things He knows. God's science is indeed comprehensive; it is not science because it is comprehensive, but because it is certain. Human science is discursive—*in fieri*—; it is not science primarily because it is discursive, but because it is certain.

Now it is interesting to note that even human "science," or rather the human act of knowing scientifically, is analogical or multi-valued with respect to its various modes. Such science is, however, justly considered a generic form of knowledge characteristic of man's definitive essence; and then it is conceived of in univocal or homologous fashion. And yet from the point of view of the act of scientific knowing it cannot truly be so conceived, since here we find diversity amidst proportional unity. Consider the multifarious orders and levels of certitude, as well as of causal principle.

Although it is true that some perfections which are essentially unlimited can be thought of as restricted to determinate natures (even the idea of "being" [*ens*] can be shrunken to signify mere identity in kind of being, so that the term will be rightly deemed univocal as predicated of specifically identical individuals)[72] nevertheless, the divine perfections cannot be envisaged legitimately in any perspective that would admit of such conceptual restriction because they are the act of the divine being itself. And that precisely is why "scientific knowledge," said of God, signifies the divine substance itself, which, as the Angelic Doctor reminds us, so exceeds the grasp of the human intellect that the ultimate reach of man's knowledge of Him consists in knowing that he does not know Him, *inasmuch as* man knows that what God is surpasses everything humanly known or knowable about Him.[73]

ceeds with certainty, demonstrating necessary connections, though it resolves all its conclusions into totally inevident, albeit simply certain, principles of faith.

72 Cf. John of St. Thomas, *Logica,* II, q. 13, a. 3 (ed. Reiser, I, 481).

73 ". . . illud est ultimum cognitionis humanae de Deo, quod sciat se Deum nescire, inquantum cognoscit illud quod Deus est, omne ipsum quod de eo intelligimus, excedere." *De potentia Dei* q. 7, a. 5, ad 14m.

?❧ Metaethics and Thomism

by Vernon J. Bourke

☆ ☆ ☆ ☆ ☆ ☆ ☆ ☆ ☆ ☆ ☆ ☆ ☆ ☆

IN RECENT English works it has become rather common to distinguish three levels of practical discourse: moral, ethical, and metaethical.[1] In such a division moral sentences express a man's personal attitude toward certain problems in his own life—or they may express the moral code of a given people or culture. Using Maritain's language, one might say that such a view of moral discourse is practico-practical. It is not necessarily philosophical; its basis may be accepted without much reflection.

Ethical discourse is philosophical and reflective. In ethics one solves none of one's own moral problems. Linguistically, the ethician makes statements about moral discourse. One could attempt to distinguish the moral from the ethical by saying that the moral is first-intention discourse, while the ethical is in a second-intention relation to the moral. This is neat but not adequate. These old-fashioned logical terms narrow the thing down to thinking, to cognitive experience alone, even to that special sort of cognition which is conceptualization. Both morality and ethics seem to have wider horizons than this.

If a man says, "I ought to pay my taxes today," or if he feels that, "Joe shouldn't have pushed Fred off the cliff," he is on a moral level. Besides knowledge, his discourse implies a certain attitude, some affective commitment on his part.

If another man says, "The statement, 'I ought to pay my taxes today,' is the expression of a duty,"—then this whole statement belongs in ethical discourse. Just as the economist, *qua* economist, makes no investments, so the ethician, as such, solves no concrete moral problems.

---

[1] See for instance: Paul Edwards, *The Logic of Moral Discourse*, (Glencoe, Ill.: 1955), pp. 19-42.

At this point the Thomist may be thinking that this is nothing new, that it is the traditional distinction between prudential reasoning and moral (ethical) science. There is some similarity but the likeness is not complete. For one thing, prudence suggests right reasoning and, of course, man's moral discourse is often wrong. It is useful to have some name for that generic process by which we work out our own moral problems; it is not formally ethical but it may be called moral. Elsewhere,[2] I have tried to establish a terminology to take care of a similar distinction between moral reasoning to a conclusion in which one *knows* what is to be done, and the moral reasoning which ends in an *action* which terminates the process. The former process is the *cognitive* moral syllogism; the latter is the *operative* moral syllogism. However this does not entirely take care of the difficulty. Ethics is not identifiable with any group of conclusions to the cognitive moral syllogism. Ethics moves on a different level toward generalized conclusions, while the moral syllogism (in both types) terminates in a particular conclusion. This emphasizes a point which Thomists always must face if they endeavor to understand their contemporaries in philosophy. Thomistic ethics implies a whole theory of knowledge and reality which is either not known, or is consciously rejected, by most other philosophies today. Contemporary ethics is usually nominalistic. Generalized statements are used but not as descriptive of real universals. Indeed, any philosophy nowadays which stresses the reality of essences or universals is liable to be labelled "platonism."[3] So, the distinction between moral and ethical discourse cannot be identical with the division between prudential reasoning and practical science.

In any case, the foregoing suggests the possibility of a third level of practical discourse, that of *metaethics*. There is a tendency now to initiate a horde of meta-disciplines. A few years ago, metaphysics was in disrepute; recently it has been imitated, nominally at least, by other so-called ultimate studies, meta-logics, meta-mathematics, meta-linguistics and so on. In a nut-shell, metaethics is concerned with statements about ethics. The present article would be an example of metaethical procedure. As conducted by language analysts (who have introduced the term) metaethics is not a system of

morality. The individual philosopher who works in metaethics
may be a utilitarian, a hedonist, a pragmatist, possibly even a de-
ontologist. His moral commitment, or lack thereof, may show only
in the examples which he discusses. Metaethics, then, examines
the groundwork and methods used in *any* type of ethics.

There is even a possibility that metaethics could be associated
with Thomistic ethics. It is to the consideration of this possibility
that the present paper is directed. Is there room and need for an
overview of the ethics of Thomism, analogous to the sort of thing
that analysts do in metaethics? I am going to suggest that there is.
It matters little whether we use the name, metaethics. What is important is that we become aware of the difference between writing
and thinking *about* ethics, and working out ethical problems. It
is quite possible that many things discussed in metaethics have no
place, for instance, in a course or textbook for undergraduate students of ethics. It is also possible that advanced research in ethics,
and the training of teachers of the subject, require some concentrated attention to the problem of metaethics.

Let us consider, first of all, the way in which treatises of Thomistic ethics start. There is usually a chapter or so devoted to the kind
of study that ethics is. Granted that it always develops that Thomistic ethics is a demonstrative science, and that its degree of precision
is less than that of some other parts of philosophy or science, what
are we doing in this introduction? The prolegomena to ethics are
often lengthy excursions into matters involving logic, epistemology,
and general theory of reality. Are these introductory notes ethics?
They remind one of the program notes to a symphony concert or
the effort of a painter to give his views on painting. The program
notes are not music, nor is the esthetic or technical explanation
art. Likewise, to decide whether ethics is a demonstrative science
is partly a logical matter. There is a theory of proof, originating in
Aristotle's *Posterior Analytics,* which most Thomists use. Do they
first do some ethical reasoning and then reflect on this process to
see the character of what they have done? Or do they make an
initial option for this sort of syllogistic and then go on to apply it
to human problematics? Whatever the answer may be, it would
seem a good thing to be aware of the importance of examining this
initial step. A Thomist does not need to be told about the effects
of a small error in the beginning.

But the problem of the character of ethical procedure is not merely a logical one. Some people see that it is also metaphysical. Yet the presuppositions of the ethician are not extensively and thoroughly treated in the usual book of Thomistic metaphysics.

The predicate "good" has been the subject of much discussion in twentieth century ethics. Thomistic metaphysics may have a wonderful explanation of it. But where is this explanation in a modern monograph? Suppose we observe Joe helping Fred and we judge or assert that Joe's action is good. Do we mean that Joe's act is a participant in the transcendental good?[4] If so, then any act that Joe does is good. Surely we mean more than this: we are asserting that Joe's act is *morally* good, that it is distinguishable from other possible acts which could be of contrary character, morally bad. Viewed as a class, morally good acts are considered to resemble each other in a manner that is not typical of morally bad acts. Is there, then, a universal which is moral goodness? What would be the metaphysical status of such a universal? Is it some special kind of relation between the action and some real term of reference? If so, what is this term of the moral relation? Is it human nature (individually or specifically)? Is it some law? Is it some supreme being? These and like questions arise from ethics but it is doubtful that they can be wholly answered by ethics.

Similar questions are asked about the contrary moral category, evil. The quick handling of evil in the ordinary treatise of Thomistic metaphysics, saying that it is simply a privation of good, has alienated many thinkers who are impressed by other things in Thomism. If we think concretely of a bad action (as the Russian novelists do), we may come to realize that it occurs quite as positively as any good one.[5] On this score, the evil act participates in transcendental good. (It is well known that some texts of St. Thomas, springing from the tradition of Dionysius, suggest the opposite: that the more evil an action is the less goodness and reality it has. There must be something wrong here; the logical conclusion would be that the greatest sins have the least reality! This may be good platonism, for evil does not really belong in a platonic world, but it is not good thinking.) Evil action also implies a relation to

---

[4] Elizabeth Salmon, *The Good in Existential Metaphysics*, (Milwaukee: 1953), pp. 64-73, adverts to the problem of the relation between transcendental good and moral good.

[5] Cf. G. P. Klubertanz, "The Empiricism of Thomistic Ethics," *Proceedings of the American Catholic Philosophical Association*, XXXI (1957) 22-23.

a moral scheme of reference—just as important as the relation of the good act, with just as many, or more, real consequences. Indeed there are more possibilities of evil action than of good. Where are these problems treated in metaphysics? Often they are not. Yet it is on 'issues such as these that a moral philosophy will find acceptance or rejection.

It is not hard to find more work for metaethics. The Thomistic ethician seems to assume that ethics is a purely cognitive discipline. He is aware that prudence has its appetitive parts (this is quite evident in St. Thomas' analysis of the three acts of prudence[6]) but he is inclined to see ethics as simply another kind of knowledge. This it may be. Some readers of Aristotle's *Nicomachean Ethics* understand ethics in this remote and almost speculative way. It is a question whether Thomistic ethics, however, should be regarded as merely a demonstrative science. Perhaps it is also a wisdom. Consideration of the end of human life is basic and formal to the ethics of Aquinas. This end is a principle for all ethical procedure; moreover, this end is God, the First Cause of all. A discipline of such a character comes very close to satisfying the Aristotelico-Thomistic definition of a wisdom.

Ethics is extremely sensitive to the personal attitudes and affective-appetitive dispositions of those who work at it. This sensitivity may be observed at many points in the development of Thomistic ethics but nowhere more definitely than in the discussion of the end of human life. Thomists say that the end is a formal principle in practical science.[7] Now one way of determining the ultimate end of man is metaphysical. One studies the nature and capabilities of men and concludes (in the Thomist tradition) that there is a specific nature in all men, with a built-in finality directed to an eventual culmination of human energies in a continued act of knowing and loving the perfect Being. Let us agree (of course many contemporary philosophers will not) that this reasoning is valid. Is the finality of human nature simply that of the intellect? Is the work of the ethician completed when he comes to an intellectual grasp of this relation of man to his end?

---

[6] Integral parts such as docility, promptness, decisiveness, and caution suggest affective or appetitive dispositions. For an interesting parallel view of prudence see: Bernard Baruch, *My Own Story*, (New York: 1957), Chap. VII.

[7] A whole study could be written on the origin and validity of this axiom: such a study would belong in metaethics.

It is possible that the role of *right appetite* extends beyond prudential reasoning and into the area of ethics. This rectification of human tendencies has a long history in mediaeval thought. It shows very clearly in the position of St. Anselm of Canterbury. For him, man is inclined toward goods of a lower order by the *affectio ad commoditatem*, to higher goods by the *affectio justitiae*.[8] Prescinding from the precise distinction here involved, we can see that this teaching (with its origin in St. Augustine) recognizes basic appetitive dispositions toward the good for man. Later, St. Bonaventure represents a tradition in which synderesis disposes the will of man to favor the moral good and to repel moral evil. This is an inborn disposition, an aspect of right appetite. Thomas Aquinas made synderesis a habit of the practical intellect but retained the notion of a natural rightness of the appetite in man.[9] Maritain is one of the few modern Thomists who have seen that this appetitive rectification may have some repercussions in ethics.

Today, there is a type of positivism which asserts that ethical statements are non-cognitive or emotive. Such a position denies truth value to ethical judgements or utterances. Non-cognitivists claim that ethical statements cannot be true, for they are neither tautologous (analytic), nor are they simply empirical (reducible to sense data). Years ago, the Cambridge school tended to deny that ethical sentences could have any meaning. But it could hardly be maintained that such utterances are mere nonsense, so today they are said to have non-cognitive or emotive meaning. Ethical sentences are hortatory, approbative, emotive, and persuasive in value. This concession seems to have disturbed those Thomists who have bothered to read Ayer and his friends.

However, it may be that the non-cognitivists are partly right. They may have put their finger on something important. Ethical conclusions are not of the same character as those of mathematics or physics. For one thing, the ethician aspires to some practical influence on human conduct. To live well it is not necessary to know mathematics, nor is it necessary to have a formal knowledge of ethics. Yet some of the things which ethicians discuss must be faced by every man who is concerned about his own conduct. More-

---

8 S. Anselmi, *De concordantia*, PL, 158, 536; cf. J. R. Sheets, "Justice in the Moral Thought of St. Anselm," *The Modern Schoolman*, XXV (1948) 132-139.

9 *Summa Theologiae* I-II, q. 57, a. 5, ad 3m: "The truth of the practical intellect depends on conformity with right appetite." Cf. *In decem libros Ethicorum expositio* IV, lect. 4, n. 1174.

over, Thomists say that ethical judgments are normative. This implies that such propositions cannot be regarded as merely abstract or speculative truths. Doubtless there is something wrong with denying all cognitive meaning to ethical sentences; this does not mean that we should ignore the affective-appetitive character of these utterances. If I say that four equals two plus two, I need not be much concerned if another man says, "So what!" But if I say that murder is bad, I may well be worried if another man says, "So what!" Thomists are perhaps too little interested in what might be called the "public relations" aspects of their ethics. They have been satisfied to erect neat "systems" but have not been much concerned with convincing their contemporaries that ethics can have consequences.

There are other reasons for regarding ethics as more than a cognitive discipline. Readers of Gilson know how he has emphasized, in the last two decades, the impossibility of young people mastering metaphysics and a purely philosophical ethics.[10] One of his reasons goes back to Aristotle's *Nicomachean Ethics*. There we are told that the appetites of youngsters are in a turmoil, making it most difficult for them to think about profound and ultimate matters. (I prescind from the truth or falsity of Aristotle's dictum.) The point is that Aristotle, Aquinas, and Gilson would all be classified as cognitivists in ethics—but they have all been aware of the immediate effects of appetitive dispositions and attitudes on the work of the ethician.

Such considerations bring us to recognize a certain validity in the efforts of continental ethicians to discover the relations between the *Sein* and the *Sollen,* of British thinkers to determine the meaning of the predicate, *good,* and of American ethicians to relate facts to values. The statement, "Fred is in this room," admits of empirical verification and is factual. That "Fred ought to be here," is not so obviously a factual claim. Indeed it does not express a simple fact but a very complicated judgment.

It must be admitted that Thomist ethicians often handle value judgments as if they were nothing but truths of fact. Some writers give the impression that moral values can be seen as existing re-

---

10 "Thomas Aquinas and Our Colleagues," in *A Gilson Reader,* ed. A. C. Pegis (New York: Doubleday, 1957), pp. 290-292.

alities.[11] Reflection suggests, however, that ethical statements are not as directly and immediately verifiable as factual assertions. Whatever *recta ratio* means in the thought of St. Thomas Aquinas, it is not as simple as factual experience. It involves an elaborate process of reasoning from what is given in human experience to conclusions which may be "intuited" finally, but only after an extremely complicated series of inferences. To suggest that all that an ethician has to do is to go around intuiting real values is a parody on the thought of Thomas Aquinas. Mathematical conclusions, such as the numerical value of pi, are not verifiable on inspection, or by simple sensory experience. And ethical propositions appear to be much more intricate than those of mathematics. Surely there is room for much more work here, work for the metaethician.

Very important in a demonstrative discipline are the principles, the starting-points which give direction to the demonstration. We k n o w that Thomists consider that man's practical intellect is equipped with a special habit (synderesis) enabling it to understand the starting-point of all practical discourse. The formula for the first practical principle, so known, is: *Good should be done; evil should be avoided.*[12] It is odd that few other types of ethics advert to, or make any use of, such a first proposition. In a way, Kant seems to offer an alternative in his famous categorical imperative. Yet the Kantian maxim: *Act so that your individual action may become a universal rule of action,* is in no way equivalent to the principle of synderesis. Kant's rule endeavors to offer a way in which one can tell what acts are good. St. Thomas' rule does not; it tells you to do them, when they are good, not to do them, when they are evil. This indicates the futility of trying to make a rationalistic deduction of specific moral duties from the principle of synderesis.

We cannot take the "Good should be done" rule and proceed as if we were Kantian formalists. It is not an *a priori* judgment intuited before we have any sense experience. That it is known in the first stages of moral and ethical reasoning is accepted by all Thomists. However, some writers consider it to be intuited (and

---

[11] "It is this concept of intuition, by which moral values are apprehended as objective realities, which is a distinctive feature of Thomistic moral philosophy." Gerard Esser, S.V.D., "Intuition in Thomistic Moral Philosophy," *Proc. Amer. Cath. Philos. Assoc.,* XXXI (1957) 176.

[12] *Quaestiones disputatae: De veritate,* q. 16, a. 1 and 2; *Sum. Theol.,* I-II, q. 94, a. 2.

so, apparently, analytic), while others take it as an induction from
sensory experience (and so, synthetic).[13] Many things remain to
be examined here, both as to the original grasping of such a practical principle and to the eventual application of it to special
problems.

There is, of course, a rather wide-spread impression that Thomistic ethics (in spite of its air of rational procedure and its claim of
starting with sense experience) is actually a theological approbative theory.[14] Thomists are thus taken to be people who *believe*
in the precepts of the Decalogue and the Sermon on the Mount,
and who erect a purported system of ethics on these items of faith.
There are many examples of such a religious ethic in the writings
of Protestant and Jewish scholars of our day.

This is a point which requires careful metaethical consideration. Does a Catholic ethician approach his problems with the
same attitude that we find in ethicians without a strong religious
commitment? Here we touch on a larger controversy which has
engaged the attention of Gilson during much of his mature life.
It is the question of the status of a Christian philosophy.[15] The
difficulty is especially acute in reference to ethics. Is the Catholic
committed in such a way that he cannot bring an open mind to
ethical discussions? If we answer affirmatively, then how can he
be classified unless as a theological approbative ethician? If we
answer negatively, we must admit that leading Thomists (Gilson
and Maritain, for example,) and the apparent weight of papal pronouncements are against this negative. Frankness would seem a
virtue in approaching this problem, for one should not assume the
mantle of the philosopher while breaking the rules of the craft.

Maritain has made his position clear.[16] He thinks that the Christian ethician is consciously subordinating his ethics to theological
principles. So too, Gilson's general support of the Christian philosophy theme seems to imply a similar decision regarding the Chris-

---

[13] Father Esser *"Intuition in,"* *op. cit.,* pp. 168-175 offers an explanation closely
related to A. C. Ewing's intuitionism; P. Hoenen (*Reality and Judgment according
to St. Thomas,* (Chicago: Regnery, 1952), pp. 164-182, has developed a theory of
first principles arising from sense data.

[14] For the terminology: T. E. Hill, *Contemporary Ethical Theories,* (New York:
1950), pp. 97-113. Hill does not put Thomism in this classification; see *infra,* note 20.

[15] For a recent history of the controversy: Maurice Nédoncelle, *Existe-t-il une
philosophie Chrétienne?* (Paris: 1956).

[16] Bernard Wall (trans.), *Science and Wisdom,* (New York: 1940), pp. 70-220.

tian ethician.[17] However, both Maritain and Gilson distinguish
the Christian philosopher from the Catholic theologian. And many
Catholic thinkers do not accept the notion that their philosophy
is subordinated to theology. They think that they are entitled to
be called philosophers. They think that they are doing what Aristotle, or G. E. Moore, or C. L. Stevenson, would regard as ethics.
It is another unresolved question for metaethics.

The relation of Thomistic ethics to other disciplines treating
human conduct needs to be studied.[18] Should the ethician try to
learn something from the social sciences, from philosophies of law,
from esthetics, from the various branches of psychology? A negative answer would seem hasty, even obscurantist. Much information about man's conduct is offered as matters of fact or interpretation in these studies. Both Catholics and non-Catholics work in
these related fields; surely their efforts are not wholly to be ignored.
Of course, it is a mistake to assume that data from these disciplines
are all factual, or on the same level of facticity, or of equal reli-
ability. If a social scientist reports that eight per cent of the people
in a certain state commit suicide each year, this is a first-level fact
and verifiable. On the other hand, if he reports that the members
of a certain tribe do, or do not, believe in a supreme being, this is
not so obviously a fact. One would have to know how this information was obtained, how queries were worded, what was the scientist's understanding of the term, supreme being. Such a report
does not seem to me to record a first-order fact. Surveys of moral
opinions, attitudes, and theories are often less than factual. The
use of statistical techniques gives such reports the appearance of
scientific data. But the gathering of the crude information, before
statistical analysis, is open to much variation in precision and re-
liability. The ethician need not grant the same importance to
second-order statistical "facts" that he would to a more immediately verifiable report. Still further removed from facticity are
those generalizations and hypotheses, in the social sciences, which
are called "laws" of human behavior. They are often found to be
but the personal opinions of the scientist, or hangovers from long-

[17] Both the *Christian Philosophy of St. Thomas Aquinas*, (New York: Random
House, 1956), and the *History of Christian Philosophy in the Middle Ages* (New
York: Random House, 1956), treat the point in their opening pages.
[18] Cf. Herbert Johnston, "The Social and the Moral Sciences," *Catholic Educa-
tional Review*, LV (1957) nos. 7-9; offprinted in 37 pages.

forgotten theories which have unconsciously guided the scientist to conclusions of extremely doubtful status.[19]

What, then, is the Thomistic ethician to do with the evidence of these sciences? He can hardly incorporate it whole hog into his subject. Apart from the various degrees of facticity noted above, he will find definite conflicts between various schools of sociology, psychology, and so on. Discrimination must be exercised. Comparisons must be made. A whole new group of problems thus arises in making an appraisal of the information from these "soft" sciences. This is a task for which the ordinary ethician is ill-equipped. The comparative study of the ethical import of the various sciences of human behavior appears as another area for the attention of the metaethician.

Legal theories provide a special difficulty. Jurisprudence has been studied for thousands of years. Various cultures, philosophies, political organizations, and ethnic groups, give rise to diverse notions on the origin and nature of the laws which govern man. Thomism, for instance, is often identified with natural law ethics.[20] But natural law means one thing to the Stoics, another thing to Thomas Aquinas, and still another to Hobbes or Rousseau. With divergent notions on the nature of reality and knowledge come different meanings for law and nature. How is the ethician, *qua* ethician, to settle the great problems which extend beyond the horizons of practical philosophy? By working at ethics, does he equip himself to accept or reject realism? Can he, by ethical procedures, discover the most reliable analysis of human nature?[21] The study of the history and meaning of legal views, and their relevance to ethics, is beyond the scope of ordinary ethics.

Thomistic ethics is a very complex position. This makes it hard to classify in a history of ethics. It is a teleological ethics. The problem of the goal, or end, of human life, led to many theories in ancient times. Following Varro, St. Augustine enumerated 288 opinions regarding the nature of man's ultimate end.[22] It may be

[19] See Alexander Macbeath, *Experiments in Living,* (London: 1952), pp. 19-21, for an amplification of this theme.

[20] Hill, *op. cit.,* pp. 248-253, so classifies the ethics of Thomism, giving Gilson and Maritain, among others, as examples of natural law ethicians.

[21] Thomistic ethicians divide man's higher psychic functions into two kinds: cognitive and appetitive. British ethics sticks to the threefold division of associationistic psychology; cognition, affection, and conation. The difference is very important in a theory of moral values.

[22] *City of God,* XIX, 1.

that Thomism coincides with one of these teleological views. There is still some argument as to which one. However, in contemporary ethics teleological classification means little. Present-day philosophy has very little use for final causes. It is advisable to consider other bases for the classification of ethics.

Histories of modern ethics divide theories on the basis of their explanation of moral judgment. Hedonism, utilitarianism, deontologism, and so on, can be distinguished in this way. Should the critical factor in deciding whether to do a moral action, or not, be the amount or quality of the pleasure associated with its accomplishment, or the contribution which the act makes to the public welfare, or the conformity of the act to duty as grasped by the moral agent? There are many other theories of moral judgment. Where does Thomistic ethics stand here? In stressing happiness and the personal rewards for good living, Thomism appears to some to be a eudaimonism. In its emphasis on justice, charity, and the consequences of human action, Thomistic ethics resembles social utilitarianism. And while it does not regard moral duty in the formally Kantian way, still Thomism stresses the obligatory force of conscience. Sometimes it appears that Thomists wish to embrace all the better known criteria of moral judgment and to call them their own. This does not make it easy to situate such an ethics.

A historian of philosophy might say that, at least, Thomistic ethics is an intellectualism, as opposed to a voluntarism. We have seen earlier that this is not clearly so. The notion of right appetite, the influence of moral habits, take the ethics of modern Thomism beyond the limits of moral intellectualism. Similar problems come up if we attempt to consider it a formal or a material ethics. Indeed, some of the discussions now conducted by non-cognitive ethicians have a familiar ring to Thomists. There are affinities between the procedure of emotive ethicians and the old studies of voluntariness, moral predication, and the relation of technical to non-technical language.

It is, then, hard to place Thomism in contemporary ethical classifications. Oddly, it appears to resemble evolutionary ethics in its stress on finality. Yet evolutionism looks to a non-existent goal, while Thomistic ethics sees man's happiness as the approach to an already existing Being. This whole problem of classification is a metaethical one.

We have seen that the term, metaethics, has been coined as a name for thinking and talking about the sort of problems which arise, not *in* ethics, but *about* ethics. One of these problems has to do with the kind of study that ethics is. Another centers in the meaning of good, when used as an ethical predicate. This leads to difficulties about the status of moral evil. The respective roles of cognition and affective appetition in ethical procedure provide another such problem. The fact-value relation requires more study. More thinking and writing might be done on the starting-point of Thomistic ethics. The relation of ethics to theology and the social disciplines constitutes a vast area of supra-ethical problematics. Lastly, we have noted some of the difficulties which occur in classifying Thomistic ethics. To these and similar matters metaethics is directed.

ૐ John of Paris as a Representative of Thomistic Political Philosophy

by Marc F. Griesbach

☆ ☆ ☆ ☆ ☆ ☆ ☆ ☆ ☆ ☆ ☆ ☆ ☆ ☆

UNTIL recently, the Dominican, John of Paris was known to most students of mediaeval philosophy vaguely, if at all, as the author of a late thirteenth century *Correctorium Corruptorii* in defense of certain teachings of St. Thomas Aquinas.[1] Martin Grabmann, on the basis of the *Correctorium* and a commentary on the *Sentences,* had judged him to be "without doubt one of the most prominent representatives of the oldest school of Thomists."[2] The historians of mediaeval political theory had also recognized him as a figure of considerable importance. Jean Riviere, recalling that St. Robert Bellarmine had ranked the Parisian among the defenders of the doctrine of the indirect power of the Pope in temporal affairs, the *"sententia media et catholicorum theologorum communis,"* gave him a prominent place in his monumental work, *Le Problème de L'Église et L'État au Temps de Philippe le Bel.*[3]

Then in 1942, a modern edition of Quidort's political treatise, *De Potestate Regia et Papali,* together with a detailed introductory

---

[1] *Le Corruptorium Correctorii "Circa" de Jean Quidort de Paris,* ed. J. P. Müller, O.S.B., *("Studia Anselmiana,"* IX [Rome: 1941]).

[2] Martin Grabmann, *Studien Über den Einfluss der aristotelischen Philosophie auf die mittelalterlichen Theorien Über das Verhältnis von Kirche und Staat,* (Munich: 1934), p. 33.

[3] J. Riviere, *Le Problème de l'Église et de l'État au Temps de Philippe le Bel,* (Paris: 1926), p. 300.

33

study, was published in France by Dom Jean LeClercq, O.S.B.[4]
This scholar, also regarding Quidort as a moderate in political
philosophy, declared him a "faithful disciple of St. Thomas," one
who "gathered together the elements (of political theory) scattered
throughout his works," and "pursued (Thomistic) principles to
their ultimate consequences."[5] Finally, Father John Courtney Murray, S.J., writing in the American Jesuit quarterly, *Theological
Studies*, accepting Dom LeClercq's historical judgments on Quidort's Thomism, went on to inquire whether the doctrine and
practice of the Church is not today orientated toward Quidort's
theory of the indirect power. In what is in many respects a remarkable article, Father Murray answers his own question affirmatively, recognizing in the *De Potestate Regia et Papali* a Thomistic doctrine of the relationship between political and ecclesiastical
authorities which could show the way to the solution of the Church-
State problem of today.[6]

If Father Murray's judgment is correct, then here, it seems, is a
mediaeval work worth knowing by all who would bring to bear on
contemporary problems the principles of St. Thomas Aquinas. But
before this judgment is accepted as correct, a careful look at the
treatise seems to be in order, for Quidort has always been something of a controversial figure.

Certain questions therefore suggest themselves: Who was this
man? What are his principal teachings in the *De Potestate et Regia
Papali?* How "Thomistic" is the treatise? In what respect, if any,
does it suggest the solution to current Church-State controversies?
Hence, this essay.

Comparatively little is known about John of Paris. The date
given for his birth varies widely, from about 1240 to 1269, with
the most reliable documents tending to suggest the earlier date.[7]
He died in 1306. The fact that there were several thirteenth and
fourteenth century writers called John of Paris obscures most biographical details. As a Dominican, Quidort was a member of the
community of St. Jacques in Paris to which St. Thomas had also

[4] Jean LeClercq, O.S.B., *Jean de Paris et l'Ecclesiologie du XIIIᵉ Siècle*, (Paris:
1942). Citations from Quidort will be from this edition.

[5] *Ibid.*, pp. 85, 97, 149, 152, 157, 162, 163, 165.

[6] John C. Murray, S.J., "Contemporary Orientations of Catholic Thought on
Church and State in the Light of History," *Theological Studies*, X (1949), 177ff.

[7] *Cf.* LeClercq, *op. cit.*, pp. 6-9.

belonged. A listing and analysis of his principal works was given by Grabmann.[8]

The *De Potestate Regia et Papali* was written near the end of 1302 or in the early months of 1303 during the course of the controversy between Pope Boniface VIII and Philipp IV (The Fair) of France. Quidort has been accused by Richard Scholz and others of being the leader of the French opposition against Boniface and of perhaps instigating the outrage upon the Pope at Anagni.[9] LeClercq, though conceding that Quidort's name appears high on the list of those who petitioned for a council against the Pope, denies, however, that the *De Potestate Regia et Papali* is a mere polemic, holding that it is a serious attempt to come to grips with philosophical issues.[10]

Quidort states in the *proemium* of the treatise that he conceives his task to be one of discovering the *via media* between the opposite errors of those who would deny all material goods to the Church and to churchmen—the Waldensians—and those who, like Herod of old, assume that Christ was born to be an earthly king ruling a secular kingdom. To that end he examines the nature and origin of political power (the *regnum*), then of the ecclesiastical power (the *sacerdotium*), and finally, their relationship. After a positive exposition of his doctrine he discusses an array of traditional opposing arguments in the course of which he further clarifies his own position.

The first fact that strikes the reader of the *De Potestate Regia et Papali* is the author's emphatic rejection of the old mediaeval notion of Christendom as a unitary political-ecclesiastical society in which the state was somehow included within the Church.[11]

---

[8] *Studien zu Johannes Quidort von Paris*, (Munich: 1922). For additional biographical data cf. F. Lajard, "Jean de Paris," in *Histoire Litteraire de la France*, XXV (Paris: 1869), 244ff.

[9] For an account of that conflict beyond suspicion of a papal bias, cf. Ernest Renan, "Nogaret," in *Hist. Lit. de la France*, XXVII, 261 ff.

[10] *Op. cit.*, pp. 23-24.

[11] There is perhaps no question in mediaeval political history that has been more disputed than this one of the notion and the fact of Christendom, the *Respublica Christiana*. Among recent articles, cf. Alfons M. Stickler, S.D.B., "Concerning the Political Theories of the Mediaeval Canonists," *Traditio*, VII (1949-51), 450ff; and Gerhart Ladner, "The Concepts of *Ecclesia* and *Christianitas* and their Relation to the Idea of Papal *Plenitudo Potestatis* from Gregory VII to Boniface VIII," *Miscellanea Historicae Pontificae*, XVIII, (Rome: 1954), 49-77. For an historical account of the evolution of the notion of Christendom and the various forms it took

From the first, his dominant purpose appears to be to establish the independence of the political regime—in particular, of the *Regnum Franciae*—from the Church. To this end he argues: (1) that the traditional supremacy of the spiritual over the temporal power involves no juridical subordination of the one power to the other; (2) that this is true because the spiritual power is in no sense the cause of the temporal power, since both are derived immediately from God; (3) that the authority of ecclesiastical prelates is fundamentally a power of ministry of the Sacraments, distinct and separate from the power of the political ruler, whose authority is supreme in temporal affairs; (4) that each of the authorities possesses an indirect power in the domain of the other.

As Dom LeClercq and others have pointed out, the entire argument of the *De Potestate Regia et Papali* is conducted in a way that shows the author thoroughly conversant with the vast mediaeval storehouse of philosophical, theological, scriptural, and canonical literature. The impression is given that every pertinent scriptural text, patristic pronouncement, canonist claim, mediaeval allegory, and philosophical distinction is taken into account. LeClercq's contention that Quidort also makes abundant use of the writings of St. Thomas Aquinas (though without giving any indication that he is doing so) is easily verifiable.

Nowhere is Quidort's indebtedness to St. Thomas, and to Aristotle before him, more evident than in the discussion of the nature and origin of political society. *Regnum,* we are told, is "the rule of a perfect multitude ordained to the common good, by one."[12] It is government of a *perfect* multitude (as distinguished from a domestic society, which is imperfect). It is ordained to the *common good* (as opposed to the various forms of tyranny, in which the ruler aims at his own good). It is a government *by one* (as distinguished from aristocracy and polycracy). It is derived from the natural law and from the law of nations, for man is by nature a social animal (as indicated not only by his material needs, but also by his power of speech).

To prevent the disintegration of human society, there must be a ruler, preferably one man, whose function it is to direct the community to the attainment of the common good of all, which (as

in the minds of its principal proponents, cf. Etienne Gilson, *Le Metamorphoses de la Cité de Dieu,* (Louvain-Paris: 1952), espec. Chap. III.

[12] *De Potestate Regia et Papali*, ed. cit. p. 176.

any good Aristotelian knows) is *vivere secundum virtutum.* The civil ruler, a *minister Dei,* is *justitia animata et custos justi;*[13] his function is to lead men to virtue. Does not Aristotle himself say that as the soul is greater than the body, so is the legislator greater than the physician, since the legislator has care of souls, the physician of bodies?[14]

In accord also with St. Thomas, Quidort argues that the *regnum,* whose end is that the community live virtuously, is further ordained to the higher, more ultimate, eternal end of man, which is attained through Christ and His appointed sacerdotal ministry. For "the one to whom pertains the more ultimate end is more perfect than, and directs, the one whose concern is an inferior end." From this Quidort concludes merely that the sacerdotal power is greater *in dignity* than the secular power. (*Et ideo dignior est sacerdotalis potestas seculari potestate.*)[15]

Against those who would claim more for the sacerdotal power, Quidort observes that the spiritual power, though greater in dignity, is not the cause of the temporal power any more than gold, which is more precious than lead, is the cause of the latter.[16] Hence, the spiritual power is not in all respects the superior. There is a domain—temporal affairs—in which the authority of the secular power is superior to that of the spiritual power, and another domain—spiritual affairs—in which the ecclesiastical authority is preeminent. For inasmuch as the two types of authority are derived independently of each other from a third power (God) superior to both, the one is subject to the other only insofar as the Supreme Power has subjected it. Again it is manifest that Quidort has been served well by a classic Thomistic distinction.[17]

Answering an objection based on the principle of the subordination of an inferior art to the ends of a superior art, the Parisian observes that an art ordained to a superior end does not rule an inferior art absolutely, but only with regard to what is necessary for the superior art's attainment of its end. He then proceeds to deny that anything in the political order is essential to the attainment of man's ultimate end, since this end can be reached in diverse ways (through tyranny as well as by just rule).[18] Logically then,

---

13 *De Potestate,* V, 184, 15-16.   14 *Ibid.,* XVII, 225, 33-34.   15 *Ibid.,* V, 184, 3.
16 *Ibid.,* 184, 34-35.
17 *Ibid.,* 184, 16-33. Cf. St. Thomas, *Scriptum super libros Sententiarum* II, d. 44, *expositio textus.*
18 *Ibid.,* XVII, 227, 22-37.

we are led to infer that there is no matter whatsoever in the domain
of the political to which the authority of the ecclesiastical power
extends.

John observes further that *rule* need not always be *per modum
auctoritatis*, but can be instead *per modum dirigentis*. In this event
an immediate superior does not have coercive authority and the
right to impose sanctions—functions that would belong rather to
a superior power. Now since there is over the whole world a supreme power—God Himself—Who established both ecclesiastical
and political regimes, all rule over the temporal power *per modum
auctoritatis* should be left to God.[19]

The author contends, moreover, that the argument from subordination of ends has validity only where the inferior is strictly a
means, not a good desirable in its own right. But the virtuous life
of the community *"habet rationem boni et appetibilis secundum
se."* Hence the argument for judirical subordination fails.[20]

Quidort similarly manages to defeat all attempts of the opposition to cling to the old mediaeval hierarchical system wherein
power was subject to power, the temporal to the spiritual. All that
he will allow of the traditional supremacy of the spiritual power
in his essentially dualist[21] theory is a pre-eminence in dignity. Aside
from that, the two domains, mutually autonomous under God, are
juridically independent and supreme in their respective spheres.

To reach this conclusion Jean Quidort had both to define the
ecclesiastical authority in such a way as to restrict it as completely
as possible to the sanctuary and to justify the self-sufficiency of the
political order. His method of procedure toward these two objectives is worthy of note.

In describing the origin and nature of the *sacerdotium* John
begins with an almost *verbatim* transcription of a famous passage
in the *De Regno* of St. Thomas:[22] since man is ordained, not only
to the virtuous life which is the end of the *regnum*, but also to
the further supernatural end, eternal beatitude, there must be an
authority to direct men thereto. Now if this supernatural end

19 *Ibid.,* 227, 4-13.   20 *Ibid.,* 227, 13-22.

21 All mediaeval doctrines of the relationship between temporal and spiritual
powers could, of course, be called dualist in a sense, since all admitted some sort of
duality of powers. Until Quidort, however, this dualism, so well expressed in the
famous letter of Pope Gelasius to the Byzantine emperor, Anastasius (cf. PL, 59,
41), was never regarded as final.

22 *De Potestate* II, 178, 16-28. Cf. St. Thomas, *De regno ad regem Cypri,* I, 14.

could be reached through natural means, the task of leading men
to it would belong to the king, that is, to the temporal ruler. But
since eternal life is attainable only through divine grace, this function must belong to that King Who is not only man but also God—
Jesus Christ, Himself.

At this point, where Aquinas goes on to conclude: *"Unde ab eo
regale sacerdotium derivatur,"* Quidort abruptly drops the text of
the *De Regno* and, good Thomist that he is, finds in another context, a conclusion more to his liking.[23] Christ, he observes, instituted the Sacraments as a means of conferring upon men the
effects of His Passion; and since these Sacraments must be administered throughout time, certain men are commissioned by Him
to dispense them to the faithful. These men are called *"sacerdotes."*

John then goes on to define the sacerdotal power: *"Sacerdotium
est spiritualis potestas ministris ecclesiae a Christo collata ad dis-
pensandum fidelibus sacramenta."*[24] But lest this rather restrictive
definition be thought to apply only to the priesthood, not to higher
prelates, he explains that *episcopi* or *magni sacerdotes* are superior
to ordinary *sacerdotes* only in that they have authority in cases of
reserved absolution and the power to confer the priesthood upon
others.[25] The power of the supreme pontiff, the *maximus sacerdos,*
differs from that of other prelates only extensively; he is in the
whole Church "as another bishop is in his diocese."[26]

Elsewhere the Parisian is more explicit in restricting the papal
power. He concedes only that the Pope is the *"principal among
the ministers of the Church,"* the *"principal* vicar of Christ in
spiritual affairs."[27] In other passages, which have sometimes earned
for the author of the *De Potestate* the title "Father of the Gallican
Church," he asserts that lesser prelates receive their authority "in
no way from the Pope, but from God immediately, through the
consent or choice of the people."[28] The Pope is without proprietary
rights over Church domains, but is the *"generalis dispensator"* of
ecclesiastical goods. As such, he is strictly accountable for his stew-
ardship, bound to restitution in illicit use, and subject to deposi-
tion should he prove incorrigible."[29] Like any other person of

23 *Ibid.,* 179, 1-12. For St. Thomas, *Summa contra Gentiles* IV, 56.
24 *Iibid.,* 179, 19-21; cf. also XII, 207, 37.   25 *Ibid.,* III, 179, 29-35.
26 *Ibid.,* X, 197, 9: ". . . *quidquid papa potest quilibet episcopus potest, nisi
quod papa potest ubique....*"
27 *Ibid.,* XVIII, 230, 12-13; cf. also VII, 189, 30-32.   28 *Ibid.,* X, 199, 31-35.
29 *Ibid.,* VI, 187, 33-35; 188, 21ff.

authority, he has jurisdiction only consequent upon agreement among men, and can, through agreement to the contrary, be deprived of his office.[30] Moreover, though his is the "highest created power," the total power of the college of cardinals is equal to, or even greater than, the Pope's.[31] With full finality Quidort sets forth a principle which is provocative, to say the least: ". . . *orbis maius est Urbe, et papa cum concilio maior est papa solo*" (the world is greater than Rome, and a Pope together with a council is greater than the Pope standing alone.)[32]

Nor do these seem to be merely minor irregularities within an otherwise orthodox doctrine, as Dom LeClercq and Father Murray suggest.[33] They are, in fact, integral to, and thoroughly consistent with, the author's stated purpose to restrict the scope of the ecclesiastical, and especially of papal, power. It is quite obvious that if even ecclesiastical prelates receive their authority not from the Pope, but immediately from God, then surely as much can be said for political rulers. And, according to Quidort, where there is no causal dependence, there is no subordination. The strategy seems unbeatable: nullify the Pope's claim to anything like universal power even within the Church, and you neutralize any attempt to vindicate papal supremacy over the secular domain.

Quidort is not lacking, however, in more direct arguments to make this latter point. He contends, for example, that since the Pope does not "institute the king *ut rex*," he has no authority over him *as a king*. Of course, if the king happens to be a Christian, then *as a Christian* he is subject to the supreme spiritual authority, since the king was "instituted *de fide*" through the spiritual power.[34]

The full force of this distinction becomes clear only in an application which the author makes of it: If the king sins as a Christian, (e.g., against Faith or the Sacrament of Matrimony) he is subject to ecclesiastical punishment like any other Christian; but if he should sin as a king, (i.e., in his official political acts) he is outside the jurisdiction of the spiritual authority.[35] Thus the entire order

---

[30] *Ibid.*, XXV, 259, 9; cf. also 255, 12ff.   [31] *Ibid.*, 258, 6-10.

[32] *Ibid.*, XX, 243, 7.

[33] Cf. LeClercq, *op. cit.*, pp. 116ff. Cf. also Murray, "Contemporary Orientations," *op. cit.*, p. 195.

[34] *De Potestate* XVII, 226, 1-5. Cf. Hugh of St. Victor, *De Sacramentis*, II-II, 4, PL, 176, 418.

[35] *Ibid.*, XIII, 214, 27-36.

of politics (though not the private life of the political ruler) is separated from ecclesiastical jurisdiction.

At least as important to the internal consistency of the *De Potestate* as these limitations imposed upon the ecclesiastical authority, is the author's notion of the self-sufficiency of the political order. Now, as the work of Etienne Gilson has made manifest,[36] one of the most meaningful measures applicable to a theory of the relationship between temporal and spiritual authorities is the man's doctrine óf nature and grace. It is just such a test that Quidort allows an objector to apply to his doctrine by arguing, in the language of St. Augustine,[37] that without the true justice, which is present only where Christ (through His vicar) is the ruler, there can be no genuine political society.[38]

The Parisian comes right to the point. He asserts simply that the *perfect* justice which is required of the *regnum* can exist apart from the rule of Christ (hence independently of the spiritual authority), since the acquired moral virtues can exist *perfectly* without the theological virtues, receiving from them only a further accidental perfection.[39]

The theory of an autonomous political order is thus provided with the philosophical and theological foundation it requires. Natural in origin, with an end of its own, perfectly attainable by natural means alone, the *regnum* is essentially independent of the *sacerdotium*. The natural order of politics is not only distinct, but separate and self-sufficient apart from the ecclesiastical authority.

This is not to say that the domains of the temporal and the spiritual powers are totally isolated from one another according to the doctrine of the *De Potestate*. Quidort sees the Pope, though lacking any direct power in temporal affairs, as still able to bring about *indirectly* certain effects in the political order. This aspect of Quidort's teaching, it will be recalled, especially commended it to Cardinal Bellarmine, as well as to some more recent scholars.[40]

---

[36] Etienne Gilson, *Dante et la Philosophie*, (Paris: 1939), pp. 200ff.

[37] Cf. *De Civitate Dei*, II, 21; PL, 41, 68.   [38] *De Potestate* XI, 204, 25-30.

[39] *Ibid.*, XVIII; 229, 22-25: ". . . dicendum est quod virtutes morales acquisite esse possunt perfecte sine virtutibus theologicis nec ab ipsis perficiuntur nisi quadam accidentali perfectione . . ." In contrast, cf. St. Thomas, *Summa Theologiae* I-II, q. 65, a. 2 and II-II, q. 23, a. 7.

[40] Cf. St. Robert Bellarmine, *De Summo Pontifice*, V, 1; ed. Naples (1856), p. 524. Cf. also Riviere, *op. cit.*, p. 300, and Murray, "Contemporary Orientations," *op. cit.*, pp. 210ff.

Though it is not always clear what a modern proponent of the theory of *indirect power* may have in mind, John succeeds in making his position quite unequivocal. Some actions of the sacerdotal power, he observes, may have repercussions in the temporal order. To preach, for example, that stolen goods must be returned could have an indirect effect upon the distribution of property. Similarly, although such ecclesiastical sanctions as interdiction and excommunication are spiritual, the imposition or the threat of excommunication might *indirectly and accidentally* bring about certain effects in the temporal order.[41]

A hypothetical case enables the Parisian to explain how this indirect or accidental power works: if the king, for example, were to commit an ecclesiastical offense, such as a sin of infidelity (in which, as we have seen, the king *as a Christian* is subject to the sacerdotal power) the Pope could excommunicate him. If the king still proved himself incorrigible, then the Pope could exert a form of "spiritual pressure" such as the threat of excommunication upon the people should they continue to obey him.[42] Conceivably, as an indirect result of the Pope's spiritual sanctions, the people themselves (not the Pope) might start a rebellion and overthrow the king. On the other hand, as has already been pointed out, if the king should commit a sin in his official status as a ruler (*peccaret in temporalibus*), the Pope would have no jurisdiction over him.[43]

Indirect power, as conceived by Quidort, is not, however, an exclusive prerogative of ecclesiastical prelates. If the Pope should commit a temporal offense, the political ruler can punish him "like any other malefactor." If he commits a spiritual offense (e.g., simony or heresy) jurisdiction over him belongs to the cardinals; but if these prelates are themselves unable to "remove the scandal from the Church," they can call upon the political ruler to depose him.[44]

Quidort goes so far as to say, perhaps with contemporary fourteenth century events in mind, that where there is danger of rebellion, and the Pope unduly stirs up the people by abusing his spiritual power, and the Church does not act against him, the tem-

---

[41] *De Potestate* XIII, 216, 5-7.

[42] In contrast to this, cf. remarks of St. Thomas in *Sum. Theol.* II-II, q. 12, a. 2.

[43] The barons and peers of the realm, who would have the right to "correct" the king in such cases, could, however, according to John, request the assistance of the Church if unable to handle the affair themselves. Cf. *De Potestate* XIII, 214, 27-36.

[44] *Ibid.*, 215, 17-24.

poral ruler can take up his "sword" against him, not, of course, as the Pope, but as the enemy of the republic.[45]

This, in summary, is the doctrine of the *De Potestate Regia et Papali*—a distinctively "modern" treatise on the relationship between political and ecclesiastical authorities. This is not an essay on the *Regnum Christi;* it is not another description of the hierarchical organization of a Christian world into one sacral society. There is here no *regale sacerdotium,* no *Summus Sacerdos* to whom "all the kings in Christendom are to be subject as to our Lord Jesus Christ."[46] Having rejected the mediaeval *dictum* that there can be no perfect natural virtue without charity, Quidort is only consistent in granting to the political regime the autonomy of a society perfect and self-sufficient in its own right. Has he, in all this, also remained a faithful follower of St. Thomas Aquinas? This is the question to which we must next turn.

Dom Jean LeClercq, in declaring Quidort a faithful Thomist, lays considerable stress upon the undeniable fact that the *De Potestate* contains numerous, and often lengthy, excerpts from the writings of St. Thomas.[47] What Dom LeClercq does not take into account, except in passing, is that John Quidort repeatedly finds it necessary to alter significantly the materials that he borrows from his Dominican confrere, by deleting passages, inserting qualifications, combining statements from different contexts and various other devices, in order to escape the conclusions of the original.[48] A textual comparison of those parts of the treatise in which the author is most indebted to St. Thomas with the corresponding passages in Aquinas' own writings leaves Quidort's Thomism sufficiently suspect to call for a close comparison of certain key doctrines of the two men.

. There are two Thomistic texts of particular importance in this respect, since in them St. Thomas considers questions closely paralleling some of those discussed by the author of the *De Potestate.* They concern directly the question of the relationship between temporal and spiritual authorities.

The first, one of the clearest expressions of St. Thomas' doctrine on the authority of the spiritual power, and of the Pope especially,

---

[45] *Ibid.,* XXII, 250, 30-32.   [46] St. Thomas, *De Regno,* I, 14.   [47] *Op. cit.,* p. 34.

[48] This becomes unmistakably evident when one juxtaposes passages of Quidort's treatise with corresponding passages from the writings of St. Thomas (cf. my unpublished doctoral dissertation: *The Relationship Between the Temporal and Spiritual Powers in John of Paris and James of Viterbo,* (University of Toronto: 1955).

in relation to temporal rulers, occurs at the very end of book II of the work on the *Sentences*.[49] The occasion is a text which Peter Lombard had quoted from St. Augustine: *"Si illud jubeat potestas quod nqn debes facere hic sane contemne potestatem, timendo potestatem majorèm."*[50] The question which this suggests to St. Thomas is: "whether the greater power ought always to be obeyed rather than the lesser."

Aquinas answers by distinguishing two situations which may prevail between an inferior power and a superior. Either the inferior power owes its origin entirely to the superior, or the two are derived independently of each other from a third power superior to both. In the first situation, which prevails, for example, between the emperor and a proconsul and also between the Pope and every other spiritual power in the Church, the subordination is total and the superior power is to be obeyed rather than the inferior in all cases. In the second situation, however, the one power is the superior of the other only in those matters in which the supreme power has subordinated the other power to it, and only with respect to those matters is the first power rather to be obeyed.

Applying this principle to the question we are here considering, St. Thomas observes that secular and spiritual powers are both derived from God independently of each other (the second situation). The secular power therefore comes under the spiritual power only insofar as God has subordinated it, namely, "in those things that pertain to the salvation of the soul" (*scilicet in his quae ιd salutem animae pertinent*), and in those things ought rather to ϳe obeyed. In the things that pertain to the good of civil society (*ad bonum civile*), on the other hand, the secular power is to be obeyed rather than the spiritual. "Render to Caesar the things that are Caesar's" (Matt., XXII, 21).

This is not the end of St. Thomas' answer, however. He continues:

> Nisi forte potestate spirituali etiam saecularis potestas conjungatur, sicut in papa, qui utriusque potestatis apicem tenet, scilicet spiritualis et saecularis, hoc illo disponente qui est, sacerdos et rex, sacerdos in aeternum, secundum ordinem Melchisedech, regnum non corrumpetur in saecula saeculorum.[51]

[49] *In II Sent.* d. 44, *expositio textus.*
[50] St. Augustine, *Sermon* LXII, Chap. 8; PL, 38, 420-421.
[51] *In II Sent.* d. 44, *expositio textus,* ad 4.

The aforementioned limitation upon the authority of the spiritual power does not apply in the case of the Pope. For he holds the apex of both powers, the secular power being "conjoined" in him to the spiritual power, this by the divine disposition of Christ Himself.

The interpretation of this last sentence of the text has given rise to unending controversy concerning this aspect of St. Thomas' political teaching. More than a few Thomists, understandably uncomfortable with these words of their master, and inclined to think that a pronouncement by St. Thomas must somehow be regarded as eternally valid, have continued to seek some explanation of this statement that would minimize the temporal authority therein attributed to the Pope.[52] Whereas Quidort quoting this very text, simply omitted the last sentence, one who attempts a faithful exposition of St. Thomas' own doctrine must somehow reckon with it.[53]

Moreover, a similar difficulty seems to occur with respect to the conception of the supreme spiritual power in the text which brings to a climax St. Thomas' teaching in the *De Regno* (I, 14). Having declared that the end of civil society is virtuous living, St. Thomas there goes on to assert that through virtuous living the individual man, and therefore civil society, is ordained further to the ultimate end, eternal beatitude. Now since this end cannot be attained through the power of human nature, but only by divine means, it is divine, not human, government that leads men to their ultimate end. But government of this kind pertains to our Lord Jesus Christ, Who is not only man but also God, not only Priest but also King, and from Whom there is derived a "royal priesthood" *(sacerdotium regale)*.

---

[52] Professor Gilson points to this current attitude toward the political thought of St. Thomas in *Dante et la Philosophie*, pp. 205-206, espec. note 1, p. 206. Cf. for example, Charles Journet, *L'Église du Verbe Incarné* (Bruges: 1951), p. 297, where he wonders how such a "curious passage" is to be interpreted.

[53] *De Potestate* V, 184, 16-33. Although no complete exposition of St. Thomas' doctrine is attempted in this essay, it should be observed in justice to Quidort that the"*nisi forte*" statement does not change St. Thomas' theory of distinct civil and ecclesiastical jurisdictions, but merely asserts that the Pope's case does not come under the theory for the reason that he "holds the apex of both types of authority." One can therefore hold intact the Thomistic theory of civil and ecclesiastical powers without accepting the statement of (alleged) fact as to the Pope's unique position. Quidort's break with St. Thomas goes deeper, however, striking at the very theory of hierarchical subordination of powers.

To this royal priesthood rather than to secular rulers, the author of the *De Regno* explains, the administration of this divine government has been entrusted—"and especially to the Highest Priest, successor to Peter, Vicar of Christ, the Roman Pontiff, *to whom all the rulers of the Christian People must be subject as to our Lord Jesus Christ Himself.*"[54]

St. Thomas' argument seems clear: since the end of civil society, only an intermediate end, is itself ordained to the ultimate end, which is the concern of the spiritual authority, political power is subsumed under the supreme spiritual ruler. The supremacy of the papal power is due, of course, to the fact that the Pope is a *spiritual* sovereign leading men to their ultimate end; but this authority extends, nevertheless, to all temporal affairs and over all secular rulers.

In both of these texts St. Thomas, while maintaining the distinction between the two powers, holds also most emphatically the subordination of the temporal power to the spiritual, especially to the supreme authority of the Pope. If they be taken to mean what they say, then their author, in contrast to the writer of the *De Potestate Regia et Papali*, still lives and thinks in the world of mediaeval Christendom.

The more we compare the specific teachings of the *De Potestate Regia et Papali* with the doctrine set forth in the writings of St. Thomas, the more striking are their differences—John's textual indebtedness notwithstanding. For though Quidort seems perfectly willing to go along when St. Thomas apportions to political and ecclesiastical authorities respectively jurisdictions in civil affairs and in things pertaining to the salvation of souls, and though he argues with St. Thomas that the virtuous life, which is the end of civil society, is further ordained to the higher end of eternal beatitude, Quidort, nonetheless, resists with the whole force of his argument the consequence—that, therefore, in Christendom all political rulers are ultimately subject to the supreme ecclesiastical head.[55]

[54] Loc. cit.

[55] The reason for this seems to be that, unlike St. Thomas, Quidort recognizes no spiritual formality within political affairs. *Temporalia* and *spiritualia* are for him materially distinct *things*, whereas St. Thomas' distinction between the things that pertain *ad salutem animae* and *ad bonum civile* is one of formalities, of formal aspects of things. The effect of John's doctrine is thus to remove political affairs from all spiritual jurisdiction—a genuine separation of Church and State.

The author of the *De Potestate* grants to the political order an autonomy quite incompatible, we have seen, with the mediaeval notion of Christendom which is the very rock upon which St. Thomas' political teaching is built. In the one theory, the political ruler comes under papal jurisdiction only in regard to his personal moral and religious life, there being no *spiritualia* in the political order itself; in the other, the civil ruler is, in his very official acts as a ruler, subject to the supreme over-all spiritual jurisdiction of the Pope. Whereas in the fourteenth century treatise the ecclesiastical power, conceived of as derived only from the Priesthood of Christ, not from His Kingship, is restricted as closely as possible to the ministry of the Sacraments, in the Thomistic tract there is derived from Christ the King and Priest a *regale sacerdotium* with authority to *govern* men with respect to their ultimate end as well as power to serve them in their spiritual needs. It is true that even according to Quidort's conception of the indirect power the strictly ecclesiastical acts of the Pope can have political repercussions although not nearly such drastic ones as the "accidental" laying of the material sword upon an incorrigible ecclesiastical enemy of the republic. The Supreme Pontiff of the *De Regno,* however, has *authority* in temporal affairs and over temporal rulers whenever the ultimate beatitude of Christians is at stake.

That there are points of agreement between the political teachings of these two men is undeniable; but the contention that Quidort's treatise is, in its essential nature or its spirit, a genuine expression of St. Thomas' own doctrine seems, on the basis of these differences, inadmissible.

It may be objected that this conclusion stems from an unduly literal interpretation of St. Thomas, that his doctrine in reality was much more modern than mediaeval. Was he not the one, after all, who introduced into the mediaeval political discussion, with his clear conception of the *droit naturel* of the state, the *Politics* of Aristotle as well as the distinction between nature and grace? How in the light of this can such texts as *In II Sent,* d. 44, *expositio textus,* ad 4, and *De Regno* I, 14, be taken at face value? Could it not be that Quidort did not accept these texts as they stand simply because he recognized them to be incompatible with the more fundamental principles of Thomistic political philosophy?

Cardinal Bellarmine, it should be noted, was already disturbed by Aquinas' statement that "the Pope holds the apex of both powers," and made several attempts to tone it down.[56] He as well as numerous scholars since his time attributed to St. Thomas the doctrine of the *potestas indirecta in temporalibus.*[57] Those who would soften or disregard these texts on the ground that taken literally they involve a contradiction in St. Thomas' teaching, often point to texts from the *Summa Theologiae,*[58] where the authority of non-believers over Christians is discussed. St. Thomas maintains there that the distinction between believer and non-believer does not of itself abrogate the temporal authority of the latter over the former, for that distinction is *ex jure divino,* while civil authority is *ex jure humano,* and *jus divinum,* which is *ex gratia,* does not abolish *jus humanum,* which is *ex naturali ratione.* Does this principle not contradict the texts we have seen?

No one would deny that according to this principle the order of nature must be clearly distinguished from the order of grace, and that civil authority does not depend on the supernatural life of grace. But civil authority is not itself denied by the thesis that the Pope's authority extends even to political rulers and the affairs which fall within the political domain. In the way already specified, the authorities remain distinct. If sometimes the same "things" come under the authority of both, it is under distinct formalities— as pertaining *ad bonum civile* or *ad salutem animae.* The aspect of temporal affairs that brings them under papal jurisdiction is a moral and spiritual one only. There is nothing in all of this that cannot be reconciled with other Thomistic principles; nor does there seem to be any grounds for saying that St. Thomas either held the doctrine of *indirect power* as it was formulated by Quidort or that he set forth the principles from which it necessarily follows.[59]

The most important claim made for Quidort by Father Murray remains to be considered; for it could still be that, by virtue of his very break with the "mediaevalism" of St. Thomas Aquinas, this fourteenth-century Dominican was able to construct the "modern" ecclesiastical doctrine toward which contemporary theology seems

[56] Bellarmine, *op. cit.,* V, 5; p. 530; and see Ladner, "The Concepts," *op. cit.,* pp. 70ff.

[57] Cf. Charles Journet, *La Juridiction de l'Église sur la Cité,* (Paris: 1931), pp. 117ff.

[58] II-II, q. 10, a. 10; and q. 12, a. 2.

[59] On this interpretation of St. Thomas' position, cf. the remarks of Gilson in *Dante et la Philosophie,* pp. 205-206.

to be oriented and from which could come the solution to the Church-State problem of today.[60]

Father Murray, in holding that the Church has adopted in our day the indirect power doctrine of Quidort, observes that the Church has come through history and experience to an increasingly perfect respect for the autonomy of the state, and consequently to a more purely spiritual exercise of its power in the temporal sphere.[61] No longer identified with the state, as in the mediaeval *Respublica Christiana,* the Church can no longer regard the state as her "right arm." In a modern democratic society she exerts her influence rather as an "immanent spiritual principle" speaking through the voices of the citizens. Whereas in the past the Church influenced the political order "through her action on the conscience of the king," today she confronts immediately, not the temporal power (the government), but "the citizen, armed with all the institutions of popular rule."[62]

It is not within the scope of this essay to determine whether this unquestionably profound insight of Father Murray's is entirely accurate and a complete description of what in fact is the mode of operation of the Church in a modern democratic society like that of the United States. On the basis of his observations it is possible, however, to judge the correctness with which he has identified this concept of the spiritual authority with the position of Quidort.

In pointing to the difference between the way in which the Church today brings its influence to bear upon the social order and the manner in which the popes of mediaeval Christendom sought to achieve their aims in the temporal order, Father Murray argues from the *mode of exercise* of the spiritual power. The difference between the old and the new, he indicates, lies in the *means* used to bring about an effect; in other words, the mode of efficient causality on the part of the Church has changed.

Profound and pregnant with consequences though the change so described be, this does not seem, however, to involve the question of whether or not the Church has *authority* with respect to a formality of things political. The whole discussion of means, in fact, implies that the Church does have such authority.

Now it is one of Quidort's main points that ecclesiastical rulers have no authority over temporal rulers as rulers. The king *ut rex*

---

[60] Murray, "Contemporary Orientations," *op. cit.,* pp. 212-213.   [61] *Ibid.*
[62] *Ibid.,* pp. 214-215, 223.

is in no way subject to the ecclesiastical authority. The political order is immune even from that exercise of the spiritual power which may indirectly have repercussions in the temporal order. Quidort, in fact, as we have seen, regards nothing in the political order as pertaining necessarily to the salvation of souls, for a tyrant, no less than a just ruler, can be the means of leading the sinner to God.[63] Thus the kind of indirect action of the spiritual power in civil affairs which Father Murray describes, not only fails to find its formulation in the *De Potestate* of Quidort, but is expressly excluded from it.

Finally, it might be objected that the problem of means is the crucial issue in the Church-State conflict of today, that the question of authority is secondary, and perhaps better left unstated. Hence Quidort might still well serve the Church's cause. Admitting the importance of the problem of means, and granting that it is not always advantageous to proclaim ecclesiastical authority indiscriminately, there is a danger, however, that in our concentration on the question of means we lose sight of the more fundamental question of authority. In this direction the *De Potestate* of Jean Quidort would seem to point.

---

[63] *De Potestate* XVII, 227, 26-40: "... Et sic est de potestate regia quia secundum eam populus non solum dirigitur in Deum secundum quod rex ea utitur ut rex, sed etiam secundum quod ea utitur rex ut tyrannus in quantum scilicet tyrannus principum est in ultionem peccatorum ut dicit Job quod regnare facit Deus hypocritam propter peccata populi ..."

ဦ Two Questions Concerning the *Esse* of Creatures in the Doctrine of Jean Quidort *by Ambrose J. Heiman, C.PP.S.*

☆　☆　☆　☆　☆　☆　☆　☆　☆　☆　☆　☆　☆　☆

A S EARLY AS 1922, Monsignor Grabmann, in a pioneer study,[1] presented Jean Quidort not only as a d e f e n d e r of St. Thomas[2] and as an important political thinker,[3] but also as an independent student of philosophical and philosophico-theological problems. In the same study, he suggested the central importance of the first three questions of Quidort's *Lectura* on the Second Book of the *Sentences*. A previous paper[4] studied the second of these questions, that is, the problem of the relation of essence and *esse.* In the present paper we propose to examine the first and third questions: the kind of *esse* that is proper to creatures, and the way in which it is produced by God.

The fact of creation and of the divine conserving are postulates of Quidort's argument at this point. Since, then, God causes creatures to be and must continually cause them to be if they are to continue in existence, Quidort asks whether the *esse* of a creature is a permanent *esse* (*factum esse*) or whether it is only a continuous becoming.[5] He argues that if the *esse* of a creature were a continu-

---

[1] M. Grabmann, *Studien zu Johannes Quidort von Paris, O. Pr.*, ("Sitzungsberichte der Bayerischen Akademie der Wissenschaften, Philosophisch-philologische und historische Klasse," [Munchen: 1922]), Abh. 3, 43.

[2] *Cf. Le Correctorium Corruptorii "Circa" de Jean Quidort de Paris*, ed. J. P. Müller, O.S.B. ("Studia Anselmiana," IX ([Rome: 1941]).

[3] *Cf.* J. Leclercq, *Jean de Paris et l'Eccésiologie du XIIIe Siècle* (Paris: 1942).

[4] A. J. Heiman, "Essence and *Esse* according to Jean Quidort," *Mediaeval Studies* XV (1953), 137-146.

[5] *Lectura* II, 1, fol. 79ra. All references to the *Lectura* shall be made to Ms. 2165 of the Nationalbibliothek in Vienna. Where it is quoted, it shall be quoted according to this Ms. with corrections from Ms. 889 of the Bibliotheque Mazarine and Ms. B III, 13 of the Universitätsbibliothek of Basel. For a complete study of these manuscripts

ous becoming, either that *esse* would be one and the same throughout the becoming, or there would be a constant succession of one
esse to another. But if it remained the same, the *esse* of the creature
would precede its becoming. On the other hand, if there were a
constant succession of *esse's,* either there would be a continual adding of *esse* to *esse* resulting in a multiplicity of *esse's* in one being,
or there would be a corruption of the one *esse* upon the advent of
the other. Each alternative, however, is impossible: there cannot
be a multiplicity of *esse's* in one creature; there is no ascertainable
cause for such a corruption of *esse.* One who maintains that the
esse of a creature is a continuous becoming, therefore, is caught between two impossible alternatives: the *esse* which he posits cannot
be the same throughout the existence of the creature, nor can there
be a succession of *esse's* in the same creature.

Nevertheless, God is continually giving *esse* to every creature,
and as soon as He ceases to give *esse* the creature ceases to be. In
attempting a solution to this problem, Quidort distinguishes between successive beings such as time and motion, and permanent
beings such as whiteness, man, and horse. The *esse* of a successive
being is indeed a continuous becoming. Successive beings are only
as long as they are becoming; once they have become they no longer
are. Permanent beings also become. When, however, they have
become they continue to be, and their becoming is distinct from the
duration they have once they have become. Now such beings may
become in two different ways. Some permanent beings come to be
through motion. Such is the case with all things that result from
natural causes. Such beings *become* before they *have become,* for
they *are not* until the motion by which they come to be has ceased.
Their becoming, therefore, precedes their having-come-to-be both
in nature and in time. Hence their *esse* is not a becoming but a
permanent state of having-come-to-be. Other permanent beings,
however, are brought into existence by a simple act of their efficient
cause. This is the case in creation as it is in the production of the
rays of the sun. Such beings come into existence instantaneously;
their becoming does not precede their having-come-to-be. Their
becoming and their having-come-to-be are really the same, differing
only in the mind: having-come-to-be is predicated of them abso-

together with the other manuscripts of this Book of the *Lectura, cf.* J. P. Müller,
"Les reportations des deux premiers livres de Commentaire sur le Sentences de Jean
Quidort de Paris O.P.," *Angelicum* XXXIII (1956), 361-414.

lutely, but becoming only in relation to the time whose terminus is the instant in which they are produced.

But what is the nature of the *esse* a creature acquires by becoming—of the *esse* a creature possesses once it has come to be. In the case of a permanent being, it is, as we have seen, other than its becoming. Is it, nevertheless, merely another kind of becoming? Quidort tells us that there were some who, impressed by the diversity between the *esse* of a creature and the *esse* of God, maintained that only the *esse* of God is fixed and stable, whereas the *esse* of every creature is in continual flux and, by reason of its constant dependence upon the action of God, is continually becoming.[6] They recognized the distinction between successive being and permanent beings and advanced two explanations of this diversity. Successive beings, they held, are in a constantly changing relationship to their causes; for this reason, they are always dependent upon their causes, both immediate and mediate. Permanent beings, on the other hand, are dependent upon their immediate causes only in their becoming. Once they have become, the immediate causes no longer exert any influence upon them, although they always remain dependent upon some mediate cause. This is true, they maintain, whether the immediate agent be natural or artificial. Thus, the form of a house is a certain disposition, composition and order of parts in a whole. During its becoming, this form is in constant dependence upon the builder; if he ceases to build, the house ceases to become. Once, however, the house has been built, the action of the builder is no longer necessary. But this form also supposes a certain natural proclivity (*virtus*) in the materials used, by reason of which they are capable of receiving and conserving the order that is the form of the house. It is dependent upon each of these materials in accord with their several natures not only that it become but also that it be. If, however, the form is so dependent upon the materials, so is the *esse,* for *esse* is through form. The house will continue to be even in the absence of the builder; its *esse,* however, will remain in continuing dependence upon the materials of which it is composed.

The same can be said of natural things. The becoming of the form of the generated depends upon the action of the generator; its *esse,* however, depends upon an intrinsic natural proclivity (*virtus*) which embraces the several proclivities of the various elements

---

6 I have been unable to locate the thinker to whom Quidort refers at this point.

of which the generated is constituted and which are held in a harmony proper to the generated form. If, then, the operation of the
generator ceases, the becoming of the form will cease; but if the
generated has already become, such cessation will have no effect
upon it whatever, for the generated is no longer dependent upon
its immediate cause.

The *esse* of a permanent being is, then, not a continuous becoming if we look at it only in its dependence upon its immediate
causes, the particular extrinsic agents which immediately cause the
being to become. These agents are necessary only for the becoming.
But universal agents are necessary not only that such a being become but also that it continue to be. Thus, in the case of generable
and corruptible things, the action of the heavenly bodies is required
both for becoming and for continuing to be; when the action of the
particular agent ceases, the action of the universal agents, the heavenly bodies, continues; if it ceased, the generable and corruptible
thing would cease to be. In relation to such agents, the *esse* even
of permanent beings is a continuous becoming. But just as the
heavenly bodies are universal agents in relation to all generable
and corruptible things, so is God the universal agent in relation to
all created things whatsoever. Therefore, just as a generable and
corruptible thing would cease to be if the heavenly bodies would
cease to influence it, so also if God were to cease to act upon the
creature, that creature would fall into nothingness. In relation to
the divine causality, the *esse* of every creature is a continuous becoming.

Some, Quidort adds, find a second difference between successive
and permanent beings. Both, they say, are continually becoming.
But whereas there is a continual renewal and corruption in successive beings, there is none in permanent beings. To illustrate their
point, they cite two examples: the water that spouts forth from a
fountain is continually renewed, but the ray of light that comes
from the sun, while continually becoming, is not renewed for it
is always the same ray.

Quidort has already indicated that, in his view, to say that the
esse of permanent beings is a continuous becoming is entirely unintelligible. Here he adds that the example which is used by those
who maintain that it is a continuous becoming, the ray of light in
the air, is misleading. Light has a diverse *esse* in the sun from that
which it has in the air. In the sun it has a real *esse;* in the air, only

an intentional *esse*. The light that is in the air is not a purely natural form; it is like an image in a mirror. Now the likeness of a man in a mirror remains only as long as the man stands before the mirror. As soon as he moves away, the image, because of the weakness of its *esse*, disappears. The presence of light in the air is exactly parallel. Because of the weakness of the *esse* of that light, it cannot remain in the air if the sun is removed. It is, therefore, rightly said to be constantly becoming. But created things cannot be classed with such a ray of light or with an image in a mirror. They are subsisting things and receive their natural forms according to an analogy, according to a perfect proportion. They have, therefore, not an intentional *esse* but a real *esse*. They become, but once they have become their *esse* cannot be said to be a becoming.

While, then, it is true that light in the air is perpetually becoming, this is only by accident. Of itself that light has a permanent *esse*. It is only because the sun is continually moving and, therefore, is constantly varying in its relation to a particular part of the air that there is, at each and every moment, a new generation of that ray of light. This new generation results from the new direction of the sun in relation to the air. If, then, the sun were immobile, so that it would always be in the same relation to a particular part of the air, there would be but one light generated and conserved, and its source would be the simple and unfailing light of the sun. The relation of God to creatures, however, is unchanging; it is like that between an immobile sun and a ray of light in the air exposed to that sun. God conserves the original *esse* given to the creature; it is neither necessary nor a fact that a new *esse* is constantly produced.

Turning to the arguments adduced by his opponents, Quidort admits that there is some truth in them. We cannot deny that the action of the particular agent may cease with the production of the effect, and that the action of the universal agent is, nevertheless, still required. Just as the action of the heavenly bodies is needed for the conservation of generable and corruptible things even after the action of the particular efficient cause has ceased, so also the divine action always remains in relation to every being, and every being depends upon this divine action even after the particular agents have ceased to act. But this fact does not demand that we conclude that all creatures are continually becoming. Let us suppose that we place a seal upon water that is perfectly still. As soon

as the seal is placed in the water an impression is formed. Moreover, that impression will be constantly dependent upon the presence of the seal. As long as the seal remains in the water, the impression will be there; but the moment that the seal is removed,
the impression will cease to be.[7] But we cannot say that the impression is constantly becoming. It is made at the moment the seal is
placed in the water and is conserved as long as the seal is present.
It depends upon the seal for its conservation, for its duration, but
it is conserved without any new operation of the seal. In the same
way, creatures are produced by the act of God and are conserved in
esse by that act. There is no question of a constant renewal of that
act, of a constant reception of new *esse* or of a constant becoming.

Moreover, to maintain that permanent creatures are continually
becoming, but without a constant renewal of *esse*, is unintelligible.
How can there be a continual flux where there is no before and
after? Either what is present before gives way to what comes after,
or it does not. If it does not, then the becoming or flux which is
posited is contrary to the very notion of transmutation and succession. But if it does give way, then there is a renewal and the very
supposition of a flux without renewal is denied. It might be suggested that there is a renewal in the flux of *esse* but not in *esse* itself.
But even this explanation cannot be granted, for the priority and
posteriority in motion is always derived from the priority and posteriority in the mobile. If there is a renewal and succession in the
flux of *esse*, that renewal and succession must also be found in the
esse itself. A becoming without renewal is an impossibility.

Henry of Ghent had also attacked, in language strongly remi-
niscent of Quidort, the position of those who held that the *esse* even
of a permanent creature is a continuing becoming.[8] After examin-

---

[7] Perhaps an echo of Grosseteste, *De Unica Forma Omnium*, ed. Bauer ("Beiträge
zur Geschichte der Philosophie des Mittelalters," IX [Münster: 1912]), p. 111.

[8] Compare, for example, Henry's criticism in *Quodlibet* V, 11 (ed. Venice, 1613). I,
fol. 250va: *Si esse creaturae esset in continuo fieri, aut ergo illud esset unum et idem,
aut semper aliud et aliud. Non idem, quia iam habitum esset antequam fieret. Non
aliud et aliud, quia tunc aut praecedens corrumperetur adveniente sequente, aut non,
sed simul cum ipso maneret. Non primo modo, quia non est assignare causam corruptionis. Non secundo modo, quia tunc essent diversa esse simul, aut unum fieret
ex pluribus et esset augmentum* with Quidort's in *Lectura* II, 1, con., fol. 79ra: *Si
esse cujuslibet creaturae esset in continuo fieri, aut illud esset unum et idem, aut
aliud et aliud. Non idem, quia tunc jam habitum esset antequam fieret et sic esse
creaturae antecederet suum fieri; non aliud et aliud, quia tunc praecedens aut corrumperetur adveniente sequente, aut non si simul cum ipso maneret. Non primo
modo, quia non est assignare causam istius corruptionis; nec secundo modo, quia tunc*

ing and criticizing the arguments of his opponents, Henry notes[9] that there are efficient causes upon which the effect depends only for its becoming; if such a cause be withdrawn, the *esse* of the effect is in no way affected. Upon other causes, however, (God in relation to every creature, the sun in relation to light in the air) the effect is dependent not only for its becoming but also for its *esse*. If such a cause be withdrawn, the being ceases to exist. This does not mean that it is by one act that the effect is caused to become and by another act that it is caused to continue to be. These acts are numerically one; to make and to conserve are one, and conversely to become and to be conserved are one. Thus creatures have a caused *esse*, which they possess without any succession or renewal.

Nevertheless, this *esse* is not like the *esse* of God. The divine *esse* is fixed and stable; the *esse* of creatures is fluid and mobile. This, however, does not mean that there is a continual flux or change either in the *esse* itself or in its becoming. There is a certain fixity and stability in the creature's *esse*, but it derives not from the creature but from God. Of itself the creature is prone to nothingness; a potency for *non-esse* is always joined to the act by which a creature has *esse*. It does not enjoy a perfect simultaneity since it always lacks something of perfect act, nor a perfect simplicity since it is always composed of potency and act. Nevertheless, the act which it does have is simultaneous and simple, for its fluidity and mutability are only potential. There is no actual flux or change in its *esse*; its *esse* is not a continuous becoming.

Quidort seems to have Henry in mind when he tells us that some have tried to modify the position of those who hold that a created *esse* is a continuous becoming. According to this modified doctrine, to become and to be conserved are really identical; their distinction is purely in the mind. Thus to become and to have a permanent *esse* would be really identical, and we could say, with truth, that from one viewpoint certain creatures have a permanent *esse* whereas, from another viewpoint, they become as long as they exist.

This opinion would also distinguish between the way in which generable and corruptible things depend upon the heavenly bodies and the way in which every creature depends upon God. The

---

essent diversa esse simul, aut unum esse esset ex pluribus, et tunc esset augmentum et semper majus et majus.

[9] *Quod.* V, 11 (ed. cit.) I, fol. 250va ff.

action of the heavens upon generable and corruptible things is through motion.[10] Now there is a relation which varies constantly between an agent that operates through motion and that upon which such an agent operates.[11] Therefore, it cannot be by an act numerically one that the heavens contribute to the production of things on the one hand, and to their conservation on the other. God, however, does not act upon creatures through motion, but by an action that is simple.[12] Therefore, the action by which He gives *esse* is not numerically distinct from the act by which He conserves *esse*. Hence also, the divine act of conserving is not a series of acts but is rather the continuation of the one act by which God makes the creature to be. At the beginning, indeed, there is a production of something new, for a new form is acquired by the subject; but beyond this no new impetus is to be found, for no motion is involved. Hence the action of God in producing and conserving *esse* is like the action of an immobile sun in producing and conserving a ray of light in the air. If the sun did not move, the ray of light which it produces in the air would be conserved without any new activity, that is, without any new production of light on the part of the sun.[13] So also God conserves the *esse* of creatures, not indeed by constantly giving them *esse,* but by conserving that *esse* which He gave at the outset. Thus, on the part of God, giving and conserving *esse* are really identical; on the part of creatures, therefore, becoming and *esse* are also identical for it is by the act of giving esse that a creature becomes, and by the act of conserving *esse* that it continues to be.

Quidort answers that there is no necessary parallel between making and conserving on the one hand, and becoming and being conserved on the other. A distinction in God that is not real does not demand that the corresponding distinction in creatures cannot be real. For verification, we need only turn to the divine ideas. Everything that is in God is God, and, therefore, not really distinct, yet the diverse ideas are the cause of the real diversity of creatures. The effect does not necessarily have the conditions of its cause, for, as is the case here, the effect may fall short of the unity, identity, and simplicity of its cause. Moreover, the identity of becoming and being conserved would mean that creatures are always being cre-

10 *Cf.* Henry of Ghent, *Quod.* IV, 15 (ed. cit.) I, fol. 217 rb.
11 *Cf.* Henry of Ghent, *Quod.* V, II (ed. cit.) I, fol. 217va.
12 *Cf. ibid.,* fol. 251vb-252ra.
13 *Ibid.*

ated, that is, the creation of each creature would continue throughout the span of that creature's existence. But none of the *auctoritates* teach this; it is not a part of the deposit of faith, nor is it in accord with the ordinary way of speaking.

Quidort prefers to say that permanent creatures have their becoming only in the first instant of their creation or production; after that instant they have a permanent *esse* in relation to every agent whatsoever. Hence, becoming and permanent *esse* are not simultaneous; in fact *esse* is related to becoming in the same way as motion is related to the terminus of motion, if we allow for the diversity between becoming and motion. Just as motion and the terminus of motion are not simultaneous, so also becoming and permanent *esse*.

If we are truthfully to say that a being becomes, two things are required. First of all, there must be a dependence upon the efficient cause similar to that dependence which is found between motion and the heavenly bodies. If motion is to continue, the influence of the heavenly bodies must continue; as soon as the latter ceases, the former also comes to an end. And there must also be a certain initial action that comes and goes. If either of these requirements are lacking, a thing cannot be said to be becoming. Because the first condition is not fulfilled, created things cannot be said to be continually becoming in relation to their particular causes, for they do not continue to be dependent upon these causes once they have been brought into existence; a house, once it has been built, no longer needs the builder in order to continue to exist. On the other hand, it is because the second condition is not fulfilled that the image of an unmoving object in a stationary mirror is not said to be becoming. In this case there is, after the first, no new impetus given by the thing mirrored, although there is a continual dependence of the image upon it. The same thing would be true of the light in the air, if the sun were immobile.

In the first instant in which God produces or creates a thing both of the above requirements are realized: the creature is dependent upon God, and there is present a first impetus by which *esse* follows *non-esse*. But after that first instant, the second condition is lacking: nothing more is added. Although there is a continual dependence upon the action of God, so that if God were to withdraw His influence the being would immediately fall into nothingness, the creature cannot be said to be becoming. A permanent

creature, therefore, is not in continual becoming. After the first
instant, in which it is truly becoming, it has a permanent *esse*: an
esse, nevertheless, that is continually dependent upon the action
of God.

In the second question, Quidort turns to the problem of the
relation between *esse* and essence. He concludes that the essence
and *esse* of a creature are really distinct; his principal argument is
that the created *esse* is caused by God.[14] In the third question,[15] he
considers the divine causality of *esse*: is that causality immediate,
or does the *esse* of a creature flow immediately from its own essence
or, perhaps, from some other created being?

Godfrey of Fontaines, in his eighth *Quodlibet*,[16] asked whether
a substance can be the immediate active and efficient cause of its
own accidents. He insisted that all accidents are caused by a principle extrinsic to their subject. In the case of inseparable accidents,
however, this cause is the generator of the substance. Nevertheless,
there is a sense in which the substance can be called the cause of
the inseparable accidents. That through which something comes
to be is said to be its cause. The inseparable accidents come to be
only through the substance, that is, the substance is the immediate
effect of the action of the generator; the accidents, in a way, are but
mediate effects. This statement, however, must be carefully understood. It must not be interpreted to mean that the generator causes
per se only the substance from which the accidents flow inseparably,
but rather that the generator causes *per se* both the substance and
the accidents; the accidents, however, only in the substance already
existing in act. In relation to these accidental forms the substance
occupies a position similar to that of matter in relation to the substantial form, for matter is, in a way, the subject of the substantial
form. As matter cannot be said to be the efficient cause, principal
or instrumental, of the substantial form, so the substance cannot
be said to be the efficient cause of the accidental forms. On the other
hand, just as matter is necessary for the becoming and being of the
substantial form and is, therefore, spoken of as the material cause,
so also is the substance rightly called the material cause of its inseparable accidents, for the accidental form can be caused only in
it. And since the agent cannot effect accidents except in a substance-

14 *Cf.* A. J. Heiman, "Essence and *Esse* according to Jean Quidort" *op. cit.* p. 144.
15 *Lectura* II, 3, fol. 81rb.
16 *Quod.* VIII, 2; *Le Huitiéme Quodlibet de Godefroid De Fontaines*, ed. J. Hoffmans ("Les Philosophes Belges," IV [Louvain: 1924]), pp. 18-33.

in-act, it can be said that the agent effects the accidents by means of
the substance and that the substance is the cause of its inseparable
accidents. The substance, however, in no way partakes of the causality of the agent, but remains only the subject upon which the
agent operates: the material cause.

This position of Godfrey furnishes the point of departure for
Quidort's discussion of the efficient cause of *esse*. Quidort puts it
as follows. Some, he tells us, maintain that not only *esse* but every
property of a creature flows from some source extrinsic to the essence of that creature. Since nothing can be both the subjective
and the efficient cause of the same effect, they argue that nothing can
be the efficient cause of what is produced within itself. Now the
substance in which properties inhere is by its intrinsic principles
constituted the subject of these properties. But if it were at the
same time their efficient cause, it would be so by reason of these
same intrinsic principles. Thus the subjective and the efficient
cause would seem to be identified. In other words, to say that the
constitutive principles of a substance are the efficient cause of any
of the properties of that substance would be equivalent to saying
that these properties can find their subjective and their efficient
cause in one and the same thing, which, they maintain, is impossible. In fire there is heat, but heat cannot flow from the intrinsic
principles of fire. Fire is generated from fire, and the form of fire
in the generated fire finds its efficient cause in the generating fire.
In the same way, according to this view, the form of heat in the
generated fire is caused by the form of heat in the generating fire,
not by any principles intrinsic to the generated fire.[17] There is,
then, only one sense in which it can be said that a subject is the
efficient cause of its own properties and this is only a very secondary
one: the efficient cause first introduces the substantial form of the
subject of the property, and then introduces the form of the property through the substantial form already produced (Godfrey calls
this causality, but material causality only). The intrinsic principles
of the substance are not truly efficient causes, but only media
through which the efficient cause of the properties operates.

This position, Quidort suggests, is not in entire accord with experience. There are instances where, it is clear, properties flow not
from their substance but from extrinsic principles. When, for instance, fire acts upon air, the form of heat appears first; the form of

[17] *Ibid.*

fire, only later. In this case, the property precedes the substantial form, and since what is prior cannot be caused efficiently by what follows it, at least in such a case, the property does not flow efficiently from an intrinsic source but from the generator of the substance. Moreover, if the generating fire is removed, the heat that has been generated soon disappears: confirming evidence that, in this case, a property is caused by principles extrinsic to its subject.

The production of a property, however, usually follows rather than precedes the production of its substance (Godfrey seems to say that it always follows); heat is usually produced only after a fire has been lighted. When this is the case, Quidort is not at all sure that the properties are caused by an extrinsic generator. They seem to flow, he observes, from the intrinsic essential principles of the subject of which they are properties. If this is not the case, how are we to explain the fact that the subject cannot be caused without them?

Quidort pursues the question no further at this point. He limits his discussion to the production of *esse*. Whatever be the case, he says, concerning the other properties, the *esse* of no creature proceeds from the intrinsic essential principles of that creature. Just as light in the air is not from the air but from the sun, and heat in water is not from the water but from the fire that heats the water, so also the *esse* of every creature comes to the creature from some extrinsic agent and not from its intrinsic principles.

If, he says, there were a being whose *esse* flowed from its intrinsic essential principles, it would be of the very essence of that being to be; it would contain the sufficient reason for its own existing; it would be able to bring itself into existence. It is, however, impossible that any being cause itself to be; even God is not the cause of His own existing. The *esse* of a creature, therefore, must be caused from without.

An examination of the way in which *esse* is predicated of a subject leads to the same conclusion. Quidort distinguishes three modes of predication. One thing may be predicated of another because it belongs formally to the essence of that of which it is predicated, or because it flows as an effect from the essence of the subject, or because it is united to the subject in a purely accidental way. If we maintain that the *esse* of a creature flows from intrinsic essential principles, *esse* must be predicable of the creature at least in the second way, if not in the first; it either flows as an effect from that of which it is predicated or it belongs formally to its essence. *Esse,* if this were true, would be at least as essential to the creature as risibility is to man. But whatever is predicated of a subject in either of these two ways cannot be separated from that subject. Risibility belongs inseparably to man, so much so that it is true to say that even if no man existed, man would still be correctly described as a risible animal. If, then, *esse* were predicable of a creature in either of the first two modes, that is, if *esse* flowed from intrinsic essential principles, it would be just as impossible for a creature not to be as it is for a man not to be risible.

Only the essence of God, however, cannot not-be. Essences, according to Quidort,[18] are of four kinds: (1) There are essences which are indifferent to *esse* and *non-esse* as well as to *esse* in one supposit or in many. Such are the essences of all generated and corruptible things. (2) Other essences are indifferent to *esse* and *non-esse,* and to *esse* in one supposit or in many if they be considered from the viewpoint of their forms, although they are not actually many because the form so fulfills the matter that matter does not and cannot desire another such form. (3) A third kind of essence is that of the angel. The angelic essence is indifferent to *esse* and *non-esse,* but not to *esse* in one or in many supposits and this by reason of its very form. (4) The divine essence cannot not-be; it is not indifferent to *esse* and *non-esse.* Nor can the divine essence be multiplied; it is not indifferent to *esse* in one supposit or in many. The divine essence alone, then, is not indifferent to *esse* and *non-esse;* only the divine essence cannot not-be.

But if every being other than God can cease to be, that is, can not-be, the *esse* of no created being can flow from the intrinsic essential principles of that being. It must, in every case, come from without. But what is its source? Quidort invokes a principle which he learned from the *Liber de Causis:*[19] the same order must be found in causes as is found in effects; the more universal the effect, the more universal is its cause. Now *esse* is common to everything that is. It is, therefore, the most common effect, the universal effect, and can find its sufficient reason only in an efficient cause that is universal. Since God is the only universal efficient cause, He alone can be the efficient cause of the *esse* of creatures.

[18] *Lectura* II, 13, fol. 86rb.

[19] Prop. I, *Die pseudo-aristotelische Schrift über das reine Gute, bekannt unter dem Namen* Liber de Causis, ed. O. Bardenhewer (Freiburg im B., 1882), p. 163; *cf.* also XVII, pp. 179-80.

Does it follow that God is the sole and immediate cause of *esse*? The author of the *Liber de Causis* did not reach this conclusion. It might be argued that God alone bestows *esse* of His own power, but that He can endow others with a power that is properly His so that they might be able to give *esse*, not indeed by reason of any efficiency that is properly theirs, but only because of this participation in the efficient power of Him who has it in His own right.

But to give *esse* to a thing, that is, to make it simply to be rather than to be this or that, is equivalent to bringing it into existence from nothing; to give *esse* is to create. When God created the angels, He created both their essence and their *esse*. To create an angel is not to make its essence to be an essence, for the essence is always an essence; nor is it to make the *esse* to be *esse*, for *esse* is likewise always *esse*. It is to place the essence under the *esse*, and the *esse* in the essence, so that the whole is created by one creation, and the whole exists by one act of being.[20]

For Quidort, then, there is a sense in which essences are eternal. This statement, however, must be carefully interpreted lest it seem to mean that creation is not from nothing but from a pre-existing essence. If we turn, for a moment to the teaching of Henry of Ghent, we find that he distinguishes a two-fold relationship between God and the creature: on the one hand, in the order of knowledge; on the other, in the order of volition.[21] In the former, God is the exemplary cause; in the latter, the efficient cause.[22] God brings creatures into existence in time, but He is their exemplar from all eternity. The divine ideas are eternal; they have an *esse* of their own; they are the essences of things.[23]

Quidort refers to this doctrine of Henry.[24] While he is ready to admit, as we have already noted, that there is a sense in which essences are eternal, he disagrees with the position of Henry. Essences are eternal only in the sense that an essence is an essence from all eternity; and, in the same sense, it is just as true to say that *esse* is *esse* from all eternity. Here there is no implication that the essence of this particular being existed from all eternity and that its coming-to-be is but the addition of *esse* to an already existing essence. For to say that the exemplar is eternal is not to say that that of which

20 *Lectura* II, 5 ad 3, fol. 83ra.
21 *Quod.* IX, 1 (ed. cit.) II, fol. 58v.
22 *Quod.* IX, 2 (ed. cit.) II, fol. 65v.
23 *Ibid.*, fol. 68r.
24 *Lectura* II, 5 ad 3, fol. 83ra.

it is the exemplar is eternal. On the contrary, experience teaches us that an exemplar may precede what is made according to it. Thus a builder may have an idea of the house he is to build long before he begins the actual construction. Essences, it is true, are related to God as to their exemplar; as such, it is true that these exemplars are eternal. But it does not follow that the essences which are con- stituent of things are eternal. God, the exemplar, precedes these es- sences eternally; there is an eternal duration separating the ex- emplar from its exemplate. And this is possible because of the very nature of an exemplary cause. But an efficient cause will not permit such precedence to its effect. As soon as any being begins to be an efficient cause, the effect that flows from such efficiency begins to be; an effect always coexists with its efficient cause. Therefore, as soon as God begins to be the efficient cause, the effect begins to be. Since there can be no precedence of efficiency to effect, God is the efficient cause only in time; but since an exemplar can precede that which is made according to it, God can be the exemplary cause from all eternity. The doctrine of divine exemplars, therefore, in no way contradicts Quidort's original position. There is no precedence of essence to *esse;* essence and *esse* are both results of the creative act. When, therefore, a thing is made to be, that is, when *esse* itself rather than this or that kind of *esse* is given, neither essence nor *esse* precedes. But beyond essence and *esse* there is nothing. Therefore, to make a thing to be in this sense is to create it.

If, then, God were to communicate to a creature the power of conferring *esse,* He would give to it a participation in His own creative power. A creature, however, by the very fact that it is a creature, is a secondary agent and cannot act as a primary agent. Now a secondary agent presupposes the action of a prior agent in its acting; what is more, it requires also, and for the same reason, the effect of that prior agent as the matter upon which it acts. Since it is impossible for a creature to be a primary agent, and since every secondary agent demands a matter upon which it acts, whereas cre- ating implies that there is no matter upon which the creator acts, it is evident that God cannot communicate His creative power to His creature; He cannot give to a creature the power of conferring *esse.*[25]

A creature, therefore, cannot be the principal cause of creation. But Quidort is prepared to go even further. No creature, he main-

[25] *Lectura* II, 5, fol. 82vb.

tains, can be even an instrumental cause in the creative act. His argument is based upon the very nature of an instrumental cause. An instrument has a two-fold activity. There is, first of all, the operation that is proper to it as a being in its own right, an operation that it exercises in virtue of its proper form. But since it is at the same time an instrument, there is a second mode of activity which it manifests that belongs to it only in so far as it is moved by the principal agent. Now this instrumental activity can be exercised only in view of that operation that is proper to the being used as an instrument. The proper operation, therefore, must precede the instrumental; the proper effect will precede the instrumental effect. But in creation nothing can precede the creative act, for creation is precisely a production from no pre-existing subject. Therefore, the proper action of an instrumental cause cannot be presupposed by the effect of the creative act. But if such causality is excluded by the very nature of the creative act, it is evident that no creature can cooperate instrumentally in creation.

The *esse* of a creature, therefore, can proceed only from the creative act of God. It cannot flow from the intrinsic essential principles of what is to be, nor can it result from the agency of any secondary cause. God alone, the universal agent, can produce the universal effect that is *esse*. And God cannot communicate this power to any creature. No creature, acting even by a delegated power, can confer *esse* efficiently nor even instrumentally.

If, however, *esse* cannot flow from the intrinsic essential principles of a thing, what is meant when it is said that form gives *esse*? Quidort answers[26] that the *esse* given by form is not *esse* as such, but rather this or that *esse*. If we are to understand this principle correctly, we must carefully distinguish form in so far as it is form from form in so far as it is a formal cause, and from form in so far as it is neither. Form informs matter, and thus, in relation to matter, it is properly designated form. But it would be incorrect to call it the formal cause of matter, for form does not make matter to be matter. Form is properly called the formal cause only of the composite; and it is only to a composite that it can be said to give *esse*, for it makes a man to be a man. In relation to *esse*, however, it is neither the form nor the formal cause; it neither informs *esse* nor makes *esse* to be *esse*. When, therefore, we say that form gives *esse*, we mean only that it is the form that makes this particular composite

[26] *Lectura* II, 3, ad 2, fol. 81vb.

to be the composite that it is. What is given by the form is not an actual *esse,* but only a quidditative *esse.* The form, indeed, has *esse* only in virtue of this actual *esse.* If, therefore, the causality of the first principle, the causality of God, and actuality were removed from form, form would neither give *esse* nor even have *esse;* in fact, there would be no form.[27] We must beware, therefore, of making form either the formal cause or the efficient cause of *esse.* The formal cause is entity; the efficient cause is God.[28]

For Quidort, then, the *esse* of every creature is distinct from its essence and is added to that essence. It cannot, however, flow from the essence but must be caused by God; essence and *esse* are caused by one divine act. God's causality does not cease with the giving of *esse.* If the creature is to continue to be, it must be conserved at every moment of its duration by the divine causality. This does not mean, however, that the *esse* is only a continued becoming. Although the divine act of making and of conserving are really identical, becoming and *esse* are distinct in a permanent creature. The creature begins to be and then continues to be; its beginning-to-be is a becoming but its continuing-to-be is a permanent *esse.*

[27] *Quod.* I, 2; *Nine Mediaeval Thinkers,* ed. A. J. Heiman ("Pontifical Institute of Mediaeval Studies, Studies and Texts," [Toronto: 1955]), 276.
[28] *Cf.* A. J. Heiman, "Nine Mediaeval Thinkers," *op. cit.,* p. 144 ff.

A Phenomenological Approach to Realism

by Robert J. Henle, S.J.

☆ ☆ ☆ ☆ ☆ ☆ ☆ ☆ ☆ ☆ ☆ ☆ ☆ ☆

I T IS THE PURPOSE of this paper to present an approach to that evidence upon which, ultimately, philosophical realism as well as the realism of the common man rests. It is never an easy matter to bring basic evidence under personal philosophical reflection; a steady and, indeed, courageous effort is always indispensable.

The climate of contemporary thought is, however, particularly unfavorable to the sort of realism I am proposing. Hence, before going on to the evidence itself, a preliminary discussion of some of the assumptions which, from the start, rule out realism and prevent any serious consideration of its case is necessary.

Anti-Realist Assumptions

When a discipline reaches a certain maturity, having attained an inner homogeneous structure of fact, concept, and argument, an investigation of its methodology becomes possible. We isolate the methodology and set it down as a prolegomenon to the study of the discipline itself. Thus we are able to dictate beforehand the conditions of proof, the range of competency, and the criterion of legitimacy for the discipline. In a highly sophisticated intellectual culture like our own, which has been long preoccupied with questions of methodology, we come to think of the methodology as prior to and determinant of the discipline, and, when generalized, as prior to and determinant of all intellectual effort. No doubt, from the standpoint of logic, this sort of analysis of disciplines is legitimate, even indispensable, but to absolutize this priority is to limit intellectual legitimacy to those conditions already recognized in what-

68

ever disciplines we consider established. We come to forget that in the order of discovery we cannot determine conditions of proof until after we have solved the proposed problems. We actually discover the logic of mathematics, for example, only by examining successful mathematical thinking. I do not mean that we accept this logic *because* it succeeds in a pragmatic sense; but that, on inspection of successful mathematical thinking, we see such and such procedures and we see, by inspection, their validity. Without examples of mathematical thinking, there would be no method to perceive. I am saying that in all cases of evidence, we either do or can come to see its validity by intellectual insight. Consequently, there is no way of laying down, *a priori*, an exhaustive list of the types of legitimate evidence. Yet, we have come to assume and to demand evidence of a certain type.

It is part of the heritage of Cartesianism that, on the side at least of rationalism and idealism, genuine philosophical proof is expected to be of an abstract kind. It is only since Descartes that we have had a series of efforts to *prove*, in an abstract sort of way, the existence of an external material world. The assumption that only such a proof will be valid is to be found in all types of rationalism, even in certain rationalistic types of Thomism. Unless one is willing to reconsider this assumption, the case for realism is closed before trial.

On the other hand, we have an empirical tradition which demands proof within the limits of a certain type of factual evidence, often identified with the type of evidence proper to experimental science. Within the framework of Humean epistemology or of logical positivism, there is no evidence for realism.

In short, the present situation in philosophy makes it necessary to request a suspension of accepted ideas of evidence prior to the examination of the case for realism. In this sense, realists must ask for a "fresh start," an open-mindedness in the matter of proof and evidence, not merely to establish their case but also to obtain a hearing at all. If the conditions of proof which realists must meet are laid down from current philosophical positions, realists will have nothing to say. A sympathetic attention to realist arguments requires then a powerful reflective effort to escape (at least temporarily and for the sake of argument) from the pervasive assumptions regarding conditions of proof—an effort all the more difficult, since, as Gilson pointed out, the non-realist is so unaware of the vast gulf which here separates him from the realist.

Modern thought commonly presents the possibility of only two types of philosophical structure. The great rationalists—Spinoza, Wolff, Hegel—present us with the idea of a philosophical system, logically interrelated, deductive, and, in a sense, closed and complete. Those who rebel against the vast ambitions of such systems tend, on the other hand, to see philosophy as constantly evolving, tentative, really without a single certitude that can claim any permanence. A realistic philosophy is neither of these; yet, in the face of current modes of thought, it is difficult even to explain what sort of structure it has. Since it is experiential, it cannot be *a priori* and deductive; since it is an effort to understand reality, it cannot be complete and closed. Since it is evidential, it will establish insights, arguments, and understandings with definitive though not exhaustive conclusiveness. It is difficult to categorize its structure in current terms, since it lies wholly outside of the assumptions of contemporary philosophy. It mediates the entrenched dichotomies, but not by a theoretical compromise. Rather it destroys the dichotomies at the start by a more comprehensive approach to evidence and by rejecting, on evidential grounds, the assumptions common to both sides of the dichotomies. If realism is expected to follow the patterns set within modern philosophy by Descartes or Locke or Spinoza or Hume or Kant or Hegel or Dewey, realism will have nothing to present. It is in the paradoxical position of being more experiential than empiricism yet intellectual, of being certain yet not concluded.

There is another pervasive modern influence which has conditioned o u r mentality against realism. The modern scientific movement, because of its vast success, both practical and theoretical, has penetrated all our thinking. It has seemed to discredit all other modes of knowing and has brought us, consciously or unconsciously, to accept the scientific mode of thinking as the univocally ideal one, if not the only valid and fruitful one.[1] It supplies the principal models for epistemological analysis and establishes the principal criteria for judging validity. Philosophers themselves have accepted these models and standards, have tried to make philosophy dependent upon science and conformed to its ideals of

[1] For an extreme example of this attitude, see Homer W. Smith, "Objectives and Objectivity in Science," *The Yale Scientific Magazine*, XXIII, (February, 1949), 2.

method.[2] I do not think any of us has escaped the pressure of this absolutizing of scientific method. But, again, unless we are willing to consider, at least, the possibility of other valid methodologies, realism need not be heard; it will be condemned out of hand.

Thus, realism does not compete on equal terms with other philosophies in the arena of modern thought. It cannot play the game according to the rules commonly assumed for philosophical discussion. It cannot join the discussion at the purely theoretical level, for it is opposed, in its very origins and foundations, to basic contemporary assumptions. This is why I have thought it necessary to prefix this brief and inadequate discussion of assumptions as a sort of prolegomenon.

The Method of Inquiry

And so we return to the problem of making a "fresh start." In a sense, of course, men must always make a fresh start in order to become philosophers, for philosophy is essentially a personal understanding and depends upon personal grasp of evidence. In this respect philosophy is quite unlike science. Scientists can build on the work of others without forever repeating the experiments and deductions others have made. It is enough that the experiments have clearly been shown to be repeatable, under controlled conditions, by competent practitioners. But, if a scientist need not reproduce all the experiments upon which his science depends, the philosopher must personally repeat all the essential experiences on which philosophical understanding depends. He cannot build on the insights of other men any more than he can grow by another's digestion. Much less can he accept and peddle the conclusions, the phrases and terms, of another's philosophy. Surely he needs the aid of others, the guidance and inspiration of the great thinkers of the world, but this essentially consists in discovering for himself, under their guidance, the same experiences and the same reflections. Philosophy is essentially personal, yet, for all that, it is not subjectivistic, for we do indeed have essentially similar experience and share a common intelligence.

It is for this reason that scientific exposition, once the difficulty of technical terms is overcome, is essentially easy while philosophical exposition remains always difficult. The philosopher must aim

[2] *Cf.* Hans Reichenbach, *The Rise of Scientific Philosophy*, (Berkeley: University of California Press, 1951).

to induce in his readers the same experiences and the same reflection as he himself has. Perhaps exposition is not the proper mode of philosophical communication and teaching. Plato's description of philosophical inquiry seems to me still the best.

> For in learning these objects it is necessary to learn at the same
> time both what is false and what is true of the whole of existence
> and that through most diligent and prolonged investigation, as
> I said in the beginning; and it is by means of the examination
> of each of these objects, comparing one with another—names,
> definitions, visions, and sense perceptions proving them by
> kindly proofs and employing questioning and answering that
> are devoid of envy—it is by such means, and hardly so, that
> there bursts out the light of intelligence and reason regarding
> each object in the mind of him who uses every effort of which
> mankind is capable.[3]

We must approach the enterprise of a "fresh start" as far as possible unhampered by assumptions, postulates, or preconceptions, but, above all, with a determination to take into account the evidence, all the evidence, the evidence in its fulness. I realize, of course, that, in speaking of "evidence," I am already using a sophisticated term which immediately raises the haunting spectre of methodological disputes. Even if we substitute a seemingly undetermined word like "fact," this, too, turns out to be a chameleon sort of term, taking its shading from backgrounds of epistemological theory. Yet somehow we must get behind or beyond theory to the underlying "given," the irreducible data which are prior to all theorizing.

It seems to me that the very fact that we are able to communicate at all—and we do so communicate—shows that we have some common experience and some basic common convictions. At the level of highly sophisticated theory, we become, often enough, mutually unintelligible, and our criticisms ineffective, yet there remains a basic communication between the adherents of even the most diverse theories. In this basic communication, our experiences of knowing, of thinking, of intelligence are, at least, very similar, and, however divorced from common ways our systems may seem, there are common points of fact which none of us can, in fact, ignore. We are men before we are philosophers and philosophers because we

[3] *Epistle* vii. 344b.

are men, and we cannot forget, as philosophers, those things that are experiences common to all of us as men.

And indeed it seems obvious that, in the history of human culture, all theories relate somehow to something encountered, unavoidably, in experience. No science or theory has even been elaborated as an explanation of something with which man has no contact of any kind, real or imaginary. People find plants and develop botany; man observes the spots of moving light in the night skies and begins to be an astronomer; we find ourselves reasoning and, reflecting on this process, discover the laws of logic. So also all discussions of knowledge relate to a certain experience or set of experiences—a certain "given" which men have found and, even prior to all theories, called by a distinctive name—the experience of knowledge.

Monsieur Jourdain of Molière's *Le Bourgeois Gentilhomme* was delighted to learn that, without knowing its definition or laws, he had actually been speaking prose all his life, however imperfectly. Thus, any man, who comes to a philosophical understanding of knowledge, must be able to see that *this* is what he had been doing all his life, however imperfectly.

Where, then, and how does any man make contact with this "given"? Where does he first discover it in human experience? It would seem obvious that knowledge is first discovered within personal experience by "reflection" on "acts" of spontaneous knowledge which even the child and the untutored savage (the mediaeval *rusticus*) have or make or suffer. For all our experimentation, no one has isolated "knowledge" from conscious experience. We may build up a collection of centipedes; capture and cage the platypus; produce pure hydrogen and cap it in a test tube. But knowledge cannot be chopped out in objective chunks, or cabined, cribbed, and confined outside of conscious experience. We first make contact with knowledge there, and there we must look if we would observe it in its natural habitat. This would seem to be an irreducible starting-point from which no one has ever wholly freed himself and to which, in the last analysis, we must all return. It is clear, then, that the very "given" of knowledge dictates a certain approach to it. If it "exists" or is "given" only in conscious experience, we must "look" at it there and this "looking" we call "conscious reflection."

Does this bring us, right at the start, to the "discredited" method of "introspection"? Well, what if it does? If there is no other place to look directly at the experience all the world has called "knowing," then introspection it must be. It may well be that, for certain purposes of experimental psychology, introspection has proved an inadequate and unreliable instrument, but this does not necessitate abandoning all use of it. And indeed we cannot. Even those who have attempted to study knowledge solely on its "objective" or "external" side really know what they are talking about and what they are explaining only from a prephilosophical introspection. Without this, their whole effort to make knowledge the object of external observation would be meaningless. Introspection and reflection must be used at least to identify that which is being discussed; only through it is the specific and concrete "given" of knowledge discovered and a *common* basis for explanation established.

We must, therefore, "look" at knowledge as it goes on or is given, and this "looking" we shall call conscious reflection. This reflection must not be a casual interior glance, a mere "identifying" of the "given," but rather a prolonged gaze, a continuous and concentrated effort to "see" what knowledge is really like, for, as Chesterton has said, it is not easy to see something as it really is, even (or perhaps especially) when it is pervasive and obvious. On the other hand, we must abstain, initially, from all efforts to theorize, to infer, or to "explain." We wish, at first, only to report what is seen. Thus an examination limited exclusively to the "given" brings us to a first methodological stage which approximately coincides with the "phenomenology" described by Professor Wild, ". . . the disciplined attempt to describe and analyze the immediate data of awareness as they are given."[4]

---

[4] *The Return to Reason*, (Chicago: Henry Regnery, 1953), p. vii. The phenomenological method here described must not be identified with the philosophy of Husserl. Thomism itself stands in need of a thorough but preliminary phenomenology. As a living philosophy, it has suffered many of the same pressures as other modern philosophies and too often has allowed itself to be forced into a rationalistic framework. Faced by the modern type of problem, Thomism has had no way, without a phenomenology, to maintain its unique grounding in experience. In this situation rationalistic Thomists have become far less experiential than was either Aristotle or St. Thomas. A phenomenology will not only ground Thomism in its own right here and now, not only open up intercommunication between all modern thinkers, but will also make it more loyal to its historical origins. Professor Gilson has noted that traditional metaphysics has lacked a phenomenology which it needs.

"Mais il n'est pas moins nécessaire à la métaphysique de l'être de s'appuyer sur une phénoménologie qu'elle dépasse sans pourtant s'en séparer. C'est pour avoir manqué de ce lest salutaire, qu'elle s'est si souvent perdue dans le vide de l'abstrac-

It is an indispensable peculiarity of this kind of description that we do not here report facts beyond others' experience, as a traveler does in describing foreign countries to his home folk. We are not trying to communicate through vicarious experience; rather, the method sets up, through its reportorial description, pointers and guides which will enable others to find and identify and "see" the same data within their own personal experience. By the same token, the process is not a demonstration, a logical proof, but a "monstration," a pointing-out. We have analogous experiences. "See that cloud there?" "Where?" "Up there, to the left of the large mass." "Yes, yes." "See how it resembles a camel, the hump towards the north and down there the four feet." "Yes, yes, I see it; it is indeed very like a camel." So two experiences are found to agree; a common "given" is established. This is our purpose: to sift experience and our descriptions of it till we reach a common agreement on a mutually and truly discovered given.

Derivative Knowledge

When an adult begins—when, let us say, he moves from being just a man to being a philosopher—to reflect upon the pieces of knowledge which he possesses or fancies he possesses, he readily discovers that these pieces display marked differences. He knows that the world is round, that Columbus landed in the West Indies, that his little girl likes candy, that $f=ma$ is a formula of physics, and so on. Obviously, a great deal of his "knowledge" is derivative and second-hand. He has never had first-hand experience of the shape of the earth; he knows it because he learned it in school, or because he knows the proofs developed by geographers and astronomers, but he only understands what it means and accepts it as fact because of prior knowledge. Let us exclude from our first investigation all the knowledges which are obviously derivative and if one makes trial of this, he will find, I think, the greater part of his knowledge is in this category.

Direct Acts of Underived Knowledge

We thus find ourselves reduced to instances of origins of understanding as well as factual acceptance, to instances that seem to display an immediacy and directness not characteristic of conclusions

tion pure et qu'elle a cru pouvoir user du concept comme d'un équivalent du réel. *L'être et l'essence*, (Paris: J. Vrin, 1948), p. 728.

or elaborations. Let us take, then, a simple case. I take a block of wood in my hands and examine it. Before I found this block of wood, before I saw it and handled it, I knew nothing of this block of wood. True, before it entered my experience, I knew, somehow, something which I subsequently use to understand it. I may, for example, say at once that it is a "book end." I previously knew something of books and how they are held upright. I may call it "wood"; I previously knew this strange noise "w-o-o-d" and its significance—certain characteristics by which I recognize the sort of thing meant. I come to this piece of wood equipped with, so to speak, ready-made "understandings" which I apply to it. As I consider this concrete experience, I see, however, that this previous knowledge equipment is usable only because here and now, as this piece of wood enters my conscious experience, I know it directly. It is this direct knowledge of the piece of wood which determines my selection of previous knowledges and my application of them to this wood. Thus, by reflection, we can distinguish these two kinds of knowledge and can set aside, for the moment, the previously acquired knowledge. Obviously, as it functions in this instance, it is derivative and lacks the immediacy we are looking for. What we are interested in is my direct knowledge given or gained in *this* experience.

Sense and Intellectual Awareness

As I hold the wood in my hand and reflect upon the concrete experience, I become aware of the high complexity of this simple, everyday act of knowing. I can, in fact, distinguish different layers or aspects or factors within the concrete unity of the act. I can distinguish an experience in which I am immediately aware of certain "qualities": the wood is "smooth"; the wood is "cool"; the wood is "hard"; and so on. This awareness itself is double: I am aware in a sort of "feeling" way, I shall call this the level of "sensing." At the same time and in the same concrete act I am aware at a level of consciously and self-consciously possessed recognition. *I feel* that the wood is cool; *I know* the wood, the coolness and the feel of it. I shall designate this level as the "intellectual level."

I am here merely pointing to a primitive distinction within awareness. That sense-awareness and intellectual-awareness are radically different kinds of awareness, and what these differences are can only be "seen" by continued reflection and by a similar use of many different sorts of knowledge experiences. Since I am only schematizing the line of reflection, let me simply assert the fact of these two types of awareness and let this rough characterization serve for the present.

Here I must point to a difficult but extremely important fact. The level of intellectual awareness is not related to the level of sense awareness, as an inference to a premise, or even as a second-step to a first-step. There is an experiential interpenetration of the two levels, such that the intellectual awareness (with its accompany-self-awareness) is in as immediate contact with the objects of sensing as is the sense awareness itself. It is very difficult to express or describe this unique and concrete experience which is unlike any other experience we have. Perhaps nothing in the data of our knowledge experience has been so obscured and disfigured by theory. Sense and intellect were sharply not merely distinguished but separated, by Descartes, for example; the intellectual was reduced to the sense, by Berkeley, for example; the intellectual was ignored, by Hume. It seems to me obvious that, in the direct act of knowing a material thing, the sense and intellectual levels interpenetrate, maintaining distinctive characteristics indeed, being, that is, what they are, yet not compartmentalized, not operating like successive stages in an assembly line, but together in a mutual immediacy.

Let us return to the experience itself, for we must remember that our method requires us to examine the complexity of the act while maintaining its concreteness and its experiential unity. No facet or factor can be allowed to assume, in our reflection, an abstract and independent status.

The Immediacy of Knowledge in Direct Acts

Now, we find that within this experience we can say of the wood, "This is a thing" and "This is an extended thing." Let us reflect upon this situation. The awareness, at both the sense and intellectual levels, which is (partially) expressed in these statements, depends upon the presence of the wood in my hands. Remove it and I cannot so speak because I am not so aware. Place it there and I am able confidently to make these assertions.

When I am directing my attention to the wood I hold in my hand, I find that the experiential awareness is not an awareness, initially and simply, of some concept, idea, image, or feeling—some modification of myself. On the contrary, in the immediate experience of the wood, I am quite *unaware* of whatever concepts, images, or subjective modifications may be present. The experience itself in its concrete totality presents itself to my reflection as an awareness of an existing extended thing. It is factually false to say that by my direct acts of underived knowledge I immediately know only concepts or ideas from which I must, somehow, infer an existing object. On the contrary, in my direct acts of underived knowledge, my knowledge and the attention of my mind terminate immediately at the existent thing.

Since the seventeenth century it has been widely accepted that we know first and immediately subjective modifications of our own minds or bodies, concepts or ideas. This assumption was common to both rationalists like Descartes and empiricists like Hume; it was taken over, almost without examination, by Kant. It has reached the status of an obvious fact. A genuinely independent examination of our knowing experience yields a quite different report. The assumption stands in contradiction to the facts. Reid and others have pointed this out. Thus Professor Joad has gone so far as to say, "Almost I would go to the length of maintaining that we never know our own ideas."[5] What Professor Joad asserts is true of our immediate acts of underived knowledge. It requires an interruption of the act itself, a realignment of activities and indeed discursive argumentation to discover the concepts and ideas through which we know. What is obvious is that we know directly an existing thing. Since it is the *thing* that we *know*, the activities *by which* we know are no part of *this knowledge*.

The realist, therefore, challenges the assumption that in acts of underived knowledge our awareness is limited to the immanent products or operations of our own consciousness. And he challenges it, not on another assumption or because of philosophical consequences, but as a matter of fact and experience.

Partial Subjectivity of Sense Experience; Objectivity of Direct Intellectual Knowledge

Let us describe the factual situation from a slightly different standpoint. The sum-total of "objects" which, in this experience, stand over against awareness are not adequately reported as an assemblage of sense data, of coldness, smoothness, roundness sensed. Reflection on experience shows that this is a distorted description:

⁵ C. E. M. Joad, *Decadence*, (New York: Philosophical Library, n. d.), p. 130.

(1) because our awareness does not terminate at sense qualities but at a thing (*"this* feels cold" is a report of immediate experience); (2) because our awareness of the thing is not simply a sense aware- ness; intelligence penetrates to the object through the sense aware- ness; (3) because what is immediately understood of the wood is not only sense qualities but non-sense aspects—"This is a thing," "It exists," "It is extended." The sense data description is an ab- straction which ignores evidence and omits precisely the crucial evidential facts.

The complex apprehensions within our awareness as we con- sider the piece of wood in our hands cannot be expressed in a single statement. We must say: "The wood feels cold"; "This is a thing"; "This exists"; "This is extended"; and the like. I have already pointed to the distinction between sense-apprehension and intel- lectual-apprehension. I have tried to point to the sense-apprehen- sion by describing it as a sort of "feeling" experience. The wood "feels" cold; it does not "feel existently" or "thingly." The very expressions we use for the sense-level experiences convey (what I reflectively discover with clarity) that these "felt" qualities involve a subjective factor. We find that there is, indeed, a certain sub- jectivity and relativity in strict sense-apprehension. This fact was recognized from the very beginning of philosophy.[6] Wine, said the Greeks, tastes sweet to a well man, but bitter to the diseased man. What feels cold to the warm hand feels warm to the cold hand. But, in the concrete experience, the relativity of sense-experience is seen to be immaterial to the objectivity of our apprehension of an existing thing. The relativity is in the quality of sense-experience, not in the total concrete object of the sense-intellect apprehension. Whether the wood feels hot or cold to me, whether at first it feels hot and later cold, I nonetheless apprehend a thing existent and extended. The quality of the sense experience does not touch the immediate intellectual-apprehension.

If we reflect now on the content of intellectual apprehension, we find that we discover in the immediate apprehension of the wood itself what we express by saying: "This is an extended existing thing." We use *these* words and, if one wishes to speak logically, we apply *these* corresponding concepts, because we find, in this case, an existing extended thing. The meaning of the words and

[6] *Cf.* D. J. B. Hawkins, *The Criticism of Experience,* (New York: Sheed and Ward, 1945), pp. 24-41.

the content of the concepts are verified or realized in the piece of wood of which I am aware. These meanings (which are here simply "understandings" of the wood) do not reveal (as did "coldness," for example) any relativity or subjectivity; they are the very expression of a *discovered objectivity*. The act of immediate knowledge is an encounter with an "other," a really existing extended thing; it is an encounter which is not merely physical or material but conscious; it is an encounter the meaning of which I immediately grasp. It is from this encounter (repeated a thousand times in daily experience) that there arises my understanding of "objectivity," of "existence," of "thing," of "extended." All of these are seen to be non-relativistic; they are in some sense "absolute," unqualified by subjective experience.

Intellectual Knowledge and Intelligibility

Here we can increase our understanding of intelligence. For here it consciously apprehends precisely an "existent," in its own existence, in its otherness and independence. This cannot be and is not *sensed;* it is intellectually understood. The act of knowing takes conscious possession of a thing which is not the act of knowing, not its subjective qualifications and not existentially a part of my consciousness. The understandings of things, which cannot be sensed, I call intelligibilities, because they are apprehended by operations at the level I have called intellectual. Intelligibility is not some added magical property of the things presented in my experience; it simply names the objective reality of the thing as I find it open to my intellectual apprehension. The intelligibility of things is simply the objective reality of things: the intellectual understanding of things is simply the grasp of their objective reality.

To summarize: What I am saying is that, if a man maintains a prolonged meditative reflection on any simple instance of the sort here described, if in doing so he washes his mind of all theories, abstractions and preconceived expectations, he will find that in this experience he immediately encounters an independently existing extended thing; that this encounter is an immediate intellectual awareness, however partial and fragmentary, of an objective reality; that his intellectual awareness goes beyond subjective states, indeed, through them as through transparencies to the objective.

Further, I am saying that in this instance (and a thousand others) the nature of intelligence is seen to be not a qualified way of experiencing, but a power of understanding realities and hence a power correlative to reality or existence.[7] One does not *assume* that reality is intelligible; one *finds* that it is intelligible. The full elaboration of the intelligibility of the real requires other reflections and other experiential facts, indeed, inference and argumentation, but the basic point is found here in any simple immediate act of underived knowledge. It is from this starting-point that a realist moves to a full metaphysical understanding of the traditional dictum *ens est verum*.

Special Difficulties of This Procedure

I should like to pause here and call attention to several difficulties in this method. It is inherent in our descriptive technique that attention can be called, only step by step, part by part, to the elements, moments, or factors which are found in interrelated unity in every moment of the experience on which we are reflecting. Our purpose is not to isolate and consider separately the various elements, but to point to them in the complexity of experience. Unfortunately, while it is possible to apprehend them simultaneously, it is not possible to talk about them simultaneously. Hence, the piecemeal descriptive analysis employed should not itself be reified but should be related to and checked by the experience itself. Unfortunately, by the same token, a certain amount of repetition is unavoidable since each aspect is actually interrelated with all the others and must constantly be tied back into the total concrete picture.

Secondly, I am fully aware that what I am trying to do will appear to many, at least at first sight, to be superficial, non-philosophical, and perhaps naive. If I may inject a personal note, I am

[7] Intellectual awareness displays a great versatility and variety of operation and occupies a commanding position in our conscious life. In order to distinguish sense from intellect, philosophers have made use of various facets of intellectual activity, many of them more clear-cut than the characteristic pointed out in the text. For example, a very common method is to appeal to the universalizing power of intelligence which is not displayed by sense. This yields a sharp distinction but it has several disadvantages. First, it is inadequate, since it uses only one achievement of intelligence; secondly, it points to an activity at a second level of reflection, not to the presence of intellect in immediate knowledge of the individual; thirdly, it tends to reify the "universals" and to give priority to universality over intelligibility and so artificially creates the problem of universal knowledge versus singular realities.

also aware how extremely difficult it is for anyone nurtured in the main lines of the modern philosophical tradition to immerse himself in this sort of experiential reflection and (an even harder thing) to take it seriously. I have myself lived through these difficulties, held to the search by puzzling over why men as men and often enough as philosophers have been, as a matter of fact, tenaciously and incorrigibly realists while modern philosophers in general have been unable to find any adequate grounds for it and have found themselves constantly driven from realistic positions. Having struggled with all these difficulties, I am now convinced that the reason for the situation is threefold: (1) the evidence for realism has been systematically ignored and indeed *a priori* excluded—through assumptions—from consideration; (2) the experiential data have been in modern times described in an inadequate and falsifying way; (3) in the resulting absence of evidence, the numerous apparent difficulties against realism have become real and insoluble difficulties. (To illustrate briefly from history, once the problem had been set as it was by Descartes and Locke, the appearance of a Hume became, logically and psychologically, possible—indeed almost inevitable.)

The Intentionality of Knowledge

To resume our reflection. When, in this complex but unified act of knowledge, I encounter the external real existent "this," which is the piece of wood, and express my awareness, "This is a real thing," I see, by reflection, that all the activities of knowing are indeed my activities, the awareness is indeed the awareness of a determined individual subject—myself. Yet my awareness goes immediately, through these activities yet without making them part of the object known, to another "this," thus transcending the activities and the determinations of the self. This characteristic of knowledge which is factually discovered in experience has been called its intentionality. Notice that this is a primitive characteristic which knowledge displays in its simple and direct form; yet it is to be found in its more elaborate exercises. For example, when I am speaking of Paris with a friend, recently returned, and I ask whether Paris is still gay under spring skies, whether Notre Dame still has its glorious glass, whether the taxis still drive madly about, I am thinking not of images or concepts but of the real Paris, the Paris so many miles away, so independent of me. My mind, through its concepts, "intends" a real object. Obviously, were knowledge not "intentional," all this would be sheer fooling; we would indeed be closed in like miners buried in a fall-in, left to groundless inference and guessing. Knowledge is intentional whether the data and evidence for the knowledge are immediately apprehended (as in the case of the piece of wood) or are indirectly grasped, not being now immediately present to awareness (as in the case of Paris). Indeed, knowledge displays its intentional character even when no decisive evidence is at hand, either immediately or indirectly. When we suppose an objective state of affairs as merely possible, it must be conceived intentionally, i.e., as a possible state of *real* affairs. Thus, were not knowledge intentional, the detective in our stories could not propose his first (and, by the rules of such stories, therefore most certainly wrong) reconstruction of the crime.

We come to see that intentionality is a primitive character of knowledge, then, by a prolonged and ever-deepening reflection on cases of immediate apprehension, such as ours of the piece of wood. Since it is thus discovered experientially as a fact, a thousand theoretical difficulties may indeed deepen our understanding of and our wonder at its uniqueness but cannot bring us to reject it. *Contra factum non valet illatio.* Once again, if we approach knowledge not experientially but abstractly, after the manner of the idealists and the rationalists, intentionality will be sieved out through abstract logic and be forgotten. Unfortunately, this is what actually happened. For intentionality was almost forgotten in the logicizing decay of scholasticism and was theoretically ignored (it was employed practically, of course) through most of the subsequent modern development. Brentano was one of the first to call attention to this oversight and thus to restore to certain modern thinkers some conscious recognition of intentionality.[8]

The Intelligibility of Being

I have already rather briefly pointed to the meaning of the term "intelligibility" and given some examples of a discovery of intelligibilities in direct knowledge. Among these was the intelligibility of "existent thing." If I may again repeat, we find this intelligibility

[8] *Cf.* L'intentionalité et les reductiones," *La Phénoménologie et la Foi*, ed. Revmond Vancourt, (Paris: Desclée, 1953), pp. 31-39.

[9] For a longer effort, likewise at least partially phenomenological, to present the basis of a realist metaphysics, see my *Method in Metaphysics*, (Milwaukee: Marquette University Press, 1951).

in the piece of wood itself as presented in experience, and, indeed, it is from the immediate experience that we gain, by intellectual insight, an understanding of this intelligibility. I know what "existent" means only because I encounter "existents" in experience. The fact is that I do have such an intelligible grasp on the "existent," on the determinate individual existent in its own objectivity. It is perfectly true that "existent" cannot be analyzed into prior concepts since it is itself a primitive intelligibility. It cannot be logically located in prior categories, since it is radically unique and hence either denatures or is denatured by any category we attempt to apply to it. Yet all the world knows, however vaguely and imperfectly, what "existent" means. It is not the business of the philosopher to get rid of this primitive understanding, impatient with it because it is recalcitrant to logical manipulation or the clarifying simplifications of reductionism. There it is: the primitive intelligibility, given in experience, forced upon us at every turn and constantly intruding itself into philosophy even after a neat naturalism has thought its exorcism final. It is our business to accept what is thus given and by long, hard meditative reflection to deepen our understanding of it and to describe its full wealth.

In short, immediate experience lays open to human intelligence the primitive and inclusive intelligibility of (now merely to transpose our terminology) being, not the *a priori* and empty concept of the rationalists, rightly derided by empiricists, but the understanding of being as it is in real things, an understanding that can never be closed and neatly catalogued. The development of realist metaphysics is simply a long intellectual effort, first, to see ever more deeply into the myriad experiences which reveal beings and to deploy the full richness of these ever-growing insights. Thus, the principle of contradiction, as a metaphysical principle, is only a statement of the intellectually recognized absolute character of a concrete existence. The elaboration of the transcendentals—the classic one, true, and good—of the realist tradition is only an unfolding of the full meaning of being as it is found in experience. The inferences and argumentations of metaphysics all proceed from the seen implications of concrete existents. Obviously, a detailed justification of realist metaphysics would demand a complete exposition of this discipline, a task impossible here.[10] I have at-

---

[10] For a systematic presentation of realist metaphysics, see George P. Klubertanz, S.J., *Introduction to the Philosophy of Being*, (New York: Appleton-Century-Crafts, 1952); and *cf.* Wild, *op. cit.*, pp. 36-37.

tempted merely to point to those pieces of evidence which force one to realism and to indicate by what loyal meditation on experiential reality one moves along the road (always arduous but especially for those who must rebuild their own step by step) to realism.

Conclusion

In this paper, I have attempted to point out by taking one of a thousand possible instances where one must look for evidence of the sort which establishes realism. I have given a kind of minimal schema of that evidence. It is perceived in a thousand such experiences perhaps inaccurately, unreflectively, confusedly. But it makes every man a common sense realist and even keeps every philosopher a practical realist. It is this evidence, massive in its immediacy and pervasiveness, which, when examined by critical reflection and probing meditation, presents the groundwork of both a realistic epistemology and a realistic metaphysics.

Realism does not present itself as one side of an "option," which distinguishes temperaments: the "tough-minded" from the "soft-minded," the naive from the critical, the crude from the refined. It does not present itself as a system structured on reasonable or useful postulates which work out well, in theory and practice, and, without imperative urgency, simply recommend themselves to sensible people. It presents itself as the result of the data of experience, of ineluctable evidence; primitive, massive, all-pervasive, which, while never adequately describable, yet grows all the stronger and firmer as critical reflection tests and examines it. It is not an assumption; it is not a postulate; it is not an option; it is the acceptance of things as they are.

ॐ Some Mediaeval Doctrines
On Extrinsic Titles to Interest

by Herbert Johnston

☆ ☆ ☆ ☆ ☆ ☆ ☆ ☆ ☆ ☆ ☆ ☆ ☆ ☆

URING the present century one of the most significant features of the world of scholarship has been a searching and fruitful study of the life and thought of the Middle Ages. Among the vast number of topics thus opened to investigation and debate, that of mediaeval teachings on the morality of usury in its various forms has attracted a certain amount of attention.[1] Any doctrine on the morality of usury and any examination of such doctrine, would be incomplete without the supplementary consideration of extrinsic titles to interest. The purpose of this paper is to bring together some of the mediaeval teachings on this last subject. Before these teachings can become intelligible, however, a brief explanation of the more basic doctrine on usury itself will be necessary.

The most clear, complete, and consistent of the mediaeval positions on the morality of usury is that of St. Thomas Aquinas.[2] It

---

[1] Though of unequal merit and written from different points of view, the following may be mentioned as representative works that deal more or less expressly with the subject: Patrick Cleary, *The Church and Usury* (Dublin: M. H. Gill & Son, Ltd., 1914); J. L. Benvenisti, *The Iniquitous Contract* (London: Burns, Oates, and Washbourne, Ltd., 1937); Andrew Beck, A.A., "Usury and the Thelogians," *Dublin Review*, 203 (July, 1938), 78-89; T. P. McLaughlin, C.S.B., "The Teaching of the Canonists on Usury," *Mediaeval Studies*, I (1939), 81-147, II (1940), 1-22; Bernard W. Dempsey, S.J., *Interest and Usury* (London: Dennis Dobson, 1948); Benjamin N. Nelson, *The Idea of Usury* (Princeton: Princeton University Press, 1949); Raymond de Roover, "Joseph A. Schumpeter and Scholastic Economics," *Kyklos*, X (1957), 115-146; John T. Noonan, Jr., *The Scholastic Analysis of Usury* (Cambridge, Mass.: Harvard University Press, 1957). The last named work was not available until after this paper was finished.

[2] For a much fuller account of the Thomistic doctrine on usury, including the

is developed partly from passages in the *Nicomachean Ethics*,[3] and partly from the idea of *mutuum* found in the *Corpus Iuris Civilis*.[4]

The whole argument is based ultimately on a certain conception of the nature of money. Barter is awkward, the argument runs, because of the difficulty of making commensurate the vastly different types of goods or services to be exchanged. Yet their relative values must be established if exchange is to take place at all. It was for this reason (and also to serve as a store of value) that money was invented. Money, then, is primarily a measure of the price of goods or services to be exchanged. As a result of this primary function, money will also serve as a medium of exchange. In this capacity, its principal use is to be spent in the purchase of something. And in being spent in such transactions, the substance of the money exchanged is, as it were, consumed or used up, for it is lost to, or alienated from, the one who spends it.

This fact puts money in that important class of things which, in the language of Roman law, are "weighed, measured, or numbered," are consumed in their proper use, and become the subject of the loan called *mutuum*. The important point about things consumed in their immediate and proper use is that their use is identical with the consumption of their substance. The use of wine, for example, is that it be drunk, and the use of bread is that it be eaten; and such use involves the consumption of the wine and the bread. It follows, then, that the use of things of this sort cannot be separated and treated separately from the things themselves. But this is exactly what a lender attempts to do when he requires a borrower to return more than he borrowed. It is to charge him for the loaf of bread (the one that he returns) and also for his eating it. The lender who does this attempts to separate the inseparable; what he actually does is to sell what does not exist, that is, the use of the thing apart from the thing itself, or to sell the same thing twice. And since money is consumed in use when it is spent in exchanges, to sell the use of money, that is, to take usury, is to do the borrower an injustice.

documentation, see Herbert Johnston, "On the Meaning of 'Consumed in Use' in the Problem of Usury," *The Modern Schoolman*, XXX (January, 1953), 93-108.

[3] Aristotle, *Nichomachaean Ethics* v. 5.

[4] For the basic texts, confer Justinian, *Institutes*, Bk. III, 14, preface; *ibid.*, II, 4 preface and section 2. In the Krueger edition these are vol. I, pp. 35-36 and 13-14 respectively. Confer also, *Digest*, Bk. XLIV, title 7, sec. 24. *ed cit.*, I, p. 764. Also Bk. XII, title 1, second quotation, volume I, pp. 190-191; Bk. VII, title 5, second quotation, *ed. cit.*, vol. 1, p. 138.

It should be pointed out that when it is said that money is consumed in use by being spent, the consumption in question does not involve, as it does with wine and bread, the destruction of a physical substance. The notion of consumption is applied to money in the sense of the alienation of the medium of exchange from the purchaser. Once he spends a certain sum of money, a certain claim on goods and services, a man cannot possibly recover that identical money, that identical claim. And he cannot use money without so alienating or consuming it, for to use money is normally to spend it. It is not the physical nature of the money used that is in question, for that may be metal or paper or bank balances or anything else that men agree upon. What is in question is the substance of money considered as medium of exchange; and in this sense money is really consumed or used up when it is spent.

St. Thomas also develops a secondary argument against demanding more than the principal in a loan. Since the use of money is inseparable from the money itself, a lender cannot give the borrower the use of a sum of money without giving him ownership of the money itself. There remains, of course, the obligation of returning an equivalent amount, yet the actual control over the money, which constitutes ownership, must be transferred to the borrower. To demand further money for its use, then, is to demand something for the use of what belongs to someone else; it is to charge a man for using what is his own. This is clearly unjust.

In this doctrine, the practice of taking usury, that is, of selling the use of money, is condemned on the basis of a conception of money as consumed in its normal use. The condemnation is absolute and admits of no exceptions. The purpose for which the borrower intends to use the loan is not the point, and is irrelevant to the discussion. Further, the amount of the return exacted by the lender makes a difference of degree only; any return at all is excessive when the facts of the situation require that none be demanded.

All of the mediaeval moralists whose doctrine is to be examined here agree on the absolute character of the condemnation of usury, though their basic reasons for that condemnation differ in important respects. But they also agree that under certain circumstances the lender is entitled to the return of more than the principal. They call this return "interest," though with a meaning different from the modern one, and designate by it the amount that "is between" what the lender has at the end of the loan period and what he should in justice have. As the term suggests, then, interest in this usage is not a price paid for the use of money, that is, it is not usury under another name; it is an indemnification for a loss, direct or indirect, suffered by the lender in making or collecting the loan. If the borrower is the occasion of this loss, it is a requirement of justice for him to make it good to the lender. And in demanding that his loss be made good, the lender is not exacting usury. He is rather asking for interest, which is another thing, on a title extrinsic to the loan itself.

On this much, the mediaeval writers are agreed. On the exact circumstances under which interest may legitimately be claimed, that is, on the nature and the application of each extrinsic title to interest, they are not entirely agreed. Not all of the mediaeval moralists whose work we shall consider recognize or even give consideration to the same titles. Altogether, however, they at least discuss four extrinsic titles to interest.

One of these, called *damnum emergens,* is a loss arising directly from the making or the collecting of the loan. An example would be the liquidation of assets at a loss to raise the money for the loan. The lender might claim interest to the amount of the loss sustained.

A second title, called *lucrum cessans,* is an indirect loss resulting from the lender's forgoing a profit that he could have made by using the money in some other legitimate way. An example would be the diverting of money from a profitable investment into a loan.[5] The lender might claim at least some interest for the profit that he was giving up in order to make the loan or for the profit that he missed because the loan was not repaid on time. The first of these reasons comes very near the modern concept of opportunity cost.

What is often recognized as a third and distinct title, *poena conventionalis,* is a penalty generally assessed against a borrower who fails to repay the principal of the loan on the agreed date. Actually, this should not be called a separate title to interest. For if it is interpreted as a purely penal clause, then it is a penalty assessed to discourage tardiness in a borrower, the proceeds of which are to be distributed to the poor rather than kept by the lender as damages. But the whole idea of interest was precisely that of dam-

---

[5] For an explanation of the mediaeval notions of investment and of loan, and a discussion of the erroneous distinction between "production loans" and "consumption loans," see Johnston, *op. cit.,* pp. 104-105, n. 26.

ages, a sum collected and retained by the lender to make good a
loss suffered through his making the loan. And if this title is so
interpreted as the lender's claim on the borrower for damages, there
lies behind it the implicit notion that failure to return on time the
amount borrowed will bring loss to the lender, either directly or
indirectly. The only thing added is the assumption that the lender
will suffer loss if the borrower fails to repay him when he was expected to do so. *Poena conventionalis,* then, is a device for deciding
when *damnum emergens* or *lucrum cessans* will really apply as extrinsic titles to interest; it is not itself a distinct extrinsic title to
interest. It was, however, regarded and treated as a separate title
by many, though not by all, mediaeval writers on the subject.

Also sometimes recognized as another title to interest is the one
called *periculum sortis,* the risk of losing the principal loaned. The
idea here was that of the insurance principle. The lender might
ask the return of a little more than the principal to make up for
the occasional loss that he would suffer in making loans.

Though there is space here only to suggest and not to develop
the arguments, the title called *periculum sortis* is open to serious
objections from the point of view of commutative or exchange justice. For the lender need not make any particular loan if he thinks
it looks risky. If he does make it, he may require such security as
would practically eliminate the possibility of loss. Further, he always has access to legal measures as at least some assistance in preventing loss. To ask for a stronger guarantee than this would seem
to be asking for something more than this world can supply, to be
asking that the contingent order be made the necessary order.[6]
And why should the reliable borrower be penalized for the shortcomings of the unreliable one? It might well be argued that these
marginal loans should not be made at all, and that the real reason
for their being made is the desire of the lender to profit from lending
money rather than risk that money in legitimate but hazardous
investments. The title could then be regarded as a safeguard against
risks that need not be incurred.

The chief and perhaps the only support of *periculum sortis* as
a legitimate title to interest would be from the point of view of
social justice rather than of exchange justice and would apply to

[6] Cf. Frederick E. Flynn, "Wealth and Money in the Economic Philosophy of
St. Thomas" (doctoral dissertation, Notre Dame, 1942), p. 72; McLaughlin, *op. cit.,*
I, 147.

institutional rather than to private and casual lenders. For however careful a professional creditor may be, he is almost bound to
suffer an occasional loss. If he cannot make up this loss from the
only source open to him, that is, his debtors, he will probably cease
lending. And society at large will be the loser. From this point of
view, then, *periculum sortis* might be called a legitimate title to
interest for an institutional lending agency which carefully followed a conservative policy. It could hardly be called a legitimate
title to interest for a merely occasional lender or for one who ran
unnecessary risks in lending. However, those mediaeval moralists
who discuss the title do not make this distinction; it may be presumed, then, that they are speaking of it and judging its validity
as a title of general applicability.

Let us now turn to those men for a brief examination of their
teaching. Though the subject of usury received at least some attention from several moralists in the twelfth century, the first known
treatment of extrinsic titles to interest occurs in the early thirteenth
century *Summa Theologiae* of Robert Courson. The title *poena
conventionalis* is here admitted as a purely penal clause, but not
as damages that the lender may keep. If he fears that the borrower
will be negligent about repaying the loan on time, Robert explains,
the lender may add a penalty for tardiness provided he intends to
distribute among the poor the proceeds of the penalty rather than
keep them for his own use. But if his intention is to acquire something beyond the principal, he is a usurer.[7] Another passage contains a reference to what seems to be *lucrum cessans,* but the text
is obscure and, at least for this writer, does not allow a definite interpretation of Robert's position.[8]

The doctrine of St. Thomas Aquinas on extrinsic titles to interest has been variously interpreted. The texts are not completely
unambiguous; they do, however, seem to support the conclusion
that he recognizes *damnum emergens* and *lucrum cessans,* but only
if the loan has not been repaid on time. The validity of *damnum
emergens* is clearly expressed.[9] So too, however, is the fact that the
borrower is bound to make good the lender's loss only if he has failed

---

[7] For the text involved, see G. Lefèvre, "Le Traité 'De Usura' de Robert de
Courçon," *Travaux et Mémoires de l'Université de Lille,* X (1902), 65-67. Cf. Mc-
Laughlin, *op. cit.,* I, 140. For the place of this treatise in Robert's *Summa,* see V. L.
Kennedy, C.S.B., "The Content of Courson's *Summa,*" *Mediaeval Studies,* IX (1947),
81-107.

[8] See Lefèvre, *op. cit.,* pp. 13-15.   [9] *Summa Theologiae* II-II, q. 78, a. 2, ad 1.

to repay the loan on the agreed date. For the lender can blame only his own carelessness or stupidity if he suffers loss even within the period of the loan.[10]

Lucrum cessans is also a title to interest. Here, however, the borrower need repay only part of the profit that had been expected. The reason is that anyone who possesses money that he can invest has a profit only virtually and not actually, and may, indeed, realize no profit at all.[11] For "profit does not arise from money alone, but from diligence and work."[12] A lender may not, then, stipulate for this compensation in his original agreement with the borrower.[13] Accordingly, he may claim any interest at all on this title only when the principal is not returned on the agreed date of repayment.[14]

Giles of Lessines, a late thirteenth century Dominican, is generally credited with being the author of the *De Usuris in Communi et de Usuris in Contractibus*,[15] a treatise long ascribed to St. Thomas Aquinas and found in Vol. XXVIII of the Vivès edition of the latter's works. The date of the work has been placed between 1277 and 1285.[16]

Giles recognizes the validity of *damnum emergens*, though only if the lender suffers a loss through, for example, having to sell his possessions or borrow money at usury to replace what the lender is keeping from him by not repaying his loan on time. *Lucrum cessans*, however, is not a valid title, because in this case the lender suffers a loss only *per accidens* through not making his intended profit; such profit need not be restored to him.[17] Though he does not mention *periculum sortis* explicitly as a title to interest, Giles seems to imply it in a passage discussing credit transactions. Here he allows the seller to raise his price at the time of the sale because of a loss which he sees threatening him through delay or trouble

---

[10] *Quaestiones disputatae: De Malo* XIII, 4, ad 14.

[11] *Sum. Theol.* II-II, q. 62, a. 4, c., ad 1 and ad 2.

[12] . . . lucrum non causatur tantum ex pecunia, sed ex industria et labore. *Scripta super libros Sententiarum* IV, d. 15, q. 1, a. 5.

[13] *Sum Theol.* II-II, q. 78, a. 2, ad 1.   [14] *In IV Sent.* d. 15, q. 1, a. 5.

[15] See, among others, Pierre Mandonnet, O.P., *Des Ecrits Authentiques de S. Thomas d'Aquin* (Fribourg en Suisse: 1910), p. 152, no. 115; Martin Grabmann, O.P., "Agidius von Lessines, O.P.," *Divus Thomas* (Freiburg), Series III, II (1924), 45-48.

[16] P. Glorieux, *Répertoires des Maîtres en Théologie de Paris au XIIIè Siècle*, (Paris: J. Vrin, 1933), I, 128.

[17] *De Usuris*, c. 20; *Opera Omnia* of St. Thomas Aquinas, ed. Vivès, XXVIII, 607 a-b. Cf. c. 7, p. 585 b.

in recovering the sale price at the future date of payment.[18] Since *damnum emergens* applies, in Giles' doctrine, only after the borrower fails to repay his loan on time, and *lucrum cessans* is ruled out altogether, this treatment of credit transactions appears *to* amount to an admission in principle of *periculum sortis,* though Giles does not apply it explicitly to the loan contract.

A contemporary of Giles of Lessines is Henry of Ghent, a secular master in theology, whose teaching on usury and allied topics is contained in his *Quodlibeta,* composed between 1276 and 1292.[19] The subject of extrinsic titles to interest is not treated expressly but occurs implicitly in Henry's answer to a particular question concerning money entrusted to guardians. If, for example, a hundred pounds belonging to their wards is left in the hands of the guardians for a time, may the wards demand another ten pounds when the money is returned to them? Only, Henry replies, if the extra sum could be regarded as interest. If the wards could make a profit with their money or if their parents wish to have it for business purposes, and if the guardians forcibly and unjustly keep the money against its owners' wills, then the latter may claim more than the original balance. Even here, however, no set sum may be demanded; the amount of interest is to be decided by the judgment of a good man according to circumstances of time, place, and the persons involved.[20]

This answer to the question seems to imply a recognition of the title *lucrum cessans* but only when the loan is not repaid on the agreed date. This is the only title that Henry considers even implicitly, probably because his chief concern in such matters is with the morality of the purchase and sale of annuities rather than with the loan contract considered strictly as such.

In much the same category is Godfrey of Fontaines, whose *Quodlibeta* were written from 1285 to 1297.[21] His only mention of extrinsic titles to interest comes when he rules out the validity of *periculum sortis* on the authority of the decretals of Gregory IX.[22]

[18] *Ibid., c.* 10, pp. 595 b-596 a.   [19] Glorieux, *op. cit.,* I, 388-389.

[20] *Quodlibeta Magistri Henrici Goethals a Gandavo* (Paris: 1518), *Quodl.* XIV, q. 13, fol. 570 r.

[21] Glorieux, *op. cit.,* I, 397-398.

[22] *Quodlibetum Duodecimum,* q. 13; *Les Quodlibets Onze-Quatorze,* ed. J. Hoffmans (Louvain: 1932), Les Philosophes Belges, V, 125.

Duns Scotus expressly admits the validity of *poena conventionalis,* and uses an example that implies *lucrum cessans* as well. The
lender, he says, may include in his contract with the borrower the
stipulation that if the loan is not repaid on time the latter will have
to pay him damages because, for example, he needed the money
for trading; as long as he warns the borrower beforehand, he is
doing no more than preserving himself from loss. Scotus adds that
the lender's intention should be considered honest if he would
rather have his money repaid on time and collect no damages than
receive the penalty attached to tardiness.[23] This last condition is
a recognition of the possible abuses to which the practice of penaliz-
ing an unpunctual borrower would be open. It was because of this
danger that Robert Courson insisted on the purely penal nature
of *poena conventionalis.* In allowing the lender to keep whatever
he receives on this title, even with an added condition as a safeguard, Scotus introduces the notion of *poena conventionalis* as a
claim for damages.

The remaining titles may not be included in the agreement
with the borrower; and to these alone, for reasons that are not made
clear, Scotus reserves the name of *interesse.* These titles are *damnum emergens,* intended to cover a considerable loss arising from
the debtor's failure to repay the loan, and *periculum sortis.*[24]
There is no mention of the *lucrum cessans* implied in the consideration of *poena conventionalis.* Curiously, Scotus bases his recognition of *periculum sortis* on the decretal *Naviganti* of Gregory IX,
a decretal which expressly rules out risk as a valid title to interest.[25]

Though direct access to the texts of the fourteenth century
moralists is not possible at this writing, secondary sources indicate that their number is small and that they contributed no
important innovations to the subject of extrinsic titles to interest.[26]
Apart from these, the next moralist to discuss extrinsic titles is the
French mystic who was also Chancellor of the University of Paris,
John Gerson (1363-1429). In a laconic passage, Gerson allows the
lender to take more than the amount of the loan for any of four
reasons: to save his *interesse,* as a punishment for the borrower's

---

[23] *In IV Sent.* d. 15, q. 2, no. 18. In 12 vols. (Lugduni: 1639), IX, 172.
[24] *Ibid.*   [25] Cf. McLaughlin, *op. cit.,* I, 147.
[26] Noonan, *op. cit.,* pp. 120-121.

negligence, because of the latter's kindness, or simply to make up for his own trouble.[27]

The third circumstance concerns a gift made freely by the borrower to the lender as a mark of gratitude and has nothing to do with extrinsic titles to interest. The second can be identified as *poena conventionalis*. In another passage Gerson deals with this title in almost the same manner as Scotus did.[28]

The first circumstance could be *damnum emergens*, if *interesse* means actual loss only, or it could be *lucrum cessans* as well, if *interesse* also means profit lost because the money was lent rather than invested. Gerson gives no indication which meaning he intends.

The fourth circumstance also presents difficulty. It does not pertain to what some modern moralists have called a service claim, for this latter refers to an advantage given the borrower. Possibly it means recompense for the trouble undergone in collecting a loan from a recalcitrant debtor, though there is nothing in *pro sola propriae vexationis redemptione* that directly suggests this interpretation. A more likely guess is that Gerson is referring to the inevitable expense, including overhead, of making an institutional rather than a strictly personal loan, an expense that the borrower must make good if the institution is to be able to continue making loans. It would be anachronistic to suggest that Gerson is referring to and justifying interest charges by the *montes pietatis*.[29] Yet such institutions as "parishes, religious fraternities, gilds, hospitals and perhaps monasteries" were already attempting "to turn the flank of the usurer" by lending money cheaply.[30] It is quite possible that it is this practice, one apparently unknown to moralists of an earlier century, that Gerson has in mind here.[31]

Gerson's Italian contemporary, St. Bernardine of Siena (1380-1444), allows the lender to receive interest on the titles *damnum emergens* and *lucrum cessans* when the borrower, through his own

[27] *De Contractibus*, Propositio Octava; *Opera Omnia*. In 5 vols. (Antwerp: 1706), Vol. III, col. 179 A.

[28] *Ibid.*, Propositio Sexta, Vol. III, col. 178 B-C. Cf. *Sermo Contra Avaritiam*, Vol. III, col. 1010 D.

[29] See F. R. Salter, "The Jews in Fifteenth-Century Florence and Savonarola's Establishment of a *Mons Pietatis*," *The Cambridge Historical Journal*, V (1936), 193-211.

[30] R. H. Tawney, *Religion and the Rise of Capitalism* (New York: Mentor, 1926), p. 53.

[31] See above, pp. 90-91.

fault, neglects to return the principal when it is due.[32] Further, and this is a new and important development, there is one instance in which it is lawful to stipulate in the original agreement for interest on these titles. If someone is about to invest his money in a definite trading venture or to save himself from an imminent loss, and out of the goodness of his heart lends the money instead to one who begs him for it, he may lawfully impose the condition that the borrower must recompense him for his loss and for the profit he is giving up. St. Bernardine hastens to point out that this interest is not to be received on the basis of any power of profit regarded as inherent in the money itself; and if the circumstances just described are not present, the creditor may receive back only the amount of his loan.[33] Here, though, for the first time, *damnum emergens* and *lucrum cessans* are recognized as titles to interest even *within* the loan period.

The reason behind this innovation is interesting. In dealing with the sale of goods on credit, St. Bernardine explains that if someone obliges a needy neighbor by selling him provisions which are then cheap, but which he had intended to sell at a time when they would probably be much dearer, he may demand the higher price which he had expected to receive in the future. One reason why the seller may thus raise the price of his goods is that he should keep himself from losing a probable profit. The second reason advanced by St. Bernardine, and one that seems closely related to the first, is that:

> what, in the firm purpose of its owner, is ordained to some probable profit, has not only the character of mere money or a mere thing, but also, beyond this, a certain seminal character of something profitable, which we commonly call capital. Therefore, not only must its simple value be returned, but a superadded value as well.[34]

In applying the Augustinian doctrine of *rationes seminales* to money, St. Bernardine restricts its application to the case in which

[32] *Sermo* XLII, *Opera Omnia*, 5 vols. (Venice: 1745), II, 252 b. Cf. *ibid.*, p. 249 b; *Sermo* XLI, II, 239 a.

[33] *Sermo* XXXVI, II, 209 a-b. Cf. *Sermo* XXXIV, II, 201 b.

[34] ... illud quod in firmo proposito Domini sui est ordinatum ad aliquod probabile lucrum, non solum habet rationem simplicis pecuniae, sive rei, sed etiam ultra hoc quamdam seminalem rationem lucrosi, quam communiter capitale vocamus. Ideo non solum reddi habet simplex valor ipsius, sed etiam valor superadjunctus. *Sermo* XXXIV, II, 197 b.

the owner of the money had been on the point of using it in a venture which would probably be profitable. In so doing he is but making more explicit the principle involved in his allowing *lucrum cessans* to be included in the agreement if the lender had been about to invest his money in a probably profitable enterprise.

Duns Scotus already used the term *capitale,* but in the sense of the principal of a loan. To the best of this writer's present knowledge, St. Bernardine is the first to use it in its modern sense.[35] At first sight, he does not seem to be making any great departure from earlier teaching. St. Thomas, for example, teaches that the owner of money already has a virtual profit (see above, p. ??), but emphasizes the point that this profit is as yet only potential, and cannot be treated as though it were actual. And since many circumstances may arise which would prevent this potentiality from being actualized, the lender is not to stipulate in his agreement with the borrower for interest to recompense him for giving up so doubtful a profit, though he may collect something on this title if his loan is not repaid on time. St. Bernardine, in attributing a seminal character to money destined for investment, is pointing out the same fact of potential profit but emphasizes the probability of its being actualized. For this reason the lender may, in this one case, stipulate in the agreement for interest as a compensation for giving up so probable a profit.

Nevertheless, although the difference seems only one of emphasis, it entails important consequences. According to St. Thomas, a man may not transfer his money from investment in a commercial enterprise or from the purchase of a capital investment, in which cases he may take what profit is produced but must risk his money to do so, to a loan in which he need undergo no real risk (for the debtor is legally obliged to repay the loan, and the creditor has, presumably, taken adequate security) and yet is guaranteed a profit in the form of interest. According to St. Bernardine, on the other hand, a man who was about to invest his money in this way may lend it instead, and, with no real risk to himself, secure a profit in the form of interest. St. Thomas, in the thirteenth century, did not consider business investments safe enough for the lender to consider himself sufficiently sure of a profit to stipulate in his agreement for interest on that title. St. Bernardine, in the fifteenth, did

---

[35] Cf. Noonan, *op. cit.*, p. 126, n. 108.

consider business investments (at least as he knew them in northern Italy) safe enough for that condition to be made.

Each may have been right in his conviction, and the latter is insistent that this potential profit belongs only to money which is about to be invested in an enterprise which will probably yield a profit, and that the lender is not to demand interest on the title *lucrum cessans* from the mere fact that he possesses money. The power of producing profit is not, in other words, regarded as inherent in the very nature of the money itself; to have money is not yet to have an actual profit. St. Bernardine did not elevate the observed fact that money, in the economic circumstances of his time and locality, could usually be invested profitably, into the immutable law that it is a source of profit by its very nature and hence can be rented at a price. He would, with St. Thomas, insist that "profit does not arise from money alone." Nonetheless, his possibly well justified commercial optimism led him to make no distinction between real capital goods and the money which purchases them (*rationem simplicis pecuniae, sive rei*), and to apply what is basically the modern notion of capital to both. This is a long stride toward later interest theory, by far the longest taken by any moralist yet considered.

In treating *poena conventionalis*, St. Bernardine follows Duns Scotus closely and, in places, almost verbatim. A lender may stipulate in the loan contract that interest will be demanded if the principal is not repaid when due, as long as he will be damaged by having to wait longer than expected for his money and provided he warns the borrower beforehand. St. Bernardine also repeats Scotus' condition that the creditor must prefer to receive the principal alone on the due date rather than both principal and interest after a delay. He adds that if the borrower fails to pay back the principal on time through no fault of his own, it is not lawful for the lender to insist on the payment of interest.[36]

At no time may interest be made the primary object of lending. If a man lends another a sum of money, expecting that the borrower will not repay the loan on time and so will be bound to pay a further sum in interest, he is guilty of usury, because he does not make the loan freely. Interest may be taken to avoid a loss, but not to make a profit.[37]

---

[36] *Sermo* XLII, II, 253 a-b.   [37] *Ibid.*, p. 252 a.

A contemporary of St. Bernardine's is the Dominican archbishop and social reformer, St. Antoninus of Florence (1389-1459). The texts in which he discusses extrinsic titles are confusing because they involve what appear to be contradictions; they are also too long and involved for their interpretation to be argued here. The most probable conclusion, though, seems, to this writer, to be that St. Antoninus admits the justice of receiving interest on the titles *damnum emergens* and *lucrum cessans* when the borrower neglects, through his own fault, to repay the principal on time.[38]

If this tentative interpretation is correct, St. Antoninus does not, as St. Bernardine does, admit the validity of *lucrum cessans* even within the loan period. And he insists that money is not of itself a source of profit, but rather that it is made profitable through the careful operations of merchants.[39] Nevertheless, he takes the same position as St. Bernardine on money as capital; indeed, he expresses that position even more definitely, though he does not, as St. Bernardine did, offer any explanation. A borrower whose money has been kept beyond the agreed date may claim interest on the title *lucrum cessans* if he had been going to invest it, on the agreed date of repayment, in a given enterprise. The reason is that "such a thing from that time takes on the character of capital," or, again, that "his money now has the character of capital."[40]

Carrying this account to the middle of the fifteenth century has stretched the term "mediaeval" to its limits and perhaps beyond. The account itself has been that of an almost uniformly consistent chronological development of doctrines on extrinsic titles in the direction of their ever broader and more inclusive application.

At the beginning of the thirteenth century, Robert Courson allows *poena conventionalis,* but only as a purely penal clause and not as damages to be collected. Later in the century, St. Thomas Aquinas recognizes the validity of *damnum emergens* and *lucrum cessans,* but only if the loan is not repaid on time. Giles of Lessines admits *damnum emergens* under the same condition and *periculum*

---

[38] *Summa Theologiae,* 4 vols. (Verona: 1740), Pars II, tit. I, cap. 6-7; Vol. II, col. 77, 97-103. Noonan's interpretation of the texts and his conclusion that St. Antoninus admits these titles even within the period of the loan, do not appear conclusive to this writer. To support this statement, though, it would be necessary to analyze the texts at greater length than is possible in this paper. Cf. Noonan, *op. cit.,* p. 128.

[39] *Ibid.,* col. 99 C.

[40] . . . res talis ex tunc assumit rationem capitalis . . . pecunia ejus jam habet rationem capitalis . . . *Ibid.,* col. 98 D, E.

sortis as well, at least in principle. Duns Scotus expands the earlier notion of *poena conventionalis* to cover damages to the lender, and also recognizes *damnum emergens* and *periculum sortis,* and implies *lucrum cessans.*

In the fifteenth century, John Gerson follows Scotus in his treatment of *poena conventionalis* and also permits *damnum emergens* and possibly *lucrum cessans* as well. His most important contribution to interest teaching, however, lies in his expanding the notion by allowing interest *pro sola propriae vexationis redemptione,* quite possibly a reference to the growing practice of institutional rather than personal lending and a recognition of the inevitable expense associated with such activity.

Finally, in the doctrine of St. Bernardine of Siena, we again find the Scotist version of *poena conventionalis* and also *damnum emergens* and *lucrum cessans* applied, under certain definite conditions, even within the period of the loan. Such an extension of the applicability of *lucrum cessans* is based not only on optimism concerning the state of business, but on the radically new concept of money as capital in the modern sense. At this point St. Antoninus also appears on the scene. He and St. Bernardine restrict the application of this concept to a particular sum of money destined for a particular investment. Yet as soon as the money which purchases capital goods is itself regarded as a capital good, the traditional mediaeval doctrine on usury becomes untenable, whether or not the innovator grasps the full implication of his own idea. For that earlier doctrine is based on a conception of money as consumed in use, and all the conclusions that flow from it will follow only as long as that conception is maintained. And it is simply not consistent with the notion of money as capital. Though its full implications will be long in achieving recognition, this radically novel concept turns directly away from the traditional mediaeval doctrines on usury and extrinsic titles, and already announces the advent of modern interest theory.

ᚾᚱᛉ St. Thomas' Treatment of the Axiom, "Omne Agens Agit Propter Finem" *by George P. Klubertanz, S.J.*

☆ ☆ ☆ ☆ ☆ ☆ ☆ ☆ ☆ ☆ ☆ ☆ ☆ ☆

CONTEMPORARY interest in formal logic, axiomatics, and theory of knowledge has brought attention to bear on the "principles" of various philosophers. But we have no right to assume that the formal statement of principles is a necessary requirement for philosophizing, or even that complete formalization is consistent with all types of philosophy. M. Etienne Gilson has recently pointed out that St. Thomas, for one, has not so structured his thinking.[1] A detailed textual investigation of St. Thomas' treatment of the so-called "principle of causality" has shown that for the Angelic Doctor the proposition that "every finite being has a cause" is the conclusion of a demonstration.[2] Studies on some of the common axioms[3] used by St. Thomas show that he sometimes treats them in the same way that he uses for "*dicta authentica*";[4] and that he analyzes them only within particular, limited contexts. In view of this, it is worthwhile to call attention to St. Thomas' formal and relatively full analysis of *finis* in the *Summa Contra Gentiles*.[5] He also does this when commenting on Aristotle's *Physics*[6] and *Metaphysics*.[7] A rapid investigation of St. Thomas' works

[1] Etienne Gilson, "Les principes et les causes," *Revue Thomiste*, LII (1952), 39-63.

[2] Joseph Owens, C.SS.R., "The Causal Proposition—Principle or Conclusion?" *The Modern Schoolman*, XXXII (1955), 159-71, 257-70, 323-39.

[3] Several unpublished theses on axioms like, "Quidquid recipitur," have been written at Saint Louis University.

[4] Cf. M. D. Chenu, O.P., "Authentica et magistralia," *Divus Thomas* (Placentiae), XXVIII (1925), 257-85.

[5] *Summa Contra Gentiles* III, 2-24.

[6] In octo libros Physicorum expositio II, lect. 11-14.

[7] In duodecim libros Metaphysicorum expositio I, lect. 11; V, lect. 1-2.

shows, in addition, over seventy-five passages where the doctrine of *causa finalis* is expounded in a briefer fashion.

Though St. Thomas sometimes uses without explanation the axiom, *"Omne agens agit propter finem,"*[8] he also at other times offers what looks like a proof for it.[9] It seems therefore strange to see Thomists calling it a "self-evident principle,"[10] or giving a logical proof for it.

[8] Explicitly in *Questiones disputatae: De vertitate*, q. 22, a. 1, sed contra 3; *De potentia Dei* q. 1, a. 5; *In II Phys.* lect. 5 (Pirotta, 379); lect. 8 (420); *De malo* q. 1, a. 1; *Summa Theologiae* I, q. 22, a. 2; q. 44, a. 4; I-II, q. 1, a. 2; q. 6, a. 1; q. 9, a. 1; q. 28, a. 6; q. 94, a. 2; q. 109, a. 6; II-II, q. 45, a. 1 ad 1; In libros posteriorum Analyticorum Expositio I, lect. 16, II, lect. 8.

The expression is explicitly stated, but in a slightly modified form, in *Scripta super libros Sententiarum* I, d. 35, q. 1, a. 1; II, d. 37, q. 3, a. 2; d. 38, q. 1, a. 1; *S. C. G.* II, 30; III, 162; *De potentia Dei* q. 3, a. 15; *In II Phys.* lect. 11; *Sum. Theol.* I, q. 23, a. 7; I-II, q. 17, a. 8; q. 90, a. 1.

It is expressed in the form of a double negative in *S.C.G.*, III, 17, 107; and *Sum. Theol.* I, q. 5, a. 2 ad 1; q. 7, a. 4.

[9] In addition to the passages mentioned in notes 5, 6, and 7, other texts are: *In I Sent.* d. 45, q. 1, a. 3; II, d. 25, q. 1, a. 1; *S.C.G.*, I, 37, 44; II, 23; *De potentia Dei* q. 1, a. 5; *In II Phys.* lect. 5 (368-69), lect. 10 (468); *In I Metaph.*, lect. 4 (70-71); II, lect. 4 (316-19); *Sum. Theol.* I, q. 23, a. 7; q. 44, a. 4; I-II, q. 1, a. 2.

[10] Most Thomists know that most of the manuals of Thomistic metaphysics speak of the "principle of finality," and say that it is "per se known." Some authors have treated this principle at length. Reginald Garrigou-Lagrange, O.P., has given the fullest exposition in *Le Réalisme du principe de finalité* (Paris: Desclée de Brouwer, 1932); according to him the principle is evident a priori, by the simple understanding of the terms (p. 117). There is an indirect proof, *ex absurdo* (p. 118-19). There is no middle term that could be used for a proof, but there is an "explanation" of the principle in the general principle of sufficient reason (pp. 118). Though Father Garrigou-Lagrange speaks of the basis of the principle in tendency, the intentionality of action, he immediately speaks of its opposite as being indetermination (p. 119). George M. Buckley, *The Nature and Unity of Metaphysics* (Washington: Catholic University of America Press, 1946), says, "The end is the sufficient reason which explains the action of the agent . . . the principle of finality is analytical, analogous, and also necessary according to the second mode of perseity" (p. 201). James F. Anderson, *The Cause of Being* (St. Louis: B. Herder Book Co., 1952), says that the ultimate ground of finality is the composition in all finite things of essence and the act of existing (p. 149). Msgr. Louis De Raeymaeker, in his *Philosophy of Being*, trans. by Edmund H. Ziegelmeyer, S.J. (St. Louis: B. Herder Book Co., 1954), gives a brief history of the various doctrines about this principle (pp. 259-60), and concludes by saying that it is proved by an analysis of particular concrete beings (pp. 260-61), and later gives the analysis from indifference (pp. 270-71). A. Chollet, writing on causality in the *Dictionnaire de théologie catholique* (Tome II, part 2), argues from adaptation in living things and from the tendency to stability in the non-living (columns 2017-19); he holds that the principle of causality is a "part" of the principle of sufficient reason (column 2030), and that the judgment is analytic (2031). Francis Aveling, writing on cause in the *Catholic Encyclopedia* (vol. III), derives our knowledge of causes from experience,

In order to discuss St. Thomas' texts, it is first necessary to find a suitable English translation for *finis*. Technical terms are difficult enough to translate in themselves. The difficulty is made more complex by the sorts of objections that modern philosophers raise against the so-called "principle of finality" and the attempted answers of Thomists.

Originally, the word *finis* meant "boundary" and "limit."[11] In the first instance, the reference was the boundary of a field; the meaning was naturally extended to signify any termination or determination. What does it mean in the context of St. Thomas' philosophy?

One helpful consideration can be found in St. Thomas' arguments against the possibility of an actually existing infinite multitude.[12] Having expounded the difference between a per se and an accidental multitude, he argues that neither kind of infinite multitude can exist in the real order. We are not interested here in the argument drawn from the nature of a real multitude as numerable. But the next argument proceeds thus:

> Likewise, the multitude of real things is created, and every created thing is included under some certain intention of the Creator, for *no agent does anything in vain.* Hence it is necessary that all created things be comprehended under some certain [i.e., definite] number.

We can note in this argument the opposition between the certain, definite intention of the creative cause, and the rejected indefiniteness which is likened to "emptiness" (*in vanum*), or "meaninglessness," "aimlessness."[13]

and interestingly enough avoids any reference to a principle and its deduction (pp. 463, 466).

[11] For the history and meanings of *finis*, see *Harper's Latin Dictionary*, ed. by Charlton T. Lewis and Charles Short (New York: American Book Co., 1907), pp. 751-52, *s.v.* It is worthy of note that the Greek word τέλος has an entirely different derivation from τέλλω, to make, or τέλλομαι, to become (see the *Greek-English Lexicon* of Liddell, Scott, and Jones [Oxford: Clarendon Press, 1940], pp. 1772-74, *s.v.*).

[12] *Sum. Theol.* I, q. 7, a. 4. Compare: "Ad hoc quod aliquid sit finis alicuius motus continui, duo requiruntur: quorum unum est quod sit ultimum motus. . . . ," *In II Phys.* lect. 4 (348); "Nullum carens fine est perfectum, quia finis est perfectio uniuscuiusque. Finis autem est terminus eius cuius est finis; nullum igitur infinitum et interminatum est perfectum," *In III Phys.* lect. 11 (747).

[13] "*In vanum*" is translated "aimlessly" by the Fathers of the English Dominican Province in their *Summa Theologica* (London: Burns, Oates, and Washburn, n.d.), I, 80.

The gist of this argument is put positively later on: "Every agent intends to make something definite, as is clear from what was said above about the infinite."[14]

A second consideration is supplied by one of St. Thomas's "proofs" of the axiom. One of the longer texts where this argument is given is the following:

> It must be said that every agent necessarily acts *propter finem.* For if the first one of several causes subordinated to one another is removed, the others also necessarily are removed. But the first of all the causes is the *causa finalis.* The reason for this is that matter does not receive form except insofar as it is moved by the agent, for nothing brings itself from potency to act. But the agent does not move except *ex intentione finis.* For if the agent were not determined to some effect, it would not do this rather than that. Therefore, that it may produce a determinate effect, it is necessary that it be determined to something certain which has the character of *finis.*[15]

Finis in the light of these passages contains two notions: (1) it is the term, outcome, result of some action, and (2) it is definite, determined, as contrasted with the indefiniteness of potency. The traditional translation, "end," has the advantage of being well-known, and also of being derived from a place-relation in a way similar to *finis;* it has the disadvantage of implying "cessation from activity," and of having been involved in a confusion of doctrines. (The terms "finality" and "final cause" have even more unfortunate connotations — and, after all, philosophers have to take common language as it is.) "Aim" does not suggest the notion of "outcome" and "completion of a task." "Purpose" is quite inadequate, since in English usage it implies consciousness and knowledge in the agent. "Object" and "goal" are the least involved in undesirable connotations, but "object" already has other meanings in Thomism, and does not have the notion of "outcome" or "term of action." Hence, "goal" is suggested as a translation for *finis;* "goal-directedness" to replace the abstract and awkward "finality," and "telic cause" to translate *"causa finalis."*

Now that we have settled on a translation of the terms, we can return to our text and see precisely what St. Thomas is trying to prove. The crucial sentence is: "For if the agent were not deter-

14 *Sum. Theol.* I, q. 23, a. 7.
15 *Sum. Theol.* I-II, q. 1, a. 2.

mined to some effect, it would not do this rather than that." St. Thomas presumes that the efficient cause as such has an ordering (dynamic orientation) to its act and product. This ordering is not in question in the texts which we have so far seen. What is in question is the character of the terminal object. Our first text above has said that this terminal object cannot be nothing—*in vanum*. Our second one says that this object must be definite, determinate (incidentally it does not say that it must be singular or specifically determinate). There are also some texts which argue that this object must be good (or at least appear to be good).[16]

In the light of St. Thomas's analysis of act and potency, it becomes clear that the potential as such cannot be an efficient cause, for the efficient cause as such is in act. Hence, unless the efficient cause is fully determinate, it is not sufficiently actuated to produce its effect.[17] Hence, one function of the telic cause is to give the ultimate determination to the efficient cause, and to do this the telic cause itself must be a determinate goal.

It will be seen at once that this argument is not simply a summary of experience, though all its operative conceptions are derived from immediate experience. Rather, the question concerns the necessary relations between metaphysical principles (act, potency, specification, and the like), and the evidence is the evidence of those principles themselves as uncovered in rational analysis. Moreover, if the premises of the argument are granted, it does not seem that anyone would deny the conclusion. (And, consequently, it is almost useless to urge this argument against those who deny the goal-directedness of nature.)

In my analysis of this argument, I have remarked that St. Thomas "supposes" the truth of the premises. Was this remark legitimate? And did St. Thomas himself think that something more could be said about them? We can profitably look at the formal discussions referred to above, and begin with the section from the *Summa Contra Gentiles*.

After the usual introductory chapter, the third book of the *Summa Contra Gentiles* begins a discussion of telic causality. The second chapter bears the heading, "That every agent acts for a

---

[16] S. C. G. I, 44; *De potentia Dei*, q. 1, a. 5; *De Malo* q. 1, a. 1; *In II Phys.* lect. 5 (379-80), lect. 10 (468); *In I Metaph.* lect. 4 (70-71); II, lect. 4 (316-19); V, lect. 3 (781-82); *Sum. Theol.* I-II, q. 9, a. 1.

[17] *In I Sent.* d. 45, q. 1, a. 3; *In II Sent.* d. 25, q. 1, a. 1; S. C. G. I, 37, 72; II, 40; III, 107; *De Potentia Dei* q. 1, a. 5; *In II Phys.* lect. 10 (468); *Sum. Theol.* I, q. 44, a. 4.

goal"; it contains seven arguments, which, however, are not all on an equal footing. The first and fifth arguments complement each other; the third and fourth are negative versions of the second; and the sixth and seventh are again distinct. Thus, we can consider the arguments as making up four different proofs, and we will consider them according to this division.

> In those things which evidently act for a goal, we call that the goal to which the impetus of the agent tends. For when the agent attains this it is said to attain its goal, and when it fails it is said to miss its goal. This is clear in the case of a doctor working for health, and a man running toward a certain terminus. And, so far forth, it makes no difference whether that which tends to the goal be cognoscitive or not. For as the target is the goal of the marksman, so it is the goal of the movement of the arrow. Now, the impetus of every agent tends to something definite. For, a particular activity proceeds not from just any power, but from heat there comes heating, and from cold, chilling. Therefore, actions themselves differ specifically according to the differences of active powers. But an action sometimes is terminated at some product (as construction at a building, healing at health); but sometimes not (as understanding and sensing). And if the action is terminated at some product, the impetus of the agent tends by means of the activity to that product; but if it is not terminated at some product, the impetus of the agent tends to the activity itself. Therefore, it is necessary that every agent in acting intends a goal: somtimes indeed the action itself, sometimes something produced by the action. . . .
>
> Furthermore, every agent either acts by nature or by intellect. About agents by intellect there is no doubt that they act for a goal, for they act, preconceiving in their intellect that which they gain by the action, and they act from such a preconception — for this is what it means to act by intellect. Now, as in the preconceiving intellect there is the whole likeness of the effect which is arrived at by the actions of the one understanding, so in a natural agent there pre-exists a natural likeness of the effect, from which [likeness] the action is determined to this effect (for fire brings forth fire, and an olive, olives). As, therefore, an agent by intellect tends to a determinate effect by its action, so also the agent by nature. Therefore, every agent acts for a goal.[18]

[18] *S. C. G.* III, 2, "In his enim" and "Adhuc."

Of these two arguments, the first argues that, with respect to their being goal-directed, there is no difference between cognoscitive and non-cognoscitive agents. The second explains why this can be said, namely, in that a "likeness of the effect" pre-exists in both kinds of agents — in the cognoscitive, in its knowledge; in the non-cognoscitive, in its nature. Note also that both arguments argue that a goal must be definite. In both of these considerations there is nothing that we have not already seen in the first text above.

But the *Summa Contra Gentiles* text has an added point: it speaks of the "impetus" of the agent, and says that the agent "tends" to its goal. We must consider, therefore, over and above the simple notions of agent, action (and product, if there is one distinct from the activity), also the notion of appetite (for this is what "impetus" means), or tendency. It is, therefore, the presence of appetite in the agent which makes it possible to say that what is *de facto* arrived at by the agent is truly a goal and cause of activity. The existence of appetite in the agents of our experience is in this text merely pointed *to* by the expressions we have singled out, but what is important for our present purpose, is that it *is pointed to.*[19]

The second, third, and fourth arguments of the chapter belong together. We can look more briefly at this series.

> In regard to all agents acting for a goal, we call that the goal beyond which the agent does not seek anything. Thus, the activity of the doctor goes on until health is reached, and when it is, he does not strive for anything further. But in the case of every agent it is possible to find something beyond which the agent does not seek anything, otherwise actions would tend to an indefinite, which is impossible. . . .
>
> Moreover, if the actions of an agent were to go on to infinity, it is necessary either that something be produced or not. . . . It is therefore not possible that actions proceed to infinity. Therefore there must be something, after whose attainment the effort (*conatus*) of the agent ceases. . . .
>
> . . . If the *conatus* of the agent is not for something determinate, but actions . . . proceed to infinity, the active principles must also go on to infinity. But this is impossible. . . .

19 Cf. *In II Sent.* d. 1, q. 2, a. 2 ad 3; d. 25, q. 1, a. 1; III, d. 23, q. 1, a. 4, qa. 3; S. C. G. I, 37; II, 30; *De veritate* q. 22, a. 1, sed contra 3; *De potentia Dei* q. 1, a. 5; *In I Metaph.* lect. 4 (70-71), lect. 11 (179); *De Malo* q. 1, a. 1; *Sum. Theol.* I, q. 5, a. 2 ad 1; I-II, q. 1, a. 2; q. 9, a. 1; q. 17, a. 8. See also some texts on love and desire, e.g., *In II Sent.* d. 1, exp. text.; *Sum. Theol.* II-II, q. 17, a. 8; q. 132, a. 4.

In this series of arguments, there is the same set of considerations that we have met before. This time St. Thomas speaks of an agent "seeking" and "striving" as well as "tending." These terms again indicate, though they do not describe or explain, the factor of tendency as a necessary factor in agency.

The sixth argument of this chapter deals with the notions of "fault" and "monstrosity." St. Thomas points out that we do not speak of a fault if "an agent falls short of something for which it is not ordered." But what a fault is in art, that a monstrosity is in nature. And the notion of monstrosity also implies that a natural cause is ordered to some effect which is somehow missed.

The seventh and final argument of the chapter is the familiar one of indifference.

> If an agent did not tend to some determinate effect, all effects would be indifferent to it. But that which is indifferently related to many does not do one of them rather than another. Therefore, that which is possible with respect to both [sides of a contradictory] does not lead to an effect unless it is determined by something to one of them; therefore, it would be impossible that it would act. Therefore every agent tends to some determinate effect, which is called its goal.

But in contrast with the first text quoted above, the present one uses the fact of tendency in the agent, and puts tendency along with act and determination (as opposed to potency, indifference, passivity).[20]

In summary, then, three of the four proofs intended by St. Thomas to establish the proposition that every agent acts for a goal explicitly employ the evidence of tendency. Only one — the argument from our recognition of faults and monstrosities — argues from order, and this one, in its form, is very like an *ad hominem* argument. Yet this order is "dynamic," not merely formal, and so it is possible to say that even this argument implicitly rests on tendency.

So far, then, in the *Summa Contra Gentiles* two points have been established: (1) that all agents tend toward a goal, and (2) that this goal-of-tendency is always determinate. St. Thomas next asks the question, "Does every agent act for a good?"

---

[20] Cf. *In I Sent.* d. 35, q. 1, a. 1; d. 45, q. 1, a. 3; *In II Phys.* lect. 5 (368-69).

Chapter three of the third book gives nine arguments to show that every agent acts for a good.[21] Of these, eight are more or less analytic in character, as we shall see; the second last one is more or less empirical, and the editors have inserted a reference to Aristotle's *Physics* in it. Let us look first at the analytic arguments. (1) That to which an agent determinately tends must be proportioned to it, and the proportioned (or, suitable) is what we mean by good. (2) The goal is that at which the tendency of an agent comes to rest, and it belongs to the function (*ratio*) of the good to terminate appetite. (3) Every action is in some way directed to the act of existence, but existence is a good. (4) Every action is for some perfection, of the agent or of the effect, and perfection is the same as good. (5) Every agent acts inasmuch as it is in act and tends to an effect in some way similar to itself, hence, to an act, and every act is a good. (6) An intelligent agent, determining its goal for itself, does so under the aspect of good; natural agents, whose goals are determined for them by some appetite, also act for good. (7) Everything tries to avoid evil, and so everything tends to good. (8) The moved and the mover have a common goal; that which is moved is moved to some act, which is a good.

It is easy to see that these arguments are analytic, in that they take notions and conclusions already acquired elsewhere, and put them together to generate new knowledge. In this sense, they could be called apriori or deductive arguments. (Some of them, in fact, are verbal, in that they move from one synonym to another.) By contrast, the eighth argument is quite different.

> We see in the works of nature that what is better comes about either always or for the most part. For example, in plants the leaves are so disposed as to protect the fruit, and the parts of animals are so disposed that the animal can be conserved. If this happens apart from the intention of the natural agent, it will be from chance or fortune. But the latter alternative is impossible, for that which happens always or for the most part is not from chance or fortune — this happens for the lesser part. Therefore, the natural agent intends that which is better, and much more manifestly the cognoscitive agent. Therefore, every agent in its action intends a good.

---

[21] This point is also made by St. Thomas in *In II Sent.* d. 37, q. 3, a. 2; *S. C. G.* I, 1, 37; III, 107, 116; *In II Phys.* lect. 5 (379-80); *De potentia Dei* q. I, a. 5; *Sum. Theol.* I, q. 5, a. 2 ad 1, a. 4; q. 44, a. 4; I-II, q. 28, a. 6 et ad 1; q. 94, a. 2, q. 109, a. 6; II-II, q. 17, a. 8; q. 132, a. 4.

"We see," says St. Thomas, and frames an argument from experience. First, he states that in fact the effects of natural causes are good, either always or for the most part, and indicates by two examples where the evidence for such a statement is to be found. (The examples are those of Aristotle in the second book of the *Physics*, as is also the following argument.) Next St. Thomas argues that it cannot be supposed that these are chance (unintended) effects, for the latter happen only for the lesser part. Therefore, the good which is ultimately effected by the natural agent was intended at the beginning of the action. That an intelligent cause intends the good is more evident — and here St. Thomas seems to be saying that this, too, is a fact of experience.

Chapters four to fifteen inclusive consider the problem of evil: how it is caused, how it is related to nature and to will, what it is, and how it causes (or, better, can be said to cause).

Chapter sixteen then formally combines the results of chapters three and four: that the goal of everything is a good. Given the conclusions of these chapters, the deduction is, of course, a simple one, but St. Thomas seems to think it is important enough to state it explicitly.

Let us next turn to the discussion of the *Commentary on the Physics of Aristotle*. Aristotle argues in the second book that the philosophy of nature must consider the cause of natural things and happenings; that there are four kinds of cause; that all four must be considered in this discipline, and that the telic cause really is a cause. We will consider the *Commentary* beginning with this last point.

The discussion begins with the doctrine of the Ancients (the pre-Socratics) who denied that nature acts for goals. The Ancients held that consistency of action does not show the reality of goals, even when they are advantageous. This position was worked out through two examples. First, the rain which benefits crops falls, not to benefit them, but from the "necessity of matter" (mechanical necessity in modern terminology). For, given the cold of the higher regions, water vapor must condense, liquid water must fall; but that crops are benefited is accidental, since they might also be spoiled. Secondly, animals have parts that actually are suitable to them, but this does not show goal-directedness. For, we can suppose that the parts and organs of animals developed by the necessity of their composition; the animals with unsuitable organs died, and the factually successful combinations survived — without any order of nature in either case.

At this point St. Thomas interposes a comment whose basis can be found in the *Commentary* of Averroes.[22] The illustration of rain is not well chosen. For, the growth of crops is not the goal aimed at in rainfall; rather, rain is for the sequence of generation and corruption, and this goal is attained, not merely accidentally. We can note, incidentally, that the approach taken by Aristotle and the Ancients involves one serious difficulty, namely, of discovering what the goal of a natural process is. Aristotle (and Averroes who actually made the correction) seems not to have adverted to this difficulty, and it is not clear that St. Thomas realized its gravity. At any rate, he does make the comment as an aside.

Aristotle then gives four reasons why he says that nature acts for a goal. The first is an analysis of what is meant by a natural event compared with what is meant by a chance event; the former happens always or for the most part, the other rarely. The second reason is a more penetrating one, and is Aristotle's most important contribution. As a thing is equipped to act, so it acts naturally. But the things which act naturally act in such a way as to attain results (and this is a factual, descriptive statement). Therefore, things are equipped to act so as to attain results; or, they have a natural aptitude to attain them; or, natural things act for goals. *Nature* here is explicitly conceived as principle of activity, which, unless it is impeded, will attain the goals which it is equipped to produce. The third reason is that in some cases, effects are achieved both by nature and by art. But, when they happen artificially they are made for a purpose. Moreover, in both cases, the same sequence of steps occurs, the same order obtains. Therefore, things which happen naturally also are for goals. Finally, goal-directedness is evident in animals, and to a lesser degree in plants. But neither of these act from intellect, but rather from nature — and this is shown by the invariance of their activity. (The force of this last step depends on the insight that it is the special characteristic of intellect-and-will to be able to grasp and choose alternative means to a single goal.) Therefore, some things in nature act for goals.

These arguments are of different kinds. The first is a simple analytic argument working from Aristotelian notions of cause and

22 Averroes, *in hunc locum*, II, 5. c. 77; cf. also, *In IV Phys.* 5. c. 83. Averroes writes as if he is merely making explicit what Aristotle intended to say.

chance already established. The second is also analytic,[23] but at a more profound metaphysical level: in terms of nature as essentially a principle of activity (previously examined in the beginning of the second book). The existence of nature as a principle of activity is declared'by St. Thomas to be immediately known (that is, is not capable of any apriori proof),[24] though he states at the same time that it is not manifest what the nature or what the principle of activity is. For nature, as internal principle of activity, is known in sense experience. But, though nature is said to be immediately known, and activity also is immediately evident to sense experience, the judgment that nature acts for a goal is not said to be immediately known; some reflection at least is necessary. The third reason is an *a pari* argument. Aristotle says that in some cases the products of natural processes can also be produced by deliberate art, and that in the latter case there is order and purpose. And, since in both cases the steps are the same, and the end result the same, Aristotle argues that the same connections obtain between them. Therefore, the natural processes also must be goal-directed. The fourth reason shows that at least some natural things act for goals, animals especially, and also plants. But neither animals nor plants have intellects, and so they must act for goals naturally. Neither of these arguments in the present form is of interest to us, since their conclusion is particular (though for Aristotle's purpose it was enough to establish that there is the telic cause).

Aristotle next reduces the objections of the Ancients to three and answers them. The first is that there are monstrosities in nature. Aristotle gives four answers. (1) Human beings also make mistakes, but the fact of failure does not prove human actions to be without purpose. (2) Whenever an order is fixed, there is a goal, but fixed orders are found even when the results are not good — whatever the reason for the latter may be. (3) Plants less obviously act for goals than animals, hence there should be more monstrosities among plants than animals. But the conclusion is false, and so monstrosities are not signs of aimlessness. (4) If animals have no goals, the generation of animals should not have any. But animal generation is clearly ordered to the result of an adult animal; hence, also the ani-

[23] This argument, used by Aristotle and by St. Thomas in two forms (as we shall see), is by no means a mere analysis of concepts and their logical implications. It is rather an analysis (using concepts and judgments, it is true) of an existing nature presented in sense perception, as St. Thomas points out.
[24] *In II Phys.* lect. 1 (305-07).

mal itself has a goal. The second objection says that telic causes are unnecessary, since we already have material and formal causes. Aristotle retorts that he who denies telic causality denies nature (even in the sense of matter and form, it would appear). For unless nature proceeded by regular steps to definite goals, it would not be a determinate principle of activity. The third objection says that nature does not deliberate. Aristotle responds that deliberation is not a necessary condition of purpose, but only in cases where the order of means is contingent.

We can now compare the doctrines of Aristotle and St. Thomas. St. Thomas carries the Aristotelian ideas of nature, activity, and goal-directedness further in two directions. The first is the very well known and often-considered explanation of the order and goal-directedness of nature by considering all natural things as products of the Divine Art. St. Thomas does this even in his *Commentary on the Physics* and, of course, does it very often in other places in his writings.[25] This point needs no further development in the present paper.

The other direction lies in making more explicit the connection between being and activity. This point has not been discussed in detail by Thomists,[26] so that it may be useful to discuss it more fully. The best known texts here argue from God's goodness to the imitation of that goodness by creatures inasmuch as they are causes of other things.[27] This of course is a *via iudicii* argument. But since on St. Thomas' own principles our knowledge of God is derived either from creatures or from revelation, we must either find the necessary connection between being and activity in the beings of experience, or conclude that it is a purely revealed item of knowledge.

It is therefore important that in the *Summa Contra Gentiles* St. Thomas has argued the other way: it belongs to being as such

25 CF. *In II Sent.* d. 25, q. 1, a. 1; *S.C.G.* I, 44, 72; II, 23; *De potentia Dei* q. 1, a. 5; q. 3, a. 15; *Sum. Theol.* I, q. 103, a. 1 ad 1, 3; I-II, q. 2, a. 1, q. 6, a. 1, q. 12, a. 5 et ad 3, q. 13, a. 2 ad 3. In *De veritate* q. 22, a. 1, this argument is even used to prove that every agent acts for the good, as also *S. C. G.* III, 162.

26 The only explicit argument framed by Thomists that I know of is that of Fernand Van Steenberghen, *Ontologie* (Louvain: *Institut supérieur de philosophie,* 1946), pp. 98-101; he argues that a finite being *qua* finite is necessarily a principle of activity; this is somewhat like one part of St. Thomas' argument.

27 Especially *Sum. Theol.* I, q. 105, a. 5; also, *De veritate* q. 22, a. 1; *In II Sent.* d. 1, q. 2, a. 2; *S.C.G.* I, 37; III, 21, 22, 68; *De potentia Dei* q. 3, a. 7 ad 10.

to be an agent, and, therefore, God also must "have" activities.[28]
How do we know this? According to St. Thomas, we find this in the
beings of experience themselves. Beings lack some suitable goods
which they acquire by activity, and have some goods which they
give to others also by activity.[29] If natural beings did not act naturally, all their actions would be from the outside, that is, violent
or forced. Yet there is an obvious difference between the arrow
that must be shot by the archer and the spontaneous activities of
natural things. St. Thomas argues that this must be so, from several
different points of view. One is the well known axiom that every
form has an inclination,[30] which St. Thomas explains by saying that
something is suitable (that is, good) to another because of the latter's form.[31] Now, it seems that a suitability which remained purely formal (that is, merely intelligible) would not be a real suitability. Again, St. Thomas argues that things could not form a universe, could not have any real order to each other except through
operation.[32] Thirdly, the very nature of act and perfection involves
activity, for agency and actuality are evidently related,[33] and to
give being to another is also evidently a perfection;[34] hence, beings,
to the extent that they are perfect in their kind, have activities, and
cause other beings. Finally, we find in ourselves desires for activity.
Now, man is indeed unique in nature, but he does not simply stand
in opposition to nature; he is a natural being, and we can even say
that in man nature reaches consciousness of itself. Hence, to this
extent we can legitimately argue anthropomorphically[35] that, since
man as a being has tendencies, every natural being as being has a
natural tendency to activity.

Now that we have seen the whole range of St. Thomas' discussion of the axiom, "Every agent acts for a goal," we can with
profit look back at the argumentation. We have already considered

[28] *S. C. G.* II, 6.

[29] Cf. *S.C.G.* IV, 19; *Sum. Theol.* I, q. 19, a. 2.

[30] *De veritate* q. 22, aa. 3, 10; q. 23, a. 1; *S. C. G.* II, 47; IV, 19; *Sum. Theol.* I, q. 19, 2; q. 80, a. 1; *In III Ethic.* lect. 13 (515); *De potentia Dei* q. 3, a. 7.

[31] *In III Ethic.* lect. 13 (516).

[32] *De veritate* q. 21, a. 5.

[33] In St. Thomas' words, every agent acts inasmuch as it is in act. See also the interesting text, *In IV Sent.* d. 8, q. 1, a. 1, qa. 1 ad 1.

[34] *De veritate* q. 21, a. 1; *S. C. G.* II, 6.

[35] On the legitimate place of a limited kind of anthropomorphism in St. Thomas' treatment of nature, see the penetrating remarks of M. Etienne Gilson, *The Spirit of Mediaeval Philosophy*, trans. by A. H. C. Downes (New York: Chas. Scribner's Sons, 1936), pp. 87-88.

the argument that a goal must be fixed or definite, and seen that it is an analytic argument resting ultimately on experience, but immediately on an intellectual analysis of real being. The argument that every agent acts *for* a goal (or, that goals are true causes) is put by St. Thomas in various ways.[36] In the *Summa Contra Gentiles*, this is established through appetite as a middle term. Every being that has an appetite is ordered by that appetite *to* a definite goal. Hence, all such beings are truly goal-directed, or, in other words, are *for* a goal. Moreover, goals are good, since that to which an appetite tends is suited to it, and that which is suitable for a being is good for it. This is an added conclusion, developed also at the level of analysis. Only once in this discussion does St. Thomas proceed by an induction from particulars to the universal. In plants and animals, we find that their activities do lead to what is better for the beings. And we can find other examples of this in all kinds of natural beings. Therefore, all agents act for the good.

In the *Commentary on the Physics of Aristotle*, St. Thomas follows his author in arguing that chance is not consistent, that nature is intrinsically a principle of activity and consequently goal-directed, that there is a parallel between nature and art, and that at least some natural things (animals and plants) obviously act for goals. Only in one place, in the discussion of the objections of the Ancients, does Aristotle make use of the argument based on an example, that of the utility of rainfall for the growth of crops. St. Thomas remarks that this example is ill-chosen, and it seems that this remark is directed at Aristotle, since he uses the singular, *exemplum inconveniens accipit*. For the rest, the Aristotelian arguments are not from particulars to the universal, but rather rest on a metaphysical analysis of nature, activity, result, and order. In this sense, the Aristotelian arguments are like the Thomistic.

St. Thomas, however, puts the entire argument in a larger context, that of Divine creative causality. (That is why some Thomists say that St. Thomas comments on Aristotle as a metaphysician and even as a theologian.) Another interesting difference between the

---

36 On the meaning of "propter," see *Sum. Theol.* II-II, q. 27, a. 3. On the nature of the causality of the goal and the good, see especially *In I Metaph.* lect. 11 (179); V, lect. 2 (775); *In III Phys.* lect. 5 (620); IV, lect. 1 (794); VII, lect. 3 (1811). For briefer remarks, see *In I Sent.* d. 8, q. 1, a. 3; IV, d. 3, a. 1, q. 1; *De veritate* q. 28, a. 7; *S. C. G.* I, 75; II, 30; *De potentia Dei* q. 5, a. 1; *In II Phys.* lect. 4 (348), lect. 11 (481); *In II Metaph.* lect. 4 (316-19); V, lect. 3 (781-82); *Sum. Theol.* I, q. 5, a. 2 ad I, a. 4; q. 22, a. 2; I-II, q. 1, a. I, arg. 1 and ad 1; q. I, a. 2; q. 9, a. I; q. 113, a. 6 sed contra.

Aristotelian analysis and the Thomistic is to be found in this, that
the former rests most basically on an analysis of nature, whereas in
the more personal arguments of St. Thomas, the key notion is that
of appetite or tendency. This is a very real difference, though not
a conflict. In another context, I had occasion to note that the shift
from nature to powers is due to the Avicennan development.[37] It
seems likely that the same reason accounts for the present difference
also. For the way in which St. Thomas uses his analysis of tendency
is very like Aristotle's use of nature. In Thomistic usage, tendency
is the tendency of a being and is specified by nature, especially by
form (inasmuch as it is a proper accident); it is the proximate principle, whereas nature is the more remote principle, of activity.
Logically, therefore, tendency can be used wherever Aristotle had
used nature. But, in addition, tendency is closer to activity, and
can be said to be more dynamic; this probably is the reason St.
Thomas favored it.

In summary, then, we can say the following things about St.
Thomas' use of the axiom, "Every agent acts for a goal." He often
uses it as a premise without any proof. At times, he discusses it in
itself, and, in its absolutely general form presents it as a conclusion
of a kind of argument. First, in the sense that every agent acts for
something definite, he proves the axiom by showing its contrary to
be impossible, and by treating it in terms of act and potency shows
that every goal must be a definite one. Secondly, to show that
an agent is ordered to a goal, he employs the notions of nature
(when commenting Aristotle) and tendency as middle terms.
(Though "agent," "nature," "tendency," and "goal" are terms
which imply each other, they are distinct notions, not simply synonymous words.) In this argument, St. Thomas insists that nature
(and tendency) are known immediately in sense experience as well
as in our experience of our own activity. Thirdly, he shows that
every goal as such is a good (or, in the case of moral agents, at least
an apparent good), twice by indicating a kind of inductive passage
from particular instances to the universal, but much more often by
analyzing the intrinsic relations between goal, appetite (or nature),
and good. Fourthly, he explains (in *via iudicii*) natural goal-
directedness through the creative intelligence (art) of God. Fifthly,
he shows that every being as such must be an agent (and even, *ex*

---

[37] *The Discursive Power* (Saint Louis: Modern Schoolman, 1952), pp. 24-28, 34-36,
193-94.

convenientia, an efficient cause), by an analysis of being, nature, tendency, activity, and good.

In St. Thomas' view, therefore, the proposition, "Every agent acts for a goal," is not a self-evident principle, nor a truth known from the logical implications of prior logical principles, but a conclusion of a real proof resting on the immediate experience of nature and tendency. Hence, again, we can see how misleading it is to base an interpretation of St. Thomas on a few texts presumed to contain his entire doctrine. Finally, it must be considered significant that whenever an alleged self-evident principle of St. Thomas' has been investigated by means of an inclusive textual analysis, it has turned out to be not a principle at all, but a conclusion.

ဠ Hugues de Saint-Victor et Les Conditions du Savoir au Moyen Age *by Benoit Lacroix, O.P.*

☆ ☆ ☆ ☆ ☆ ☆ ☆ ☆ ☆ ☆ ☆ ☆ ☆ ☆

Q UESTION discutée[1] tout au long du moyen âge, et même encore aujourd'hui: comment en arrive-t-on à la science?[2] Il faut du talent bien sûr, de la pratique aussi et beaucoup d'intelligence. *Natura, exercitium, et disciplina* sont, au dire de Hugues de Saint-Victor (+1141)[3] qui résume ici la tradition, trois fondements indispensables, sur lesquels viennent se greffer l'étude, l'enseignement, ses procédés et ses programmes.

[1] D'après Didascalicon III, 12-19, ed. Buttimer, *Hugonis de Sancto Victore Didascalicon de Studio legendi* ("Studies in Medieval and Renaissance Latin X," [Washington, D.C.: The Catholic University of America Press, 1939]), pp. 61-69. *Johannis Saresberiensis Episcopi Carnotensis Policratici* VII, 13, ed. Clement C. I. Webb, (Oxford: Clarendon Press, s.d.), pp. 145-52. Vincent de Beauvais, *Speculum doctrinale* I, 28-31; faute d'édition définitive, utiliser avec précaution celle des Bénédictins de Douai, 1624.—Sur Hugues de Saint-Victor voir le travail récent de R. Baron, *Science et Sagesse chez Hugues de Saint-Victor* (Paris: P. Lethielleux, 1957), abondante bibliographie aux pp. 231-57.

[2] Déjà Platon, v.g. *Phédon* 82-84; surtout Sénèque, *Lettres à Lucilius;* Clément d'Alexandrie, *Stromates* I, 3sqq. ou VI, 89-90; Basile de Césarée, *Aux jeunes gens sur la manière de tirer profit des lettres helléniques*: S. Augustin, *De doctrina christiana* II, 18 sqq. Au moyen âge, en plus des textes déjà indiqués à la note précédente, voir à titre d'exemples Saint Bernard, *Sermon sur le Cantique des cantiques* XXXVI, 1-7 (PL., 183, 967-968); Pseudo-Boèce, *De disciplina scholarium* (PL., 64, 1223-1238); Guibert de Tournai, *De modo addiscendi*, ed. Bonifacio (Turin: 1953; le très monastique *De modo studendi*, ed. Verardo, *Opuscules Théologiques* I (Rome: 1954), p. 450, attribué à S. Thomas par des manuscrits du XIVe siècle.—Plus près de nous et qui ont connu plusieurs éditions: Père Gratry, *Les Sources: conseils pour la conduite de l'esprit* (Paris: 1861); A. D. Sertillanges, *La Vie intellectuelle*, (Paris: Desclée, 1944).

[3] Cf. *Didascalicon* III, 6, p. 57: Tria sunt studentibus necessaria: natura, exercitium, disciplina. in natura consideratur ut facile audita percipiat et percepta firmiter retineat; in exercitio, ut labore et sedulitate naturalem sensum excolat; in disciplina, ut laudabiliter vivens mores cum scientia componat.—Références à Cicéron, Quintilien, saint Augustin, Cassiodore indiquées par l'éditeur.

Les programmes? On commence par l'étude des Arts Libéraux, comme au temps de Cicéron, et c'est au terme de cette expérience, toute scolaire, qu'on peut espérer en arriver à la sagesse, prolongement normal d'une vie d'étude bien conduite. Or, justement, un jour que l'on interrogeait un certain sage, *quidam sapiens,* grammarien du début du XIIe siècle, sur la façon et les moyens concrets d'arriver à la sagesse, l'excellent pédagogue qu'était Bernard de Chartres (+1124/30)[4] déjà célèbre par ses bons mots, répondit tout simplement:

Mens humilis, studium quaerendi, vita quieta
Scrutinium tacitum, paupertas, vita quieta
Haec reserare solent multis obscura legendi.[5]

Trois lignes qui font fortune au moyen âge: Hugues de Saint-Victor les transcrit immédiatement dans son *Didascalicon,* après 1125; Jean de Salisbury écrit en 1159: "Je n'arrive pas à goûter la beauté de ces vers, mais j'en approuve le sens. J'estime que les philosophes devraient en avoir l'esprit imbus."[6] Comme Hugues de Saint-Victor il cite et commente; de même Pierre le Mangeur chancelier de Paris en 1164 dans un de ses sermons;[7] Guibert de Tournai vers 1264/69[8] dans un *De modo addiscendi.* Ce qu'on a appelé à l'époque, fort élégamment d'ailleurs, les *clefs du savoir*[9] devient au chapitre 28 du livre premier du *Speculum doctrinale* (vers 1240) de Vincent de Beauvais les *juvamenta studii* indispensables à tout intellectuel sérieux.

Déjà, de retrouver ces vers dans les oeuvres que nous venons de citer suffirait à dire l'importance que le moyen âge leur accorde si nous ne voulions en montrer au surplus l'originalité. Bien entendu, tout n'est pas dit ni connu des conditions du savoir au moyen

---

[4] Voir Manitius, *Geschichte der Lateinischen Literatur des Mittelalters* II, 3 (Munich: 1931), pp. 196-98 pour une notice biographique; E. Gilson, *History of Christian Philosophy in the Middle Ages* (New York: Random House, 1955), pp. 259-61 donne le contexte philosophique. Jean de Salisbury, *Metalogicon* III, 4, éd. Webb (Oxford: 1929), p. 136, rapporte la comparaison célèbre: Dicebat Bernardus Carnotensis nos esse quasi nanos gigantium humeris insidentes . . .

[5] *De studio legendi* III, 12, p. 61.

[6] *Policraticus* VII, 13, éd. cit., p. 145: Et licet metri ejus suavitate non capiar, sensum approbo et philosophantium credo mentibus fideliter ingerendum.

[7] Cf. *Sermo* 3, (PL, 198, 1730D).   [8] Cf. *De modo addiscendi,* IV, 26, p. 243.

[9] Jean de Salisbury, *Policraticus* VII, 14, p. 152, où il est même question d'une septième condition du savoir: septima discentium clavis ponitur *amor docentium,* quo praeceptores ut parentes amandi sunt et colendi.

âge quand on a rendu compte du texte de Bernard de Chartres et de ses deux premiers commentaires, celui de Hugues de Saint-Victor et celui de Jean de Salisbury. Nous espérons tout de même qu'un examen attentif des textes et de leurs sources[10] nous permettra d'entrevoir les raisons et la façon dont certains hommes de lettres du moyen âge latin discutaient de la morale de l'esprit. C'est un thème qui a toujours inquiété le moyen âge et l'a parfois profondément divisé.[11]

I

Les questions que l'on pose sont les suivantes: suffit-il pour être *sage* de savoir? Doit-on aussi se conduire bien? Y-a-t-il un lien nécessaire entre la conduite morale du vrai étudiant et sa science? Concrètement, quelle relation le sage doit-il avoir avec son milieu? Quelle attention donner aux jugements de la majorité?

Précisons pour l'intelligence de cet exposé qu'il ne s'agit ni pour Bernard de Chartres, ni pour son premier commentateur, Hugues de Saint-Victor, non plus que pour Jean de Salisbury, d'une simple discussion théorique comme pourraient en avoir des intellectuels "purs," dilettantes ou obsédés par les idées; ni même d'une discussion de principe comme en eurent certains rigoristes disciples des Pères du désert. Non. Il s'agit plutôt de morale *pratique* de l'esprit, morale des moyens avant tout. Les positions de principe sont acquises. Cicéron, Sénèque, S. Jérome, S. Augustin et leurs premiers disciples du moyen âge, Isidore de Séville, Alcuin, et Raban Maur, tant d'autres autorités, ont décidé: il n'est plus question de se demander si oui ou non il convient de lier les devoirs de la conduite aux lois du savoir. Pour Hugues de Saint-Victor,

---

[10] Au Frère C. H. Buttimer, éditeur du *De studio legendi* (cf. n. 1), nous devons d'avoir pu identifier les sources chrétiennes de Hugues de Saint-Victor; et c'est grâce à la bienveillante collaboration de Jerome Taylor, auteur d'une traduction anglaise du *Didascalicon* (avec introduction et notes, à paraître sous peu), que nous avons pu retracer aussi les sources classiques. Nous en devons autant à C. C. I. Webb, le savant éditeur du *Policraticus*. Remerciements.

[11] Rien de mieux pour s'en rendre compte que de lire à la suite les textes nombreux et variés recueillis, au XIIe siècle, par Gratien (cf. *Decretum Magistri Gratiani,* d. 36-38, éd. Friedberg, pp. 140 sqq.); au XIIIe siècle par Vincent de Beauvais, *Speculum doctrinale* I, 30-37.—Sur les différents motifs et les faits, voir Dom Leclercq, *L'amour des lettres et le désir de Dieu* (Paris: 1957), pp. 108-145, qui analyse les réactions des milieux monastiques. G. Paré, A. Brunet, et P. Tremblay, *La renaissance du XIIe siècle. Les Écoles et l'enseignement* (Paris: J. Vrin, 1933), pp. 138-206, analysent le point de vue des milieux scolastiques.

comme pour tous les esprits positifs de son temps, la réponse ne
fait pas de doute: il le faut.[12] Et même

> une science tachée par une vie impudique est à rejeter. Ainsi,
> celui qui cherche à savoir doit par-dessus tout s'efforcer à ne
> pas négliger la discipline.[13]

On l'a dit, et bien dit:

> "Mores ornant scientiam."[14]

Mais si Hugues devait seulement discuter de ce qu'il faut faire!
Mais non! La situation est beaucoup plus alarmante. Au moment
où il transcrit les vers de son confrére de Chartres, les écoles, et donc
les écoliers, sont en pleine crise de croissance.[15] Plusieurs des étudiants pour qui le maitre de Saint-Victor écrit les trois premiers
livres du *Didascalicon*, étudiants des Arts Libéraux, en sont venus
comme bien d'autres à se croire sages et magnifiques simplement
parce qu'ils lisent les grands auteurs, Platon par exemple. Se
croiraient-ils les seuls à savoir quelque chose? Il s'en trouve même
qui ne veulent plus suivre les cours: comme s'ils savaient déjà tout!
D'autres brûlent les étapes; et c'est le danger d'aborder ensuite la
lecture des Ecritures avec le même esprit frondeur. Déjà certains
étudiants bien connus se moquent de la simplicité des Pères et se
croient évidemment leurs propres et seuls maîtres à eux. "Espèces
de porteurs de nuages": *nugigeruli!*[16] L'auteur si suave du *De
Archa Noe* et du *De Arrha animae* ajoute avec une certaine aigreur
qui montre la gravité des options en jeu:

> J'en ai connu beaucoup qui ne possédaient pas encore les pre-
> miers éléments de la science et qui pourtant ne daignaient
> s'intéresser qu'aux grandes questions. Ils croyaient ne devoir

---

[12] *De Studio legendi*, III, 12, p. 61: Et ideo praeceptis legendi, praecepta quoque
vivendi, adjungit, ut et modum vitae suae et studii sui rationem lector agnoscat.

[13] *Ibid.*: Illaudabilis est scientia quam vita maculat impudica. et idcirco summo-
pere cavendum ei qui quaerit scientiam, ut non negligat disciplinam.

[14] La même idée chez Quintilien, *Institutions oratoires* i. 18; xii. 1; chez Sénèque,
Lettre 88, etc. Sénèque est même d'avis que le beau style d'un écrivain est lié à sa
conduite morale (cf. *Lettres* 75, 114).

[15] Cf. Jean de Salisbury, *Metalogicon*, qui raconte et fait sentir les événements;
Gilson, *op. cit.*, pp. 139-63, explique l'histoire des idées. Paré, Brunet, et Tremblay,
op. cit., pp. 139 sqq., montrent bien l'évolution en cours.

[16] Cf. *De studio legendi*, III, 13, p. 63.

se grandir que de cette façon; d'avoir entendu les paroles,
d'avoir lu les écrits des grands et des sages . . . Nous avons
vu X . . ., disent-ils; nous avons lu X . . . C'est leur habitude
de nous parler ainsi: X . . . ces grands, ces hommes célèbres,
ils nous connaissent.[17]

A son éponque, on ne se glorifie plus, paraît-il, d'avoir compris un
auteur, mais simplement de l'avoir lu. Orgueil de l'esprit, mépris
des traditions:

Ils croient que la sagesse est venue au monde avec eux et qu'elle
mourra avec eux. Ils trouvent que les paroles divines sont dites
si simplement qu'on n'a plus besoin de maîtres. Plutôt, ils
souhaitent que chacun puisse par sa seule intelligence scruter
les arcanes de la vérité. Aussi, plissent-ils le nez, tournent-ils
les narines devant ceux qui lisent encore les Ecritures.[18]

Ces faux étudiants qui seront demain de mauvais maîtres "ne com-
prennent pas l'injure qu'ils font ainsi à la parole de Dieu."[19] Il y a
de quoi s'impatienter: "Plaise au ciel que personne ne me connaisse
moi, mais que je sache quelque chose."[20] Impatience ou dépit?
c'est difficile à dire:

Je pense qu'il est indigne que vous m'écoutiez: moi, je ne suis
pas Platon: moi, je n'ai pas mérité de voir Platon.[21]

De toute façon, lui Hugues de Saint-Victor, *magister Hugo*, n'hési-
terait pas, s'il le fallait, de retourner à l'école pour apprendre; il
serait prêt à boire, comme dit Horace, dans un vase de terre,
même à consulter un campagnard. C'est qu'il ne faut pas rougir
d'avoir à apprendre toujours. "Ce que tu ne sais pas, peut-être que
l'autre le sait."[22]
Ah! s'il pouvait les corriger de leur orgueil! Seront-ils touchés
quand il leur dira les sacrifices qu'il a faits, lui, pour s'instruire?

Moi-même depuis que je suis jeune je vis en exil. Et je sais
le chagrin d'une âme qui a quitté le petit domaine de sa pauvre
chaumière.[23]

---

[17] *Ibid.,* p. 62.   [18] *Ibid.,* pp. 63-64.   [19] *Ibid.,* p. 64.
[20] *Ibid.,* p. 62: sed utinam me nemo agnoscat et ego cuncta noverim.   [21] *Ibid.*
[22] Cf. *ibid.,* p. 62: Sufficit vobis: ipsum philosophiae fontem potastis, sed utinam
adhuc sitiretis! rex post aurea pocula de vase bibit testeo. quid erubescitis? Platonem
audistis, audiatis et Chrysippum. in proverbio dicitur: *Quod tu non nosti, fortassis
novit Ofellus.* Allusions à Horace, *Satires* i. 2. 113; Sénèque, *Lettre* 119.
[23] *De studio legendi* III, 19, p. 69: Ego a puero exsulavi, et scio quo maerore

Maître Hugues est convaincu de l'importance, de l'*actualité*
plutôt, des préceptes du chancelier de l'école de Chartres. Il est
surtout convaincu, comme tous ceux qui répéteront les vers de
Bernard, de l'importance de cette première condition du savoir qui
est au principe de toutes les autres, l'humilité dont les enseigne-
ments, il le sait,[24] sont fort nombreux. Faut-il les rappeler? Oui.
Tous? Peut-être pas. Les plus urgents:

> Ne mépriser aucune science, aucun écrit; ne rougir d'ap-
> prendre de qui que ce soit; et lorsque tu as acquis le savoir,
> ne va pas pour cela mépriser les autres.[25]

S'il pense à ce qui arrive en fait, Hugues de Saint Victor est bien
obligé de constater, avec regret, que plusieurs des étudiants qu'il
connait craignent et rougissent d'étudier de peur que, ce faisant,
ils avouent par là, qu'ils ne savent pas tout. Voilà tout de même,
une gros souci de réputation qui va mal avec les exigences de la
vraie science! L'humilité pourrait peut-être corriger ces excès.[26]
Suivent des protestations, des supplications même, dont il a déjà
été question et qui nous mènent d'une facon plutôt inattendue à
l'une des plus belles pages d'humanisme du moyen âge latin:

> Nemo est cui omnia scire datum sit, neque quisquam rursum
> cui aliquid speciale a natura accepisse non contigerit. Prudens
> igitur lector omnes libenter audit, omnia legit, non scrip-
> turam, non personam, non doctrinam spernit. indifferenter ab
> omnibus quod sibi deesse videt quaerit, nec quantum sciat,
> sed quantum ignoret, considerat. hinc illud Platonicum
> aiunt: *Malo aliena verecunde discere, quam mea impudenter
> ingerere.*[27] cur enim discere erubescis et nescire non vere-

animus artum aliquando pauperis tugurii fundum deserat . . . Voir J. Taylor, *The
Origin and Early Life of Hugh of St. Victor: An Evaluation of the Tradition* (Texts
and Studies in the History of Medieval Education, V. ed. A. Gabriel and J. N. Garvin)
(University of Notre Dame, 1957), pp. 51 sqq; Baron, *op. cit.*, pp. 227-28.

[24] Cf. *ibid.*, 13, p. 61: Principium autem disciplinae humilitas est, cujus cum
multa sint documenta, haec tria praecipue ad lectorem pertinent. Guibert de
Tournai (*De modo addiscendi*, pp. 237-39) commente aussi, à sa façon.

[25] *Ibid.*, pp. 61-62: haec tria praecipue . . . primum ut nullam scientiam, nullam
scripturam vilem teneat, secundum ut a nemine discere erubescat, tertium, ut cum
scientiam adeptus fuerit, ceteros non contemnat.

[26] Cf. *ibid.*, p. 62: Multos hoc decipit, quod ante tempus sapientes videri volunt.
hinc namque in quendam elationis tumorem prorumpunt, ut jam et simulare in-
cipiant quod non sunt et quod sunt erubescere, eoque longius a sapientia recedunt
quo non esse sapientes, sed putari, ejusmodi multos novi qui . . . Cf. aussi n 24.

[27] *Ibid.* et. cf. S. Jérome, *Lettre* 53, 1, 2.

Hugues de Saint-Victor et Les Conditions du Savoir

cundaris? pudor iste major est illo. aut quid summa affectas
cum tu jaceas in imo? considera potius quid vires tuae ferre
valeant. aptissime incedit qui incedit ordinate. quidam dum
magnum saltum facere volunt, praecipitium incidunt. noli
ergo nimis festinare. hoc modo citius ad sapientiam pertinges.
ab omnibus libenter disce quod tu nescis, quia humilitas commune tibi facere potest quod natura cuique proprium fecit.
sapientior omnibus eris, si ab omnibus discere volueris.
qui ab omnibus accipiunt, omnibus ditiores sunt. nullam
denique scientiam vilem teneas, quia omnis scientia bona est.
nullam, si vacat, scripturam vel saltem legere contemnas. si
nihil lucraris, nec perdis aliquid. maxime cum nulla scriptura
sit, secundum meam aestimationem, quae aliquid expetendum
non proponat, si convenienti loco et ordine tractetur, quae
non aliquid etiam speciale habeat, quod diligens verbi scru-
tator alibi non inventum, quanto rarius, tanto gratius carpat.[28]

Saint Paul avait écrit aux Philippiens: "Tout ce qu'il y a de vrai,
de noble, . . . voilà votre idéal."[29] En principe, il y a du vrai en
toute lecture, et chez tous les auteurs. Hugues de Saint-Victor le
pense. Mais S. Paul, le même S. Paul, avait aussi écrit aux Thes-
saloniciens: *vérifiez tout*,[30] c'est-à-dire *choisissez*. En ce cas et
puisqu'il faut choisir, on décidera d'après le but que l'on se propose:
afin d'en arriver, par exemple, à une meilleure connaissance des
Ecritures; ou encore pour répondre aux exigences de l'apologé-
tique, aux obligations de son devoir d'état. De toute facon,

le bon ne doit pas prendre la place du meilleur. Si tu ne peux
pas tout lire, lis ce qui est le plus utile. Même si tu pouvais tout
lire, il ne faudrait pas fournir le même effort à tout. Il y a des
écrits qu'on lit afin qu'ils ne nous soient pas inconnus; d'autres,
pour être bien au courant; parce qu'il nous arrive parfois
d'accorder plus de crédit qu'elles en ont aux choses nouvelles
et on juge plus aisément une chose dont le fruit nous est
connu.[31]

[28] *Ibid.*, pp. 62-63.   [29] IV, 8.   [30] I, 21.
[31] *Op. cit.*, p. 63: nihil tamen bonum est quod melius tollit. si non omnia
legere non potes, ea quae sunt utiliora lege. etiam si omnia legere potueris, non
tamen idem omnibus labor impendendus est. sed quaedam ita legenda sunt ne sint
incognita, quaedam vero ne sint inaudita, quia aliquando pluris esse credimus quod
non audivimus, et facilius aestimatur res cujus fructus agnoscitur. L'authenticité
de ces lignes (possibilité de quelques emprunts) nous paraît assurée: unité du
style, fidélité au contexte, vigueur des *sententiae* qui révèle la gravité de la situation
et la personnalité de Hugues de Saint-Victor; des répétitions (peut-être dicte-t-il);

Nous rejoignons ici les idées chères à Clément d'Alexandrie, à Basile de Césarée et à bien autres écrivains chrétiens.[32] Si l'humilité est la première condition du savoir au moyen âge, ce n'est pas seulement que les autres, Bernard de Chartres, par exemple, en ont décidé ainsi; mais c'est une partie de la morale chrétienne qui le veut. D'où l'invitation répétée de Hugues de Saint-Victor à rester objectif et libre devant tout écrit; à mépriser en principe aucune source du savoir; à respecter même les traditions vieillies. Récapitulons:

> Le bon étudiant se devra donc d'être humble, doux, loin des désirs de la vanité et des apparâts de la volupté, diligent, soucieux d'apprendre de tous librement; qu'il apprenne à étudier une question à fond avant de juger; qu'il ne cherche pas à paraître docte; qu'il aime les découvertes des sages et qu'il veille à les tenir toujours devant sa face comme on tient un miroir devant son visage. Si au sujet de questions plus obscures peut-être, il n'est pas d'accord avec elles, il ne les méprisera pas pour autant jusqu' à penser que le seul bien qui existe est celui qu'il a pu découvrir par lui-même.[33]

L'humilité dont parle Hugues de Saint-Victor pourrait être appelée l'humilité de l'esprit, qui est soeur de la docilité et de la studiosité. Pour sa part, Jean de Salisbury se réfère à l'humilité du coeur, *soeur de la simplicité.* Aussi, ses commentaires appar-

---

le *secundum meam aestimationem* de la page 63, ligne 10 et *Didascalicon* VI, 3 comme *lieu parallèle*, autant d'indices pour attribuer à Hugues de Saint-Victor la paternité de ces conseils. Seul le procédé est ancien: celui des *Distica Catonis* si populaires au moyen âge; appel de Sénèque à multiplier les maximes, *Lettres*, 94, 108.

[32] Voir notes 2 et 11. On peut presque tout justifier par les *autorités*. Et justement l'embarras des auteurs du moyen âge c'est de retrouver chez les mêmes *patres* (v. g. S. Paul, S. Augustin, S. Jérome, Isidore de Séville, etc.) des textes qui trop facilement isolés de leur contexte, justifient et le devoir de savoir et celui d'ignorer. Après S. Paul (v.g. I *Thess.* V. 19-22 versus I *Cor.* I, 17 sqq.; *Philip.* IV, 8 versus I *Cor.* III, 18 sqq.), on pourra comparer, par exemple, Isidore de Séville dans *Etymologiae* I, 43; II, 19 et *Sententiae* III, 13 (PL, 83, 685-689). En opposant science et charité, ni S. Paul, ni S. Jérome, ni S. Augustin n'ont pu, inquiets qu'ils étaient déjà du contenu paien des Arts Libéraux, résoudre la question. Plusieurs ont pu proposer que l'étude des Arts Libéraux soit mise au service de celle des Ecritures mais c'était encore là, une solution partielle. Hugues de Saint-Victor est un des premiers, un des rares même que nous connaissons, après Alcuin (*Ep* 74; M.G.H. *Epistolae* IV, p. 117) et Lupus de Ferrière (à Eginhard 829/30, éd. Levillain [Paris 1927] I, 5-6) à prévoir que l'étude du vrai, peu importe où il se trouve, possède une valeur humaine *en soi* digne d'une créature de Dieu.

[33] *De studio legendi* III, 13, p. 64.

tiennent-ils davantage à la littérature mystique, très liés qu'ils sont
à l'allégorie et remplis d'allusions bibliques. Sont-ils plus convain-
quants pour le lecteur du moyen âge déjà habitué à la Bible? Peut-
être. Tout de même, il est possible que les exigences pratiques de
l'humilité du coeur dont il est question au VIIe livre du *Policraticus*[34] ne soient guère différentes de celles de l'humilité dont il
s'agit au livre III du *Didascalicon*. Mais, lorsque Vincent de Beauvais décide de rappeler à ses contemporains tout ce qu'il sait sur
l'humilité, il jugera bon de distinguer lui aussi entre l'humilité
de l'esprit réceptif, première condition du savoir, Hugues de
Saint-Victor devenant ici sa première source, et l'autre humilité,
celle du coeur, plutôt connaissance de soi.[35]

II

Après l'humilité, Bernard de Chartres conseille le zèle de la
recherche. L'humilité relève de la discipline, elle s'apprend, elle
s'enseigne même; le zèle de la recherche, *studium quaerendi*,[36]
exprime une ardeur au travail qui se conquiert par l'exercice, la
ténacité et la persévérance dans l'action. Ici, Hugues de Saint-
Victor emprunte à S. Jérome comme à Cicéron.[37]

Trois attitudes définissent le zèle de la recherche chez l'étudiant.
La première consiste à s'éloigner de la foule et même à ne pas tenir
compte de ses réactions. "Le vrai bien n'est pas dans le jugement
des autres; il est caché plutôt au fond de la conscience pure."[38] Peu
importe ce que les autres pensent. La sagesse ne se trouve pas
nécessairement là où se trouve le plus grand nombre de gens. Au
contraire, devrait-on dire! L'étudiant aspirera plutôt à vivre en
marge et à ne pas s'associer à ceux qui ne vivent pas comme lui.
Qu'il le sache, qu'il en prenne parti: la majorité des gens vont
différer d'opinion avec lui.[39]

[34] Cf. *op. cit.* 13, pp. 145-46.

[35] Comparer deux séries de textes, celle du *Speculum doctrinale* I, 28; celle de
IV, 38. Voir, sur "l'humilité du coeur," Leclercq, *op. cit.*, pp. 195-96.

[36] Cf. *De studio legendi* III, 14, pp. 64-67. Sens du mot *studium*, chez Cicéron,
De rhetorica I; cf. *Policraticus* VII, 13 pp. 146-48. Guibert de Tournai, (*De modo
addiscendi* IV, 24) identifie tout simplement *studium quaerendi* à l'antique vertu
de *studiositas* (éd. Bonifacio, p. 239).

[37] Cf. *Lettre* 52, 2-3; voir Cicéron, *Tusculanes* III, 6 9. Même procédé chez
Guibert de Tournai, *ibid.*, pp. 239-40.

[38] *De studio legendi* III, 14, p. 65: quia . . . sciebant verum bonum non in
aestimatione hominum sed in pura conscientia esse absconditum.

[39] Cf. *ibid.*, pp. 64-65.

La seconde attitude de l'étudiant zélé pour la recherche consiste à tout donner à son métier. Il n'est pas nécessaire de multiplier
les théories sur ce sujet quand Sénèque dit qu'en matière d'exhorta-
tion les exemples font mieux que la doctrine.[40] Tout ce que les
anciens ont pu faire pour la philosophie, tout ce qu'ils ont pu ab-
sorber! Mépris des honneurs, de la gloire et de la renommée; défi
aux coutumes établies, violentes solitudes. Des pages entières de
Sénèque, de Valère-Maxime sont là pour le raconter. Hugues suit
S. Jérome qui retient surtout l'exemple de Parménide assis durant
15 ans sur son rocher et celui de Prométhée dont la vie est mise en
danger à cause d'une méditation trop prolongée.

Ce n'est pas tout de se sacrifier et de s'immoler à la cause de la
sagesse. Reste—et c'est une troisième attitude—à poursuivre l'effort
toute sa vie. Encore faut-il assitôt préciser que le sagesse protège ceux
qui la servent. Eternelle jeunesse des sages! Longévité heureuse
d'Homère, de Socrate, de Pythagore, de Démocrite, de Xénophon,
de Platon, d'Hésiode et de combien d'autres! De S. Jérome encore,
qui l'emprunte à Cicéron, vient le mot qu'Alcuin citera un jour à
son ami Charlemagne et que transcrit avec respect Hugues de Saint-
Victor: "Pendant que toutes les forces du corps s'en vont avec l'âge,
la sagesse, elle, grandit."[41] D'ailleurs, regardez, observez! Ils ont
tous raison, tous: Alcuin, Jérome, Cicéron, de célébrer ces vieillards
studieux que l'âge rend de plus en plus ingénieux:

> Senectus enim illorum qui adolescentiam suam honestis actibus
> instruxerunt, aetate fit doctior, usu tristior, processu temporis
> sapientior et veterum studiorum dulcissimos fructus metit.[42]

Il y a de quoi encourager n'importe quel étudiant et à bien se
conduire et à bien travailler. Ceux qui ne seront pas encore con-
vaincus par les rappels de Hugues de Saint-Victor trouveront quelques années plus tard, dans le commentaire de Jean de Salisbury,
toute une page d'exemples tirés de Valère-Maxime.[43] Ils appren-
dront, par exemple, que Thémistocle parvenu à 107 ans constate
au moment de mourir que sa vraie vie d'étude ne vient que de

---

[40] Cf. *Lettres à Lucilius* 33, 94, 95, etc.

[41] *De studio legendi* III, 14, p. 65; omnes paene virtutes corporis mutantur in
senibus et crescente sola sapientia decrescunt ceterae. Cf. S. Jérome, *Lettre* 52, 2, 1.
Voir Alcuin, à Charlemagne en 796/7, dans M.G.H. *Epistolae*, IV, p. 178.

[42] *De studio legendi* III, 14, p. 65.

[43] Cf. *Policraticus* VII, p. 149; Valère-Maxime, *Actions et paroles mémorables*
VIII, 7.

commencer. Le vieux Sophocle récitait au juge ému la fable d'Oedipe. Nestor était aussi éloquent dans sa vieillesse. Caton apprendra le grec à la fin de sa vie. "Voyez comme ils l'ont aimée cette sagesse, eux qui l'ont cherchée malgré le déclin des ans."[44]
Revenons à Hugues de Saint-Victor, à S. Jérome, devrait-on dire encore.[45] Du point de vue doctrinal, rien de bien neuf. Il s'agit d'Abisag la Sunamite. D'étranges étymologies auxquelles les étudiants du moyen âge étaient familiers rappellent aux lecteurs du *Didascalicon* que s'ils persévèrent dans leur effort, ils pourront toujours compter qu'à la fin de leur vie la science les réchauffera comme la Sunamite réchauffa le corps de David vieillissant. L'audace des rapprochements prouve qu'on tient à ses idées: la science aime jusqu'à la fin ceux qui lui sont fidèles.
Au lieu de la Sunamite, Jean de Salisbury[46] invoque l'image de Jacob en lutte jusqu'au matin avec l'ange des Ecritures. La victoire arrive à la fin, au matin, après toute une vie d'application et de recherche. Il n'y a pas à hésiter sur le sens de *studium quaerendi*: le zèle dans la recherche est une condition majeure de la science qui sert et récompense ceux qui la respecte.

III

Si l'humilité relève de la discipline, si le zèle de la recherche tient surtout à l'exercise, les quatre autres conditions du savoir, *vita quieta, scrutinium tacitum, paupertas, terra aliena*, tiennent alternativement à la discipline et à l'exercice. D'abord, il y a la vie tranquille. Ceci s'entend de deux façons:[47] vie tranquille de l'homme *intérieur* qui ne se laisse pas distraire par toutes sortes d'ambitions vaines; vie tranquille *extérieure* parce que la vie d'étude demande beaucoup de temps. Que de textes de Sénèque à rappeler encore! Hugues de Saint-Victor paraît pressé. Jean de Salisbury cite en revanche six vers de Juvénal. La *sententia* est la même: l'esprit divisé contre lui-même ne peut pas se concentrer, et c'est en vain que travaille celui qui est à la merci des tracas extérieurs. Un poète, par exemple: peut-il penser en même temps à ses images et à l'achat d'une couverture? Mais non! Jean de Salisbury se rappelle de l'aveugle de Jéricho. Oui, celui-ci est guéri, mais pour-

---

[44] *De studio legendi* III, 14, p. 66: Animadverte igitur quantum amaverint sapientiam quos nec decrepita aetas ab ejus inquisitione potuit revocare.
[45] *Lettre* 52, 2 sq. Cf. *de studio legendi*, p. 67.
[46] Cf. *Policraticus* VII, 13, pp. 146-49; références indiquées par l'éditeur.
[47] Cf. *De studio legendi* III, 15, p. 67.

by Benoit Lacroix, O.P.   [129

quoi? Parce qu'il a une idée dans la tête, qu'il la répète, qu'il tient
tête à la foule. Le Christ l'écoute. C'est le Christ qui dit aussi:
celui qui s'inquiète de plusieurs choses se trouble aussi beaucoup.
Bref, Juvénal et l'Evangile viennent se rencontrer pour donner
raison à Bernard de Chartres d'avoir indiqué, comme troisième
condition du savoir, *une vie tranquille.*[48]

IV

Qu'est-ce que le *scrutinium tacitum?*[49] Une réflexion, méditation attentive et réfléchie de l'esprit; de toute façon, une autre
condition du savoir, un effet de la recherche qui viserait l'instant
même où l'esprit est actif. Cette *méditation soignée* suppose qu'on
est attentif et diligent.

Une oeuvre, toute oeuvre en fait, s'accomplit par le travail qui
la commence et l'amour qui l'achève.[50] Or, le travail exige de la
vigilance et du soin; le soin, lui, fait l'étudiant appliqué au travail
et prévoyant; la vigilance le rend attentif. On a rejoint, tant mieux
que mal, le *De Nuptiis Mercurii et Philologiae* (écrit entre 410/39)
et bien connu des étudiants des Arts Libéraux, pour assister à
l'ascension mystérieuse au ciel de *Philologia* portée vers en haut
dans une litière. Qui tient la chaise, c'est-à-dire la litière de la
sagesse? En avant, comme on devrait s'y attendre, *travail* et *amour*
personnifiés par deux jeunes femmes. Suivent *cura* et *vigilia.* Les
deux pucelles, en arrière, symbolisent la réflexion.[51]

Jean de Salisbury a évité ces complications. Il lui a suffi de rappeler l'idée maîtresse; la réflexion est une nécessité pour l'étudiant
et elle est le résultat d'une vie intérieure qui sait évaluer avec
précision les biens de cette vie.[52]

V

L'autre condition du savoir, la pauvreté, *de parcitate* "de
l'épargne" disent certains manuscrits du *Didascalicon,* est mieux

[48] Cf. *Policraticus,* pp. 149-50; Juvénal, *Satires* vii. 63-68; allusions à *Luc* X,
41 et XVIII, 35sqq; *Matt.* XX, 30sqq. et. XXI, 9.
[49] Cf. *De studio legendi* III, 17 pp. 67-68.
[50] Cf. *ibid.* p. 68: . . . studium quaerendi instantiam significat operis, scrutinium
vero diligentiam meditationis. opus peragunt labor et amor, consilium pariunt cura
et vigilia. in labore est, ut agas, in amore, ut perficias. in cura est, ut provideas,
in vigilia, ut attendas.
[51] Cf. *De nuptiis* ii. 134-135; *De studio legendi,* p. 68.
[52] Cf. *Policraticus* VII, 13, p. 150: Sed studii tunc exercitatio plurimum proficit,
cum virtus, in singulis quae legit aut audit homo, tacito apud se veri judicii scrutinio
convalescit; ibi namque ratio cuncta examinat et fructum omnium appendit in
statera.

connue. Sénèque en a tellement parlé![53] La pauvreté, pour un étudiant, consiste d'abord à éviter le superflu: affaire de discipline et de conviction plutôt que d'exercice. Hugues de Saint-Victor pourrait en dire long, mais il pense à certains qu'il connaît: à certains qui se sont vantés non pas d'avoir appris mais d'avoir dépensé. Quelle désinvolture! Au lieu de quelques belles maximes du brave Sénèque, servons à ces étudiants grotesques le vieux proverbe qui a été traduit du grec en latin: "gros ventre ne fait pas nécessairement grand esprit":

Pinguis venter tenuem non gignit sensum.[54]

Plus serein, Jean de Salisbury alligne sa pensée sur celle de Pétrone et de Lucain: . . . *Paupertas fecunda virorum . . . custos verae humiltiatis . . . socia virtutis.*[55] Des exemples, empruntés à Valère-Maxime,[56] devraient les convaincre: Démocrite sacrifie tout à la philosophie; Cratès de Thèbe jette un magot d'or à la mer pour mieux sauvegarder sa liberté intérieure; Anaxagore refuse de cultiver ses champs afin d'être plus disponible. Même Socrate, si réceptif, était un pauvre en fait. Bien entendu, le nécessaire reste nécessaire. Mais l'étudiant doit se souvenir qu'une trop grande abondance affaiblit la raison humaine. Celle-ci a besoin de sa liberté pour étudier.[57]

Pas plus original que Hugues de Saint-Victor, Jean de Salisbury sera au moins plus positif.

VI

Enfin! un des thèmes les plus chers du moyen âge, l'exil, *terra aliena*. "Ceci aussi exerce un être humain" en quête de science.[58]

[53] Cf. *Lettres à Lucilius* 4 (fin), 8, 14, 15 (fin), 17, 18, 58, 80, 81, 87, 90, 110. *Paupertas* est opposée souvent à *frugalitas*, ou encore à *fortuna*, troisième grand obstacle à la science, les deux premiers étant *negligentia* et *imprudentia* (Cf. *Speculum doctrinale* I, 29).

[54] Cf. Anselme d'Havelberg, *Epistola apologetica* (PL, 188, 1120). La source immédiate de Hugues de Saint-Victor est toujours la *lettre* de S. Jérome à Népotien, c. 11. L'éditeur du *De modo addiscendi* de Guibert de Tournai signale (p. 244, note 1) que le proverbe grec ne comporte pas de négation. Ceci change toute la perspective. Mais, d'après l'édition Labourt des lettres de S. Jérome (Collection Budé), II, 187 et celle de Buttimer (p. 68), la négation se trouve bel et bien dans le texte latin des meilleurs manuscrits: ce qui est plus normal.

[55] D'après Webb, pp. 150-51: voir Lucain, *Pharsale* I, 165-66; Pétrone, *Satyricon*, 84.

[56] Cf. *Actions et paroles mémorables* VIII, 7, 4.

[57] Cf. *Policraticus* VII, 13, p. 150: Si luxuriat animus in deliciis, rerum affluentia lumen rationis extinguit.

[58] *De studio legendi* III, 19, p. 69: Postremo terra aliena posita est, quae et ipsa quoque hominem exercet.

Précisions que le moyen âge connaît trois sortes d'exil.[59] Il y a d'abord l'exil volontaire, religieux et mystique: un moine, fils des Pères du 'désert, pélerin du Christ, laisse sa maison et se convertit au Seigneur. C'est l'exil du moine irlandais qui passe sur le continent; exil de Jean Scot Erigène, de tant d'autres . . . depuis Abraham qui en est le prototype. L'autre forme d'exil est moins fréquente. Elle dépendra davantage des circonstances qu'on ne choisit pas. C'est l'exil forcé d'Orose au Ve siècle, ou même, plus tard, en 1163/4, celui de Jean de Salisbury, ainsi que de tous ceux qui doivent laisser leur pays par suite des guerres et des persécutions. Enfin il y a l'exil plus volontaire du sage, tel que proclamé par Horace, Sénèque, vécu par Alcuin et ses imitateurs d'autrefois et d'aujourd'hui.[60] "Omnis mundus philosophantibus exsilium est"[61]: c'est l'exil que recommandent Hugues de Saint-Victor et Jean de Salisbury sous l'autorité, tous les deux, de Bernard de Chartres.

Lui, Hugues de Saint-Victor sait bien tout ce qu'il en coûte au coeur de laisser sa terre natale afin de se mettre au service de Dieu et de la sagesse. Certains de ses textes rappellent à l'historien des lettres les plus belles pages d'Alcuin qui a connu, lui aussi, les chagrins des souvenirs trop précis. Ovide avait donc raison: "Je ne sais par quelle douceur nous captive le sol natal qui ne veut pas se faire oublier".[62] Précisément, c'est le devoir du sage de réagir, de dominer sa sensibilité, d'affirmer un fois de plus sa liberté intérieure et de pouvoir, par exemple, regarder en face *les maisons de marbre et les toits lambrissés* qui l'abritent aujourd'hui et comparer avec l'intimité plus douce, mais plus lointaine, de la *petite hutte de chaume* d'autrefois . . . sans broncher.[63] "Pour l'âme exercée (du sage), en effet, c'est le principe d'une grande vertu que d'apprendre à se détacher peu à peu des choses visibles et transitoires pour en

[59] Sur l'exil religieux et mystique, imitation des Pères du désert (v.g. Athanase, *Vie de S. Antoine* 7) ou influence celtique (voir L. Gougaud, *Christianity in Celtic Lands* [London: 1932], pp. 129-31); Bède, *Opera* . . . éd. Plummer II, p. 170. Sur l'exil forcé, v.g. Orose, *Historia adversus paganos* V, 2; Léandre de Séville à sa soeur (PL, 81, 14); plus tard, Jean de Salisbury, *Lettre* 134, à Thomas Becket (PL, 199, 113). Sur l'exil du sage, v.g. *Lettres à Lucilius* 68, 102, etc.

[60] Voir la célèbre lettre d'Alcuin à Charlemagne (*Epist.* 121; M.G.H., *Epistolae* IV, pp. 176-77). Non moins épique et "secret de ma vie publique," la lettre de E. Gilson dans *Esprit* XIX (Paris: 1951), pp. 593-96.

[61] Cf. *De studio legendi* III, 19, p. 69.

[62] *Pontiques* I, 3. 35-36:
Nescio qua natale solum dulcedine cunctos
Ducit, et immemores non sinit esse sui.

[63] Cf. *De studio legendi* III, 19 (explicit) p. 69; *v. supra* n. 23.

arriver à pouvoir ensuite les délaisser".[64] A cette dernière forme
d'exil on parvient par étapes. On est d'abord celui pour qui la
patrie reste douce: homme délicat, sans nul doute. Puis on devient
l'homme courageux qui considère tout l'univers comme sa patrie.
Mais l'homme parfait, le vrai sage, est celui pour qui la terre entière,
toute terre, est une *terre étrangère*. Etape ultime: en se purifiant,
l'amour légitime de la patrie s'est éteint: il est désormais permis de
parler sagesse.[65]

Jean de Salisbury est-il du même avis? Bien sûr! Mais, il
s'exprime autrement. Le vrai sage, dit-il, doit viser à se libérer
des servitudes domestiques. Ainsi qu'Abraham, il devrait pouvoir
quitter son pays au moindre appel et se faire étranger à tout ce
qui l'empêche de chercher la sagesse.[66] La philosophie a de ces
exigences? Oui, mais elle promet de libérer ceux qui la servent, puisqu'elle accorde au philosophe ce privilège peu banal de
faire en sorte que son propre domaine lui devienne comme étranger.
Ou même, elle peut faire que le philosophe en arrive un jour à
se sentir *at home* n'importe où. En fait, un vrai sage ne souffre
jamais de l'exil.[67]

Et voilà! Parmi les écrivains du moyen âge, Hugues de Saint-
Victor est sûrement l'un des plus parfaits. C'est même, au dire de
S. Bonaventure,[68] le plus complet. Aussi, ce qu'il nous apprend
des conditions du savoir comme sa façon de s'expliquer, prennent-
ils une particulière importance.

[64] *Ibid.*: Magnum virtutis principium est, ut discat paulatim exercitatus animus
visibilia haec et transitoria primum commutare, ut postmodum possit etiam dere-
linquere.

[65] *Ibid.*: Delicatus ille est adhuc cui patria dulcis est; fortis autem jam, cui
omne solum patria est; perfectus vero, cui mundus totus exsilium est. ille mundo
amorem fixit, iste sparsit, hic exstinxit.

[66] Cf. *Policraticus* VII, 13, p. 151.

[67] Cf. *ibid.*: Terram alienam philosophia exigit et suam interdum alienam facit,
immo alienam facit suam et nullo unquam gravatur exilio.—Toute cette doctrine
de l'exil du sage fut trés vite adoptée par le christianisme qui transposera: le vrai
chrétien est un exilé (cf. *Epître aux Hébreux* XI, 33sqq.) dont la patrie est partout
où se trouve sa religion (v.g. *Epître à Diognète* V, 5). Lire le beau texte d'Orose,
Hist. adversus paganos V, 2: Inter Romanos, ut dixi, romanus; inter christianos
christianus; inter homines homo . . . Utor temporarie omni terra quasi patria quia
quae vera est et illa quam amo patria in terra penitus non est. Plus près de nous,
E. Gilson, "L'esprit de Chrétienté," *La Vie intellectuelle*, XIII, (1945) 18-36 . . .
"N'êtes-vous toutes mes paroisses lorsque je suis exilé de la mienne" (p. 19).

[68] *De reductione artium ad theologiam* 5, éd. Quarachi, Opera Omnia V, p.
321; Anselmus sequitur Augustinum, Bernardus sequitur Gregorium, Richardus sequitur Dionysium, quia Anselmus in ratiocinatione, Bernardus in praedicatione, Richardus in contemplatione. Hugo vero omnia haec.

Autour de deux lignes, Hugues et Jean de Salisbury ont réussi
à convoquer des *paiens* Virgile, Horace, Ovide, Juvénal, Valère-
Maxime, Sénèque, surtout Sénèque,[69] Pétrone, Lucain, Martianus
Capella, ainsi que les *exemples* chrétiens, plus *familiers*, précise
Jean de Salisbury,[70] d'Abraham, de Jacob, de David, même de
l'aveugle de Jéricho. Quant à S. Jérome, "la grande ombre de
S. Jérome,"[71] on le sent toujours présent. Il sert d'intermédiaire et
de directeur de conscience, comme au temps du drame d'Héloise
et d'Abélard. Enfin, de les retrouver ainsi tous réunis, anciens et
modernes, paiens et chrétiens, pour discuter des relations de la vie
morale et de la vie de l'esprit, voilà qui est loin d'être banal et qui
démontre une fois de plus à toute l'histoire de la pensée humaine,
les générosités d'un humanisme qui n'a pas fini de nous étonner.

Ajoutons qu'il s'agit là d'un autre cas d'*humanisme moral*,
pour parler à la façon d'un *quidam sapiens* de notre temps, ami lui
aussi des Arts libéraux . . . "humanisme moral qui a conduit les
penseurs chrétiens à consulter les anciens pour s'instruire de ce
qu'est l'homme."[72]

Faut-il préciser? C'est de l'homme *chrétien*, créature de Dieu,
faite à Son image et à Sa ressemblance ainsi qu'on le dit aux pre-
mières pages de la Genèse, qu'il s'agit en l'occurrence. Hugues de
Saint Victor en est conscient. Aussi, la première des fonctions de
cette morale de l'esprit est-elle, selon lui, de promouvoir la dignité
d'une *créature de Dieu*.[73]

En conséquence, celui qui a été créé à l'image de Dieu ne
devrait plus se demander si oui ou non *bien vivre* vaut mieux que
bien savoir, si la *charité qui édifie* est mieux que la *science qui
enfle*, s'il vaut mieux *pratiquer la componction* que d'en *savoir la
définition*, mais faire en sorte que tout chez lui, et l'intelligence
et la volonté, et l'esprit et le coeur, soit le plus parfait possible.
Ordonnance et non plus opposition de la vie morale et celle de
l'esprit. Bien entendu c'est à la science d'aider l'homme à mieux
vivre; mais bien vivre est déja toute une science. Ce sont plutôt

---

[69] Voir l'article de Dom Déchanet, O.S.B. "Seneca noster . . .," *Mélanges de
Ghellinck* (Gembloux: 1951), II, 753-67. *Sénèque au moyen âge*: tous les médiévistes
souhaitent une étude complète de ce thème déjà plein de promesses.

[70] *Policraticus* VII, 13, p. 149: Porro ad studium quaerendi non modo domesticis
sed etiam extraneis animamur exemplis.

[71] E. Gilson, *Héloise et Abélard* (Paris: J. Vrin, 1938) p. 61.   [72] *Ibid.*, p. 229.

[73] Hugues de Saint-Victor, *De studio legendi* I, 5, p. 12: Integritas . . . naturae
humanae duobus perficitur, scientia et virtute, quae nobis cum supernis et divinis
substantiis similitudo sola est.

les deux réunies et accordées, vertu et science, qui réhabilitent l'homme blessé par la faute et l'apparentent de nouveau aux natures divines. Qu'elles s'appellent morales ou qu'elles s'appellent intellectuelles, les actions du *lector artium* ont toutes le même et premier' rôle: conduire l'être humain, tout l'être humain, à sa perfection, à son bonheur, c'est-à-dire, selon Hugues de Saint-Victor toujours,[74] à la suprême consolation de cette vie, qui est la sagesse.

---

[74] *Ibid.* 2, p. 6: Summum igitur in vita solamen est studium sapientiae quam, qui invenit, felix est, et qui possidet beatus.

Martin Heidegger: Language and Being *by Lawrence Lynch*

☆ ☆ ☆ ☆ ☆ ☆ ☆ ☆ ☆ ☆ ☆ ☆ ☆ ☆

I

THE FIRST READING of a work by Martin Heidegger creates the impression that the usual world of discourse has been left far behind. Words to which one has become accustomed, whose meanings have some semblance of stability in philosophical discussion, suddenly appear in quite unexpected ways. Not only do they seem to convey quite different meanings, but they seem to be used with quite a different conception of what meaning is. Then, side by side with such old friends, complete strangers make their appearance—words which have a strange look about them, an odd ring to them and which may even be foreign to usually reliable dictionaries.

A few samples, selected at random, will illustrate the point. Those familiar with philosophical terminology, will recognize words like *Vorstellung*,[1] *Notwendigkeit*,[2] *Wahrheit*,[3] *Verstehen*,[4] *Freiheit*.[5] It soon becomes clear, however, that "idea," "necessity," "truth," "understanding," "freedom" do not even approximate the

---

The following signs are used in citing Heidegger's various works:
SZ—Sein und Zeit (6th ed.: Tübingen: Neomarius verlag, 1949).
WM—Was ist Metaphysik? (5th ed.; Frankfurt a.M.: Vittorio Klostermann, 1949).
HWD—Hölderlin und das Wesen der Dichtung (München: Albert Langen and Georg Muller, 1937).
WW—Vom Wesen der Wahrheit (2nd ed.; Frankfurt a.M.: Vittorio Klostermann, 1949).
Hw—Holzwege (Frankfurt a.M.: Vittorio Klostermann, 1950).
WD—Was heisst Denken? (Tübingen: N. Niemeyer, 1954).
VA—Vorträge und Aufsätze (Pfullingen: G. Neske, 1954).
EM—Einführung in die Metaphysik (Tübingen: N. Niemeyer, 1953).

[1] *WW.*, sec. 2.　　[2] *WW.*, p. 23.　　[3] *WW.*, pp. 16, 23.　　[4] *SZ.*, sec. 31, p. 142 ff.
[5] *WW.*, p. 15.

"meaning" Heidegger is trying to convey. "Idea" has its meaning wrenched into a new form—no longer is it a representation or mental likeness, but the setting forth of being in front of one as object; "necessity" is no longer a demand levied on a thing that it be so and so in every instance but, rather, the characteristic of "writhing in distress" which marks man's approach to truth, i.e. distress; "truth" is no longer correspondence or adequation with what is, but is seen to be an unveiling or a revealing—not the property of a proposition, but of "things"; "understanding" is a way in which man *is* by deciding or projecting (non-idealistically!) meaning into his world, instead of constituting a power or act of knowing; "free-dom" is, in a way, choice and the absence of determination, but it is more properly a letting-be.

Examples of familiar words that suddenly take on a strange appearance and, with it, a new connotation are, among others, *Dasein,*[6] *Existenz.*[7] They become hyphenated in form and signify "being-there," "standing-outside." And with the introduction of hyphenated forms many odd compound words and phrases occupy line after line of Heidegger's works: *In-der-Welt-Sein,*[8] *Sein-zum-Tode,*[9] *Mit-sein,*[10] *In-die-Acht-nehmen.*[11] With them come newly-compounded words like: *Unentborgenheit,*[12] *Mitdasein,*[13] *Offenständig-keit,*[14] *Zuhandenheit,*[15] *Vorhandenheit.*[16] And, perhaps, strangest of all *das Nichts* takes on a verb-form: *das Nichts selbst nichtet!*[17]

Little wonder, then, that Heidegger's works are difficult to interpret and, in many cases, impossible to translate. Many of his creations are so close to root-meanings in German that it is well-nigh impossible to capture the genius of his work in any other language—the translator must re-examine the etymological foundations of his own tongue and produce like creations. Is such novelty warranted? Is Heidegger's expression unnecessarily difficult? Are there good reasons, deeply-rooted in his own thought—or, perhaps, vision—for such an attitude to language? What follows will, perhaps, give some indications of an answer.

One reason for novelty may be found in a theme that often recurs: Heidegger considers *his* philosophy to be a new one—he believes, indeed, to be true to itself, philosophy must always seem

---

[6] *SZ.,* p. 133.   [7] *WIV.,* p. 15.   [8] *SZ.,* p. 52 ff.   [9] *SZ.,* p. 237 ff.
[10] *SZ.,* p. 117 ff.   [11] *WD.,* p. 125.   [12] *WW.,* p. 19.   [13] *SZ.,* p. 117 ff.
[14] *WIV.,* p. 12.   [15] *SZ.,* p. 71.   [16] *SZ.,* p. 73.   [17] *WM.,* p. 31.

present at the dawn of new revelations.[18] Being new, and its insights novel, new forms of expression must be devised to express
them. Above all, a new attitude must be developed to the function
of such expressions.

Heidegger's interpretation of the history of Western thought
is one factor inducing such a conviction. Neitzsche, he believes,
marks the end of the Western tradition in philosophy because he
asked the primary philosophical question: What is being? and re-
plied: Nothing. The reason is that being is a concept void of all
meaning; "being" is a word devoid of all sense. The explanation
of that emptiness, Heidegger believes, is that after Plato and Aristotle the whole Western tradition of philosophy insisted on considering being as *das Seiende.* Forgetting the true being *(das Sein)*
of being, Western metaphysics insisted on interpreting its object,
being as being, as *das Seiende als Seiende.*[19] And Neitzsche was
simply bold enough to declare that tradition dead.

Whereas the Western tradition of philosophy is dead, philosophy is not dead. Philosophy *is* and, like everything present, must
look to the past and advance to the future. Therefore, the new
philosophy will look back beyond Plato to Heraclitus and Parmenides who first raised the question of being and sought, in Heidegger's view,[20] to answer it in terms of *to-be* rather than of *what-is;*
it will seek to advance from their insights into *to-be* toward new
revelations of the truth of *To-be.* To express its revelations philosophy must look back to the root-meanings of the philosophical
lexicon created by those early philosophers, for in their early insights into *To-be* they, too, created a philosophical language
founded in the etymological-roots of their Greek tongue. Heidegger feels it necessary to do the same for his German tongue. To
understand Heidegger's attitude to and use of language, then, one
must turn to his treatment of being: language is, indeed, in a very
profound sense, being.

[18] Cf. Jean Wahl, *Vers la Fin de l'Ontologie* (Paris: Société d'Éditions d'Enseignement Supérieur, 1956), p. 23.

[19] *WM.,* p. 7, 17. "Weil Sein für alle Metaphysik seit dem Anfang des abend-
ländischen Denkens besagt: Anwesenheit, muss das Sein, wenn es in höchsten Instanz
gedacht werden soll, als das reine Anwesen gedacht werden, d.h. als die anwesende
Anwesenheit, als die bleibende Gegenwart, als das ständige stehende 'jetzt'. Das
mittelalterliche Denken sagt: nunc stans. Das aber ist die Auslegung des Wesens der
Ewigkeit." *WD.,* p. 41.

[20] EM., Die Besshränkung des Seins (Sein und Werden).

II

What, then, is language?

On the surface that seems to be a simple and straightforward question. But is it? What does it ask? Does it mean: what kind of thing is language, i.e. what do we call "language"? If that is the point of the question, the answer might be: we call words and combinations of words "language," because they are the "things" which compose it. Language may then appear, as it did to some, to be a conventional creation, the work of man's art.

Does it mean: what kind of thing is language, i.e. what is it *for?* If so, we might reply: language is for communicating. Its purpose is to present the content of one man's experience to others. It is the expression outwardly of what is within a man.

Does it mean: what kind of thing is language, i.e. what is the *essence* of language, what makes language to be language? To *that* question, the answer might be: meaning. Whether "meaning" is interpreted or defined as essence known, or as verifiable fact, or as something of the sort, language is the kind of thing that it is because language has the task of signifying, the task of pointing to "meaning."

Does it mean: what is the being, i.e. the *to-be* of language? If so, the question may concern either the *to-be* of language or the *to-be* that makes language to be. In this event, to find our answer, we may have to "examine" or experience the *to-be* of language, not "signifying" or "expressing" as it is usually conveyed, but the *To-be* in which language shares in order to be. But then we are led to the question of origin: what makes language to be? And the *only* possible answer to that question is: *To-be.* But, then, what is *To-be?*

Our simple and straightforward question is, then, a most complicated one. Where will we turn for our answer? Heidegger has no hesitation: the first three formulations of the question are alike in looking upon language as *das Seiende,* language considered as *what-is.* But how understand being *(what-is)* except as be-ing *(to-be)?* Indeed, confining attention to *das Seiende* may very well mean that we will miss its true being *(to-be)!* What, indeed, is being?

Philosophy has always sought the answer to *that* question; indeed, it owes its origin to the *asking* of the question.[21] The answer might be: a tree, a house, a stone, a man. Each of these is a being.

---

[21] *WW.,* p. 23.

But what is being *as* being? One might say "Being" and mean Being-as-a-whole, i.e. the sum total of all beings is being. But that still does not say what the being of all that is, is. Is it "Being-as-such" —for being-as-such makes all beings to be beings? But, then, what is being-as-such? One reply might be: the to-be of what-is τὸ ὄν and τὰ ὄντα may lead us to οὐσία; ENS and ENTIA may lead us to ENTITAS; *das Seiende, das Seiende als Solche in Ganzen* may bring us to *die Seiendheit*. But the question remains: what is εἶναι, ESSE, *das Sein?*[22]

The obvious answer just given: the *to-be* of *what-is*, really misses the point. It tells us of the *to-be* of *what-is;* it fails even to *ask*, let alone *answer*, the question: what is *to-be?* On this score, Western thinkers have consistently failed to ask the proper question. One consequence of this failure has been that metaphysics has always grown under the patronage of and under the inspiration of physics: metaphysics has tried to find being-as-such in the being of *what-is*. Even the *to-be* which St. Thomas finds in the pure act which is God is, according to Heidegger,[23] the *to-be* of a being *(ens increatum)*. Conversely, in their preoccupation with *what-is*, physicists (after Plato)have forgotten the true reality of φύσις. Nature is not, as they usually conceive it, essence; it is, rather, being *(to-be)*, i.e. growth.[24] The real question, then, is: what is *To-be?*, rather than: what is the to-be of *what-is?* Returning, then, to the question about language asked above, the last formulation alone should be explored: for it, too, led us to ask: what is *To-be?*

How does *To-be* make language to be? Heidegger's reply is couched in different terms in various works. Language is the response of *Dasein* to the possibilities of being;[25] language results from man's thought about Being;[26] man's freedom reveals the truth of *To-be* and language expresses it;[27] language results from man's erupting into *To-be;*[28] language comes to be through the λόγος, which is *To-be*.[29] Let us examine each of these formulations in turn with a view to uncovering the true being of language seen in its origin.

Examining the question: what is *to-be?* as a *question* reveals one important fact, a fact which will prove invaluable in our search for an answer. The question demands that he who asks it, be; the

---

[22] *WM.*, p. 16.   [23] *Cf.* Wahl, *op. cit.*, p. 33.   [24] *WW.*, p. 16; *WD.*, p. 135.
[25] *SZ.*, p. 161.   [26] *WW.*, p. 24.   [27] *WW.*, p. 15.   [28] *Cf.* Wahl, *op. cit.*, p. 187.
[29] *WD.*, p. 142.

question is really a self-questioning. Seeking the proper being to
answer the question leads us to the only self-questioning being we
know—man, the being Heidegger names *Dasein*.[30] Answers to
questions concerning *To-be* and the *to-be* of language must come,
then, from the *to-be* of *Dasein*.

The *to-be* of *Dasein*—its *existence*—is never complete; *Dasein*
is characterized by the permanent relation of instability it maintains with itself.[31] *Dasein* is the kind of being whose *to-be* is always
to, i.e. toward, being. The *existence* of *Dasein* is never *existentia*,
in the usual sense of the term or as indicating indifferently the existence of *any* being. The existence of *Dasein* is *Existenz* and might
better be called Ex-isting: it is being-toward-being, being which is
to-be-more-than-it-is.[32] And inasmuch as it does have such *Existenz*,
Dasein is at all times in control of the *to-be* which it *is*. Its *to-be*,
the possibility it actually *is*, depends on *Dasein* itself—especially
on its decision. Hence, *Dasein* is free and has to decide its *to-be*.
Dasein is, then, as it exists: *Das 'Wesen' des Daseins liegt in seiner
Existenz*.[33]

How does *Dasein* exist? Its *to-be* is *Da*, there. *Dasein* is in
the world;[34] its *to-be* is revealed by its "attitude" to the world (an
attitude, or, more properly, a way of being called *Besorgen*). Its
world is constituted by *(a)* mere beings, i.e. beings which *are* merely
in front of *Dasein*: *Vorhandenes; (b)* by beings which are useful to
Dasein in becoming the being it wants to be, i.e. the tools or beings
which *are* at hand for *Dasein*: *Zuhandenes;* and *(c)* by other beings
whose *to-be* is *Existenz*, i.e. *Mitdasein*. In short, *Dasein* is a kind
of intersecting point at which *Welt, Mitdasein*, and *Existenz* come
together.[35] That is the primitive situation in which *Dasein* "experiences" its being—an experience or sentiment Heidegger calls
Befindlichkeit, a sense of finitude or contingency, a *feeling* of challenge in the face of a being that has to be chosen and affected in the
midst of and confronted by the uncertainty of other beings.[36]

In facing that challenge, however, in deciding the being it will
be, Dasein gives a meaning to the beings or instruments it uses to
ex-press itself, i.e. to push itself out into being. Pro-jecting of itself
into being not only gives determination to *Dasein*, but meaning
to its world. The world's meaning is, in a very correct sense, due
to the projects man makes; it is a meaning, however, which is *ex-*

---

[30] *SZ.*, p. 11.   [31] *SZ.*, p. 12.   [32] *SZ.*, pp. 41-42.   [33] *SZ.*, p. 42.
[34] *SZ.*, p. 143.   [35] *SZ.*, p. 137.   [36] *SZ.*, pp. 135 ff.

istential, not essential or conceptual.[37] However, unless the meaning thus projected were articulated or set into a structure or context, unless the interpretation *Dasein* gives to its world were in some way common—unless, in short, *Dasein* expressed *existentially* meaning-in-common, it would not *be.* And that is precisely the existential being of language. *Rede,* Heidegger's term[38] for that aspect of the *to-be* of *Dasein,* is the existential root of the formal symbols, the words, which we call language.[39] The *to-be* of language is, therefore, the *Existenz* of Dasein. Heidegger can say[40] very truthfully, then, that *Dasein* is what it says. Conversation, i.e. talking in formal words, should reveal man's existence and, hence, the truth of *To-be*—not, be it noted, the essences man knows nor the truth of *What-is!*

Existenz is described in somewhat different contexts in *Vom Wesen der Wahrheit* and *Was ist Metaphysik?* One might be led to think that the essence of truth would be found existentially in *Verstehen* as a projecting of meaning. It is to be found, however, in the freedom of *Dasein,* in its *letting-be* of *what is.*[41] *Das Wesen der Wahrheit enthüllt sich als Freiheit.* Decision or self-autonomy remains, but it is seen to involve *Dasein* opening itself up to *what-is*

---

[37] *SZ.,* pp. 144-46.   [38] *SZ.,* p. 161.

[39] "Die Versuche, das 'Wesen der Sprache' zu fassen, haben denn immer auch die Orientierung an einem einzelnen dieser Momente genommen und die Sprache begriffen am Leitfaden der Idee des 'Ausdrucks', der 'symbolischen Form', der Mitteilung als Aussage; der 'Kundgabe' von Erlebnissen oder der 'Gestaltung' des Lebens. Für eine vollzureichende Definition der Sprache wäre aber auch nichts gewonnen, wollte man diese verschiedenen Bestimmungstücke synkretistisch zusammenschieben. Das Entscheidende bleibt, zuvor das ontologisch–existenziale Ganze der Struktur der Rede auf dem Grunde der Analytik des Daseins herauszuarbeiten." *SZ.,* p. 163.

[40] "Das Sein des Menchen gründet in der Sprache; aber diese geschieht erst eigentlich im Gespräch. Dieses ist jedoch nicht nur eine Weise, wie Sprache sich vollzieht, sondern als Gespräch nur ist Sprache wesentlich. Und was wir sonst mit Sprache meinen, nämlich einen Bestand von Worten und Regeln der Wortfügung, ist nur ein Vordergrund der Sprache. Aber was heisst nun ein 'Gespräch'? Offenbar das Miteinandersprechen über etwas. Dabei vermittelt dann das Sprechen das Zueinanderkommen. Allein Hölderlin sagt: 'Seit ein Gespräch wir sind und hören können voneinander'. Das Hörenkönnen ist nich erst eine Folge des Miteinandersprechens, sondern eher umgekehrt die Voraussetzung dafür. Allein such das Hörenkönnen ist in sich schon wieder auf die Möglichkeit des Wortes ausgerichtet und braucht dieses. Redenkönnen und Hörenkönnen sind gluck ursprünglich.˙ Wir sind ein Gespräch—und das will sagen: wir können voneinander hören. Wir sind ein Gespräch, das bedeutet zugleich immer: wir sind ein Gespräch. Die Einheit eines Gesprächs besteht aber darin, dass jeweils im Wesentlichen Wort das Eine und Selbe offenbar ist, worauf wir uns einigen, auf Grund dessen wir einig und so eigentlich wir selbst sind. Das Gespräch und seine Einheit trägt unser Dasein" *HWD.,* p. 8.

[41] *WW.,* p. 15.

by letting it *be*. Projecting takes on the character of a being-open-to (an opening-up-to) or a revelation (unveiling) of being. Indeed the fundamental meaning of truth: ἀλήθεια, is said to be revelation or unconcealment *(Un-Entborgenheit)*.[42] Heidegger insists that the ' existence of *Dasein* is not *existentia* but *ex-istence*, described as an *ex*-posing of *Dasein* to the revealed nature of what-is-as-such.[43] In short, *Dasein* comes to be what it is by throwing itself open to or putting itself out into the world that reveals *To-be*. Thus, Heidegger repeats[44] that historical man began to exist when the first thinker experienced the openness or unconcealedness of being *(what is)* and wondered: what is being *(what-is)?*

To say that man ex-ists means: the history of man's essential possibilities is arranged by the un-veiling of *what-is-in-totality (das Seiende in Ganzen)*. But letting-be or ex-isting in this sense is one with freedom: the *to-be* of *what-is* is its opening itself up or its self-revealing, its shining-out.[45] And man's participating in that *to-be*, his *to-be*, is his own opening up to *what-is* which reveals *what* he is. A deadly danger lies hidden here, however. It is that we might take a revelation of *what-is* for a revelation of *what-is-in-totality*. Each revealing of *what-is-in-totality* in a *what-is* really involves a *concealment* of totality by a particular way of being (by a *what-is* covering up *what-is-in-totality*). In short, the ex-istence of *Dasein* not only reveals the truth of *what-is* but the untruth of pre-essence: *das vorwesende Wesen*.[46] In this way, freedom thrusts man into the very mystery of being. There, open to the truth of *what-is*—but aware that that truth stands in front of original being —he has to rely on his own resources and practical needs to build up a world which has meaning for him.[47]

The greatest temptation for him, one that threatens his very being, is to insist that the truth he *does* see is the original truth: that the truth he sees in *what-is* is the truth of *To-be*. For the question: what is *das Seiende im Ganzen?* may mean: *what kind* of reality is it? or, what is the being fundamental to all being: what is *das Sein des Seienden?*[48] The basic question is not concerned with *das Seiende* but with *das Sein!* Man's freedom may reveal *what-is*, but that freedom may be lost in practical involvements and techniques unless he recalls that *To-be* is primary. His freedom

---

[42] *WW.*, p. 19, p. 15; *VA.*, p. 229.   [43] *WW.*, p. 15.   [44] *WW.*, p. 16.
[45] *WW.*, p. 16.—*To-be* as *aufgehenden Anwesen*. Cf. *VA.*, p. 142.
[46] *WW.*, sec. 6, p. 19 ff.   [47] *WW.*, p. 21.   [48] *WW.*, p. 23.

for ex-istence is guaranteed by thinking about *To-be*. In that thinking (about *Sein*), however, his freedom is put into words— not words as the expression of opinions but, rather, the articulation or expression of the truth of what-is-in-totality.[49] Words, then, *should* reveal *To-be*, but may stand in the way of such revelation if they are taken to be expressions only of *what-is*.

Hence, the sentences with which Heidegger concludes *Was ist Metaphysik*:

> Thinking, obedient to the voice of Being (i.e. Sein, *To-Be*), seeks the word through which the truth of Being (*To-be*) finds its way into speech. The language of historical men only rings true when it issues from the Word. But if it does ring true, then the testimony of the silent voice of its hidden source beckons it on. Thinking of Being (*To-Be*) stands guard over the word and fulfills its destiny in that guardianship—its destiny being care (Sorge) for the use of language. The thinker's speaking arises from this long-guarded speechlessness and from the careful clear- ing of the ground thus revealed. The poet's naming is of like origin. And yet, inasmuch as like is only like as it is diverse, and since poet and thinker are most thoroughly alike in their care of the word, so, too, are these two at opposite poles in their very essence. The thinker bespeaks Being; the poet names the Holy.[50]

Heidegger is telling us that thought in obedience to the voice of Being (i.e. *Sein,* or *To-be*) seeks the Word and through the latter finds its way into language. Thus, thinking of *To-be* stands guard over language and in that guardianship achieves its destiny, care (Sorge) for the use of language. But surely in these very formulae we seem to have come full term. For have we not returned to themes quite familiar to the Western tradition Heidegger finds sterile? Language expresses the Word (*verbum or* λόγος) which is, in turn,

---

[49] *WW.*, p. 24.

[50] *WM.*, p. 46. "Das Denken, gehorsam der Stimme des Seins, sucht diesem das Wort, aus dem die Wahrheit des Seins zur Sprache kommt. Erst wenn die Sprache des geschichtlichen Menschen aus dem Wort entspringt, ist sie im Lot. Steht sie aber im Lot, dann winkt ihr die Gewähr der lautlosen Stimme verborgener Quellen. Das Denken des Seins hütet das Wort und erfullt in solcher Behutsamkeit seine Bestim- mung. Es ist die Sorge für den Sprach-gebrauch. Aus der langbehüteten Sprachlosig- keit und aus der sorgfältigen Klärung des in ihr gelichteten Bereiches kommt das Sagen des Denkers. Von gleicher Herkunft ist das Nennen des Dichters. Weil jedoch das Gleiche nur gleich ist als das Verschiedene, das Dichten und das Denken aber am reinsten sich gleichen in der Sorgsamkeit des Wortes, sind beide zugleich am weitesten in ihrem Wesen getrennt. Der Denker sagt das Sein. Der Dichter nennt das Heilige."

man's thought about Being. No. The agreement is only apparent. Heidegger feels the difference is profound. What, indeed, *does* it mean to think? And *is the* λόγος being *(das Seiende)* or essence *(das Wesen)?*

Is thinking best exemplified by the rigidly disciplined discourse of logical argument? Is thinking an act that produces or handles thoughts, i.e. representations, concepts, ideas? Is one called a "thinker" in virtue of his scientific knowledge or training? Is it the purpose of thinking to discover highly abstract laws, theories, hypotheses or sketches of reality or to solve the puzzles of the world?[51] And what is meant by λόγος? Is it a word (in language)? a sentence? a concept? essence? Affirmative answers to these questions are signs of *essential* thinking, of thinking concerned with *what-is. That* interpretation of thinking is the mark of the impact of Plato and Aristotle on Western thought.[52] To discover the truth about thinking we must return to the sources of philosophic thought in Heraclitus and Parmenides: thinkers who have heard the voice of Being.[53]

Parmenides gives Heidegger the lead in one very emphatic statement: χρῆ τὸ λέγειν τὲ νοεῖν τ'ἑον ἔμμεναι. How are we to translate or interpret this statement? "It is necessary to say and think that Being is," or "This is necessary: for speaking as well as thinking, Being is," or "It is necessary that speaking and thinking be beings." What, indeed, does it mean taken word by word? χρῆ may be rendered, in German, *Notig* or *Es brauchet;* λέγειν might be *Sagen,* and *νοεῖν, denken.* But what do they mean? If λέγειν leads us to λόγος and, hence, to logic, does logic (the doctrine of *thinking*) bring us to νοεῖν (logical thinking)? No. According to Heidegger, λέγειν does not refer to language and the attendant circumstances of speaking but, rather, to the act of putting or placing indicated by the German *legen.*[54] Thus, if one proposes a motion (*vorlegt*), he be*speaks* it; if one thinks about a matter, he turns it over (*überlegen*) in his mind. The notion of *putting* is primary. Thus, λέγειν and *legen* have to do with *das Liegende* — what is put, placed or situated. *Legen ist Vorliegenlassen.* Thus, if we *say* one thing of another, we let it lie in front of us as this or that, i.e. we let it shine forth. The essence of λέγειν and of λογός is *zu-einem-Vorschein-Bringen* or *Vorliegenlassen.*[55]

[51] *WD.,* p. 79 ff.   [52] *WD.,* p. 40.
[53] *EM.,* Die Beschränkung des Seins (Sein und Werden).
[54] *WD.,* p. 121.   [55] *WD.,* p. 123.

Heidegger's interpretation of λόγος, as fundamentally a *putting forth*, or letting-shine, is confirmed for him by the role he conceives λόγος playing in the thought of Heraclitus. λόγος *puts* things in the sense that it gives change or being a kind of stability by gathering together "moments" of *to-be*. In that act of composing (the inspiration of the poet, i.e. the composer!), being *(To-be)* speaks to us so that we can say *what-is*. But to speak truly, we must let being *(To-be)* speak, we must let being lie in front of us, shine forth upon us.[56']

In this context, how should we interpret νοεῖν? What do we do when we think? What is the *to-be* of thinking? Harking back to the fragments of Parmenides, Heidegger translates νοεῖν by *In-die-Achtnehmen*.[57] To think is not so much to grasp *(nehmen);* it is, rather, to let that which lies before us come in to us *(ein Ankommenlassen des Vorliegenden). Acht* refers to the gathering together in which that which lies before us is preserved.[58] In thinking, we let *what-is* be, we allow being *(Seiende)*, as λόγος or as a gathering-together of *to-be*, to speak to us. Thinking is closer to recollecting than to demonstrating.

We may also ask what is the meaning of τ'έον ἔμμεναι? Does it mean: what one says and thinks, the object of speaking and thinking, is τ'έον ἔμμεναι? Does it indicate that being is the subject which speaks and thinks? Or is the phrase intended to throw some light on the *to-be* of speaking and thinking by referring us to the *to-be* of *what-is?* In answer, Heidegger once n.ore refers[59] to Parmenides and a fragment in which ἐον is used for ἔμμεναι. The phrase would then become τ'έον ἐον. Does ἐον, then, have two meanings in the phrase? Yes. But that is exactly what happens in the case of any participle. Thus, for example, the word *Blühendes* may mean: *(a)* that which blooms, i.e. a rose bush or apple tree, or *(b)* being in bloom, i.e. in bloom as distinct from being faded. In short, the participle functions as noun and verb. τ'έον ἐον would be a parallel case: *Blühendes: blühend: blühen; Seiendes: seiend: sein*. We may render τ'έον ἔμμεναι, then, *Seiendes seiend*. And then the phrase χρῆ τὸ λέγειν τὲ νοεῖν τ'έον ἔμμεναι means: it is necessary to let Being as Being *(Seiendes als Seiendes)* lie before us and pay attention to the being *(seiend* as verbal, i.e. *sein)* of Being.[60] To this point,

---

[56] *EM.,* Die Beschränkung des Seins (Sein und Denken)—especially Heidegger's interpretation of Heraclitus, fragment. 2.
[57] *WD.,* p. 125. [58] *WD.,* p. 128. [59] *WD.,* p. 132. [60] *WD.,* p. 137.

however, as Heidegger realizes, we have only substituted words of one language for another. How may we TRANS-late the words?

What words are these Greek words translating? What original expression is cast into the Greek symbols?

The words of language translate the words of being, the λόγος in which *To-be* expresses itself. *To-be* is a being-present which presents itself in beings. In this way, τ᾿έον expresses, in Greek, the presence of *To-be;* ἔμμεναι expresses the *being* present of *To-be:* in German, *das Anwesende anwesen.*[61] Unless *To-be,* being-present, held sway, there would be no present (thing), no object, no being. It was the virtue of early Greek thought to let that presence be present, to pay attention to the *being-present* of what-is-present; it was the misfortune of later Greek thought to concentrate on the present *(Anwesende)* and withdraw its attention from its *being* present. Indeed, it is only when *To-be* is allowed to express itself that the essence of thinking and speaking will be revealed. τ᾿έον ἔμμεναι explains the "it" of the English translation ("*it* is necessary") of χρῆ: the *being*-present of what-is-present demands that λέγειν be *Vorliegenlassen,* that νοεῖν be *In-die-Acht-nehmen.*[62] Language and thought, then, find their original being in *To-be.*

III

Language then, is a boon to man, the field of "the most innocent of pastimes" ("Diss unschuldigste aller Geschafte"—Holderlin III, 377), but at the same time a menace to his existence.[63] *To-be* speaks to him in words and reveals *what-is:* among other things it reveals what *he* is. Language reveals to man that he is free, a thinker or poet rather than a rational animal. He is a speaker or even a conversation. The truth about language reveals the truth of *To-be,* as the truth of *To-be* reveals the truth about language. But where the truth of *To-be* is forgotten in concern for *what-is,* the truth about language is lost. And then language becomes a menace to man. Gossip will make a non-entity of him! Believing that language expresses *what-is,* as distinct from *To-be,* he finds himself bound by the necessities (needs) of *what-is*—a slave to essence, abstraction, technique. His freedom is gone.

This conclusion, then, seems imposed upon us: Heidegger's experience of Being as a *To-be* which precedes or lies beyond *What-is,* a *To-be* which is revealed in, and in turn reveals, the nature of man as a thinker or speaker, demands a new approach to and a

61 *WD.,* p. 141; *VA.,* p. 142 ff; *VA.,* p. 229.   62 *WD.,* p. 146.   63 *HWD.,* p. 4.

novel use of language. Words in language do not *contain* a meaning in the sense of embodying essence; they contain what might be called *existential* meaning (not as revealing the *Existenz* of *Dasein* but, rather, as revelations of the *To-be* of Being). They might be described as signs indicating the attunement of man's being with Being, directions pointing to "experiences" of *To-be,* rather than formulations of *what-is.* Or it might be expressed thus: Heidegger would have us look *through* words at the primitive expressions of *To-be* in Nature (as revealing *To-be,* not as essence!) Hence, the need he feels to re-examine the etymological roots of words and their early usages. Hence, his habit of creating new words and new word-forms to help us open ourselves to *To-be.*

At least one fundamental question remains—a question that suggests a veritable host of other queries. In constantly asking: What is *To-be?* have we *really* been asking the basic question? Many descriptions have been forthcoming, each careful to stress the primacy of the non-essential, dynamic character of *To-be.* But may we still not ask: Is *To-be?* Has the analysis presented, even in Heidegger's later works, been of a *To-be* which *is?* Or has it been a descriptive analysis of man's awareness of *To-be*—of a *To-be* which *is* in human experience? May the reason explaining why metaphysics always seems to slip through his fingers be this: a *To-be* which *is* has never been touched? Is not the *To-be* of metaphysics hidden from the beginning? If it is, may it not be that existential analysis *itself* hides it? Perhaps analysis of this kind *precludes* the possibility of metaphysics instead of leading to the threshold of metaphysics!

‿‿ The Interpretation of the

Heraclitean Fragments

by Joseph Owens, C.SS.R.

☆ ☆ ☆ ☆ ☆ ☆ ☆ ☆ ☆ ☆ ☆ ☆ ☆ ☆

The Problem of Interpretation

HE ONE HUNDRED or more fragments that remain from the
ancient scroll of Heraclitus have been gathered from widely
different sources.[1] They are taken as they have been found
quoted in authors ranging from the fourth century B.C. to the thirteenth A.D. In these writers they are used in extremely varied contexts and cited for surprisingly different purposes. As they stand,
they have defied all modern efforts to arrange them in any systematic
or doctrinal order.[2] One of them is known, through ancient testimony, to have stood at the very beginning of the scroll, and a
second one came shortly after it. But the order in which the rest

---

[1] The first modern collection is that of Schleiermacher in *Museum der Alterthums-
Wissenschaft*, I (1808), 315-533, containing seventy-two fragments. The standard
edition now is that of Diels-Kranz (DK), in the fifth to eighth editions (1934-1956) of
H. Diels' *Die Fragmente der Vorsokratiker*. However, I. Bywater's edition, *Heracliti
Ephesii Reliquiae* (Oxford: Clarendon Press, 1877), has not yet been rendered entirely obsolete. There are recent editions by R. Walzer, *Eraclito* (Florence: G. Sansoni,
1939), and C. Mazzantini, *Eraclito* (Florence: Chiantore, 1945). A history of the editions may be found in Walzer's work, pp. v-vii. The exact number of the fragments
depends upon what one accepts as original sayings of Heraclitus and what one considers to be doubtful or spurious or merely later paraphrases of Heraclitean sayings
made by quoting authors. The number goes as high as 144 considered genuine by Y.
Battistini, *Héraclite d'Ephèse* (Paris: Editions "Cahiers d'Art," 1948), besides the
nineteen looked upon as uncertain or apocryphal. On many of the 132 fragments listed
as genuine in DK, there is still considerable dispute, while *Fr.* 129 (DK), placed with
the doubtful and spurious, is regarded as "certainly genuine" by G. S. Kirk, *Heraclitus:
The Cosmic Fragments* (Cambridge: University Press, 1954), p. 390.

[2] Except for the first two, the fragments are listed in DK according to the al-
phabetical order of the authors who quote them in their fullest form. Attempts to
arrange them in some kind of doctrinal order have been far from convincing.

of them followed is unknown and apparently offers no hope of ever being satisfactorily restored.

The very type of philosophical doctrine that the fragments contain, moreover, has been open to serious dispute. It has been presented basically as a *cosmology* after the manner of the early Milesian teachings, as a doctrine that seeks to explain the genesis and processes of the universe through a primary principle called fire. It has also been regarded as fundamentally a *metaphysical* doctrine, in the sense that its deepest purpose is to interpret reality by seeing a universal flux as the innermost core of things. This has been understood as denying all permanence and stability and even the presence of any *being* in the universe, and has been placed in direct opposition to a more or less contemporary doctrine of Parmenides. Finally, the Heraclitean wisdom has been viewed as essentially a *moral* doctrine, with physical teachings developed only through the requirements of its moral teaching.

How is one to proceed in judging these different interpretations of the fragments? There need be little doubt that the fragments themselves, since they are sufficiently numerous, have to be the final criterion. The testimonia regarding their meaning are conflicting, often unrealiable, and sometimes patently false. The contexts in which they were quoted quite apparently isolate them only too frequently from their original setting and give very little indication of their exact meaning on the Heraclitean scroll. In most cases there is no guarantee that they were being quoted directly from the place that they occupied in their original surroundings and not from a setting given them later in some secondary source.

When the fragments are taken in themselves, however, they are found couched in a style that at once gives rise to a special difficulty in probing their philosophical thought. It is a style that is terse, rounded, oracular. It makes no attempt to analyze or prove. It merely projects its meaning globally and vividly. In one of the fragments, Heraclitus suggests his own notion of an oracular response. It "neither speaks nor conceals, but indicates."[3] A better

---

[3] *Fr.* 93 (DK, 22B); trans. K. Freeman, *Ancilla to the Pre-Socratics* (Oxford: B. Blackwell, 1948), p. 31. Cf. *Fr.* 92. On the bearing of these fragments upon Heraclitus' own style, cf. W. Jaeger, *The Theology of the Early Greek Philosophers* (Oxford: Clarendon Press, 1947), pp. 111-112 and 121. Similarly: "Car, bien que ces deux fragments parlent de la Sybille et d'Apollon de Delphes, au fond, nous y voyons les propriétés du style que le sage d'Ephèse estime le plus, et qu'il s'efforce de réalizer dans son écrit." A. M. Frenkian, *Etudes de Philosophie Présocratique: Héraclite d'Ephèse*

description of the Ephesian's own style would be hard to find. The style does not seem meant to be intentionally obscure; in fact, much of what it expresses has from earliest times been recognized as lucid and brilliant.[4] On the other hand, it does not lend itself to any systematic development of philosophical doctrines. It expresses them rather as a whole, and leaves them to sink gradually into the mind of the reader through prolonged and sympathetic reflection.

Such is the form in which the Heraclitean wisdom has been expressed. In accordance with the norm that in a Greek philosopher content may not safely be separated from form,[5] the peculiar style of the Ephesian sage can hardly help but play a key role in the interpretation of the fragments. In general, the oracular note hints strongly enough that Heraclitus is speaking in the apocalyptic manner prevalent in his time,[6] and is offering to his fellow-men truths above every-day knowledge. In particular, each fragment has to be considered as a whole, viewed from all angles, and then grasped, as far as possible, in its entire meaning. Attempts at fine distinctions between words expressing similar notions like wisdom, knowledge, insight, and so on, can hardly have any place here. It is rather a matter of taking what the words meant in general to the people of

(Cernauti: Glasul Bucovinei, 1933), p. 21. "So jedenfalls macht es Heraklit selbst." F. J. Brecht, *Heraklit* (Heidelberg: C. Winter, 1936), p. 136. "Cette forme d'expression est celle des oracles . . . ," N. Boussoulas, "Essai sur la Structure du Mélange dans la Pensée Présocratique," *Revue de Métaphysique et de Morale*, LX (1955), 298.

[4] Cf. Diogenes Laertius, *Lives and Opinions of Eminent Philosophers* (DL), II, 22; IX, 7; 16. The earliest mention of Heraclitus as the "obscure" or "dark" philosopher (ὁ σκοτεινός, Latin *tenebrosus*) seems to be that of Cicero, *De finibus* ii. 5, 15. who gives as the reason the obscurity of the Ephesian's comments on nature. Cicero writes as though the epithet was already well established. It is used without comment in the possibly later pseudo-Aristotelian treatise *De Mundo*, 5. 396b20. The name "riddler" had been applied to him by the Skeptic philosopher and satirist Timon of Phlius, in the third century B.C. (DL, IX, 6). Aristotle, *Rhetoric* iii. 5. 1407b12-18, cited his composition as difficult to read because it often does not make clear whether a word goes with what precedes or with what follows. On the legend of Heraclitus as "the weeping philosopher," cf. Kirk, *op. cit.*, p. 8, and C. E. Lutz, "Democritus and Heraclitus," *Classical Journal*, XLIX (1953-54), 309-314.

[5] On this norm in regard to Plato, cf. J. Stenzel, *Plato's Method of Dialectic* trans. D. J. Allan (Oxford: Clarendon Press, 1940), pp. 1-22; in regard to Aristotle, cf. W. Jaeger, *Aristotle* trans. R. Robinson (Oxford: Clarendon Press, 1934), pp. 6-7, 25, n. 1.

[6] Cf. Jaeger, *The Theology of the Early Greek Philosophers*, pp. 109-110. Jaeger's observation, *Paideia* trans. G. Highet (New York: Oxford University Press, 1939), I, p. 173, that "The speculations of the early physicists were not guided by logic, but by other kinds of spiritual activity" holds all the more in the case of Heraclitus. "Héraclite, il ne faut pas l'oublier, *voit* ce qu'il pense: . . ." Battistini, *op. cit.*, p. 21.

the time, and then trying to fathom what Heraclitus could have wished to express in saying something just the way he did.

Needless to insist, all the resources of modern scholarship have to be used to guard as far as possible against merely subjective and arbitrary interpretations. Each fragment is to be studied in the context or contexts from which it has been taken. The meaning that the quoting author ascribes to it has to be carefully examined and his motive for giving it that meaning investigated. The likelihood that it could or could not have had that meaning on the original scroll of the Ephesian has then to be probed. Elements that come from later environments or from errors in transmission have to be recognized as such and eliminated. The labor required for this task is, of course, tremendous, as any serious acquaintance with recent work on the texts will readily show.[7]

Once the text has been established, there still remains the problem of determining as far as possible its original meaning and genuine significance. This last step is naturally the most hazardous. After all the available critical information has been gone through, one is still left with the really basic questions. Why should Heraclitus have expressed himself in this way? What could have been his reason for calling attention to this or that fact? Why should he have bothered making this or that observation?

As an instance, one may take the sixtieth fragment in the Diels-Kranz collection: "The way up and down is one and the same." The meaning of the individual words offers in this case no special difficulty. The saying is found quoted in different contexts by a number of ancient authors. It was interpreted from cosmological, metaphysical, or moral viewpoints. Quoted in a cosmological setting, it was looked upon as describing the changes in the cosmos downward from fire to sea to earth, and upward from earth to sea to fire.[8] This interpretation is quite evidently forced and difficult and seems to have been made in view of an already adopted conception of what Heraclitus' philosophy was. If the Ephesian really had wished to express that cosmological doctrine, why would he

---

[7] Kirk's *Heraclitus: The Cosmic Fragments* is a model of such a study. Yet instances of difficulties still remaining after so close an investigation of the fragments treated, may be found noted in G. Vlastos, "On Heraclitus," *American Journal of Philology*, LXXVI (1955), 337-368; W. Gerson Rabinowitz and W. I. Matson, "Heraclitus as Cosmologist," *Review of Metaphysics*, X (1956), 244-257, and other studies occasioned by the appearance of Kirk's monumental work.

[8] DL, IX, 8-9. On the ancient interpretations, cf. Kirk, *op. cit.*, pp. 105-112.

have selected this manner of speaking? The sentence in itself just
does not express or even "indicate" in any recognizable way that
teaching. Yet, to judge by the frequency with which this sentence
was quoted, it seems to have occupied an important position on the
scroll, ahd so should have been a vivid and forceful expression of
some key Heraclitean doctrine.

It has also been interpreted from the metaphysical viewpoint as
signifying the coincidence of opposites in a given instance.[9] But
again, why should Heraclitus have used such a simile if his purpose
were to illustrate the doctrine that opposites are the same? The
image that the words evoke is that of a road going in one direction,
and so remaining the same road, while it goes up a hill and descends
into the next valley. From the standpoint of Heraclitus' own surroundings, it readily suggests a road from one city to another on
the rugged Ionian coastal strip. It was quoted in the same context
as the fragment using the simile of hand-writing — the writing goes
straight ahead even while going up and down and back and forth
and around. The road, accordingly, would continue to be the same
as it went up and down. The image would be quite inept to convey the notion of a metaphysical coincidence of opposites. The
"up" and the "down" remain very really distinct.

The fragment has also been interpreted from a moral viewpoint as referring to the changes in human fortunes, or to the jour-
neyings of the soul. These notions fit the image much more closely.
But again, one has to inquire if that is exactly what Heraclitus could
have meant in using the simile. It is a question of finding out what
one can about the particular or general context in which the fragment occurred on the scroll, and then asking what Heraclitus could
have had in mind when he chose such a simile to force home the
teaching that he wished to impart.

Another instance may be seen in the sixth fragment: "The sun
is new each day." This statement has been given cosmological interpretations in accord with more general tenets on the cosmic
processes and a metaphysical interpretation in terms of the universal flux.[10] Could it, on the other hand, be a physical comment used

[9] Hippolytus, *Refutation of All Heresies* ix. 10. 4, ed. P. Wendland (Leipzig:
1916), p. 243. Regarding the simile used in Fr. 59 (DK), cf. *infra*, n. 63.

[10] Cf. K. Reinhardt, "Heraclitea," *Hermes*, LXXVII (1942), pp. 235-244; Kirk,
op. cit., pp. 264-279. Battistini lists separately as his seventh fragment "Le soleil est
nouveau chaque jour car il participe du pouvoir dionysien"; *op. cit.*, p. 32. This version is from Proclus, *Tim.*, 334D.

for a moral purpose? If so, might it not be meant to press home the fact that each rising sun brings new circumstances and new problems for the day? Again, the contexts in which the fragment was quoted have to be investigated to see if they yield any information about its meaning on the original scroll. If, as in this case, the particular context on the scroll cannot be at all established, then the over-all tenor of the Heraclitean writing has to be considered and the question asked: Why would Heraclitus make use of such an observation, in view of the general character of his teaching? Why would he consider the notion appropriate for conveying the doctrine upon which he was pondering at the moment?

This approach may appear extremely unsatisfactory for dealing with a philosophic text. It may seem appropriate for interpreting poetry or art, but hardly adapted to a critical examination of philosophical doctrine. Yet it seems to be the method required by the form in which the Heraclitean fragments have been cast, a form of expression that does not lend itself to the treatment proper for examining what has been written in a didactic style. True, such a method can hardly be expected to produce general agreement or to arrive at critically conclusive results in particular instances. Other interpreters will react differently and will insist on seeing other meanings in the fragments, and will be able to make out an acceptable case for so doing. However, if it is the approach indicated by the literary form of the fragments, it has at least a claim to be examined, in order to see if it does not give a better and deeper understanding of the Heraclitean sayings than either of the others.

With these preliminary remarks about form and style in mind, one may proceed more easily to assess the three main lines of interpretation that have been proposed in the long history of the fragments.

The Cosmological Interpretation

The origin of the cosmological approach to the fragments can readily be traced. Aristotle, looking for vague traces of his own material cause among his predecessors, mentioned how Thales and Anaximines respectively had made water and air the first material principle from which all things in the universe developed, and "Hippasus of Metapontum and Heraclitus of Ephesus, fire."[11] Theophrastus, in drawing up the physical doctrines of the Greek phi-

---

[11] *Metaphysics* i. 3. 984a 7-8.

losophers, followed the lead given by Aristotle and presented Heraclitus as a cosmologist who had taught that the universe was derived,
quite after the general manner of the early Milesian teachings, from
fire as from a first principle. The whole Greek doxographical tradition stemmed from Theophrastus and it established firmly in this
sense the long accepted interpretation of Heraclitus as an Ionian
cosmologist. He is still viewed in this light by numerous modern interpreters.

It is true that Heraclitus does speak of the cosmos as a fire that
is kindled and quenched, and of fire changing into sea and earth,[12]
as though fire were the stuff from which the universe emerges. The
fragments expressing these thoughts have been handed down as
quoted against a Stoic background and in the doxographical tradition, and so their meaning in that sense was fixed. But the fragments taken just in themselves do not express exactly that meaning.
Another fragment describes the role of fire in a way that places the
doctrine in a setting quite other than the Milesian background.
"All things are an equal exchange for fire and fire for all things, as
goods are for gold and gold for goods."[13] This fragment gives utterance to a notion considerably different from the general trend
of the Milesian teachings. The metaphor is that of a common cur-
rency in terms of which all marketable goods can be bought and
sold. Would Heraclitus ever have expressed himself in this way if
he had before his mind the notion that the cosmos developed from
an original matrix or plasm in the manner of a living process, as in
the doctrines of Thales, Anaximander,[14] and Anaximines? The
fragment does not convey any notion like that. It indicates a common medium by which things can be evaluated, not a common
principle from which things originate.

Another fragment, if given a cosmological interpretation, would
seem to rule out any interest on the part of Heraclitus in the problem of an original material principle. "Beginning and end in a
circle's *circumference* are common."[15] There is no hint as to what
the original context of this fragment may have been. Nothing in-

---

[12] *Frs.* 30 and 31 (DK).   [13] *Fr.* 90 (DK); trans. Kirk, *op. cit.*, p. 345.

[14] ". . . Anaximander believed that in this living matrix the nascent world developed either like an egg or like an embryo in the womb." W. K. C. Guthrie, *Classical
Quarterly*, XLIX (1956), 42. For a different view of Anaximander's doctrine, cf. G. B.
Burch, "Anaximander, the First Metaphysician," *Review of Metaphysics*, III (1949-50),
137-160.

[15] *Fr.* 103; trans. Kirk, *op. cit.*, p. 113. Cf. Orphic *Fr.* 6 (DK, 1B).

dicates that its significance was primarily cosmological. But if it is meant at all to express vividly a general principle of Heraclitus' thought, it would exclude any tendency to seek the origin of things in an absolutely primary stuff. On the other hand, it would fit in quite well with the conception of a perpetual exchange of things in circular succession. Why would Heraclitus bother to make such an observation? The fragments show no interest in geometrical questions. The thought could hardly have had any significance on the scroll except as an illustration of some other truth. One may say that the fragment was intended as an instance of the relativity doctrine, and so has a metaphysical bearing. But even if true, this interpretation would mean that the saying illustrated the general coincidence of beginning and end, in a circle, for instance. So if the fragment has any general bearing at all, it should rule out an over-all explanation of the universe in terms of an original basic material, as with the Milesians. There is nothing, moreover, in the fragments that suggest a *predominant* interest of Heraclitus in following the pattern set by the Milesian cosmologies.

It seems quite unlikely, then, that the role given to fire by the Ephesian was that of a primal stock for cosmic generation and development. Fire, rather, was regarded by him as a common medium of exchange in the cosmic processes. This was enough to allow Aristotle to see in it some vague traces of his own common substrate of change, but it is not enough to require that Heraclitus' over-all thought be interpreted from a cosmological viewpoint. Certainly, a number of the fragments express cosmological doctrines, but nowhere, when they are taken in themselves and apart from the doxographical tradition, do they imply that these doctrines are to be regarded as the key for interpreting his thought as a whole.

The Stoics invoked the patronage of Heraclitus for their own cosmological views. The cosmic Fire was identified with wisdom, as it was in Heraclitus,[16] and was called by them the *Logos*. In the Stoic background the term λόγος in that cosmic sense has been associated with the doctrines of Heraclitus, and in certain of the fragments has been interpreted with that significance. In the other fragments, Heraclitus employed the term λόγος in the ordinary meanings that it had at the time. He used it in senses of "word" or

---

[16] *Frs.* 64 and 66. Cf. W. C. Kirk, *Fire in the Cosmological Speculations of Heracleitus* (Minneapolis: Burgess, 1940), pp. 24-26; K. Reinhardt, "Heraklits Lehre vom Feuer," *Hermes*, LXXVII (1942), 25-27.

"doctrine,"[17] of "fame,"[18] or of "measure."[19] These were readily recognizable meanings in the common usage of the times. The fragments show no tendency to give the term any special and technical meaning. The use of the term in the sense of a cosmic principle cannot be found previous to the Stoics. Plato and Aristotle show no awareness of any such cosmic meaning of λόγος in Heraclitus. If the fragments, in accordance with their peculiar style, are meant to express their meaning vividly and forcefully, they could hardly be expected to use the term λόγος in a way that was not in current recognition at the time. The signification of λόγος in the cosmic sense of the Stoics, or in the theological sense of the early Christians,[20] may therefore be disregarded as a key to the interpretation of the fragments, in spite of the popularity that it still retains among modern commentators.[21]

The Metaphysical Interpretation

Using the term "metaphysical" in the sense of a basic explanation of all reality, this interpretation means that the fundamental tendency of Heraclitus' thought is to remove any stability from things and explain everything in terms of a universal flux. As in the case of the cosmological interpretation, its origin is not hard to discover. Plato had been given his early philosophical training by the "Heraclitean" Cratylus, of whom practically nothing is known except what can be gathered from Plato's and Aristotle's writings. Cratylus blamed Heraclitus for saying that you cannot step into the same river twice; rather, you could not step into the *same* river even once. Nothing, accordingly, ever remained the same; things were all in a perpetual flux. Plato draws from this doctrine the conse-

---

[17] *Frs.* 87 and 108.   [18] *Fr.* 39.   [19] *Frs.* 31, 45, and 115.

[20] On the lack of doctrinal similarity, cf. M.-J. Lagrange, "Le Logos d'Héraclite," *Revue Biblique,* XXXI (1923), 96-107. W. Kranz, "Der Logos Heraklits und der Logos des Johannes," *Rheinisches Museum,* XCIII (1950), 88-93, presents the case for literary influence on the opening verses of the fourth Gospel. On the other hand, V. Macchioro, *Eraclito* (Bari: Laterza, 1922), p. 137, saw in Heraclitus the "profeta incompreso del pensiero cristiano."

[21] For the case against a cosmic sense of the term λόγος in Heraclitus, cf. O. Gigon, *Untersuchungen zu Heraklit* (Leipzig: Dieterich, 1935), pp. 2-6. On the opposite side, cf. Kirk, *Cosmic Fragments,* pp. 35-40. Sometimes both meanings are joined together; e.g.: ". . . daher ist 'Logos' dasselbe wie 'Sammlung' und dann auch das Sammelude, von dem alle Sammlung ausgeht. Folglich *meint Logos die Sammlung,* die alle Dinge zueienander in Beziehung setzt, indem sie diese auf das ursprünglich Sammelnde als den Grund jeder Sammlung bezieht." J. B. Lotz, "Hörer des Logos, der Mensch bei Heraklit von Ephesus," *Scholastik,* XXVIII (1935), 556.

by JOSEPH OWENS, C.SS.R. [157

quence that knowledge and speech would be impossible. Aristotle interprets it as expressing a denial of the first principle of demonstration and as involving the consequence that Cratylus finally could but point his finger and not attempt to express anything in words.[22] Against this background Heraclitus' deepest thought has been interpreted as a denial of *being* and a thoroughgoing explanation of all reality in terms of becoming.

The keynote of this interpretation has been the formula suggested by Plato: "All things are flowing."[23] This saying does not occur among the fragments of the Heraclitean scroll. The river simile, however, is used in several fragments.[24] Whether just one of these is the original and the others paraphrases, and if so which one, is still a matter of controversy.[25] But the image used can hardly have been meant to express a universal flux doctrine. The river is understood as remaining the same river; the people who step into it are considered to remain the same men. Small wonder that Cratylus could not see in it an expression of the universal flux! Yet Plato for purposes of dramatic contrast had to represent Heraclitus as teaching a complete denial of being, as opposed to Parmenides, who was represented in the same dramatic setting as maintaining a complete denial of becoming. It is not hard, though, to make out a good case that the universal flux doctrine of the "Heracliteans" has its intellectual descent from the poem of Parmenides rather than from the scroll of Heraclitus.[26] The cosmological background

[22] Cf. Plato, *Theaetetus* 156A-183A; Aristotle, *Metaph.*, i. 6. 987a29-34, and iv. 4. 1005b24-25; 5.1010a11-15; 7.1012a25-26.

[23] *Cratylus*, 439C. So: "Le premier élément de la métaphysique d'Héraclite, celui qui domine tous les autres et les conditionne, c'est le principe de l'écoulement universel. Tout coule!" P. Bise, *La Politique d'Héraclite d'Ephèse*, (Paris: Alcan, 1925), p. 70. Similarly, O. Spengler, *Der Metaphysische Grundgedanke der Heraklitischen Philosophie* (Halle: C. A. Kaemmerer, 1904), p. 5. "The central point of his doctrine is, on the contrary, the constant flux of things, including fire." J. B. McDiarmid, "Theophrastus on the Presocratic Causes," *Harvard Studies in Classical Philology*, LXI (1953), 94.

[24] *Frs.* 12, 49a, 91 (DK), and Bywater, *op. cit., Fr.* 41. An historical schema of these fragments may be found in Kirk, *Cosmic Fragments*, p. 375.

[25] Cf. Vlastos, "On Heraclitus," *op. cit.*, p. 338-344; Rabinowitz and Matson, "Heraclitus as Cosmologist," *op. cit.*, p. 250-254; A. Rivier, *Museum Helveticum*, XIII (1956), 158-164; G. S. Kirk, *Museum Helveticum*, XIV (1957), 162-163.

[26] Cf. K. Reinhardt, *Parmenides und die Geschichte der griechischen Philosophie* (Bonn: F. Cohen, 1916), pp. 241-247. On the Heracliteans, cf. E. Weerts, *Heraklit und Herakliteer* (Berlin: E. Eberling, 1926), pp. 84 ff., and "Plato und der Heraklitismus," *Philologus*, (Suppl.) XXIII (1931), Heft 1. B. Wisniewski, on the other hand, upholds the dependence of the flux teaching, as well as the Protagorean view of knowledge, on

against which this metaphysical interpretation of the Heraclitean doctrine was presented is the origin of all things from water,[27] not from fire.

In point of fact, the "universal flux" interpretation runs counter to the express teaching contained in some of the fragments. For Heraclitus, all cosmic changes take place according to *fixed* measures. The unity and rational pattern of the cosmos is repeatedly stressed. The emphasis is on what is *common*, in spite of all particular differences. Moreover, the very doctrine of opposites in the fragments requires that the *notion* of each opposite be stable and definite. The example used by Aristotle to show that Heraclitus denied any difference between opposites is that the good and bad are the same, understanding this to mean that goodness and badness are identical.[28] In the fragments, Heraclitus states that sea water is beneficial for fish, harmful for men,[29] that for donkeys chaff is preferable to gold,[30] that vetch bring happiness to oxen,[31] that some things are unjust to men though just to god.[32] But the meaning of these observations, evidently enough, is that the same thing can be good in relation to one species and bad in relation to another. It in no way implies that the *notion* of goodness passes over into that of evil. The two notions are kept carefully distinct in their import. In the fragment "Cold things warm themselves, warm cools, moist dries, parched is made wet,[33] the notions remain stable while the particular things change successively from one characteristic to the other. There is no assertion of any coincidence of opposites in a metaphysical sense.

The other fragments used by later interpreters to show that Heraclitus held this identity of opposites likewise reveal no coincidence in a metaphysical context. The statement that day and

---

the Heraclitean sayings; "Protagoras et Héraclite," *Revue Belge de Philologie et d'Histoire*, XXXI (1953), 490-499.

[27] Cf. Plato, *Crat.*, 402AD; *Theaet.*, 180D. K. Deichgräber, "Bemerkungen zu Diogenes' Bericht über Heraklit," *Philol.*, XCIII (1938-39), 25, notes that the coincidence of opposites, later associated with the cosmic fire by the Stoic and early Christian commentators, has no part in the doxographical summaries found in Diogenes Laertius: "Characteristisch ist für die echt aristotelische Anschauung vom Wesen der herakliteischen Philosophie, dass sie als reine Physik interpretiert wird, dass also auch das Prinzip der coincidentia oppositorum, das im Grunde erst von einigen heraklitisierenden Stoikern und dann von den Christen (Hippolytus) wiederentdeckt wird, in diesem Bericht keine Rolle spielt."

[28] *Top.*, viii. 5. 159b30-33; *Phys.* i. 2. 185b20-25.   [29] *Fr.* 61 (DK)   [30] *Fr.* 9.
[31] *Fr.* 4.   [32] *Fr.* 102   [33] *Fr.* 126; trans. Kirk, *Cosmic Fragments*, p. 149.

night are one[34] is made in a background suggesting that day and
night are successively different phases of the one twenty-four hour
cycle. Such also is the case with winter and summer — they are the
one year. So, presumably, war and peace, satiety and hunger, are
looked upon as successive phases of definite cycles. Every one of
them is included in the widest unity of all, the divine: "god is
day-night, winter-summer, war-peace, satiety-hunger, and undergoes alteration in the way that *(fire),* when it is mixed with spices,
is named according to the scent of each of them."[35] The simile indicates that the same reality can successively take on different and,
from a narrower viewpoint, opposed aspects. There is no question
of identifying these aspects, or of having one notion pass over in
Hegelian fashion into its opposite. Rather, the doctrine, expressed
very forcefully in some of the fragments,[36] requires that the notions
of the opposites found in ever-varying things remain firmly distinct from each other, even while the particular things characterized
by those notions change incessantly, in order to maintain a balanced
tension. If one of the opposites disappeared into the other, the tension between them would likewise vanish, a tension that is essential
to the Heraclitean constitution of reality.

The general manner of expression throughout the fragments,
moreover, gives only too evident witness that Heraclitus attached
a very particular and definite meaning to each opposite. He shows
no hesitancy whatsoever in respect to the fixed significance of words.

The metaphysical interpretation of the fragments, then, has
its origin quite apparently in Plato's literary device of setting in
extreme contrast the philosophical doctrines of being and becoming, and attributing the doctrine of universal becoming to Heraclitus. This interpretation evidently enough does not spring from

---

[34] *Fr.* 57. On the interpretation, cf. Kirk, *op. cit.,* pp. 155-157.

[35] *Fr.* 67, following trans. Kirk, *op. cit.,* pp. 184. Cf.: "This does not mean however that the contraries mutually neutralize one another, so that the balance is zero.
With Heraclitus, the balance is positive in each single case: . . ." H. Fränkel, "Heraclitus on God and the Phenomenal World," *Transactions of the American Philo-
logical Association,* LXIX (1938), 243. Heidel, *Proceedings of the American Academy
of Arts and Sciences,* XLVIII (1913), 704-708, and Fränkel, in his article (pp. 234-244),
suggest "oil" instead of "fire" for the simile in *Fr.* 67.

[36] *Frs.* 10, 51, 54, 65 (cf. context in Hippolytus, *Refut.* ix. 10. 7, ed. Wendland, p.
243.27), 84a, 125. A recent expression of the Heraclitean notion of becoming reads:
". . . le devenir dont il s'agit ici n'est pas un devenir *de* l'Etre, mais un devenir *dans*
l' Etre." J. Brun, *Rev. de Métaph. et de Morale,* LXII (1957), 15.

the fragments themselves. Rather, it is patently incompatible with
much of their teaching.

The Moral Interpretation

A third interpretation in antiquity considered that the sayings
of Heraclitus were intended primarily to expound a moral doctrine. Diodotus, a grammarian who wrote a commentary on the
scroll, called it "A helm unerring for the rule of life." Others gave
it similar moral titles like "A guide of conduct."[37] Diodotus, moreover, declared expressly that it was not a treatise on nature, but on
πολιτεία, and that the parts dealing with nature had only a paradigmatic role.[38] This estimate of Diodotus need not be dismissed
cavalierly by understanding the term πολιτεία in the sense of government or civil constitution and claiming that it was "ridiculous"
or "absurd" for him to think that it was a work on politics. The
title that he gave the book upon which he was commenting shows
clearly enough that he understood πολιτεία in its sense of the Greek
citizen's daily life and the Heraclitean scroll as a guide to living
that life correctly. He regarded it as a treatise on human conduct.
If this grammarian is Diodotus of Sidon, whose brother was a Peri-
patetic, he could be expected to think against a background in
which "political" and "moral" teaching coincided. But in any case,
what he was saying would be in modern language that the Heraclitean scroll was not a treatise on the physical world but upon
moral conduct, and that the passages containing physical doctrine
were introduced only in function of its moral teaching.

As Diodotus read and commented upon the scroll, then, he did
indeed see in it physical doctrines. These, however, had only a
secondary role. They were developed in function of the moral
teachings, or at least were used merely to illustrate them. Do the
fragments actually bear out this estimate of the sayings?

The first two fragments, whose place at the beginning of the
scroll is sufficiently attested, do in fact purport to introduce a moral
teaching. The first fragment bears upon what men *do* in their
waking hours. It states that Heraclitus is undertaking to propound
"words and deeds." This was the epic conception of human con-

---

[37] DL, ix. 12, trans. R. D. Hicks.   [38] *Ibid.*, ix. 15.

duct,[39] though the Homeric formula could also mean "word and thought."[40] The second fragment urges men to live in accordance with what is common, and not according to any private wisdom. These fragments introduce clearly enough a discourse that intends to tell men how they should live. The opening lines of the scroll were intended to present a moral treatise.

The first fragment has been translated in various ways. The key words in its opening sentence are capable of different meanings. But if they are taken according to the natural meaning that each word would have at the time in the incipit of an Ionian treatise, λόγος means the scroll or treatise or discourse itself,[41] τοῦδε in this situation means "the following," and the present participle of the verb "to be" (ἐόντος) in the context means "real" or "true."[42] The fragment, accordingly, may be translated:

> The following *logos*, ever true, men are found incapable of understanding, both before they hear it and when they once have heard it. For although all things take place in accordance with this *logos*, they seem like people of no experience, when they make experience of such words and deeds as I set forth,

[39] ". . . to be a speaker of words (μῦθον) and a doer of deeds," *Iliad* ix. 443. Cf. Jaeger, *Paideia*, I, pp. 6-7. The statement of Heraclitus seems to be paraphrased in *Frs.* 73 and 112; cf. Kirk, *Cosmic Fragments*, pp. 44-45 and 390-391.

[40] Cf. R. Schottländer, "Drei vorsokratische Topoi," *Hermes*, LXII (1927), 444-446.

[41] There does not appear to be any one English word that will adequately translate the term λόγος in this Ionian sense. On the notion, cf. W. Jaeger, *Studien zur Entstehungsgeschichte der Metaphysik des Aristoteles* (Berlin: Weidmann, 1912), pp. 138-144. In this signification a λόγος meant primarily what it said, what is told; cf. Kranz, "Der Logos Heraklits und der Logos der Johannes," *op. cit.*, p. 81-82. It continued to refer more basically to the utterance even after it was set down in written form and had come to denote the papyrus scroll; cf. Jaeger, *op. cit.*, p. 140. On the history of the word λόγος, cf. E. L. Minar, "The Logos of Heraclitus," *Classical Philology*, XXXIV (1939), 323-341. English words like "discourse," "treatise," "account" do not seem to express correctly the bearing of λόγος on both the written scroll and its intelligible content. Nor is *logos* confined to the prosaic or didactic notion of "treatise" or "discourse." It means "legend" (trans. Godley) at Herodotus, ii. 81; cf. ii. 123. "Message" would perhaps be too loaded in the direction of an oracular pronouncement, though λόγος was used at the time in the sense of an oracular response, cf. Pindar, *Pythian Odes*, iv. 59.

For the use of λόγος in incipits parallel to the present one in Heraclitus, cf. Diogenes of Apollonia, *Fr.* 1 (DK, 64B); Ion of Chios, *Fr.* 1 (DK, 36B); and the incipit attributed to Pythagoras in DL, viii. 6 (DK, 14 *Fr.* 19; I, 105.12).

[42] Cf. J. Burnet, *Early Greek Philosophy* (4th ed.; London: [reprint] Black, 1952), p. 133, n. 1; Jaeger, *Theology of the Early Greek Philosophers*, pp. 225-229, n. 11. On the case for linking "ever" (ἀεί) with "true," cf. W. Capelle, "Das erste Fragment des Herakleitos," *Hermes*, LIX (1924), 190-203. On the case for joining it with "capable of understanding," cf. A. Busse, *Rheinisches Museum*, LXXV (1926), 206-207.

explaining each in accordance with its nature and declaring how
it is. But the rest of men do not know what they are doing after
they have awakened, just as they forget what they do while they
are asleep.

This fragment, leading up to what men *do* when awake, seems
intended to explain human conduct in such a way that an individual's life will be brought into conformity with the fundamental pattern according to which all things take place. The
second fragment, which came shortly after the first and is introduced with a "therefore," apparently continuing its thought, states
that a man's conduct should be based upon the common, and not
upon any private wisdom: "Therefore one should follow the common; but though the *logos* is common, the many live as though they
had a private wisdom."[43] Solidarity with the world around means
living as awake. It gives life meaning and solidity. To live according to a private wisdom, on the contrary, is to live in a meaningless
dream-world. The λόγος of Heraclitus proposes to expound this
common wisdom. In such a background it is quite to be expected
that Heraclitus distinguished between himself and his λόγος,[44] for it
is not setting forth any private wisdom of his own, but the common
wisdom that is accessible to all,[45] though difficult for them to attain.[46]

[43] *Fr.* 2. Cf. *Fr.* 17.

[44] "If you have heard not me, but my logos, it is wise for you to admit that all
things are one." *Fr.* 50; trans. Jaeger, *Paideia*, I, p. 182. In *The Theology of the Early
Greek Philosophers*, p. 121, Jaeger translates ". . . not to me but to the *logos* [as I have
proclaimed it] . . .," still distinguishing, however, between Heraclitus himself and his
teaching. The manuscript reading is δόγματος instead of λόγου. The emendation
is necessary philologically, but not because of any impossibility of the writer's placing
himself in opposition to his teaching, especially against the background of Heraclitus'
initial distinction between private and common wisdom. For the case that this fragment militates against the acceptance of the term λόγος as the message of Heraclitus,
cf. Kirk, *Cosmic Fragments*, pp. 37-40.

[45] The capacity to understand the common is possessed by every one; cf. paraphrases (Kirk, *Cosmic Fragments*, pp. 55-56) given in *Frs.* 113 and 116. *Fr.* 16 "How
could any one escape the notice of that which never sets?" (trans. Kirk, *ibid.*, p. 362;
for interpretation, cf. *ibid.*, pp. 364-365) seems to refer to the cosmic fire that steers all
things, and so to the ever manifest cosmic order.

[46] *Fr.* 123 "The real constitution of things is accustomed to hide itself" (trans.
Kirk, *ibid.*, p. 227) and *Fr.* 22 "Those who search for gold dig much earth and find
little" (trans. Kirk, *ibid.*, p. 231) appear to stress the difficulty and labor required in
order to attain wisdom. One quite possible interpretation of *Fr.* 11 "Every animal is
driven to pasture with a blow" (trans. Kirk, *ibid.*, p. 258) is that men have to be driven
to the true pastures of their souls by tongue-lashings like those of Heraclitus, and so
his urgings are quite in order. The concluding sentence of *Fr.* 1 would seem to refer
to those who are not fortunate enough to hear read to them the λόγος of the Ephesian.

With a play on the Greek expressions "capable of understanding," "with intelligence," and "common," adding to the vividness
of his style, Heraclitus emphasizes that intelligence is based upon
what is common, just as a city-state is based on its law (νόμος), in
fact ultimately on one all-pervading law, the divine.[47] The solidarity experienced in the civilized life of the Greek city-state is
used to embody the notion of "the common." Apparently the feeling of solidarity in communal action, inherited from centuries of
prehistory,[48] is understood to make life real and meaningful. But
the vision of Heraclitus is penetrating far beyond the individual
city-state and is conjuring up a unity common to all city-states and
all human laws and customs. In this sense "the common" becomes
identified with "the divine." In that unity alone does that which
is wise consist.[49] It is the understanding of how all things are steered
through all,[50] whether or not it be called by the name of Zeus.[51]

The general conceptions of these fragments are clear enough.
They group together the notions of wisdom, the common and the
divine, just as the notion "god" is understood by Heraclitus as the
common universe which includes all the opposites.[52] Wisdom consists in understanding the common unity of direction that all things
exhibit. In relation to the divine, all things are beautiful, good,
and just, but some of them become unjust in relation to men.[53]
The human ἦθος or habituated way of viewing things does not
entail true insights; but the divine ἦθος does.[54] The respective
ἦθος, then, determines a man's destiny, [55] even the eyes and ears
being bad witnesses for any one who has a barbarian soul.[56]

Throughout these fragments, the basic contrast between the
common and the particular viewpoints, as laid down in the first
two, is being exploited. Particular knowledge is of no avail to any
one who lacks the habituation of Greek education and culture and
who does not base his wisdom on the common or divine ἦθος. But

[47] *Fr.* 114.
[48] F. M. Cornford, *From Religion to Philosophy* (London: E. Arnold, 1912), pp.
59-88, uses the theme of this influence to bolster his theory that Presocratic philosophy is a transcript of traditional mythology.
[49] *Fr.* 32; cf. *Fr.* 50.   [50] *Fr.* 41.
[51] On the likelihood of the identity of "the wise," at least radically, in these last
three fragments, cf. Kirk, *Cosmic Fragments*, pp. 387; 394.
[52] Cf. *Fr.* 67.   [53] *Fr.* 102.   [54] *Fr.* 76.
[55] *Fr.* 119. Cf. Epicharmus, *Fr.* 17 (DK,23B), where τρόπος is used instead of ἦθος.
[56] *Fr.* 107. On the contemporary meaning of *ethos* as the customs or culture of a
people, cf. B. Snell, "Die Sprache Heraklits," *Hermes*, LXI (1926), 363-364.

even though particular knowledge is in itself unable to give wisdom,[57] nevertheless, wide acquaintance with particular things is required by true wisdom.[58] Heraclitus is quite obviously speaking
of a type of knowledge that depends on the disposition or habituation acquired through Greek culture, knowledge that while requiring wide speculative acquaintance with particular things, is
nevertheless not based on that acquaintance but fundamentally
upon the affective part of the soul.[59] This indicates what was later
called practical knowledge, a knowledge meant for action.

If, as the opening fragments imply, the purpose of the Ephesian's
discourse is to show men how to live, and is based upon the distinction between a particular viewpoint as meaningless and only
the common viewpoint as meaningful or intelligible, then all this
fits into a coherent notion of wisdom. The common civic life in-
culcated by the Greek παιδεία is viewed as based upon what is common in the fullest sense, the divine. The purpose of human action
is to attain to the full that solidarity and common unity, which
alone can give reality and intelligibility to human life. But for any
one thinking in this way an initial problem arises. The same particular things can be good for one agent, bad for another.[60] In fact,
the good and desirable change for the same individual as he finds
himself in differing circumstances,[61] or as he regards it from different viewpoints.[62] The moral opposites can never be located fixed-
ly in any particular thing. Circumstances are always changing and
requiring new and different decisions. To be consistently brave,
moderate, and just, one has to vary one's particular conduct according to the ever-changing circumstances. To go forward steadily
in the same direction one has to keep incessantly changing the
direction of one's course, as new circumstances arise. This seems to
be the truth that Heraclitus is inculcating with the simile: "Of
letters [*or*, of writers] the way is straight and crooked; it is one and
the same."[63] The hand in writing has to keep continually changing
its direction in order to proceed straight ahead in the expression
of one's thought.

[57] Cf. *Fr.* 40, also *Frs.* 108 and 129.   [58] *Fr.* 35; cf. *Frs.* 47 and 55.
[59] Cf. *Frs.* 18, 86, and the context of *Fr.* 19.
[60] Cf. fragments cited *supra*, nn. 29-32.   [61] Cf. *Fr.* 111.
[62] Cf. *Frs.* 48, 56, 79, and paraphrases in *Frs.* 82 and 83. On *Fr.* 58, cf. Rabinowitz
and Matson, "Heraclitus as Cosmologist," *op. cit.*, p. 248, n. 8.
[63] *Fr.* 59; trans. Kirk, *Cosmic Fragments*, p. 97. The text of Hippolytus evokes the
image of the screw-press, giving the same general meaning, but much less vividly.

Such appears to be the fundamental intuition of Heraclitus. Only in a continually deviating way can human conduct make progress in one and the same direction, and the solidarity of one's life with the common world around be maintained. From this viewpoint one may inquire into the nature of the physical world. What kind of world is required by these exigencies of human conduct? It has to be a world where particular things, which give rise to the different circumstances, are always changing, even from one opposite to the other. Yet it has to be a world in which a common unity of direction pervades all the particular changes. It has to be a world that throughout all the incessant changes preserves the balanced tensions that keep its measures fixed and make things able to perform their specific functions, as is the case with the bow and lyre.[64] Such is the ordered universe that the very nature of human conduct postulates. Fire, so mobile in its constitution and yet always acting according to the fixed requirements of a definite nature, serves to explain that universe and in it is located the guiding role and nature of wisdom.[65]

Accordingly, one's life should not be allowed to stagnate in any rigid moulds of tradition — we must not act just as our parents did.[66] Rather, like the mixed drink,[67] the integrity of one's life is maintained only when it is continually stirred. Therefore, ceaseless struggle is the only way of preserving the common unity,[68] and to remove strife from the universe would mean destroying the world order.[69]

Reading the statements of Heraclitus from this moral viewpoint, the viewpoint indicated clearly enough by the two opening fragments, one sees what Diodotus meant when he said that the work of Heraclitus was a moral treatise, not one on nature, and that the physical doctrines in it had only a paradigmatic role. The physical doctrines serve to elucidate and substantiate the moral ones, by showing what type of physical world is required by the exigencies

[64] Cf. *Fr.* 51.
[65] *Fr.* 30; cf. *Fr.* 94. On the general Heraclitean doctrine of fire, cf. W. C. Kirk, *Fire in the Cosmological Speculations of Heracleitus,* and K. Reinhardt, "Heraklits Lehre vom Feuer," *op. cit.,* p. 1-27.
[66] *Fr.* 74. Cf. Battistini, *op. cit.,* pp. 21 and 46.
[67] *Fr.* 125. Cf. *Fr.* 84a "It rests by changing" (trans. Jaeger, *Paideia,* I, p. 182; cf. "In changing, it takes its rest," *Theology of the Early Greek Philosophers,* p. 123).
[68] Cf. *Frs.* 10, 53, 65, 80.
[69] Cf. Aristotle, *Eudemian Ethics* vii. 1. 1235a25-28, and other references in DK 22A22.

of human action. The common wisdom revealed by the demands
of human action is explained in terms of the most mobile of visible
things, fire. It is the fire that runs through the universe and steers
and guides the cosmic processes. The wisdom involved in the unity
of things is indeed identified with this definite nature, fire, or at
least is made an aspect of it; for in Heraclitus there is as yet no
notion of the supersensible, even in regard to thought and the soul.
The moral approach, accordingly, shows why Heraclitus was led
to see in fire the medium of exchange for all things rather than a
primal stuff for cosmic generation. Similarly, it explains his emphasis on the doctrine of the opposites as incessantly changing yet
united into one common whole, without any derogation of the
fixed meaning that each exhibits.

The notion that the non-human world should be interpreted
in function of one's own conduct may seem strange today. But
could it have caused any surprise in the times of Heraclitus himself? The method of the early physicists was to describe the world
in terms of the vital processes that they experienced within themselves.[70] Heraclitus, instead of remaining on the biological level,
is rather taking specifically human action and making it the starting-
point for his teachings about the universe as a whole. It is a universe in which death is seen justified by the very willingness of men
to accept birth and life.[71]

Conclusion

Of the three approaches for interpreting the Heraclitean fragments, the first and second do not seem tenable, notwithstanding

---

[70] ". . . a strange symbolist belief that the non-human world could be interpreted
through human life." Jaeger, *Paideia* I, p. 173. Cf. *supra*, n. 14. Cornford notes that for
Pythagoras "The world must have a certain character if it is to respond to the needs
of the soul," *Classical Quarterly*, XVI (1922), 139.

[71] Cf. *Fr.* 20. H. Cherniss, "The Characteristics and Effects of Presocratic Philosophy," *Journal of the History of Ideas*, XII (1951), 333, notes "the revolutionary
notion that the meaning of the world is to be discovered not by looking outward
towards phenomena but by probing one's own soul." In this way "die erkenntnis der
wahrheit ist gebunden an die selbsterkenntnis." Weerts, *op. cit.*, p. 24. ". . . seine
Wahrheit ist Wahrheit für uns und durch uns; . . ." F. J. Brecht, *Heraklit* (Heidelberg:
C. Winter, 1936), p. 16. "Compared with the philosophers who preceded him, Heraclitus was the first philosophical anthropologist." Jaeger, *Paideia*, I, p. 182. Mazzantini
sees in him "forse il primo moralista ellenico," *op. cit.*, p. 24. "Heraklit bedurfte einer
bestimmten Naturphilosophie, um seine Gottes- und Seelen-lehre darauf bauen zu
können. Er war ein Religionsstifter, der mit seiner Lehre Trost und Hoffnung bringen
wollte." A. Stöhr, *Heraklit* (Vienna, etc.: E. Strache, 1920), p. 9.

the prestige of their modern advocates. The first, the cosmological interpretation, does not account for the preponderant number of fragments that have a moral import.[72] This interpretation, moreover, makes a forced reading of those fragments that deal with physical tenets. It does not correctly express the type of doctrine that is indicated by the notion of fire as a medium of exchange. It seems to have no other origin than the effort to fit Heraclitus into the Greek doxographical tradition.[73] Finally, it hardly gives a picture that does justice to the profound wisdom of the great Ephesian, a wisdom that has stood the test of centuries.

The second interpretation, that of the universal flux, is at manifest variance with the text and the spirit of the fragments. The keynote of the Heraclitean sayings is their insistence on the common, a "common" that has to be achieved in a world where particulars change incessantly but always according to fixed and definite measures. The origin of the universal flux interpretation is clearly enough Plato's dramatic contrast of Heraclitus with Parmenides, rather than any exigence of the Ephesian's own sayings.

The third interpretation, the approach from the viewpoint of human conduct, seems to be the one required by the text of the fragments when they are read in themselves and outside the two predominant grooves of traditional interpretation. This way of understanding them, besides being indicated by the introductory fragments, fully respects the oracular form in which they were written. It does not try to interpret them as though they were didactically written texts. It lets them overflow in the full wealth ot meaning that can be found in them. It gives them a worth far beyond the historical, and recognizes in them the ability even today to evoke insights into the basic problems of moral philosophy. Without going anywhere near the extreme that would see in them the

[72] Kirk, *Cosmic Fragments*, treats about half the Heraclitean fragments as open to interpretation in a cosmic sense. Of these, however, only *Frs.* 30, 31, 64, 66, 67, 76, 90, 94, and 126 seem to have a definite cosmological meaning, and even with them it is not hard to see how they were adapted to press home moral considerations. "Nowhere throughout his work is there any trace either of a purely didactic attitude or of a purely physical theory of the universe." Jaeger, *Paideia*, I, p. 177.

[73] Cf. *supra*, nn. 11-15. It seems to have been unknown to Plato. "It has long since been noted that in all Plato's references to Heraclitus the doctrine of the elemental fire is never mentioned . . ." H. Cherniss, *Aristotle's Criticism of Presocratic Philosophy* (Baltimore: Johns Hopkins Press, 1935), p. 380.

solution to the major problems of present-day thought,[74] the moral approach gives them an abiding and highly pertinent value, for it finds vividly indicated in them the fundamental character of practical science, and a surprisingly subtle penetration into the problem of establishing true universality in the continually shifting subject-matter found in the moral world. It allows one today as much as ever in the past to find continued profit in pondering over the sayings that remain from the λόγος of the ancient Ephesian sage.

[74] E.g. "Dans ses oeuvres gît la pensée fondamentale et, en tout cas, les principes premiers qui peuvent mettre fin à la crise de la pensée moderne et concilier enfin ces deux soeurs maintenant étrangères, la philosophie et la science." R. Bertrand, *L'Univers cette Unité* (Paris: La Colombe, 1950), p. 11. Nevertheless, there need be little doubt about the permanence and continued actuality of Heraclitus' thought: "On n'en a donc jamais fini avec Héraclite." Battistini, *op. cit.*, p. 26. ". . . les vérités qu'il a révélées aux hommes brillent d'une éternelle jeunesse." M. Solovine, *Héraclite d' Ephèse* (Paris: Alcan, 1931), pp. ix-x. G. Burckhardt, *Heraklit* (Zürich: O. Füssli, n.d.), p. 16, lists a few instances of the influence of Heraclitus on modern thinkers. A discussion of Heraclitus' doctrine against the background of present-day thought may be found in Ludwig Binswanger, "Heraklits Auffassung des Menschen," *Die Antike*, XI (1935), 1-38.

Some Reflections on *Summa Contra Gentiles II, 56* by Anton C. Pegis

☆ ☆ ☆ ☆ ☆ ☆ ☆ ☆ ☆ ☆ ☆ ☆ ☆ ☆

I

THE Aristotelianism of St. Thomas Aquinas is a historical problem of notorious and even baffling complexity whose most interesting aspect is its very possibility. How, historians have asked, can St. Thomas interpret the historical Aristotle in the way that classical Aristotelians before and after him have not followed? To consider the most baffling problem of all, how can St. Thomas propose as Aristotelian a view of the intellectual soul as the substantial form of the body that has satisfied no major participant in the long Aristotelian debate on the meaning of *De Anima,* II, 1-2 and III, 5?

To St. Thomas, as is well known, it was both evident and evidently Aristotelian that the intellectual soul was, *qua* intellectual substance, the substantial form of the body. Yet this was the very point on which two eminent Aristotelians, namely, Alexander of Aphrodisias and Averroes, amply proved by their celebrated divergence on the separation of the intellect from the soul that their common premise involved the impossibility of an immaterial form of matter. In his own *De Anima,* Alexander had argued that the human intellect, being part of a soul that was the form of matter, was corrupted with the corruption of that form.[1] In the twelfth cen-

[1] On the corruptibility of the intellectual soul in Alexander of Aphrodisias, see his *De Anima* (ed. I. Bruns, *Supplementum Aristotelicum,* II, 1: *Alexandri De Anima cum Mantissa* [Berlin: G. Reiner, 1887] pp. 1-187), pp. 12, lines 6-25; 15, 27 to 16, 27; 17, 9-15; 21, 22-24; 24, 18 to 25, 4; 81, 23-28; 84, 22 to 85, 5; 89, 19 to 90, 1; 90, 2 to 91, 5.

On the interpretation of Alexander, see the work of Paul Moraux (*Alexandre d'Aphrodise* [Paris-Liège, 1942]), which however presupposes a strongly Thomistic interpretation of Aristotle. The classic exposition of Alexander remains that of E. Zeller, *Philosophie der Griechen,* ed. E. Wellman (5th ed; Leipzig: 1923), III, 1; pp. 813-31. On the first penetration of Alexander's *De Intellectu* (pp. 106-13 of the Mantissa) in the Latin world, see G. Théry, *Alexander d'Aphrodise* (Paris: J. Vrin, 1926).

tury, Averroes could not understand how a separate and unmixed intellect could be material and corruptible. He was particularly scandalized that Alexander could have proposed this notion as an interpretation of their common master Aristotle. On the contrary, the intellect was for Averroes immaterial and incorruptible, and for this reason it was separate from the soul that was the substantial form of the body, though operating within it.[2] The conflict between the Exegete and the Commentator has been, since the entry of Averroes into the Latin world, the central theme in the history of Aristotelian psychology.[3]

In the thirteenth century, Siger of Brabant struck directly at the core of the Thomistic position: the human soul could not be at once a subsistent form and a substantial form: *anima intellectiva non potest habere rationem per se subsistentis et, cum hoc, unum facere cum materia et corpore in essendo.* Between Siger and St. Thomas stood the teaching of Aristotle, including the Aristotelian dilemma. As a substantial form, the soul would be related to the body as shape to wax and would thus be a material form. But if the intellectual soul was not such a material form, then it was separate in being from the body. In that case it was united to the body as operating within it. In Siger's words:

> Dicendum est igitur aliter secundum intentionem Philosophi, quod anima intellectiva in essendo est a corpore separata, non ei unita ut figura cerae, sicut sonant plura verba Aristotelis, et eius ratio ostendit. Anima tamen intellectiva corpori est unita in operando . . . Sunt igitur unum anima intellectiva et corpus in opere.[4]

[2] See *Averrois Cordubensis Commentarium Magnum in Aristotelis De Anima,* ed. F. S. Crawford, (Cambridge, Mass.: The Mediaeval Academy of America, 1953), II, Comm. 4, p. 393, line 196 ff.

[3] See, for many textual indications, Bruno Nardi, *Sigieri di Brabante nel Pensiero del Rinascimento Italiano* (Rome: Editioni Italiane, 1945).

[4] Siger of Brabant, *De Anima Intellectiva,* III; in P. Mandonnet, *Siger de Brabant et l'Averroisme latin au XIIIᵉ siècle* (2nd ed.; Louvain: Institut Supérieur de Philosophie, 1908), II, 151, 154.

On the general interpretation of Siger of Brabant at the present time, see E. Gilson, *History of Christian Philosophy in the Middle Ages* (New York: Random House, 1955), pp. 388-99, 717-25. For the present state of Sigerian research, see A. Maurer, "The State of Historical Research in Siger of Brabant," *Speculum,* XXXI, (January, 1956), pp. 49-56; F. Van Steenberghen, "Nouvelles recherches sur Siger de Brabant et son école," *Revue Philosophique de Louvain,* LIV, (February, 1956), pp. 130-47; Géza Sajó, *Un traité récemment découvert de Boèce de Dacie* (Budapest: Akadémiai Kiado, 1954), pp. 14-37.

Early in the fourteenth century, John of Jandun was as little able as Siger to conceive the philosophical possibility of a substantial form that was not material. To him the position of Averroes (and Aristotle) was philosophically irrefutable. Hence, if as a Christian he ultimately disagreed with Averroes, he did so *sola fide*, not on philosophical grounds.[5] It seemed nothing short of miraculous to him that a unique substantial form was not itself extended in an extended body; it was just as miraculous that a form individuated by the individuation of corporeal matter could be the subject of universal notions and, unlike the sense powers, know in a way that transcends the conditions of matter:

> Quod enim aliqua forma dans esse materiae praecipue sine quacumque alia forma substantiali non sit extensa secundum extensionem corporis, hoc non video nisi e solo miraculo divino contingere posse; et quod aliqua forma individuata individuatione materiae corporalis recipiat comprehensionem universalem diversam a comprehensione sensitiva, hoc non video possibile nisi solum per divinum miraculum et huiusmodi similia.[6]

But there is more. If it required a miracle to believe with St. Thomas in the notion of an immaterial substantial form of matter, John of Jandun was left with only two available philosophical possibilities, namely, the mortalist position of Alexander and the separatist position of Averroes. Not only did he follow Averroes and

---

[5] "Sed quamvis haec opinio sit Commentatoris et Aristotelis [the opinion of Averroes on the non-plurification of the intellect], et quamvis etiam haec opinio non possit removeri rationibus demonstrativis, tamen ego dico aliter. Et dico quod intellectus non est unus numero in omnibus hominibus, immo ipse est numeratus in diversis secundum numerationem corporum humanorum, et est perfectio dans esse simpliciter. Hoc autem non probo aliqua ratione demonstrative, quia hoc non scio esse possibile; et si quis hoc sciat gaudeat. Istam autem conclusionem assero simpliciter esse veram et indubitanter teneo sola fide. Et ad rationes contra istam opinionem responderem breviter concedendo tanquam possibilia apud Deum omnia illa ad quae illae rationes deducunt tanquam ad impossibilia." (John of Jandun, *Super Libros de Anima Questiones Subtilissimae,* III, q. 7 (ed. Venice, 1552, fol. 66 Ca). On John of Jandun, see the introductory study of S. MacClintock, *Perversity and Error: Studies on the "Averroist" John of Jandun* (Bloomington: Indiana University Press, 1956).

[6] John of Jandun, *ibid.,* fol. 56vab. The text continues: "Et puto quod qui per alium modum nititur solvere rationes quasdam contra istam positionem ipsa [read: *ipse* with the edition of Florence, 1507, fol. 61vb] ex insufficientia solutionis magis redderet hanc positionem improbabilem quam sustineat eandem. Et ideo non plus de isto ad praesens. Quare etc." (*ibid.*)

Siger of Brabant, criticizing the position of Alexander in surprising detail, but he credited Siger with distinguishing two kinds of substantial forms in the philosophy of Aristotle. In one sense, any form joined to matter, giving it existence as its perfection, is a substantial form. The intellectual soul is not a substantial form in this sense. In a second sense, a "form of the body" is a form that acts or works within the body to which it is specifically joined for such a purpose: *sumitur forma corporis pro operante intrinseco appropriato corpori*. In short, the intellectual soul *non est forma dans esse corpori*. Hence the conclusion of John of Jandun:

> homo distinguitur ab aliis per intellectum proprie dictum tanquam per operans intrinsecum quod in operando unite se habet ad corpus secundum naturam; et per animan cogitativam distinguitur ab aliis sicut per forman constituentem ipsum in esse substantiali specifico.[7]

Two hundred years after John of Jandun, Pietro Pomponazzi had the occasion to say some remarkable things on this same Aristotelian problem. And surely what was most remarkable about the *De Immortalitate Animae* (published in 1516) was the attitude of Pomponazzi toward St. Thomas. As he saw it, the Aristotelians of his day were almost all convinced of the Averroistic interpretation of the *De Anima;* nevertheless, this interpretation was to him not only absolutely false but also unintelligible, monstrous, and completely foreign to Aristotle:

> Quamvis haec opinio [that of Averroes] tempestate nostra sit multum celebrata et fere ab omnibus pro constanti habeatur eam esse Aristotelis, mihi tamen videtur quod nedum in se sit falsissima verum ininintelligibilis et monstruosa et ab Aristotele prorsus aliena.[8]

---

[7] John of Jandun, *op. cit.*, III, q. 5 (fols. 58Hb, 59 Da, 60Db). The whole of this question (fols. 57Cb-60Ea) is directed with considerable vigor against Alexander of Aphrodisias. For the reference to Siger of Brabant, see fol. 60Ca, where, in spite of the printed reading "Remigius de Brabantia," the identification is certain because John of Jandun goes on to designate the *De Anima Intellectiva* by its *incipit*, "Cum anima sit aliorum cognoscitiva."

[8] Gianfranco Morra, *Petrus Pomponatius: Tractatus de Immortalitate Animae* (Bologna: Nanni & Fiammenghi Editori, 1954), cap. IV, p. 48. There is an English translation by W. H. Hay, II, revised by J. H. Randall, Jr. and annotated by P. O.

To prove the error of the Averroistic notion of a separate and unique intellectual soul for all men, Pomponazzi thought it adequate to do nothing more than refer his reader to what the glory of the Latins, Divus Thomas Aquinas, had written against Averroes with such devastating results. From the *Summa Contra Gentiles* to the *De Unitate Intellectus,* St. Thomas had set forth an unassailable refutation of Averroes; so much so, that the Averroists had no better defense against him than to resort to vituperation.[9]

The notion of a separated and unique intellectual soul for all men, therefore, was not an Aristotelian doctrine; it was a gratuitous Averroistic fiction, and St. Thomas had so proved. So thought Pomponazzi. Admittedly, for St. Thomas to have proved that the position of Averroes was *not* Aristotelian would have been, in the perspective of the history of Aristotelianism, a monumental achievement. For the moment let us not contest it. Let us suppose that St. Thomas did accomplish what Pomponazzi attributed to him; moreover, let us make this supposition in order to learn from Pomponazzi an important lesson. For the Thomistic victory over Averroes can be interpreted in more than one way, and the way of Pomponazzi is both surprising and instructive. Averroes, let us grant, was wrong and St. Thomas proved it. Did this mean that St. Thomas was right? Not at all, since proving Averroes wrong was no more than a purely negative result; the correct interpretation of Aristotle was still an open question and still awaited an answer. Where did St. Thomas stand on this positive issue?

As Pomponazzi saw it, the common problem at stake was to endow man with an intellectual soul and to determine what (if anything) in man remained immortal in the union of soul and body. The spokesman for the doctrine of an individual immortal soul joined to the body as its substantial form was to Pomponazzi St. Thomas Aquinas. Here in five propositions is his summary of the Thomistic teaching on soul and body:

> Primum itaque est quod intellectivum et sensitivum in homine sunt idem re.
> Secundum quod tale vere et simpliciter est immortale, secundum quid vero mortale.

Kristeller, in *The Renaissance Philosophy of Man,* ed. E. Cassirer, P. O. Kristeller and J. H. Randall, Jr. (Chicago: The University of Chicago Press, 1948), pp. 280-381.
[9] *De Immortalitate Animae, ibid.*

Tertium quod talis anima vere est forma hominis et non solum
est motor.
Quartum quod eadem anima est numerata ad numerationem
individuorum.
Quintum quod huiusmodi anima incipit esse cum corpore,
verum quod venit de foris atque a solo Deo producitur non
quidem per generationem, sed per creationem; haec tamen
non desinit esse cum corpore, verum a parte post est
perpetua.[10]

Now Pomponazzi had no doubt about the truth of this whole position. Sacred Scripture, which was to be preferred to reason and to
experience because it came from God, had sanctioned it. Where
Pomponazzi experienced some doubts, however, was on two points.
Did the teaching of St. Thomas so exceed the limits of nature as to
presuppose something from faith or revelation? Moreover, was this
teaching in agreement with the doctrine of Aristotle, as St. Thomas
held?[11] To Pomponazzi the answers were not far to seek. By ap-
pealing to reason, to experience, and to Aristotle, he proved to his
own satisfaction *(a)* that the human intellect had no operation independent of the body;[12] *(b)* "that the Commentator, St. Thomas
or anyone else who thinks that according to Aristotle the intellect
is truly immortal is far from the truth";[13] and *(c)* that Aristotle was
so far from believing in a life after death that he never mentioned
it.[14]

By taking such a position in the Aristotelian debate on the intellect, Pomponazzi has done much more than merely agree with
Alexander of Aphrodisias against Averroes. He has, in fact, accomplished two things. He has put his finger on a genuine Thomistic contribution to the interpretation of Aristotle's *De Anima;*
moreover, he has forced the student of St. Thomas to consider carefully the distance separating this exegetical contribution from its
author's personal teaching on the soul and the foundations of that
teaching. Without considering here the larger question of the relative merits of Averroes and St. Thomas as interpreters of Aristotle,

[10] *De Immortalitate Animae,* cap. IV; ed. cit., pp. 74, 76.
[11] "Sed quod apud me vertitur in dubium est an ista dicta [i.e., the five proposi-
tions] excedant limites naturales, sic quod vel creditum vel revelatum praesupponant,
et conformia sint dictis Aristotelis, sicut ipse Divus Thomas enunciat" *(De Immortalitate Animae,* cap. VIII; ed. cit., p. 82).
[12] *De Immortalitate Animae,* cap. IV; ed. cit., p. 50.
[13] *De Immortalitate Animae,* cap. IV; ed. cit., p. 66.
[14] *De Immortalitate Animae,* cap. VIII; ed. cit., p. 102.

we can usefully examine the very precise textual problem raised by Pomponazzi.

In developing the definition of the soul in *De Anima* II, 1-2, did Aristotle intend to exclude the intellect from the soul? As we know, St. Thomas has given a detailed account of this question in the first chapter of the *De Unitate Intellectus contra Averroistas*. The import of this account should be weighed both by those who accept and by those who reject the Thomistic interpretation of the Aristotelian psychology. On the basis of a minute analysis of *De Anima*, II, 1-2, St. Thomas has argued that the definition of the soul in these chapters is intended to apply to all souls, that there is no question in Aristotle's text of the separation of the intellect from the soul, and that the unmixed and separate nature of the intellect which Aristotle reserves for later study (namely, in *De Anima*, III, 4-5) means in the context that the intellect does not have an organ, as do the sense powers: it is not intended to prove that the intellect is a substance separated from the soul.[15] Let us grant to

---

[15] In evaluating what St. Thomas did in *De Unitate Intellectus*, Chapter I, it is important to limit ourselves to the precise points at issue. Is the soul for Aristotle the *actus corporis?* Is his consideration of the soul a universal one, so that the intellect is intended by him to be a part of the soul defined in *De Anima*, II, 1. 412 b6 and redefined causally in *De Anima*, II, 2.413 b11-13? Whatever interpretation of the *De Anima* we adopt, St. Thomas seems to be clearly right in holding, against Averroes, that the Aristotelian answer to these questions is in the affirmative. Whether and how this Aristotelian answer can be justified are relevant but later questions, and they amount to asking whether there can be a non-material form of matter. Even so, there is nothing in *De Anima*, II, 1-2 to favor the Averroistic view that the intellect is not part of the soul. To this extent, St. Thomas has scored against Averroes by showing that there is no basis in this text of Aristotle requiring the inference that the intellect is a substance separate from the body. Averroes' inference is a construction, quite understandable, but still a construction.

In granting to St. Thomas a limited victory over Averroes, let us also notice what he does with the elements of the victory. For this purpose, let us mark a dividing point in the first chapter of the *De Unitate Intellectus*. It occurs when St. Thomas, having completed the exposition of Aristotle's teaching on the soul and the intellect, goes on to ask how a soul that is the substantial form of the body can have a power that does not act through a bodily organ (*De Unitate Intellectus*, I, ed. L. Keeler, [Rome: Gregorian University Press, 1936], p. 18, Nos. 26-27). How, in other words, can there be an incorruptible form of corruptible matter (p. 22, No. 32)? Moreover, St. Thomas raises this issue after showing that for Aristotle the intellect is incorruptible (pp. 21-22, No. 31). This problem then leads St. Thomas to undertake a truly remarkable piece of exegesis, namely, that Aristotle "so posited the intellectual soul to be a form that he yet held it to be incorruptible" (p. 23, No. 33). Here, let us acknowledge, both St. Thomas and Averroes are beyond the text of the *De Anima;* here, too, we can sympathize with St. Thomas' conclusion that the Averroistic machinery of *continuatio* to explain how intellectual knowledge takes place in the individual man is a most implausible one (p. 54, No. 85). But, in the end, when

St. Thomas a precise victory: a straightforward reading of the Aristotelian texts in question confirms his exegesis as to what Aristotle
did *not* intend to do. But let us also be grateful to Pomponazzi
for emphasizing this fact against Averroes and (no less) for limiting
its role in the interpretation of Aristotle. St. Thomas' conclusion
proves that as an interpreter of the *De Anima*, Averroes was wrong
in separating the intellect from the soul; it does not prove that St.
Thomas' own doctrine of an intellectual substance united to the
body as its substantial form was the right interpretation. There
was, for example, the position of Alexander of Aphrodisias, such
as we know it today from his own *De Anima,* such as it was set forth
in his lost commentary on Aristotle's *De Anima,* and such as St.
Thomas knew it from Averroes and, perhaps, from Alexander's
De Intellectu.[16]

Some reflections force themselves on us at this point. When
Pomponazzi agreed with St. Thomas against Averroes he was allying himself with the Alexandrist wing of the Aristotelian school
and he was opposing Averroes, Siger of Brabant, and John of Jandun, not to mention later mediaeval Averroists or Pomponazzi's
own contemporaries such as Agostino Nifo in his younger days.
But when Pomponazzi disagreed with St. Thomas' positive teaching as set forth in the five propositions listed above he was allying
himself with all the major Aristotelian commentators on a premise
that was their common guide and that separated St. Thomas from
Aristotelianism in a decisive way. This common premise was that
every form of matter, being by nature the realization of the matter
whose actuality it was, had no existence other than that of its material composite. Every form of matter was thus itself material and
corruptible. Alexander and Averroes did not disagree on this
premise as Aristotelian teaching. For anyone to propose the doctrine of an incorruptible substantial form of matter was to be think-

In No. 33 St. Thomas is faced with demonstrating his own contention, he proves
from Aristotle that the intellect is separate and survives the body (pp. 23-24, Nos.
34-36), but it is on his own teaching of form and *esse* that he rests his explanation
of an immaterial form of matter (p. 25, No. 38; p. 53, No. 84).

To have freed Aristotle from an Averroistic misinterpretation of *De Anima,*
II, 1-2 is an important Thomistic accomplishment; but to rest the explanation of an
immaterial form of matter on the dissociation of form and *esse* is to visualize a
metaphysical possibility that Aristotelian forms did not contain and could not fulfill.
In this sense, St. Thomas revolutionized Aristotelianism. The only question at issue
is the nature and the origins of that revolution.

16 See P. Moraux, *op. cit.,* pp. 21, 137-38.

ing and teaching outside the framework of historical Aristotelianism. Even more, to propose it as a notion whose only proper expression was the Aristotelian theory of matter and form was to precipitate a conflict and a test for Aristotelianism on the only level on which a truly decisive issue could be drawn.

From this point of view, the Thomistic doctrine of an intellectual substance as the substantial form of matter must be seen as a moment in history when an Aristotelian formula was deliberately used to express in philosophical terms a view of man that the world and tradition of Aristotelianism considered a metaphysical impossibility. For better or for worse, therefore, whatever St. Thomas accomplished after eliminating Averroistic separatism was bound to remain a singular achievement. It was either a unique philosophical transformation of Aristotelian psychology—as unique as the philosophical intuition that made it possible—or, as Pomponazzi insisted, a doctrine whose very truth was a Christian tenet and not a philosophical notion. Hence, by preventing us from locating St. Thomas *within* the history of Aristotelian psychology, Pomponazzi is forcing upon us this question: If St. Thomas did not undertake and, *a fortiori*, did not accomplish the impossible— namely, to defend on Aristotelian grounds the notion of a non-material form of matter—how could he use an Aristotelian formula to express the unity of man? Moreover, how could he expect to succeed in an effort that was a total challenge to Aristotelianism? To Pomponazzi, St. Thomas' answer, though successful, was not a philosophical one; it had therefore the success of revealed truth. In other words, while the position of St. Thomas was true, it was not philosophical because it was not Aristotelian. What, then, was it?

We can now turn to *Summa Contra Gentiles* II, 56, where St. Thomas asked for the first time in his career the question whether any intellectual substance can be joined to a body: *utrum aliqua substantia intellectualis corpori possit uniri*.[17] This question opened a new chapter in the history of Christian thought and led to a new chapter in the history of Aristotelianism.

II

Chapters 56-90 of *SCG* II are not the first account that St. Thomas has given of the relations between soul and body in man.

---

[17] *Summa Contra Gentiles* II, chap. 56, No. 1. I shall use the abbreviation *SCG* in referring to this work.

There are many passages in his *Scripta super libros Sententiarum* that deal with the constitution of man and with various problems surrounding that constitution.[18] But *SCG* II, chap. 56 is the first text in which, so far as I know, St. Thomas has formally and directly asked "whether any intellectual substance can be joined to a body." Moreover, the circumstances surrounding the question thus asked are as far-reaching as the question itself—far-reaching and surprising.

In the first place, the question whether an intellectual substance can be joined to a body is raised quite abruptly and opens a remarkably long parenthesis on man (chaps. 56 to 90) within an investigation of immaterial substances begun in chap. 46 and resumed in the last eleven chapters of *SCG* II (chaps. 91-101). Secondly, in chap. 56 St. Thomas performs an extraordinary doctrinal reduction. Whether an intellectual substance can be joined to a body is not an Aristotelian question. Whether an intellectual substance can be the substantial form of a body is an Aristotelian question, not indeed because Aristotle asked it (he did not), but because it involves an Aristotelian principle and an Aristotelian doctrine. The principle concerns the unity of the being resulting from the union of an intellectual substance and a body. How can there be a union without a unity? Only, what kind of unity? Evidently, a unity enabling us to say of the components that they constitute one being. This decision leads St. Thomas to an Aristotelian doctrine. An intellectual substance can be joined to a body—that is, constitute one being with it—if it is joined to the body in the way that a substantial form is joined to matter. This, surely, *is* an Aristotelian question. It is different from the first question by being cast as a question in an Aristotelian formula. The significance of this difference is precisely the problem that St. Thomas invites his interpreters to consider in examining the internal development of *SCG* II, chap. 56.

SCG II as a whole is a vindication of the total freedom of the Christian God as creator and of the stability and order of the universe in its very existence as a contingent creature (chap. 22). Within this large framework, there is a study of intellectual substances that undertakes to show the befittingness of the existence of intellectual creatures in a universe whose plurality, hierarchy, and order are due to the will of God and to His desire to communicate

---

[18] On this point, see the classic exposition in *SCG* II, 30.

as much perfection to creatures as they can bear (chaps. 45-46). St. Thomas then proceeds to study the nature of these intellectual substances: their endowment with will and freedom of choice (chaps. 47-48), their non-corporeal and immaterial nature (chaps. 49-50), and the consequence that no intellectual substance is a material form in the sense of having an *esse materiae obligatum* or of being *a forma non subsistens sed materiae immersa* (chap. 51); their composition in terms of *esse* and *quod est* (chap. 52), and of act and potency (chap. 53), which is to be distinguished from the composition of form and matter (chap. 54); and, finally, their incorruptibility (chap. 55). Then, without further explanation, chap. 56 opens with the following paragraph:

> Since it has been shown above that an intellectual substance is not a body or any power depending on a body, it remains for us to examine whether any intellectual substance can be joined to a body.

Interruption or no, this sentence inaugurates a revolution in Christian thought whose theological boldness is matched only by its philosophical creativeness and its historical imagination. From this moment onward, Christianity and Aristotelianism face a new phenomenon in their midst: a philosophical account of the unity of man expressed in Aristotelian terms of which Christianity had hitherto known the reality but not the metaphysical explanation, and of which Aristotelianism knew neither the reality nor the explanation.

The union of an intellectual substance to a body, assuming for a moment that it be possible, cannot be conceived as the union of two bodies or as the union of an agent and the recipient of its action. The intellectual member in the union renders the first alternative inadmissible and the stability or permanence of the union renders the second inapplicable: a unity of agent and recipient in a transitory sort of affair. What then? We are evidently looking for a union that will permit us to consider the result of the union as "one being," or something "one in being." And since, moreover, this "one in being" cannot be something indivisible (being composite) or a continuous magnitude, St. Thomas is left with one final alternative as the only suitable formula of his original question, namely, that the "one in being" is a unity which,

in its composition, has the order of a definable whole. Now such a
whole—such a *ratione unum*—is possible if its components are
related to one another as substantial form and matter. Thus, when
we examine the kind of "oneness" that can obtain between soul
and body, we find that our original question—*utrum aliqua substantia intellectualis corpori possit uniri*—was posing the following
technical issue: *utrum substantia intellectualis corporis alicuius
forma substantialis esse possit.* In other words, can an intellectual
substance be the substantial form of some body?

　　Only, what enabled St. Thomas to take from Aristotle a formulation of his original question that the history of Aristotelianism had
rendered suspect for such a purpose? Nor can it be argued that
he did not know the difficulties raised by the Aristotelian formula.
In fact, in the concluding paragraphs of *SCG* II, chap. 56 he has
summarized these difficulties in five arguments which, if true,
render his undertaking impossible at the very outset. Let us briefly
report these arguments: (1) Something one cannot be effected
from two actually existing substances, since *act* is that by which
any given thing is distinguished from another being. Now, since
an intellectual substance and a body are actually existing substances, their union cannot produce something one—*aliquid unum.*
(2) Form and matter are contained in the same genus, since every
genus is divided by potency and act. But an intellectual substance
and a body belong to diverse genera and therefore one of them
cannot be the form of the other. (3) That whose act of being
(*esse*) is in matter must be material. But if an intellectual substance is in the form of a body, its act of being must be *in* corporeal
matter, since the act of being belonging to a form cannot be separate from the act of being belonging to its matter. Hence [if an intellectual substance is a form of a body] it is not immaterial. (4)
That whose act of being is in a body cannot be separated from the
body. But according to the philosophers the intellect is separate
from the body and is neither a body nor a power in a body. Therefore, an intellectual substance is not a form of a body, or otherwise
its act of being would be in a body. (5) That whose act of being is
common to a body must have an operation common to a body.
Each thing acts according as it is a being, and the operative power
of a being cannot be higher than its essence, since the power follows
from the principles of the nature. Now if an intellectual substance
is the form of a body, its act of being must be common to it and

to the body. This means that the operation of the intellectual substance will be shared in by the body—which was proved to be impossible.

Some reflection on this turn of events will suggest that we are, after all, at a historic crossroads and that Thomas Aquinas has led us directly to it. What has prepared the way for this unexpected moment of decision? For this *is* a moment of philosophical decision, a moment when the Angelic Doctor is called upon to review the history of Aristotelianism and to show that the great commentators on Aristotle were wrong and that he, Thomas Aquinas, was right in interpreting their common master. Moreover, judging by his attitude, we are bound to say that St. Thomas did not wish to be judged on a lesser ground than this. Beginning with the impasse at the end of *SCG* II, chap. 56, he set out to show how every obstacle in the way of proving that an intellectual substance could be the substantial form of a body was refutable. He argued that the position of Plato, by conceiving man as an *intellectual substance using a body,* really denied the union and the unity of soul and body (chap. 57). He argued, secondly, that the intellect by which man is supposed to know (that is, the possible intellect) could not be a separate substance, since man would not then be himself an intelligent knower; nor, strictly, would he be a man (that is, an intelligent being) unless the intellect were a part of his own soul (chaps. 59-60). He argued, thirdly, that the position of Averroes was against the teaching of Aristotle (chap. 61). He argued, fourthly, and from another point of view, that Alexander of Aphrodisias was no less wrong as an Aristotelian in making the possible intellect a part of the soul—a power within man, therefore —and on that account declaring it corruptible (chap. 62). Similar criticisms are directed against other materialistic interpretations of the human soul or the intellect (chaps. 63-67). Fifthly, and finally, St. Thomas came to the main piece of his performance. He had reached it by showing that there was no escape from his interpretation of the way in which an intellectual substance could be joined to a body, namely, as its substantial form (chap. 68). As a corollary to this conclusion, St. Thomas then went on to refute the arguments against his basic position (chap. 69), and to show directly against Averroes that "according to the intention of Aristotle an intellectual substance is joined . . . to the human body . . . as its form" (chap. 70).

What could be more decisive? Only, that St. Thomas really achieved such a victory over the Exegete and the Commentator is hardly credible. It is as little credible that he could have pretended to an Aristotelian victory that he did not, as he saw it, achieve. Indeed, in *SCG* II, chap. 70 St. Thomas did not argue that Aristotle himself taught the doctrine of an intellectual form of matter; he argued merely that such a doctrine was according to the opinion *(secundum opinionem)* or intention *(intentionem)* of Aristotle. What is more, in the course of the chapter St. Thomas argued against Averroes that the Aristotelian heavens were not animated by *continuatio*: the intellect that moved each heavenly body had to be joined to it substantially. How this was possible on Aristotelian grounds St. Thomas did not say; he merely said that Averroes was wrong as an interpreter.

We are therefore left to speculate on St. Thomas' singular Aristotelian journey. If we ask: what forced him to think that an intellectual substance had to be joined to the body as a substantial form is joined to matter? the answer is not far to seek. St. Thomas learned from Aristotle how a composite substance can be one being, namely, if it is internally a whole and externally one in being; moreover, both of these requirements can be met if the component parts are related as form to matter. But if we ask: what enabled St. Thomas to think that an intellectual substance could be joined to matter as its substantial form? no Aristotelian answer is forthcoming. Yet St. Thomas thought, in spite of the Aristotelians, that he could successfully solve this problem so formulated, that this formulation was as necessary to the problem as it was Aristotelian, and that the solution was recognizably Aristotelian even when the original problem was not.

Let us take a further step and consider another question. Will it perhaps be said that as a Christian believer, St. Thomas knew the answer before he entered the problem? This is true, but it is not sufficient. Other theologians, before and after St. Thomas, knew and defended the unity of man and of soul and body in man. But such an appreciation of man, while understandable on religious grounds, did not prevent these same theologians from holding philosophical opinions that St. Thomas would have found (and in some cases did find) inadequate. At one and the same time St. Augustine said that man was a soul using a body and that soul and body together constituted the whole man. Had he held in the philosophical terms used by St. Thomas in *SCG* II, chap. 57 that man is an *anima utens corpore,* then, assuredly, he would have been destroying on philosophical grounds what he was, at the same time, defending on religious grounds. But St. Augustine was following St. Paul, not Plotinus.

What St. Thomas knew as a theologian—namely, that soul and body in man constitute a whole being, composite but one—did not by itself enable him to enter the Aristotelian metaphysical world and successfully solve *at the philosophical level* an embattled question among Aristotelian thinkers. His faith in the Christian revelation could have been (and was) a guiding light for St. Thomas; but for this philosophical purpose his intellect had to be ready *as an intellect* to follow the lead of faith and to create an answer to an Aristotelian question that was somehow an adequate answer —adequate because it was philosophically open to the technical data of the problem, adequate because its attachment to Aristotle was as recognizably permanent and deep as it was evidently revolutionary and transforming.

III

I have come to this conclusion in order to propose a very modest hypothesis on the interpretation of St. Thomas in relation to Aristotle's psychology. Taken as a whole, the Thomistic doctrine of man has no recognizable historical antecedents. What is Christian and religious in it does not account historically for what is philosophical; what is Aristotelian in it does not account (again, historically) for its philosophical character. If we say that the Thomistic doctrine of man is the result of the conjunction of a Christian appreciation of the reality of the human person and an Aristotelian philosophical formula used to express that reality, it remains that the conjunction itself exists only because St. Thomas, alone among thirteenth century theologians, saw its possibility. This is another way of saying that the "why" of the Thomistic vision of man escapes us, since, in knowing its components and even their mutual suitability, we are but following the very light we are interpreting.

But if the ultimate and unique "why" of St. Thomas' view of man escapes us, perhaps its shadow can be seen in the doctrinal framework of his writing and teaching. This, it seems to me, is particularly the case with the *SCG,* a work whose context and perspective present with great clarity the religious purpose, the doctrinal effort and the philosophical tools of its author. The luminous

184] *Some Reflections on SCG* II, 56

shadow of St. Thomas casts both light and warmth in this work, and those who wish to stand in the presence of a living person are invited to examine the *SCG* in order to discover, not indeed its author, but the traces of his presence.

The *SCG* is a work of apologetics for a philosophical audience, Aristotelian in technical education, and therefore demanding considerable precision on the nature and requirements of philosophical thinking. It is, moreover, a work by a theologian who set out as an apologist to acknowledge the merits of Aristotelian philosophy on the level of philosophy and to show that Christianity accepted its basic tenets, improved on them in many cases, and (in spite of its transcendence) never rejected a philosophical argument except by a proper refutation. In short, Christianity could give life within itself to a genuine philosophy, Aristotelian in origin and nature, and strictly scientific in its methodology.

The apologetic strength of this last point did not lie in insisting that Christianity and philosophy could be harmonized, in spite of the rationalistic interpretation of Aristotle proposed by Averroes; nor was it to show that Christians could be philosophers. For what apologetic value was there in arguing that Christians could become philosophers and, when they did so, followed a pagan Aristotle? St. Thomas' apologetic point lay elsewhere. It consisted in showing that what the philosophers were aiming at, what they had been trying to achieve in philosophy since the days of Plato and Aristotle, *this* was taught in a higher, fuller and more perfect way by the Christian revelation. Where the philosophers had stopped short, whether through confusion or error, or because philosophy could advance no farther, revelation had given light. Revelation had corrected philosophical errors and it had given answers that were beyond the scope and the expectation of philosophy. But this point, too, decisive as it is, does not fully cover the apologetic aim of the *SCG*. So framed and limited, its theme would consist in showing to the philosophers the wisdom of substituting belief in revelation for the life of philosophy and to suggest that, by revealing Himself in history, God had considered the important truths of human existence too necessary to mankind to be left in the hands of the philosophers.

But it was not to point out how philosophy was surpassed and superseded by revelation that St. Thomas wrote the *SCG*. On the contrary, it was to show what happened to philosophy itself when it functioned, according to the proper use of its principles, in the hands of a Christian theologian. The *SCG* contains an object lesson in Christian philosophizing, carried on by a theologian under the light of revelation, and aimed at the philosophers as a model of the nature and spirit of philosophy when it lives in the light and the service of revealed truth. Believing as a theologian that grace saves nature, and indeed that, in a Christian world, nature of its very constitution has only to be true to itself in order to be on the way to the truths of revelation, St. Thomas likewise believed that philosophy was both saved and perfected by the light of that revelation. The philosophy in the *SCG* is philosophy at home in a Christian climate; it is Christian philosophy, that is to say, a philosophy that considers its openness to the influence of revelation to be nothing less than a turning to the source of its nature. That is why, far from suffering any diminution in autonomy or rationality from its Christian state, philosophy rather experiences an advancement. An eminent example of this fact can be seen in what St. Thomas did in the *SCG* to the psychology of Aristotle.

Historically speaking, all Aristotelian psychologies that stay within the metaphysical framework of Aristotle must finally deny immortality to the individual soul. They can differ in the form of their denial by giving to the individual man either a corruptible intellect (Alexander) or by denying to him an intellect altogether (Averroes). There is no Aristotelian way out of this dilemma. If, in fact, St. Thomas found a way out it was because, maintaining the full force of the Aristotelian definition of the soul as form of matter, he found a basis on which to accomplish with an Aristotelian formula what no Aristotelian had been able to do, namely, to show how an intellectual soul and a body are joined together to constitute a substance that, in its very compositeness, is one in being and in nature. And if it be the case that Aristotle never intended to separate the intellect from the soul he was defining in *De Anima*, II, chaps. 1-2, then St. Thomas was an Aristotelian in all the elements of this classic problem except the basis of its solution.

Can one be such an Aristotelian? The exegetes and the commentators will always deny it since, whatever their differences, they are united in the ideal of returning to the Aristotle of antiquity. But history is not reversible and philosophy is not a game to be replayed. Being always original, it can take place only in the

present, just as it is only in the present that we learn from the
thinkers of the past. As conducted by St. Thomas, Aristotle's philosophical search is a living reality in the thirteenth century; it is
living in the mind of a Dominican monk who dedicated himself
to the work of meditating on the God of the Christian faith. Why
should not St. Thomas have treated Aristotelian notions as capable
of renewed life and greater development than Aristotle gave them?
In any case, by locating the problem of the unity of man within the
perspective of the idea of creation, and by disengaging the full
philosophical import of this idea from the notion of duration, St.
Thomas introduced a dimension within Aristotelian psychology
that radically reshaped the elements of an old problem in the very
process of solving it.

The idea of creation and of a creating God, whose slow emergence in history St. Thomas has more than once recorded,[19] makes
it possible to transform the Aristotelian metaphysics of being as
eternal separate substances into a metaphysics of being as seen from
the point of view of existence. The *SCG* is dominated by this
transformation. Two parallel developments are particularly noteworthy in this regard. In Book I, chaps. 13-22, St. Thomas proceeds
from the notion of God as the Prime Mover to the "sublime truth"
of God as *ipsum esse subsistens.* In Book II, chaps. 6-22, he steadily
and surely develops the idea of God as the prime, sole, universal,
and total cause of the *esse* of creatures, which in turn contains the
further idea that creation is the *ipsa dependentia esse creati ad
principium* and that God as creator is the *causa essendi simpliciter.*
Even though Plato, Aristotle, and "their followers," among whom
we must give a place of honor to Avicenna, did not all reach this
conclusion, St. Thomas yet locates them at least on the road to it.
As a Christian theologian seeing them from the vantage point of
revelation, he could appreciate, amid their differences, their common aim; and so he joined them to himself even though he knew
that they were separated from one another by their philosophies.

Within the perspective of the idea of creation, *being* is neither
a Platonic essence nor an Aristotelian substance (or ousia); it is
that which is named from an act, the act of *to be,* which is everything it is through that act, which is through itself but not in virtue
of itself, and whose constitutive principles explain both that it is

---

[19] See *Quaestiones disputatae: De potentia Dei* q. 3, aa. 5, 17; *Summa Theologiae*
I, q. 44, a. 2; *De substantis separatis,* chap. VII.

what it is and that *it* is what it is, but do not explain that it *is*. This is the lesson that St. Thomas enforces in the *SCG* II, chaps. 46-55. These remarkable chapters study the metaphysical status of pure forms, and, by dissociating *esse* from *form,* make possible the notion of an intellectual form that is neither a Platonic intelligible nor an Aristotelian intelligence, but a person with a dynamic history, irreversible and open, whose intellectual nature is free of every vestige of the Aristotelian physics and astronomy. Aristotle's theology is inconceivable without his physics; his pure forms are "separate substances" in a universe in which, because there is motion, there must be final causes, the self-enclosed and unapproachable goals of motion. On the contrary, the theology of St. Thomas places man, not matter, at the center of the universe. The creation of man in view of a divine beatitude to which he would be raised is unknown to Aristotle even in that aspect of it that is humanly knowable. In short, by placing a creating personal God at the origin of reality; by translating the old Aristotelian immaterial substance into an intellectual form that is a person; by making reality, at its core, a union of persons rather than an order of eternal cosmological exemplars; and, finally, by seeing the existence of matter from the point of view of the existence of intelligence rather than vice versa;—by such a revolution in metaphysical perspective, itself inspired by the religious message of Christianity, St. Thomas Aquinas, having created the philosophical notions that express with perfect adequacy the reality of the human person, clothed these notions in the language of Aristotle. The result, being a true creation in its own order, was as new to Christian ears as it was unknown to the Aristotelians.

The doctrine of an intellectual form of matter, so paradoxical in historical Aristotelianism, became a recognizable possibility as soon as Christianity taught the unity of the human person to the western world. Even though Aristotle did not know it, the Christian man is in his nature a diminished intellectual creature; that is why, indeed, he has a body. Only, how can such a notion come from Aristotelianism if, at the origin of the world of Aristotle, there is, not a personal God, but an impersonal intelligence regulating by its mere presence an eternal astronomical order? How, indeed. Even so, the notion of the soul as form of matter has only to live within the mind of a Christian theologian whose philosophical tool is a metaphysics of being as act, in order to become a philosophic reality. This is what happened when St. Thomas Aquinas created, in philosophy, the metaphysics of man as a composite substance, one in being, intellectual in nature, composite in the diminution of his intellectuality. This event, which enabled an Aristotelian formula to be the vehicle of an un-Aristotelian notion, is what St. Thomas has unobtrusively recorded in *SCG* II, 56.

Thomas of Sutton's Critique on the Doctrine of Univocity

by Joseph J. Przezdziecki

THE DOCTRINE of univocity, as proposed by John Duns Scotus around the turn of the fourteenth century, was to become the center of numerous controversies that were to last for centuries. It was inevitable from the start that those who had been brought up on the teachings of St. Thomas Aquinas would react rather vigorously to many of the ramifications of the Scotistic doctrine and would subject that doctrine to a most careful scrutiny. Among the first to attempt this was the English Dominican Thomas of Sutton.[1]

This great disciple of St. Thomas at the University of Oxford devotes no fewer than four of his *Quaestiones ordinariae* or *disputatae*[2] to an examination of the doctrine of univocity. In Cod. Merton College 138, the best of the manuscripts, the questions are listed as follows:

[1] On the life and literary activity of Thomas of Sutton, see F. Ehrle, "Thomas de Sutton, sein Leben, seine *Quodlibet* und seine *Quaestiones disputatae,*" *Festschrift Georg von Hertling* (Kempten-Munich: 1913), 426-50; F. Pelster, "Thomas von Sutton O.Pr., ein Oxforder Verteidiger der thomistischen Lehre," *Zeitschrift für katholische Theologie,* XLVI (1922), 212-53, 361-401. These two studies, while far from settling all questions, must be considered the starting-point of all further research into the life and writings of this mediaeval master. See also W. A. Hinnebusch, O.P., *The Early English Friars Preachers* (Rome: 1951), pp. 396-410. The author refers to most of the pertinent literature on the subject.

[2] These Questions are contained in one or more of the following Mss.: M=Oxford, Cod. Merton College 138; A=Erfurt, Cod, Amplonianus Fol. 369; B=Basel, Cod. B IV 4. For a description of these Mss., cf. J. Przezdziecki, "Selected Questions from the Writings of Thomas of Sutton, O.P.," ("Pontifical Institute of Mediaeval Studies, Studies and Texts," [Toronto: 1955]), pp. 309-10. All material from the works of Thomas of Sutton will be cited according to the Oxford Ms., corrected when necessary by one of the other Mss.

Q. D. 32: Quaeritur utrum hoc nomen ens dicatur univoce de Deo et de omnibus rebus cujuscumque praedicamenti.[3]

Q. D. 33: Utrum ens sit univocum Deo et creaturis.[4]

Q. D. 34: Quaeritur de nominibus divinis, et primo utrum nomina quae dicuntur de Deo et creaturis dicantur univoce de Deo et creaturis.[5]

Q. D. 35: Secundo quaeritur utrum hoc nomen substantia, prout est nomen generis generalissimi, dicatur univoce de Deo et substantiis causatis, et hoc est quaerere utrum Deus sit in praedicamento substantiae.[6]

Before proceeding to the subject of this study, it will be helpful if we make a few general remarks about the relationship that existed between Thomas of Sutton and Duns Scotus.

Scotus (c. 1266-1308) is a younger contemporary of Thomas of Sutton, but he died a few years before his Dominican adversary.[7] He evidently was familiar with certain of Sutton's works, as has been borne out by the Scotist Commission.[8] The doctrinal positions of Sutton, however, do not figure as prominently in the works of Scotus as do the positions of Henry of Ghent.

Like Godfrey of Fontaines, Duns Scotus, and many others, Thomas of Sutton, especially in the first two *Quodlibets* and in the earlier *Quaestiones disputatae,* often attacks the views of Henry of Ghent.[9] In later works, however, while not neglecting Henry of Ghent, Sutton devotes a great deal of time to the refutation of various Scotistic doctrines.

As far as I have been able to ascertain, Sutton never refers to Duns Scotus by name in the last two *Quodlibets* and in the *Quaestiones disputatae.*[10] But in *Quaestio Disputata* 27 he comes very

---

[3] In M on fol. 329r and in B on fol. 177v.

[4] In M on fol. 331v. Cardinal Ehrle, through an oversight, failed to include this Question among the Quaestiones Disputatae; cf. Ehrle, "Thomas de Sutton, sein Leben," *op. cit.,* p. 448. The next two questions are referred to by him, and also by Pelster, "Thomas von Sutton," *op. cit.,* p. 401, as Q.D. 33 and Q.D. 34, but this does not correspond to the numbering of the Ms.

[5] In M on fol. 333v, in A on fol. 55r, and in B on fol. 174r.

[6] In M on fol. 336r, in A on fol. 91r, and in B on fol. 176r.

[7] The date of Sutton's death cannot be fixed exactly. He seems to have died shortly after 1313; cf. Pelster, "Thomas von Sutton," *op. cit.,* p. 251.

[8] Cf. *Ordinatio* (ed. Vaticana, III, 1954), p. 418.

[9] Cf. Pelster, "Thomas von Sutton," *op. cit.,* p. 247; Przezdziecki, "Selected Questions," *op. cit., passim.*

[10] In the *Quaestiones* of Cod. Rossianus IX, 121, Sutton refers to him as Frater Joannes Duns or simply Duns; cf. Pelster, "Thomas von Sutton," *op. cit.,* pp. 216-18, 400.

close to naming him. For after having referred to Scotus' principle
of individuation as an *unitas quaedam*,[11] he writes: "Quaero enim
ab illo qui hoc dicit, utrum unitates sub specie angeli distinguuntur
seipsis per proprias naturas aut distinguuntur ex aliis."[12] The use
of the phrase *ab illo qui hoc dicit* makes it plain that he has a definite individual in mind, and that individual can only be Scotus,
as is clear from the description of the doctrine. This is confirmed
by a text in which Sutton alludes to Scotus' subtility: "Patet igitur
quod totum dictum istorum, qui tam *subtiliter* putant nova in-
venire, non est nisi ficticium puerile."[13]

As for the questions listed above, it should be noted that only
Quaestiones Disputatae 32 and 34 are against Scotus. But even this
statement needs some modification because there are many arguments in both works which cannot be found in Scotus. Some of
these arguments have undoubtedly been proposed by certain masters; most of them, however, should probably be attributed to the
respondents themselves.

Quaestiones Disputatae 33 and 35 are directed against some
unknown masters. I have suspected that Robert Cowton might be
one of these, but the examination of one of his questions revealed
that he himself is opposed to the doctrine of univocity, even though
at one point he made the following remark about the position of
Scotus: ". . . haec opinio est valde probabilis."[14]

---

[11] *Q.D.* 27; Cod. M, fol. 315vb: Quidam tamen ad rationes istas impediendas
talem proferunt cavillationem. Dicunt quod natura specifica in substantiis materialibus quam in immaterialibus non individuatur per seipsam, nec in substantiis materialibus *est individuatio per materiam* aut formam nec etiam per aliquod accidens,
sed principium individuationis tam in materialibus quam in substantiis separatis
est *unitas* quaedam sub specie, distincta ab omni alia unitate quae est sub illa specie,
sicut unitas differentiae est principium contrahens genus ad speciem et est distincta
ab omni alia unitate alterius differentiae quae est sub illo genere. Et unitas quae
est principium individuationis est quid positivum, sicut et differentia specifica est
aliquid positivum sub genere. In *Quodl.* III, q. 21 (*ibid.*, fol. 204va) the same doctrine is stated thus: . . . quidam ponunt quod causa individuationis est quid positivum,
sed non est materia, nec forma, nec tota substantia, nec quantitas, nec aliquod accidens, sed est *unitas* vel *entitas* quaedam distincta ab omni alia entitate ejusdem
speciei. The principle of individuation is also discussed in *Quodl.* I, q. 21, but no
reference is made to Scotus' position; cf. Cod. M, fols. 169v-171r.

[12] *Q. D.* 27: Cod. M, fol. 315vb. It is noteworthy that Sutton, when he describes
Scotus' position, never employs the term *haecceitas*, but either *entitas*, or *unitas*, as
Scotus himself does in his chief work; cf. *Opus Oxoniense* II, d. 3, q. 6, n. 2; XII, 128;
ibid., nn. 9-13, XII, 138ff. Perhaps the same situation exists in the unedited *Prima
Lectura*, but I did not have the text available on this point.

[13] *Q. D.* 27; Cod. M., fol. 316vb.

[14] *In I Sent.*, Prol., q. 4; Cod. Merton College 93, fol. 15rb. In this connection,

It should also be noted that it is not at all clear from the questions directed against Scotus whether the unedited *Prima Lectura* or the *Opus Oxoniense* served as the source of the arguments presented by the respondents for univocity. Sutton himself was familiar both with the *Lectura*[15] and the *Opus Oxoniense*.[16] Although the respondents were familiar with at least one of these works, they evidently saw no need of recording Scotus' arguments in his own words.

One final word on the dating of *Quaestiones Disputatae* 32 and 34. Exact dates cannot, of course, be assigned. It is very probable, however, that these questions were debated and written while Scotus was still alive. It is hardly likely that Sutton would wait a long time before challenging the position of the great Franciscan. The question raised was a burning issue and must have provoked much discussion among Sutton's students. He had to speak. This he probably did sometimes before 1305.

The Conceptus Communis

For historical reasons, and also for the understanding of Thomas of Sutton's attack upon the doctrine of univocity, it is essential to have a precise knowledge of the arguments that were employed by the proponents of this doctrine. In the writings of Thomas of Sutton these arguments are very numerous. In fact, the respondents usually argue at such great length that it is rather difficult to be brief in the presentation of their arguments, especially when a whole series of arguments is used to establish a certain point. Many of these arguments revolve around what is often called in the texts the *conceptus communis*. This "common concept" will serve as a kind of unifying principle for the series of arguments to be given below. It is hoped that this discussion will help us to catch something of the atmosphere prevailing at Oxford shortly after the year 1300.

The first argument advanced by the respondent in *Quaestio Disputata* 32 for the view that being is predicated univocally of God and of the things belonging to the various categories is highly significant, as it betrays an essentialist conception of being. The

I wish to thank Father Ballic for his kindness in sending me copies of this Question by Robert Cowton and the two Questions on univocity from Scotus' *Prima Lectura*.

[15] Cf. C. Balic, "La valeur critique des citations des oeuvres de Jean Duns Scot," *Mélanges Auguste Pelzer* (Louvain: 1947), 546-48.

[16] Cf. Pelster, "Thomas von Sutton," *op. cit.*, pp. 216ff.

respondent observes that the reason which impels some to accept
the doctrine of analogy is basically this: certain names, like "wise"
and "just," are applied to God and creatures, and yet when applied
to creatures, these names imply imperfection which must somehow be removed before they can be applied to God. For in creatures these names signify qualities, but in God they must signify
divine substance. But this reason is inapplicable to being because
being does not imply imperfection.[17] Being signifies simply that
which has essence (*habens essentiam*), just as "wise" signifies that
which has wisdom (*habens sapientiam*). Now, since being transcends all the categories, it implies no determinate mode of being,[18]
such as that of quantity or quality. Therefore being is predicated
of God and other things univocally.[19]

[17] The basis for this position, which is definitely Scotistic, as will appear from
texts soon to be quoted, is the famous doctrine of Avicenna: *ipsa equinitas non est
aliquid nisi equinitas tantum* (*Metaphysica* V, c. 1; ed. Venice, 1508, fol. 86va).
Gilson has repeatedly asserted that the Scotistic view of being as univocal is based on
Avicenna's doctrine of essence; cf. *Jean Duns Scot* (Paris: J. Vrin, 1952), pp. 84ff.
It is interesting to note that Robert Cowton, who probably lived in the same house
with Scotus at Oxford, suspects Avicenna of being the originator of the doctrine of
univocity. He writes: In ista quaestione sunt tres opiniones. Una, quod ens, ut
distinguitur contra nihil, dicit unum conceptum formaliter communem omnibus
entibus, Deo et etiam creaturae, substantiae et accidentibus. Et Avicenna videtur
fuisse auctor illius opinionis. . . . And a little later he makes this reference to Scotus
as holding this opinion: Aliqui tenentes opinionem hujusmodi sic tenent hanc
opinionem omnino esse veram et dicunt hoc quemlibet experiri in seipso, quod ipse
potest abstrahere unum conceptum entis ab omnibus et concipere ens univoco conceptu, ut ens distinguatur contra nihil, non includendo in illo conceptu limitationem
vel non limitationem effectus vel esse Creatoris vel creaturae, et per consequens ille
conceptus unus communis erit omnibus entibus, quamvis sit analogus in rebus
ipsis (*In I Sent.*, Prol., q. 4; Cod. Merton College 93, fol. 15rb). A short time later,
Peter Aureolus, in criticizing Scotus' doctrine, even refers to Avicenna's *equinitas*.
Cf. *Petri Aureoli Scriptum super Primum Sententiarum*, d. 2, sect. 9, n. 72; ed. E. M.
Buytaert, O. F.M. (St. Bonaventure, N. Y.: Franciscan Institute, 1956), pp. 494ff.
[18] The modes of being, according to Scotus, are *praeter conceptum entis*, and
it is for that reason that being can be predicated univocally. He writes: Illae igitur
differentiae quae accipiuntur ab eadem re et ab eadem realitate secundum diversas
rationes formales illius realitatis, quae dicunt modum essendi illius realitatis, non
includunt ens formaliter, quia ad illas stat resolutio conceptus non simpliciter simplicis. Unde omnia quae formaliter includunt ens habent aliquas perfectiones quae
sunt modi entitatis, qui sunt praeter conceptum entis, sicut quando ens dictur de
substantia et accidente, substantia habet aliquid formale quod non est formaliter
entitas, sed modus entis (*Prima Lectura*, I, d. 3, q. 12; Cod. Antonianus 178, fol.
23rb). And a little later: . . . concedo quod aliquid sit extra rationem entis, et haec
est principalis quaestio quae ponit quod ens sit univocum et quod sic descendit per
differentias (*ibid.*).
[19] *Q. D.* 32, *Arg.* 1; Cod. M. fol. 329rb: Tota causa quare aliqua nomina dicuntur
de Deo et de aliis analogice, et non univoce, haec est, quia prout dicuntur de creaturis

To this the opponent objects. He explains that the name "being," as used of creatures, implies imperfection because a creature
does not have the same mode of being that God has. For God is his
own being (*esse*), while in creatures "that which is" differs from
being, and this is a mark of imperfection. Therefore being is not
predicated univocally of God and other things.[20]

In replying to this objection the respondent concedes that
when an effect has a mode of being which is different from that of
its cause, then the specific name (*nomen speciei specialissimae*) is
not predicated univocally of the cause and the effect, but the general name can be. Thus, substance is predicated univocally of material and immaterial substance, and the same is true of being.[21]
In short, because the modes of being vary in different things, it is
impossible to predicate a name like that of "material substance"
of material and immaterial substances alike, for that would in effect
be the same as to say that immaterial substances are material. In
like manner, if we were to predicate a perfection, as it is in a creature, of God, we would be reducing God to the level of created
reality. Hence it is clear that the respondent has no intention of
saying that God and creatures are being in the same way. He does
claim, however, that the general term "being," according as it pre-
scinds from the modes of being in God and creatures, is univocal.

And he observes further that if being implied imperfection,
it would signify some predicamental mode of being, for it is through

important aliquid imperfectionis in suis rationibus, quod oportet removere ab eis
prout dicuntur de Deo. 'Sapiens' enim et 'justus' et hujusmodi significant qualitatem;
qualitas autem non est in Deo, nam omnia quae sunt in Deo sunt ipsa Dei substantia.
Sed ista causa deficit de ente; non enim importat aliquam imperfectionem, sed solum
significat 'habens essentiam,' sicut hoc nomen 'sapiens' significat 'habens sapientiam.'
Et cum ens sit transcendens omnia praedicamenta, nullum determinatum modum
essendi importat, neque scilicet quantitatem, neque qualitatem. Ergo hoc nomen
'ens' dicitur de Deo et de aliis univoce. For this argument, as it appears in Scotus'
Prima Lectura, cf. T. Barth, "De univocationis entis scotisticae intentione principali
necnon valore critico," *Antonianum* XXVIII (1953), 109. Robert Cowton repeats
this argument, following the *Prima Lectura* very closely; cf. *loc. cit.*, fol. 16ra-b.

[20] *Ibid.*: Dicebatur quod hoc nomen 'ens,' prout dicitur de creaturis, importat
aliquam imperfectionem, quia nulla creatura habet talem modum essendi qualem
habet Deus, quia Deus est suum esse. In creaturis autem differunt 'quod est' et suum
esse, et hoc est imperfectionis. Et ideo ens non dicitur univoce de Deo et de aliis.

[21] *Ibid.*, *Arg.* 2; Cod. M, fol. 329rb: Contra. Quando effectus habet alium modum
essendi quam sua causa, quamvis nomen speciei specialissimae non dicatur univoce
de causa et effectu, nomen tamen generale potest dici univoce de eis, sicut hoc nomen
'substantia' dicitur univoce de substantiis materialibus et de substantiis immaterialibus, quae sunt causae earum, et habent tamen alium modum essendi. Sed ens est

such modes that things belong to the various predicaments. But being does not signify any of these modes because it is the supreme genera that add modes to being. Being, therefore, considered in itself, does not signify any of these modes, nor does it signify any of the imperfection which they entail. If it did, the various predicaments would add nothing to being.[22]

The opponent rejects this view, pointing out that being signifies the various predicamental modes of being analogically, and that consequently it does not signify a concept common to the ten predicaments.[23] The respondent, however, argues once more in favor of a concept common to all the predicaments, one, namely, which abstracts from substance and the other categories.[24]

There are three other arguments that deserve special mention.

First, the same thing cannot be certain and doubtful in the same respect and according to the same concept. But *de facto* one can be certain that a given thing is a being and yet doubtful whether it is a substance or an accident. For example, all know with certainty that the powers of the soul are beings, and yet many

nomen maxime generale. Ergo potest dici univoce de illis quae habent diversos modos essendi.

[22] *Ibid., Arg.* 4; Cod. M, fol. 329rb: Praeterea. Si ens importaret aliquam imperfectionem, tunc significaret aliquem modum essendi praedicamentalem, scilicet quantitatis vel qualitatis vel alterius, quia per istos modos essendi primo limitantur res ad determinata praedicamenta. Sed nullum istorum modorum significat hoc nomen 'ens,' quia genera generalissima addunt istos modos supra ens. Et ita ens de suo nomine nullum istorum modorum significat, et per consequens nullam imperfectionem posteriorem; alioquin substantia, quantitas et alia genera nihil adderent supra ens. The same point is made in a slightly different fashion: Nomina quae attribuuntur Deo primo imponuntur ad significandum perfectionem in creaturis. Ens autem non attribuitur Deo prout significat accidens in creaturis. Si ergo non attribuitur Deo prout significat idem quod substantia, relinquitur quod attribuatur Deo secundum quod significat alium conceptum quam conceptum substantiae vel cujuscumque accidentis. Significat igitur conceptum communem omnibus, et ita secundum illum dicitur de Deo et de omnibus aliis univoce (*Q.D.* 32, *Arg.* 10; Cod. M, fol. 329va).

[23] *Ibid.:* Dicebatur quod hoc nomen 'ens' significat analogice modos essendi praedicamentales, quia ens aut significat substantiam aut quantitatem aut aliquod aliorum praedicamentorum, et non significat conceptum communem istis.

[24] *Ibid., Arg.* 5; Cod. M, fol. 329rb: Contra. Si ens dictum de substantia significaret idem quod substantia et ens dictum de quantitate significaret idem quod hoc nomen 'quantitas,' haec esset falsa: 'substantia est magis ens quam quantitas,' quia sensus esset quod substantia est magis subtantia quam quantitas. Ex quo sequitur quod quantitas sit aliquo modo substantia. Et similiter haec esset falsa: 'quantitas est minus ens quam substantia'; hoc autem falsum est. Ergo hoc nomen 'ens' non significat substantiam, nec quantitatem, sed conceptum communem omnibus praedicamentis.

are not certain whether they are the substance of the soul or its accidents. Therefore being signifies a concept distinct from the concepts of substance and accident.[25]

Although this argument is developed no further, it is evident that the respondent wishes to say that the concept of being, considered in itself, does not include the determinations of substance and accident, but is predicable of both in exactly the same way.

Secondly, the respondent also asserts that it can be proved that the truth and being of God are the univocal measure of the truth and being of creatures. He bases this conclusion on the startling affirmation that the truth and being of God are the univocal cause of the truth and being of creatures. To establish this latter point, he appeals to the authority of Aristotle, who, in the second book of the *Metaphysics*, when he wishes to prove that the first principle of things, viz. God, is the highest from the standpoint of truth and being, proceeds as follows: That is the greatest in a given perfection through which that perfection is caused in other things and predicated univocally of it and them.[26] But it is the first principle that causes truth and being in other things and it does so in such a way that both name and meaning (*ratio*) are the same. Therefore the first principle is the greatest from the standpoint of truth and being.[27] And in an appended note we are reminded that Aristotle

---

[25] *Q. D.* 32, *Arg.* 23; Cod. M, fol. 329vb: Praeterea. Idem non est certum et dubium secundum eandem rationem sive secundum eundem conceptum. Sed de aliquo est certum quod sit ens et dubium est an sit substantia vel accidens, sicut manifestum est de potentiis animae, quas omnes certitudinaliter sciunt quod sunt entia, dubitant tamen multi an sint substantia animae vel accidentia ipsius. Ergo ens significat alium conceptum quam substantiae vel accidentis. For Scotus' argument in the *Prima Lectura*, cf. Barth, "De univocationis entis" *op. cit.*, p. 105. See also *Ordinatio*, I, d. 3, *pars* 1, qq. 1-2 (ed. Vat., III, n. 27). This argument, as reproduced by Robert Cowton, in certain of its expressions, resembles the *Ordinatio;* the proof of the minor, however, is based exclusively on the *Prima Lectura (loc. cit.,* fol. 15va-b).

[26] Cf. Aristotle, *Metaphysics* ii. 2. 993b 24. For St. Thomas' interpretation of this crucial passage, see *In duodecim libros Metaphysicorum expositio,* II, lect. 2 (Cathala, nn. 292-94).

[27] *Q. D.* 34, *Arg.* 3; Cod. M, fol. 333va: Praeterea. Veritas Dei et entitas est causa univoca veritatis et entitatis creaturarum. Ergo eadem ratione est mensura univoca. Probatio assumpti: Secundo *Metaphysicae* (ii. 2. 993b 23-31) Philosophus probat quod primum principium, quod est Deus, est maxime verum et maxime ens per talem rationem: Unumquodque, per quod causatur aliquid in aliis univoce dictum de ipso et illis aliis, est maxime tale. Sed per primum principium causatur veritas et entitas in aliis secundum idem nomen et eandem rationem. Ergo primum principium est maxime verum et maxime ens. In ista ratione Philosophi habetur expresse quod verum et ens dicuntur univoce de prima causa et de causatis, non obstante quod sit causa excedens. Duns Scotus, *Prima Lectura,* I, d. 8, q. 3; Cod. Anton. 178, fol. 45rb:

expressly says that truth and being are predicated *univocally* of the First Cause and of the things caused, notwithstanding the fact that the former surpasses the latter in perfection.

And thirdly, it is argued that unless the doctrine of univocity is admitted, it will be impossible to compare one thing with another.[28] This argument is very much like the preceding, except that it has a wider scope, for comparisons can be made not only between a creature and God, but between one creature and another.

We might at this point summarize the teaching on univocity as proposed by the respondents (or respondent) in Sutton's *Quaestiones Disputatae*, bearing in mind that they are, for the most part, merely reporting in their own words arguments put forward by Duns Scotus himself.

It is clear from the texts that the respondents admit that God and creatures are not on the same level of being, for God is absolutely perfect, whereas creatures manifest varying degrees of imperfection. And the same must be said of predicamental reality because one predicament is obviously not another. From this it follows that being itself is analogical. But this is not the issue. As

---

Praeterea, ad hoc est auctoritas Philosophi secundo *Metaphysicae* (ii. 2. 993b 24). Plana vere invenitur a Philosopho, ita plana auctoritas pro alia parte. Dicit enim ibi Philosophus: Unumquodque maxime est tale quod est causa univoca aliis veri. Philosophus aperte addit 'univocam.' Sed Deus est causa veritatis in aliis. Ergo Deus maxime est verus. Veritas igitur univoce dicitur de Deo et creaturis. See also *Ordinatio*, I, d. 8, *pars* 1, q. 3 (ed. Vat., IX, n. 79). Robert Cowton, *op. cit.*, fol. 15rb: Ad idem, secundo *Metaphysicae*, dicit Philosophus quod unumquodque est magis tale quod est ratio aliis ut talia dicantur. Ideo principia sempiternorum maxime sunt vera, quia sunt aliis causa veritatis. Igitur primum principium et alia comparantur in veritate. Igitur habent veritatem univocam. Sed sicut se habent ad esse, sic ad verum. Si igitur comparantur in veritate, et in entitate; igitur univoce in utroque.

[28] *Q. D.* 34, *Arg.* 7; Cod. M, fol. 333vb: Praeterea. Non fit comparatio inter aliqua nisi secundum id quod univoce reperitur in illis, sicut habetur ex septimo *Physicorum* [vii. 4. 248b 6-7] Sed Deus et creatura comparantur ad invicem secundum sapientiam, bonitatem et justitiam, et alias perfectiones. Ergo hujusmodi perfectiones univoce conveniunt Deo et creaturis. Assumptum patet, quia Deus est sapientior et melior quam aliqua creatura. Duns Scotus, *Prima Lectura*, I, d. 8, q. 3; Cod. Anton. 178, fol. 45va: Nunc autem sicut in comparatione propria requiritur quod illud secundum quod fit comparatio sit species atoma—ex septimo *Physicorum* [vii. 4. 249b 20-21]—sic in comparatione largissima requiritur ratio communis secundum quam sit (*read:* fit) comparatio—etiam cum dico quod homo est animal perfectius quam asinus, et etiam cum dicitur quod substantia est perfectius ens quam accidens. Et ideo, si Deus est supersapientia respectu nostrae sapientiae, oportet necessario quod sapientia sit unius rationis hic inde. See also *Ordinatio*, I, d. 8, *pars* I, q. 3 (ed. Vat., IV, n. 83) Robert Cowton, *op. cit.*, fol. 15rb: Item. Secundum Philosophum, septimo *Physicorum* [vii. 4. 248b 6-7], in aequivocis non est comparatio. Sed secundum ens est comparatio. Igitur non est aequivocum.

the respondents point out time and time again, in spite of the fact
that there are differences between one thing and another, there
must be a common concept of being which is applied to these
things in one and the same way. In other words, the differences
are not taken into account in the *concept* of being. It is this prescinding from differences that makes univocal predication possible.
The *conceptus communis,* then, as interpreted by the Scotists, is
by definition a univocal concept. It signifies that which things
have in common, without signifying that by which things differ.

How does Thomas of Sutton react to the view expressed by the
respondents? For the answer to that question we must turn to the
magistral determinations of *Quaestiones Disputatae* 32 and 34.

The Critique of Univocity

It would be interesting to consider what Thomas of Sutton has
to say in reply to these and many other arguments in favor of the
doctrine of univocity, but a study of these replies is not within our
present scope. Moreover, such a study would not yield, at least in
any systematic fashion, a knowledge of the principles employed by
Sutton in his refutation of the doctrine of univocity. For a clear
presentation of these principles it will be far more satisfactory to
consider in some detail the determinations which are furnished by
Sutton in *Quaestiones Disputatae* 32 and 34.

The first of these determinations is of particular significance
for this study because Sutton's aim there is not so much to give an
account of the various types of analogy, as is the case in *Quaestio
Disputata* 34, but rather to examine the claim that the concept of
being is a *conceptus communis.*

At the beginning of the *Respondeo* of *Quaestio Disputata* 32
Sutton sets out to discover the reason why many of his contemporaries affirm that the concept of being is a univocal one. As far as
things themselves are concerned, there is no particular problem.
All authors agree that being is predicated not univocally, but analogically, of *things* in the various predicaments, and the same must
be said with regard to the predication of being of God and things
distinct from God.[29] The real problem lies in the *signification* of
being.

[29] *Q. D.* 32; Cod. M, fol. 330ra: Respondeo. Dicendum quod omnes auctores
conveniunt in hoc quod ens non dicitur univoce de *rebus* diversorum praedicamentorum, sed analogice, et hoc necesse est dicere. Et similiter dicitur ens de Deo et de
rebus aliis cujuscumque sint praedicamenti.

According to Thomas of Sutton, it is the commonness *(com-munitas)* of being that is at the root of the erroneous doctrine of univocity. For whatever is understood, whether it be a substance or an accident, being is understood. In fact, even when one does not know whether the thing understood is a substance or an accident, one at least knows that it is a being. And he goes on to point out that it is by reason of this commonness that being has a great resemblance to any genus which is a common univocal term. For when some species is understood, the genus too is understood. Thus when I understand such a species as man, I also always understand the genus animal. In fact, I can know that a certain thing is an animal, and yet not know whether it is a horse or an ass, as happens when the thing is viewed at some distance. Taking this resemblance between being and genus into account, some have been deceived into thinking that just as the genus animal has a concept common to all the species, and is thus included in the concept of every species, so being has one concept common to all things, and is thus also included in the concept of every reality.[30]

Such is Thomas of Sutton's explanation for the origin of the doctrine of univocity.[31] In his view of the matter, the theory of univocity ultimately rests on a confusion between the commonness of being and the commonness of genus. He must now establish that the two are different, and to do this is to establish that being is not a genus.

Restricting himself for the moment to the consideration of predicamental reality, Sutton states categorically that it is impossible that there should be a common concept of being which could

[30] *Ibid.*: Decipiuntur autem multi de *significatione* hujus nominis 'ens' propter suam maximam communitatem: quidquid enim intelligitur, sive substantia, sive accidens, statim intelligitur ens; etiam si de eo quod intelligitur ignoretur utrum sit substantia vel accidens, nihilominus intelligitur quod sit ens, nec de hoc dubitat intelligens quin sit ens. Et in hoc habet ens magnam similitudinem cum nomine univoco communi, scilicet cum genere. Quaecumque enim species *intelligitur*, genus est de intellectu ipsius: sive enim intelligam hominem sive equum sive leonem, semper animal intelligo. Et possum cognoscere animal et tamen ignorare utrum sit equus vel asinus, ut quando videtur asinus a remotis ambulare, certitudinaliter scitur quod est animal, sed nescitur utrum <sit B> equus vel asinus. Et ideo sicut animal habet conceptum communem ad suas *species* qui includitur in conceptu cujuslibet speciei, ita videtur multis quod ens habet unum conceptum communem ad omnia qui includitur in conceptu cujuslibet. . . .

[31] This explanation was probably suggested to Sutton by *Summa Contra Gentiles* I, 32, *Adhuc. Omne quod.* In *Q. D.* 33, Cod. M. fol. 332rb, Sutton summarizes all of the arguments proposed by St. Thomas in this chapter.

be predicated univocally of the Aristotelian predicaments.[32] The reason for this impossibility lies in the fact that being is included in our understanding of everything, and hence it is not a common notion which can be contracted to the various predicaments after the fashion of a genus which is contracted to its species by means of the specific differences. This can be proved as follows. The genus is not included in the concept of difference,[33] because if it were, the genus would contribute nothing to the constitution of a species. Being included completely in the difference, the difference by itself would be in a position to account for the species with the result that the genus would no longer serve as a part of a definition. Moreover, every definition employing genus and difference would of necessity be nugatory, for the genus would appear in the definition twice, once in its own name and again under that of difference. It would also follow that the difference is not a *part* of the species but the *whole*, for it would signify all that is signified by the species. It is evident, then, that the concept of genus is not included in the concept of difference.[34]

Now, if we turn our attention to the concept of being, it soon becomes apparent how unlike genus this concept is. In this case we are dealing with a concept that is included in the concept of whatever reality we understand, and it is for this reason that being cannot have a difference which would contract it to some species. Therefore being cannot have one concept common to the ten predicaments because that would suppose that there is something outside of being which would contract it to substance and the other predicaments. If this supposition were true, the ten predicaments would be so many species of the genus "being." It follows therefore

[32] *Ibid.*: Sed absque dubio decepti sunt. Impossibile enim est quod ens habeat conceptum communem, secundum quem dicatur de diversis praedicamentis univoce.

[33] On this point, see St. Thomas, *S. C. G.* I, 25, *Quod. autem.*

[34] *Ibid.*, fol. 330ra-b: Et ut hoc evidens fiat, considerandum est quod ens est de intellectu uniuscujusque, et ideo non est tale commune quod potest contrahi ad diversa praedicamenta per illum modum quo genus contrahitur ad species, scilicet per differentias. Genus enim non est de intellectu differentiae, quia si sic, genus nihil faceret ad constitutionem speciei, quia totus conceptus generis includeretur in differentia, et sic non minus faceret differentia per se quam differentia cum genere; et sic genus non esset pars definitionis, immo in omni definitione, in qua poneretur genus cum differentia, esset nugatio, quia genus bis diceretur, semel nomine generis et iterum nomine differentiae. Sequeretur etiam quod nec differentia esset *pars* speciei, quia per differentiam importaretur *totum* quod importatur per speciem. Manifestum [enim] est igitur quod conceptus generis non includitur in conceptu differentiae.

that being is not predicated univocally of the predicaments, for whatever is predicated univocally of specifically different things contained under it after the manner of essence (*in quid contentis*) is their genus.[35]

But perhaps being is one of the remaining four predicables, and if so, it would be predicated univocally. This, however, is impossible. For, first of all, being is not a difference, since differences are predicated *in quale* and not *in quid*.[36] Nor is being a property or an accident, for properties and accidents are predicated only accidentally of the species and the predicaments. Finally, being is not a species, because no species is as common as are the predicaments. Therefore, since these possible sources of univocal predication[37] do not express what is expressed by being, being is not a univocal notion.[38]

From the analysis given above Sutton concludes that the Aristotelian predicaments are really the ten supreme genera, and that being is not a kind of super-genus under which they can be brought. The predicaments are in reality ten different modes of predication and it is impossible to reduce one mode to another. And since each of these predicaments is an *ens per se* and not an *ens per accidens*, and since, moreover, not all beings are said to be univocal, as we have established, being must be predicated of the predicaments either equivocally or analogically.[39]

[35] *Ibid.*, fol. 330rb: Cum igitur conceptus entis includitur in conceptu cujuslibet quod intelligitur, non potest ens habere aliquam differentiam contrahentem ipsum ad aliquam speciem. Ergo ens non potest habere conceptum unum communem decem praedicamentis, quia non potest esse aliquid quod contrahat ipsum ut sit substantia, nec aliquid quod contrahat ipsum ut sit quantitas, et sic de aliis, ut sic substantia et quantitas et alia genera praedicamentorum sint species entis et contineantur sub ente sicut species sub genere. Et ex hoc squitur quod ens non dicatur univoce de ipsis praedicamentis. Omne enim quod praedicatur univoce de multis in quid contentis sub ipso et differentibus specie est genus eorum.

[36] On these two kinds of predication, cf. C. Shircel, *The Univocity of the Concept of Being in the Philosophy of John Duns Scotus* (Washington: 1942), pp. 31-2.

[37] Cf. St. Thomas, *S. C. G.* I, 32, *Adhuc. Omne quod.*

[38] *Ibid.*: Non enim potest esse differentia eorum, quia differentia praedicatur in quale et non in quid. Nec potest esse proprium vel accidens eorum, quia tam proprium quam accidens praedicatur accidentaliter de specie et etiam de unoquoque praedicamentorum cujus est proprium vel accidens. Nec etiam potest esse species eorum, quia nulla species est communior quam ista genera. Relinquitur ergo quod ex quo ens non est genus substantiae et quantitatis et aliorum, quia [*read:* quod B] nullo modo potest praedicari univoce de ipsis. Omne enim quod praedicatur univoce de multis vel est genus eorum vel species vel differentia vel proprium vel accidens.

[39] *Ibid.*: Oportet igitur necessario quod illa decem, quae communiter dicuntur

Taking up these last two alternatives, Sutton proceeds to exclude the first. It should be noted, however, that the term equivocal, as used by him here, refers only to the equivocals by chance (*aequiuoca a casu*). Like St. Thomas before him,[40] Sutton does not hesitate to employ the term equivocal in the sense of the analogical.[41] His intention here is simply to exclude the predication of being in a purely equivocal sense.

In the case of pure equivocals, since only the name is common, and this is the result of chance, it is possible equally to attribute a name to widely divergent things, predicating it of one thing with as much reason as of another. But being cannot be predicated in this way of substance and accidents. For substance is a primary instance of being whereas accidents are being only in the sense that they belong to substance. Substance is being in an unqualified sense, and exists as an independent reality, while accidents are being only in a qualified sense and exist not in themselves but in substance and for substance. All this had clearly been demonstrated by Aristotle. Consequently, since being is predicated primarily of substance, and of the other predicaments only in so far as they are referred to substance, it is impossible to admit the view that being is predicated of the predicaments in a purely equivocal sense. Therefore, the priority of substance with regard to the accidents must be taken into account in the very concept of being, and to do so is to acknowledge that the concept of being is truly analogical.[42]

---

decem praedicamenta, sint prima rerum genera, non habentia supra se aliud genus. Et distinguuntur secundum decem modos praedicandi diversos, quorum nullus reducitur ad alium; nec potest inveniri in rebus alius praedicandi modus ab istis decem. Et quia quodlibet istorum decem generum est ens per se, non per accidens, et non omnia dicuntur entia univoce, ut ostensum est, necesse est ut ens dicatur de eis vel aequivoce vel analogice.

[40] Cf. *Summa Theologiae* I, q. 13, a. 10, ad 4m.

[41] *Q. D.* 34; Cod. M, fol. 334va: Et advertendum est quod definitio aequivocorum, quae ponitur in principio libri *Praedicamentorum* I. Ia 1-2, convenit enti et sano et omnibus analogis. . . . In quatuor [*read:* quarto B] autem libro *Metaphysicae* [iv. 1. 1003a 33-b 10] accipit aequivoca magis stricte, vocans illa tantum aequivoca nomina quae primo et principaliter significant plura; cujusmodi sunt aequivoca a casu, et nulla alia. Et illo modo 'ens' et 'sanum' non sunt aequivoca, sed sunt media inter aequivoca et univoca.

[42] *Q. D.* 32; Cod. M, fol. 330rb: Sed non dicitur de eis aequivoce, ita ut ex aequo dicatur de quolibet illorum principaliter, sicut aequivocum a casu, quia substantia est primum ens, et alia non dicuntur entia nisi quia sunt primi entis. Substantia enim est ens simpliciter et per seipsam, et alia sunt entia secundum quid et propter substantiam dicuntur entia. Et hoc ostendit Philosophus in septimo *Metaphysicae*

Up to this point, in the text which we have been analyzing, Sutton has been exclusively preoccupied with the concept of being as applied to the predicaments. Why this obsessive interest in the predicaments? Would it not be far better to study the concept of being according as it applies to God and creatures? Was not that the problem raised by Sutton himself when he formulated the question which the bachelors were to discuss? Sutton is perfectly aware of all this. In fact, as appears from a rather casual remark in the concluding paragraph of his determination, all along he has, in a sense, been establishing the view that the concept of being when applied to God and creatures is an analogical one. His procedure in the question is this: if it can be established that the concept of being is analogical with regard to the diverse predicaments, *a fortiori* it will be analogical with regard to God and creatures.

But apart from this argument, Sutton also offers a special argument to show that being is predicated analogically of God and creatures. The argument is basically Thomistic, with certain evident borrowings from *Summa Contra Gentiles*, I, 32. He argues thus. God is called being essentially because He is His own subsisting being *(esse)* and possesses all the perfection of being. Everything else is called being by participation, because nothing else is its own being, nor does it possess all the perfection of being. All things apart from God only share in being, possessing it merely in a partial way, i.e., according to a limited degree of perfection designated by genus and species.[43] In fact, the distance between the

[vii. 1, 1028a 10-31] ex modo loquendi. Quando enim volumus dicere de aliquo quid est, dicimus ipsum esse hominem vel leonem vel aliquid tale quod significat substantiam, et non dicimus quod est bonum vel malum neque tricubitum neque percutiens. Sed dicendo quod est bonum vel malum, dicimus quale quid est, et dicendo quod est tricubitum dicimus quantum quid est; et tunc non dicimus quid est simpliciter et absolute, et per consequens nec essentiam simpliciter vel ens simpliciter nec ens ratione sui ipsius, sed quid quantitatis vel qualitatis, quae non sunt ratione sui, sed ratione substantiae. Et ita substantia significat quidditatem vel essentiam absolute ratione sui ipsius; alia vero genera dicuntur entia eo quod sunt aliquo modo entis primi quod est substantia—et quaedam sunt qualitates substantiae et quaedam quantitates et quaedam relationes substantiae. Quia igitur ens dicitur principaliter de substantia et de aliis non dicitur nisi in habitudine ad substantiam, oportet necessario dicere quod ens non dicitur pure aequivoce de ipsis, sed secundum prius et posterius analogice.

[43] In *Q. D.* 34, Cod. M, fol. 334vb Sutton writes: Non potest esse quod talia nomina dicantur de Deo et aliis univoce, quia prout dicuntur de creaturis sunt nomina significantia perfectiones contentas in genere praedicamentali: verbi gratia, scientia creaturae est de genere qualitatis, et similiter potentia, sapientia et bonitas. Oportet igitur quod qualitas sit de ratione cujuslibet istorum, cum genus semper

being of any creature and divine being is far greater than the distance between the being of any accident and the being of substance. There is, then, far less reason for saying that being can be predicated of God and a creature univocally than there is for saying that it can so be predicated of substance and accident, for compared to God, creatures are more in the nature of non-beings than beings.[44]

It is now clear that Thomas of Sutton is definitely an advocate of the doctrine of analogy. Let us now take a rapid glance at the nature of this analogy as it is explained in *Quaestio Disputata* 34. Sutton's remarks on this subject are important because they show in unmistaken terms that he is siding with St. Thomas against Duns Scotus and his followers.

Basing himself on Boethius,[45] Sutton distinguishes between *aequivoca a casu* and *aequivoca a consilio*, the former referring to equivocals in the proper sense and the latter to analogicals. He also accepts Boethius'[46] fourfold division of equivocals by design (*a consilio*). These are (1) *aequivoca secundum similitudinem*, (2) *aequivoca secundum proportionem*, (3) *aequivoca ab uno*, and (4) *aequivoca ad unum*.[47]

The first type of equivocals involves a certain likeness, as in the case of an actual man and a picture of him.[48] The second type

sit de ratione speciei. Sed prout dicuntur de Deo, qualitas non est de ratione alicujus eorum; qualitas enim imperfectum modum essendi importat. Unde Deus est sine qualitate bonus, et sapiens, et potens. Rationes igitur illorum nominum non sunt totaliter eaedem prout dicuntur de Deo et prout dicuntur de aliis; et ita non univoce dicuntur.

[44] *Q. D.* 32; Cod. M, fol. 330va-b: Ulterius sciendum est quod ens dicitur analogice de Deo et de quolibet alio. Deus enim dicitur ens essentialiter, quia est suum esse subsistens, habens omnem perfectionem essendi. Sed omne aliud dicitur ens per participationem, quia nullum aliud est suum esse, nec habet omnem perfectionem essendi, sed participat ipsum esse et partialiter habet aliquam essendi perfectionem secundum gradum determinatum ad genus et ad speciem; et multo longius distat esse cujuslibet creaturae ab esse divino quam esse accidentis cujuscumque ab esse substantiae. Propter quod multo minus potest ens dici de Deo et creatura univoce quam de substantia et accidente; respectu enim Dei alia sunt magis non entia quam entia [cf. St. Thomas, *De aeternitate mundi;* ed. Perrier, n. 7].

[45] Cf. *In Categorias Aristotelis*, PL, 64, col. 165B-C.   [46] *Ibid.*

[47] *Q. D.* 34; Cod. M, fol. 334rb: Sed advertendum est quod secundum expositores Philosophi dupliciter dicuntur aequivoca: quaedam enim sunt aequivoca a casu et quaedam a consilio vel a proposito. Aequivoca a casu sunt illa quibus a casu imponitur unum nomen, ut Alexander Priami filius et Alexander Macedo; et ista proprie dicuntur aequivoca. Quae autem sunt aequivoca a proposito dividuntur quadrupliciter: quaedam enim sunt secundum similitudinem, quaedam secundum proportionem, quaedam ab uno, quaedam ad unum.

[48] *Ibid.*: Aequivoca a consilio secundum similitudinem dicuntur, ut homo et

refers to what is now generally called analogy of proportionality.[49] The third type applies to equivocals which are derived from something one.[50] The fourth type embraces equivocals which are referred to some one end or some one subject.[51]

The problem now is to determine according to which of these four types names are said to be predicated analogically.[52] Sutton admits that names can be predicated of God and creatures according to each of these types, but at the same time he proposes to establish that analogy "according to proportion" is analogy in the proper sense of the term.

The first analogy which he considers is that which involves a reference to something one. According to this type of analogy, names will be predicated of God and creatures because creatures have a relation to God as their cause. In discussing this kind of analogy, Sutton repeats in rather free terms what St. Thomas says in *Summa Contra Gentiles*, I, 34.[53] He accept this type of analogy,

quod pingitur ad similitudinem hominis, quorum utrum [*read*: utrumque B] dicitur animal, sed aequivoce secundum similitudinem.

[49] *Ibid.*: Secundo modo aequivoca a consilio vel a proposito, scilicet secundum proportionem, dicuntur, ut cum 'principium' dicitur de unitate quae est principium numeri, et de puncto quod est principium lineae, et de fonte qui est principium fluviorum, et de corde quod est principium in animali . . . Et bene dicuntur aequivoca secundum proportionem et propriissime, quia proportionaliter dicuntur de diversis; sicut enim unitas est principium numeri, ita punctus est principium lineae, et sic de aliis. Eet ideo talia aequivoca dicuntur proprie analoga, et alia non dicuntur analoga proprie, sed communiter; analoga [*read*: analogia B] enim idem est quod proportio.

[50] *Ibid.*: Tertio modo aequivoca a proposito dicuntur aequivoca ab uno, quia scilicet descendunt ab uno aliquo ad multa, de quibus dicitur nomen aequivoce, ut a medicina dicitur medicinalis liber, in quo scribitur scientia medicinae, medicinale ferramentum incisivum secundum artem medicinae, medicinale pharmacum quod est opportunum ad sanitatem secundum artem medicinae. Ad omnia ista descendit haec aequivocatio ab uno, scilicet a medicina.

[51] *Ibid*: Quarto modo dicuntur aequivoca a consilio ad unum, quando scilicet diversa referuntur ad unum; et ex hoc dicitur de illis nomen idem, sicut 'sanum.' Nam cibus dicitur sanus et pharmacum sanum et exercitium sanum et urina sana, quia referuntur ad unum finem, scilicet ad sanitatem animalis. Et hoc modo ens est aequivocum ad substantiam et ad alia praedicamenta, quia ens dicitur de quantitate et qualitate et caeteris praedicamentis accidentium prout habent habitudinem ad unum, scilicet ad substantiam quae est primum ens; non tamen tanquam ad unum finem, sed tanquam ad unum subjectum.

[52] *Ibid.*, fol. 334vb: Cum autem aequivoca a ·consilio dicantur quatuor modis, ut dictum est, videndum est quo illorum modorum ista nomina dicuntur analogice.

[53] *Ibid.*: Et ponitur communiter [Et ponit Thomas, *Contra Gentiles*, lib. I, cap. 34 A] quod dicuntur secundum ordinem vel respectum ad unum, sicut 'sanum' dicitur de diversis secundum habitudinem ad unum. Non tamen sic dicuntur ad unum quod illud unum sit alterum ab illis et prius eis, sicut ens de quantitate et qualitate

but observes that, from the standpoint of knowledge, names are first attributed to creatures and only then to God.[54] But this, too, is in accordance with what St. Thomas says a little later in the same chapter.

He says much the same thing with regard to analogy involving derivation from something one[55] and analogy "according to likeness."[56]

Thus we are left with analogy "according to proportion." This is analogy in the most proper sense, and it is according to this mode of analogy that names are predicated of God and creatures.[57]

secundum ordinem ad·substantiam, quae est prior utroque illorum; sed secundum quod attenditur ordo duorum non ad tertium, sed unius eorum ad alterum, sicut ens dicitur de substantia et accidente, secundum quod accidens ad substantiam habet respectum, non secundum quod substantia et accidens ad aliquid tertium referuntur. Hujusmodi igitur nomina sic de Deo et rebus aliis dicuntur, quia res aliae habent ordinem ad Deum, et sic dicuntur ad unum.

[54] *Ibid.*: Et illud bene dictum est, considerando [ad] res de quibus dicuntur haec nomina; omnes enim res creatae habent ordinem ad Deum sicut ad suam causam. Sed considerando [ad] significationem nominum, secundum quam principaliter attenditur analogia, non isto modo dicuntur nomina de Deo et rebus aliis; non enim ideo dicitur homo justus vel sapiens quia habet ordinem ad justitiam Dei vel sapientiam, sicut ens dicitur de quantitate propter hoc quod est entis, quod est substantia. Propter hoc autem dicitur ens analogice de substantia et accidente, quia per prius imponitur substantiae et per posterius accidenti, in quantum accidens est ipsius substantiae. Non sic autem nomina dicta de Deo et rebus aliis. Non [enim B] sic imponuntur primo Deo et posterius attribuuntur rebus aliis, sed potius e contrario prius imposita fuerunt rebus aliis, deinde fuerunt attributa Deo; non tamen sic quod dicerentur de Deo ad significandum habitudinem ejus ad res alias. Et ideo videtur quod, proprie loquendo, non dicuntur ista nomina analogice illo modo, scilicet ad unum.

[55] *Ibid.*, fol. 335ra: Nec etiam illo modo quo aliqua dicuntur analoga ab uno, sicut a medicina dicitur liber medicinalis et ferramentum medicinale, quia quamvis bonitas creaturae descendat a bonitate Dei quantum ad esse, non tamen quantum [ad B] attributionem nominis. Non enim ideo dicitur homo bonus quia sua bonitas est a bonitate Dei, et similiter est de aliis nominibus.

[56] *Ibid.*: Nec adhuc dicuntur ista nomina illo modo quo aliqua dicuntur analoga secundum similitudinem, sicut 'animal' est analogum ad hominem et ad id quod pingitur ad similitudinem hominis. Quamvis enim omnes res habeant aliquam similitudinem ad Deum, ut sapientia hominis ad sapientiam Dei et bonitas hominis ad bonitatem Dei, non tamen propter hoc dicitur homo bonus vel sapiens quia habet similitudinem bonitatis Dei et sapientiae Dei; tunc enim ista nomina per posterius imponerentur creaturis quam Deo, quod falsum est.

[57] *Ibid.*: Relinquitur igitur quod nomina dicta de Deo et de rebus aliis dicantur quarto modo, scilicet secundum proportionem, prout hoc nomen 'principium' dicitur de unitate et de puncto et de fonte, ut dictum est. Et hoc facile est manifestare de singulis nominibus. Sicut enim homo cognoscit altissimas causas, et ideo dicitur sapiens, ita Deus cognoscit altissimas causas perfecte et ideo merito debet dici sapiens: unde *Job* undecimo (IX, 4) dicitur: 'Sapiens corde est.' Similiter sicut homo habet cognitionem rei per propriam causam, et ideo sciens dicitur, ita Deus omnium

This type of analogy is most unlike pure equivocity. It does, however, resemble univocity to a greater degree than any of the other types, and it is for this reason that we should not be surprised at the fact that some have mistaken it for univocity.[58]

Yet the *aequivoca secundum proportionem* are not identical with univocal notions. This can be demonstrated infallibly by simply taking into account the definition of a univocal notion. The argument will take this form. A univocal notion, by definition, has a meaning which is completely the same. But this is not true of the names which are predicated of God and creatures. Consequently these names are not univocal notions.[59]

This proof, Sutton continues, is the basis for all the arguments that are brought forward against the doctrine of univocity. He mentions two such arguments from St. Thomas' *Quaestiones disputatae: De potentia Dei*, q. 7, a. 7. The first runs as follows: Every effect of a univocal agent measures up to the power of the agent. But no creature, being finite, measures up to the power of the first agent which is infinite. Therefore it is impossible for a creature to receive a likeness of God univocally. Consequently, since wisdom, goodness and all other perfections are not present in God and creatures univocally, neither can the names be predicated univocally.[60]

causarum et effectuum ordinem cognoscit modo perfectissimo, et ita propter talem proportionem debet dici sciens. Et ideo primo Regum, [capitulo] secundo (II, 3), dicitur: 'Deus scientiarum Dominus est.' Similiter etiam sicut homo habet cognitionem principiorum absque discursu, ita et Deus omnia cognoscit absque discursu; et ideo sicut homo dicitur intelligens, ita et Deus. Job duodecimo (XII, 13): 'Ipse habet consilium et intelligentiam. . . .' Similiter intelligendum est de omnibus aliis nominibus quae absolute significant perfectionem: omnia dicuntur de Deo et rebus aliis secundum proportionem et ideo propriissime dicuntur analoga; et non sunt univoca, quia non secundum rem omnino eandem dicuntur de Deo et de rebus aliis.

58 *Ibid.*: Talia tamen quae sunt proprie analoga maxime recedunt a ratione pure aequivocorum inter omnia analoga et maxime accedunt ad rationem univocorum. Et ideo non est mirum si aliqui dicant ea esse univoca, quia quod non multum distat ab aliqua specie videtur esse illius speciei, cum tamen non sit; et illo modo talia videntur esse univoca, cum tamen non sint.

59 *Ibid.*: Quod autem non sint univoca infallibiliter demonstratur per definitionem univocorum, ut dictum est, quia univocorum est ratio totaliter eadem. Ista vero nomina non dicuntur de Deo et de aliis secundum rationem eadem [read: eandem B].

60 *Ibid.*, fol. 335ra-b: Et super ista probatione fundantur omnia argumenta quae adducuntur a doctoribus ad illam conclusionem, quorum unum est tale: 'Omnis effectus agentis univoci adaequat virtutem agentis. Nulla creatura, cum sit finita, adaequat virtutem primi agentis, cum sit infinita. Ergo impossibile est quod similitudo Dei univoce recipiatur in creatura' (*De Potentia*, q. 7, a. 7), ita ut sapientia vel

The second argument is stated by Sutton thus: When the form in the agent and in the effect does not have the same mode of being, but rather is immaterially in the one and materially in the other, that form is not univocally in the agent and in the effect. Thus the form of a house is not univocally in the soul and in matter, because in the mind of the builder it is present immaterially, but in matter it has material being. Now, that which is in God, is in him immaterially and absolutely without composition; in fact, in God it is divine being. But this cannot be said of other things. Therefore it is impossible that anything should be predicated univocally of God and other things.[61]

With this we have concluded our account of Sutton's critique of the doctrine of univocity. In its essential elements, this critique was not original; it was never meant to be such. In spite of all, however, we have witnessed here an open attack made by one of the greatest defenders of St. Thomas at Oxford against the Scotistic movement at that English university. This attack was made just as the movement was gathering strength in the first decade of the fourteenth century. And it is, indeed, a very able attack, showing great insight into the principles which dominate the metaphysics of the Angelic Doctor. At the present time it is still impossible to say to what extent Scotism penetrated Oxford, but we can be reasonably sure that the masterly intervention of Thomas of Sutton did much to check its spread. It was perhaps through Sutton more than anyone else at Oxford that the genius of St. Thomas Aquinas was able to confront the genius of John Duns Scotus.

bonitas vel alia perfectio univoce sit in Deo et in creatura; et ita ista nomina non dicuntur univoce.

[61] *Ibid.*: Aliud argumentum adducunt tale: Quando forma in agente et in effectu non habet eundem modum essendi, sed in uno est immaterialiter et in alio materialiter, illa forma non est univoce in agente et in effectu; sicut forma domus in anima et in materia non est univoce, quia in mente artificis est immaterialiter, in materia vero habet esse materiale (cf. *De Potentia*, q. 7, a. 7, *Item patet*). Sed omne quod in Deo est, est immaterialiter et simpliciter sine compositione cum alio et est esse divinum. Hoc autem in rebus aliis non accidit. Impossibile est igitur aliquid de Deo et rebus aliis univoce praedicari (cf. *De Potentia*, q. 7, a. 7, *Dato ergo*).

ଛ୬ Intelligere Intelligentibus Est

Esse *by James H. Robb*

☆ ☆ ☆ ☆ ☆ ☆ ☆ ☆ ☆ ☆ ☆ ☆ ☆ ☆

SOMETIME toward the end of January 1269 notice was given at the University of Paris that Frater Thomas Aquinas, lately returned from a nine-year sojourn in Italy to reoccupy the Dominican chair of theology in the University, would hold a *quaestio disputata* on the human soul. The statement of the problem was unique and unusual; St. Thomas had decided to initiate his new series of disputed questions on the soul by posing his topic in terms which he used at no other time throughout his career, namely: "Utrum anima humana possit esse forma et hoc aliquid"— "Whether the human soul can be both a form and an individual substance."[1]

In formulating this question, St. Thomas doubtless felt that he was responding to an urgent doctrinal need of his time, the need of reconciling Platonic and Aristotelian tendencies. The phrasing of Question One suggests, and a reading of the question confirms the initial suspicion, that the doctrine on the soul which was most dear to the Platonists, namely, the soul's subsistence and immortality, and the doctrine which was most authentically Aristotelian, that the soul is the form of the body, are not two opposed answers to two separate questions, but rather two parts of a single answer to a single question. And it is within his answer to this question that we shall situate the doctrine that man is an incarnate spirit, that for him, as for all spiritual beings, *intelligere est esse*, the *to be* is a spiritual one, a *to understand*.

---

[1] *Quaestiones de Anima* q. 1. The manuscript tradition of St. Thomas' Disputed Questions *On the Soul* and *On Spiritual Creatures* treats them as series of questions, not as single questions divided into articles. This tradition is followed in the text and notes of this paper. All texts cited in these notes will be by St. Thomas Aquinas except where noted.

II

The concluding words of the corpus of Question One certainly make clear that the unity of the question and the unity of St. Thomas' answer find their ultimate justification in the unity of the being with which they are concerned. St. Thomas locates the human soul, nay more as we shall see, he locates man himself, on the confines of two worlds: that of bodies, the world of matter and time, and that of the pure intelligences, the world of spirit and timelessness; and he does so because he is convinced that the human soul is the subsistent form of matter. "Thus, therefore, the human soul, insofar as it is united to the body as form, has a *to be* which is elevated above the body and not dependent on it; therefore, it is clear that it is established on the confines of bodily and separate substances."[2]

He is thus entitled to say to the Platonists: True, the human soul is a subsistent, intellectual substance, but it is the lowest of such substances; to the Aristotelians he can say: Granted that the soul is the form of a natural organic body, granted even that it is therefore a material form, it is nevertheless the highest of all such forms and unique. St. Thomas is determined that he will not compromise man's unity either in nature or in being. For he is suggesting that the soul's role as form of matter is grounded in its very nature as a subsistent intellect, which gives to man both his specific nature and his being, which therefore enables us to speak of man the composite as totally a spiritual being, one who is both in nature and in existence spiritual.

One of the cornerstones of his doctrine on man seems to be the celebrated line: Thus, therefore, we say that in this man there is no other substantial form than the rational soul, and that by it man is not only man, but animal and living being and body and substances and being.[3] St. Thomas is saying something rather startling, namely, that a spiritual substance not only makes man to be man, but makes man to be an animal, makes the human body to be a body, that is to say, makes matter to be material. Now it is not surprising that matter should exist with a material *to be;* but it does seem at first sight rather extraordinary that matter should exist as matter with a spiritual *to be.* Yet that is exactly what he is proposing. For in the same question he declares that every individual thing is actually a being through its form; and since an

---

[2] *Ibid.*   [3] *De Spiritualibus Creaturis* q. 3.

individual thing has unity on the same basis on which it is a being, every individual thing has unity through its form. The unity of man, therefore, as well as his very being, depends on his form, that is to say, on a subsistent, intellectual substance.[4] Thus in the real order the distinction between man's rationality and animality disappears.

> For according as the body is understood as perfected in sensible being by the soul, in this sense is it related to the ultimate perfection which comes from the rational soul as such, as a material element is related to a formal element. But since genus and species signify certain conceptual entities, a real distinction of forms is not needed for the distinction between a species and a genus but only a mental distinction.[5]

Matter, when viewed as perfect in corporeal being, capable of receiving life, is the proper subject of the soul. But that it acquires this perfection is due, not to any corporeal form, but to the specifying and actualizing activity of the rational soul itself.[6] In fact one can say bluntly with St. Thomas: The body is perfected by the soul in corporeal being. That is to say, the human body is made to be body and to be perfected in the order of bodies by an intellectual substance.[7] The human soul, then, is immediately present to the human body, giving it an act of existing, granting it being which is both substantial and specifying, conferring on man at one and the same time his nature, his being, and his unity.

III

Everyone who reads St. Thomas' *Quaestiones de Spiritualibus Creaturis* is aware of St. Thomas' debt to Aristotle. But it becomes equally clear as one reads these questions and also the *Quaestiones de Anima* that there is a dimension in St. Thomas' thinking on man that is lacking in Aristotle's. Strangely enough, the key to the difference is rooted in a text that is borrowed literally from Aristotle by St. Thomas. This is the famous text from Aristotle's

---

[4] *Ibid.*   [5] *Op. cit.,* ad 3m.

[6] *Op cit.,* ad 2m. This is not to suggest that the soul is the efficient cause of the human body; that question is another one entirely and one which does not concern the immediate problem. It does suggest that the human soul is the cause which gives to the human body both its nature as human and its being, and which causes everything material that enters into man, including that which nourishes him physically, to exist as human within a spiritual orbit of being.

[7] *Op. cit.,* ad 4m and ad 14m.

De Anima: Vivere autem viventibus esse est.[8] This text is introduced almost casually into Question One of St. Thomas' *De Anima*,
and its significance could be easily minimized or overlooked; it
serves, however, two purposes: to pose a question and to recall to
the reader's mind all that St. Thomas has had to say elsewhere concerning this Aristotelian phrase.

The question is this: If *vivere viventibus est esse,* if the *to be*
of living things is a *to live,* and if the soul gives to the human composite a *vivere,* what sort of a *vivere* is this, and what kind of an
esse is conferred? A superficial answer at this point would be easy:
the soul possesses and therefore confers a spiritual *esse,* but to this
key question, this facile answer, though true, is worse than no answer. Instead of an answer, one really has a number of new problems: What is a spiritual substance doing in the realm of matter?
What sort of an intellectual substance is the soul if, within the
depths of its nature, there is an imperative demand for its union
with matter? And even more startling perhaps: What sort of a
body is it that exists as a body with a spiritual act of existing? To
solve these problems one needs to turn to numerous texts which
throw light upon this terse philosophical formula. But before
doing that it might be worthwhile to locate this text within the
framework of St. Thomas' solution to Question One of the *De
Anima.*

At the time when St. Thomas disputed in Paris his *Questions
on the Soul,* the University was seething over the question of the
interpretation of Aristotle. Possibly no single topic was so much
mooted as that of "man" himself. One has only to read the propositions condemned in 1270 to realize this and to realize further that
these episcopal censures were aimed principally at a group of men
who are today commonly called Latin Averroists.

St. Thomas, at the beginning of the *De Unitate Intellectus,*
speaks of an error about the human soul which was current in his
time.[9] In this short text St. Thomas refers three times to an *error;*
he does not say *errors.* This error consists in making the intellect
separate from man and one for all men. This error seems to be

---

[8] Aristotle, *On the Soul,* ii. 4. 415 b 12-14. Cf. St. Thomas, *In libros De anima
expositio* II, c. 4, lect. 7.

[9] *De Unitate Intellectus contra Averroistas,* Prooemium. This text will be cited
according to the edition of Leo W. Keeler, S.J., (Rome: Gregorian University, 1946).
The numbers will be those of Keeler's divisions.

St. Thomas' preoccupation in the first three questions of the *De Anima.*

The lines of the doctrinal problem are being sharply drawn. If Averroes and his disciples are correct, then one must deny that any particular man understands for the very obvious reason that no man has an individual intellect. This point cannot be over-emphasized. St. Thomas is not beginning his enquiry from any preconceived or arbitrary definition of man. The bedrock upon which he is' to erect his carefully articulated doctrine is an evident fact, simple and immediate like all evident facts, and so fundamental that to ignore it or to deny its implications would mean yielding the very possibility of success in this philosophical investigation. It is the fact that a man understands and is aware that he understands.[10] To delineate the nature and being of the human soul without doing violence to this fact is St. Thomas' goal.

St. Thomas begins in Question One of the *De Anima* by maintaining in the face of the "materialists" that there is an activity performed by man, namely intellectual understanding, which does not depend on matter. Since a being operates insofar as it has being, and since anything receives its being through its form, the form which is the source of man's being and operation must be a form not immersed in matter like other material forms. In short, it must be an intellectual or spiritual form.

St. Thomas next attacks the "separatist" positions, treating Plato first. His criticisms of Plato's doctrine of man are well known; basically they come to this: By man, in Plato's doctrine, one does not mean the human composite of soul and body, but the soul alone. In order to save the proposition "Man understands," the Platonists are willing to sacrifice the unity of the human composite; this is a sacrifice which St. Thomas in his turn is unwilling to make. The other extreme separatist position is that of Averroes, according to whom—in St. Thomas' interpretation—man does not understand, but rather a separate intellectual substance does. In a limited sense the unity of the composite is saved, but what a composite it is! It is a composite which no longer can claim to be capable of intellectual operations. If the Averroists are correct, the fact that *this man understands* is made impossible, so actually the unity preserved is not that of an intellectual being.

10 Cf. *Scriptum super libros Sententiarum* II, d. 17, q. 2, a. 1. *De Unitate Intellectus*, c. 3, no. 68; cf. nos. 71-79.

St. Thomas locates himself between the materialists who deny that the soul is subsistent and the separatists who locate intellectual understanding in something other than the composite man. His argument can be reduced to its bare essentials: That by which the body lives is the soul. Nor, for living things the act by which they live is the act by which they exist. Therefore, the soul is that by which the human body actually exists. But, St. Thomas continues, that by which anything has existence is its form. The conclusion is inescapable: The human soul is the form of the human body. That there is intellectual operation in man and what this implies have already been developed. We realize, therefore, that this form is a subsistent, intellectual one. St. Thomas has thus established, as on many other occasions, that the rational soul is the form of the human body and that this soul is a self-sustaining being. The uniqueness of this question lies in the way in which St. Thomas relates these two conclusions to each other, as two partial answers to a single question. However, having arrived at that point in the text where he invokes the principle, *Vivere autem est esse viventium,* let us turn aside to examine this text in more detail before following our guide to his final conclusions.

IV

Few texts from Aristotle have been used more frequently by St. Thomas than the closely chiseled phrase: *Vivere viventibus est esse.* No exegesis of it, however, is more explicit and more authoritative than that of the *Summa Theologiae,* I, q. 18, a. 2: Whether life is an operation. In the preceding article St. Thomas has declared that living beings are those which move themselves, understanding motion in a broad metaphysical sense. This brings us to article two, for if life is self-motion, if *vivere* is a *se agere,* does this mean that life is merely an operation? The *Sed Contra* leaves no doubt as to the answer; it is the answer to which the body of the article is but an exegesis: "Sed contra est quod dicit Philosophus in II *De Anima*: 'vivere viventibus est esse.' " Against the objectors who insist that *vivere* is an operation St. Thomas calmly cites Aristotle: "To live, for living things, is to be." This being so, life is an *esse,* not an *operatio.*

In explaining his position, St. Thomas sets down some rather fundamental principles. Our intellect, he says, is made to know the essences of things, but the only way in which it can come to the knowledge of them is through our sense knowledge of the accidents of a being. Now, since we name a thing following the way in which we come to know it, we commonly name things from their accidents, but what we intend to do is to signify their very nature. As a result of this, names can either refer to the substantial essence of something or can refer to the properties or operations from which the names have been derived.

These preliminary remarks enable us to come to grips with the notion of *life, vita*. We call a thing living because of external manifestations, namely that it is moving itself. However, what the name "life" expresses most properly when one refers to the life of something is this: "A substance to which self-movement, or the application of itself to any kind of operation, belongs naturally. *To live,* accordingly, is nothing else than for a substance with such a nature *to be. . . .* Hence living is not an accidental, but a substantial predicate."[11] That is to say, if it is true that a being is called a being from its act of existing, then a living being is said not only to be *that kind* but even *to be* from its act of living.

In considering briefly this text, we have not merely arrived at certain basic conclusions, but we have also had proposed to us a method which will enable us to proceed very far indeed in our study of man's being. If we designate the very substantial *vivere* of man from his operations, and if the proper operation of man is the knowledge of truth, then in order to understand most adequately the being of man, we must locate him in the hierarchy of knowing beings. To do this is tantamount to understanding the grade and the mode of life that is in man.

To understand the relation of the three terms, *esse, vivere* and *intelligere,* to one another, it is necessary to see how St. Thomas begins his analysis at the very lowest level of living beings and finds them resolved into a perfect unity at the highest level of being, in God. Since beings are said to be living because they act of themselves, as distinguished from beings which are moved by others, an important principle can be set down: Since self-motion, that is, motion from an intrinsic principle, is that by which one comes to know life, the more perfectly this principle is intrinsic to the knower, the more perfectly interiorized is the activity of knowing, the more perfect will be the life of that being.

Using this principle, therefore, one can move upward from plants, to animals, to intellectual beings, and finally to God, where

---

[11] *Summa Theologiae* I, q. 18, a. 2.

is found the perfect *vivere*. In other intellectual beings, although
the intellect moves itself to some and even most things, there are
certain first principles which it must accept. It can move itself,
therefore, with respect to some things, but not with respect to all.
"Hence, that being whose act of understanding is its very nature,
and which, in what it naturally possesses, is not determined by another, must have life in the most perfect degree. Such is God; and
hence in Him principally is life."[12]

This same conclusion finds one of its most profound and detailed explanations in the fourth book of the *Summa Contra Gentiles* where St. Thomas treats the generation of the Divine Word;
it is the preamble-to that theological discussion which is of signal
interest to us. The dominating principle of this text is as follows:
Quanto aliqua natura est altior, tanto id quod ex ea emanat, magis
ei est intimum. To paraphrase: The loftier any nature is, the
more that which comes from it is rooted intimately within it. Once
again, as in the *Summa Theologiae*, St. Thomas proceeds upward
through the hierarchy of being. But instead of approaching his
solution from the viewpoint of the interiority of agent, instrument,
and end, here he stresses the three factors involved in intellectual
knowing: the act of understanding (*intelligere*), the thing understood (*res intellecta*), and the formal principle by which the thing
is understood (*intentio intellecta*). As one advances upward from
intellect to intellect, one becomes aware of the progressively decreasing metaphysical distance between these three, until in God
there is the perfect identification of intellect, formal principle, and
object understood.[13]

What purpose does this analysis serve in the solution of our
present problem: Is the act of existing of man an act of understanding, and if so, what sort of an act of understanding? A necessary one, for if *intelligere intelligentibus est esse*, to the extent that
we understand the grade of intellectuality of man, to that extent
we understand his very being. Further, we can come to understand
adequately the intellectuality of man only by contrasting his intellectual life with that of other spiritual beings. The analysis,
moreover, has pointed up several important conclusions: First,
that there are to be found diverse grades of intellectual life. Secondly, in showing that as one moves from the lowest grade of intellectual life to the highest, one finds a greater interiority of ac-

[12] *Sum. Theol.* I, q. 18, a. 3.   [13] *Summa Contra Gentiles* IV, 11.

tivity and actuality and a greater unity in being, terminating in
the transcendent and absolute unity of divine being and self-knowledge. From this we have disengaged a very useful principle: The
inferiority of a grade of intellectual understanding, and therefore
of being, can be known from the metaphysical distance which separates an intellect, its formal principles of knowing, and its object.

V

If, then, what is most distinctive of human life is its intellectuality, it is important to ask St. Thomas at this point what it is that
makes a being to be intellectual. One of his most concise statements
is the following: *Immunitas autem a materia est causa intellectu-
alitatis.*[14] "Freedom from matter is the cause of intellectuality."
Another way of putting it: "It is clear that the immateriality of a
thing is the reason why it is cognitive, and that according to the
mode of immateriality is the mode of cognition."[15] Each point in
St. Thomas' development of this conclusion, found in the *Summa*,
is deserving of separate treatment: the confinedness of those beings
which have no knowledge, their limitation to their single material
form and their inability to transcend it; the unlimitedness, the virtual, if not actual, infinity of immaterial beings; the fact that matter is that which restricts, confines, and limits form. Consequently,
immateriality is the reason that a spiritual being is a knowing being,
and to the degree of its immateriality will correspond the degree
of its intellectuality.

This principle and its application cause no particular difficulty
when applied to purely material beings and purely spiritual beings.
It is easy to see that a purely material being does not possess knowledge; it can be seen also that a purely spiritual being can, by the
very fact of being spiritual, know. What is vastly more perplexing,
however, is to distinguish between various spiritual beings. Human
souls, angels, and God are all alike in this, that they are immaterial.
Yet one is forced to say, following St. Thomas, that since they have
differing degrees of intellectuality, they have differing degrees of
immateriality. The difficulty persists: One cannot say of these
beings that one is more immaterial than another because it possesses less matter, for none of these beings possesses any matter at
all. An angel is not more immaterial than a human soul because
the human soul is more material than an angel; the human soul is
not material at all. We must look elsewhere than at the simple

[14] *Compendium Theologiae,* cap. 27.   [15] *Sum. Theol.* I, q. 14, a. 1.

difference between the material and the immaterial if we wish to
resolve this difficulty. In brief, immaterial beings have no matter.
Therefore, more or less immaterial refers to degrees of being immaterial, and since immateriality and knowing are inseparable,
one could suppose that degrees of immateriality mean degrees of
knowledge. Further, if acts of understanding are our means of
getting at the nature of a knower, then the degree of immateriality
manifested in these acts will lead us to the kind of intellectual life
such a being leads. This is equivalent to knowing the kind of being
such a thing possesses, for *vivere viventibus est esse.*

VI

St. Thomas' various approaches to the problem of the degree
of intellectuality in spiritual beings enable us to see one and the
same conclusion from three different but intimately related vantage
points: immateriality of being, interiority of life, and propinquity
of knowing intellect to the object known and the form or species
which is the means of knowing.

God, who is supremely and infinitely immaterial, without any
shadow of potentiality, is therefore most intellectual and most intelligible. Unable to be affected from without, God's life in source,
operation, and end exists in a perfect and absolutely interior identity. Moreover, in God are identified in an absolutely sublime and
to us an incomprehensible unity of being, the intellect which understands, the object understood, and the principle by which it is
understood.[16] On every count, then, God is most perfectly intellectual, and therefore the closer any created spiritual substance is
to God in its degree of being, the more perfect will be its intellectuality. Next below God, for St. Thomas, are the separate substances, pure spiritual beings, who are less immaterial than God
because in their being and in their intellectual operation potentiality makes its appearance. Their nature, not identified with their
being, is as potency to act in relation to that being, and their knowledge, though created in them and present as part of their natural
endowment, still has this element of potentiality inseparably bound
up with it: an angel is not always actually considering the knowledge it possesses habitually, but needs to move itself to a fully actual
consideration of its knowledge. Each angel, moreover, constitutes
an entire grade of being, and consequently there are as many grades
of immateriality, or as many degrees of increasing potentiality, as

[16] *S. C. G.* IV, 11.

there are pure spirits. Until finally descending, as it were, from
Pure Act, down through manifold levels of being, each of which
progressively contains less act and more potency, one arrives at the
human soul, a spiritual and immaterial substance, too, but the least
immaterial of all spiritual beings; for its power of understanding,
the possible intellect, is by nature in potency to all the intelligibles
that it is proportioned to know, and not at all in act with respect
to them; a being, moreover, whose proper object, the intelligibility
found in sensible things, lies outside it; an intellect which finds
before it an object which is only potentially intelligible to it, an
object which needs to be made actually intelligible; a spirit in
which there is a maximum of distance between the intellectual
power, the objects known, and the species by which it understands
those material things; in short, the lowest and the humblest of
spiritual beings.[17]

This descent from God to man, this falling away, as it were,
from the richest, most actual and most plenary intelligence to that
one which in itself is completely poor, barren, and potential should
raise in one's mind a question. What is the proportioned object of
such an intellect and what is the mode and means by which it perfects itself, through which it can triumph over its native poverty;
for triumph it must if it is to be truly an intellect, for any intellect
as such is open to know all being?

A comparison can make this point more acute. God actually
knows all being and this because in His essence He possesses a principle by which—since it is His *esse* and His *esse* is infinite—He adequately knows all being. The angels do not know all being adequately since they are not infinite; but the closer they are to God,
who knows all things by one likeness, His essence, the fewer are
the likenesses necessary through which an angel knows reality.
That is, through few forms, pure spirits can know many things and
know them well. The humble human intellect, a *rusticus*, a lowly
peasant, dwelling far from the royal court, needs a form which is
like the proper and specific form of the thing known and which
represents only that one thing whose form it is like. That is to say,
the human intellect is restricted to understanding forms of this
kind only—forms that are limited, multiplied, individuated in
matter, that is, the forms of material things. No other answer explains the presence in the human soul of sense powers. It is not the

[17] *In II Sent.* 3, q. 1, a. 6.

nature of spiritual beings as spiritual to have sense powers, otherwise all spirits would have them. Furthermore, sense powers, without sense organs, make no sense; and sense organs are found only
in a body. The conclusion is inevitable: The human soul is of
such a lowly degree of immateriality or spirituality, that it needs
to be united to a body in order to perform its acts of intellection
and to perfect itself as a spiritual being.

VII

Especially satisfying to St. Thomas, in view of the Averroistic
controversies which were rife at Paris at this time, must have been
the embarrassing position in which his doctrine leaves the Latin
Averroists. St. Thomas has insisted that if one looks at the Averroistic man, and focuses his attention, not on the material composite,
but on the intellect, this man becomes a Platonic man. As St.
Thomas expresses it: "Therefore, if the possible intellect is one in
all men as a separate substance, it follows that all men derive their
species from a single separate substance; and this is similar to the
doctrine of ideas and is open to the same difficulty."[18] Nothing
could be more unacceptable to an Averroist certainly than to have
it pointed out to him that his brand of Aristotelianism is reducible
to Platonism. On the other hand, if what the Averroists mean by
man is simply this material composite (intellect not included),
then their position is open to all the charges that St. Thomas levels
against the materialists.

So much for what St. Thomas refuses to hold. What he does
maintain as his own position is more significant. He insists that the
human soul is the form of the body and that the human soul is an
intellectual one. He stoutly defends the doctrine that the form of
a man is a subsistent, concrete being since it has a wholly immaterial operation, intellection. Furthermore, this self-subsisting
soul, whose existential act is a spiritual one, an intellectual one,
communicates this existential actuality to the matter it informs in
order that the human being be made complete and be able to carry
on intellectual cognition.[19]

It is to relieve its own native poverty, then, that the soul communicates its own existential act to the body. By nature the lowest
of intellectual creatures, the human soul must seek in union with
matter the means of its full perfection, both on the level of being
and on the level of action. This incompleteness of the soul is often

[18] *De Anima,* q. 3.
[19] *Op. Cit.,* q. 1, ad 7m.

taken to mean merely that the soul, apart from the body, cannot carry on its proper activity, which is to know the truth; since the soul is proportioned to knowing truth adequately only by means of phantasms, it needs to be united to a body.[20] There is a more basic answer even than this, however. No part is truly perfect when separated from the whole of which it is a part; now, the human soul is a part of man, part of human nature, and hence never has its own nature perfectly except when united to a body. For although something may have that actuality which is required for it to be subsistent, if it contains virtualities which are not actually realized, then it is not complete nor perfect in being. This is true of the human soul, for it has such virtuality that powers that are the acts of organs stem from it, and only while it is actually joined to a body as its form are those virtual powers reduced to act. Thus, when separated, it does not have the fullness nor the perfection of its own nature.[21] On the level of operation, the human soul is still more obviously deficient, for unless it be joined to the body it cannot seek those particulated and manifold means by which it overcomes its lowliness, which serve as a remedy for its native insufficiency, those intelligibles which are proportioned to such a lowly and humble intellect, that is to say, the intelligibles immersed in matter.

This natural incapacity of the soul alone either to be or to achieve itself perfectly is the hallmark of its lowliness in the hierarchy of spiritual substances, a diminished intellectual being. Nevertheless, it is intellectual and in seeking to realize itself it confers on the body a spiritual act of existing.

St. Thomas is explicit in stating that there is but one existential act for the entire human composite: It is necessary, if the soul is the form of the body, that there be one *esse* for soul and body, and this is the *esse* of the composite.[22] He is no less explicit that this *esse* belongs primarily to the soul: Although the soul has a complete *esse*, it does not follow therefore that the body is united accidentally to the soul, because that *esse* which belongs to the soul *is communicated* to the body so that there is one *esse* for the whole composite.[23] No less emphatic is St. Thomas that this existential act is of such nobility that the body cannot share in it fully. Emi-

[20] *Op. cit.*, q. 1, Sed contra 2. [21] *De Spiritualibus Creaturis*, q. 2, ad 5m.
[22] *de Anima*, q. 1, ad 13m. [23] *Op. cit.*, q. 1, ad 1m.

nently communicable, the existence which the soul confers on the
body utterly exceeds the capacity of matter.[24]

Here we are once again at the heart of that profound mystery
which is man: this composite being, spirit and matter, in which
even the matter, though an organized body, exists with no corporeal, no bodily act of existing, but with a spiritual one. How
best to name this creature? How best to call attention to the degree
of being that is his? Surely not by locating him neatly and univocally in the genus of animals. For there is about man's being far
more of spirit than of matter, and our goal must be to locate man,
not logically (for logically we can locate him in many genera), but
in the existential órder of reality. What is man's form? A subsistent
spirit. What is his existential act? A spiritual one. What quickens
his body with life, with sense and intellect? What, in short, makes
his body to be a human one, his operations those of a man? Once
again the answer is clear and inescapable: an intellectual or spiritual
substance. What sort of *being*, then, is man, if he exists with a
spiritual act of existing and is made to be the kind of being he is
through a spiritual substance? What can one say but that even in
his materiality man is totally and adequately a spiritual being, for
being (*ens*) does not bespeak quiddity but only the act of existing,
and man's act of existing is that of a spirit.[25]

Nor, does it seem to me, can there be any doubt as to where one
must turn to understand most profoundly the nature of man. One
does not turn to the animal kingdom and ask why one animal out
of all others should be in possession of truly spiritual powers. Man
is not an animal, quickened into rationality by something from
without. The difference that makes man to be distinctively human
is located in the depths of his spiritual substance. What is it?
Which of us knows since for us essential differences are unknown
and unnamed and can merely be designated by accidental differences, as a cause is designated by its effect.[26] Turn, rather, to the
innumerable host of spiritual substances and ask why the human
soul differs from all other spirits. St. Thomas does not speak here
of rationality nor of intellectuality as the basic difference. Somewhat surprisingly he chooses as the distinguishing marks *unifiable*

[24] *Op. cit.*, q. 1, ad 17m, ad 18m, and end of corpus.
[25] *In* I *Sent.* d. 8, q. 4, a. 2, ad 2m: Ens autem non dicit quidditatem, sed solum
actum essendi, cum sit principium ipsum.
[26] *In II Sent.* d. 3, q. 1, a. 6.

to a body and *not unifiable*. These "differences," rooted deep in the nature of spiritual substances, be they angels or human souls, issue into actions that differ, issue, too, into the fact that souls need to be united to bodies and that angels cannot be so joined. Whatever the difference is, it is not something extraneous to these spiritual subsisting forms; it is something in the structure of their being as spirits that makes the one capable of spiritual self-perfection without the aid of matter, and forces the other both to be and to become itself fully as incarnate in a body that it transcends and transforms. This difference, ultimately unknown to us as it is, is what makes a man to be a man, that makes human life, the human *vivere*, to be in the deepest and most complete sense of the word an *intelligere*. That is to say, for man, as for all spiritual beings, even though he be an incarnate spirit, *intelligere est esse*.

That this is St. Thomas' constant teaching seems certain. In the *Scriptum* he states that *to understand* includes *to live*, just as *to live* includes *to be*, and these are not reducible to diverse principles but to one. *Intelligere* is *vivere; vivere* is *esse*.[27]

In the *Summa Theologiae*, he makes a distinction between two meanings of the word *intelligere;* sometimes, he remarks, words such as "to sense" or "to understand" are taken to refer to operations, and sometimes they can mean the very "to be" of those who are acting.[28] In his *De Spiritualibus Creaturis* he spells this point out in detail. The human soul, he declares, insofar as it is essentially the form of the body, gives *esse* to the body. This it does insofar as it is the substantial form of man. However, insofar as it is a soul, it gives an *esse* of a particular kind, namely, a *vivere*, a "to live." Moreover, insofar as it is an intellective soul, it confers a *vivere* that is of a special type, namely, *vivere in intellectuali natura*, "to live in an intellectual nature." That *vivere in intellectuali natura* means *intelligere* the following sentence makes clear. *Intelligere* he goes on, can be used in two ways. Sometimes it refers to an operation, the action of understanding, and then it arises from a power or a habit. Sometimes, however, and this is the meaning that interests us here, it means the very existential act of an intellectual nature and only in this second sense is its principle the very essence of the intellective soul.[29]

27 *In I Sent.* d. 2, q. 1, a. 1, ad 1m. Cf. *In I Sent.,* d. 3, q. 2, a. 3.
28 *Sum. Theol.* I, q. 18, a. 2, ad 1m.
29 *De Spiritualibus Creaturis*, q. 11, obj. 14 and ad 14m.

In a later work, his *De Substantiis Separatis*, St. Thomas makes the same point. In this work St. Thomas is primarily concerned to treat of angels, but he says many things which apply with equal force to the human soul since it is an immaterial substance. The text is found in a context similar to that of the argument of the *De Spiritualibus Creaturis*—the plurality of forms. St. Thomas declares: In immaterial substances that which is their "to be" is their "to live," nor is their "to live" anything other than an "intellective to be."[30]

It seems absolutely necessary, therefore, to read any of his texts which refer the principle *Vivere viventibus est esse* to man, as though the text read: *Intelligere intelligentibus est esse*. In fact, this reading of the text illumines many another passage. The fact that the *esse* of the composite being man is an *esse intellectivum* or an *intelligere* goes a long way toward making it clear why the human body as such can never fully share in the existence of the soul, even though the body's total existence is from the soul. More important, however, it removes the apparent difficulty in seeing how man—and not merely the soul—is located on the confines of two worlds, the world of spirit and the world of matter. He belongs there because he exists in his totality and in his compositeness through an act of existence which is wholly intellectual.

The incompleteness of the human soul has already been indicated and the avenue for its completion, union with a body, pointed out. What needs to be reemphasized is that not merely the human soul but man himself is incomplete. Each being in the universe, since it is of a determined kind, is limited to the extent that it is only itself and *is not* all other things. A remedy, in the words of St. Thomas, has been provided, however, a remedy by which some beings at least, namely, knowers, can overcome the handicap of their initial insufficiency. For by knowledge it is possible that the perfection of the entire universe exist in one thing. This was the dream of the philosophers—that in the human soul, that is to say, in man as intellectual knower, might be inscribed the total order of the universe and its causes. They were right in this ambition, St. Thomas continues, but erred in insisting that such knowledge was the ultimate end of man, whereas the Christian knows that man will find his perfect achievement in the vision of God, because

[30] "De Substantiis Separatis," 9, in *Opuscula Philosophica* ed. Joannes Perrier, O.P., (Paris: 1949), 1, 164.

according to Gregory, "What is it that they do not see who see Him who sees all things."[31]

Here it is that intellect inserts itself, for corresponding to the orders of immateriality are found the orders of knowing, and only an intellect, free from all conditions of matter, is capable of knowing all being. But within this intellectual self-healing which is man's peculiar way of transcending the limitations of his pettiness is located a mode and a means of knowing that illumines the kind of reality that man is. For man, in order to know and thereby to become more and more fully all of reality, must take a hand in the process, and I use the word "hand" advisedly. Man must make his knowledge and his truth. He finds himself with a weak and lowly intellectual power, though with sense organs to relieve this impoverishment, in a world of things that are only potentially intelligible to him—the lowliest of intellectual knowers, the lowliest of knowable objects, potentiality everywhere like a murky sea. But inserted in him is a spark of the divine,[32] the agent intellect, and through this power man must make, step by step, through shadow and time, the intelligible acts which are to release him gradually but definitely from this world of shadow into a world of light. Unless he does this work, it will not be done; unless he applies the remedy, he will remain enclosed within the limits of his own meager being, "cabined, cribbed, confined." But let him go to work, making his truth, restless for more and more of reality, and in a certain and profoundly true sense, infinity is opening before him.

Man the maker. This phrase is more true than we have thought. It is not merely by way of metaphor that St. Thomas links so frequently the human intellect and human hands.[33] The relation is a profound one and is intimately connected with man as an incarnate spirit who makes his truth. The work of man's hands, conjoined with the human intellect, and engaged in the world of matter about him, is all that is material in human civilization, good or bad. A Hermes of Praxiteles, a Christ by Epstein, a horn cup for ale, the china of Sevres, the tenement houses, the Cathedral of Chartres, the wine that joys the soul of man, the heroin that en-

[31] *Quaestiones disputatae: De veritate*, q. 2, a. 2..

[32] In his *Commentary on the Epistle of St. Paul to the Romans*, cap. V, lectio 3, St. Thomas does not hesitate to call the human soul "divine": ". . . propter divinitatem animae rationalis."

[33] For example, *In II Sent.* Prologus; *In II Sent.* d. 1, q. 2, a. 5, ad 3m; *In II Sent.* d. 3, q. 3, a. 1, ad 1m; *De veritate* q. 22, a. 7; *Sum. Theol.* I-II, q. 5, a. 5, ad 1m.

slaves—all the works of the hands of men reveal not only the fecund creativity of human spirit, but in some way the very intelligibility of the real, as we come to know better the potency of marble after seeing what the causality of a Michelangelo effects. Here is the level where the lines of the conflict, crucial in our time, between the natural and the artificial seem to be drawn. They may be opposed, but not necessarily so, surely. If properly understood and related to man's spiritual needs, the artificial can serve further to unveil the intelligibility of the natural.

Here, too, is the point where intelligibility incarnate in matter meets spirit incarnate in human flesh; this is the point where the moral issues which the material world poses arise. For it is through its relation to man, incarnate spirit, and his end, the direct vision of God, that all material aspects of culture (and our civilization is inseparable from matter) need to be transformed and spiritualized. If this culture serves, in the most humble way, the enlargement of human life and happiness, order is preserved and that peace which is its tranquillity. But let these material things become ends, instead of means of a transcendent spiritual purpose, and we have a serious disorientation, one of the perversions of reality so common in our time, truly a sin against nature, the nature of man as knower, the nature of things as knowable.

At this same point is situated the role of history in human life. One can even say, this is the only place where there is history. For of all spiritual beings, man is the only one who has a history, man who through space and time works out his destiny step by step to achieve his end. The incarnation of spiritual substance which is man, his very existence, an *esse* that is a *tendere*, but a special kind of *tendere*, namely, an intellectual one, an *intelligere*, provides, therefore, the natural basis upon which the supernatural transformation of history, likewise an Incarnation, the Word made flesh, was erected.

All this, it seems to me, and no doubt a great deal more, is included in St. Thomas' commitment that the *to be* of man is a *to understand*. In an Aristotelian age (and the phrase is St. Thomas' own),[34] he had set out to solve an Aristotelian problem on the constitution of man. Without yielding any of the cardinal points of Aristotle's metaphysics or psychology, but rather by placing the problem and its solution within the framework of his own meta-

[34] *In III Sent.* d. 5, q. 3, a. 2.

physics of being, St. Thomas seems to have preserved both the substantial unity of man and the subsistent actuality of the intellective soul. In doing so, he avoided what the Platonists of his time feared most of all, the debasing of man to the stature of a material being. Instead, he used the psychology of the Philosopher to locate the human soul and to situate man himself at a point in reality to which even the Platonists could not object; that is, among the spiritual substances. Man may be the lowest of intellectual substances, but he has full claim to citizenship in their kingdom.

But if St. Thomas' doctrine of the nature of man and his being seemed to him to answer a contemporary doctrinal need, it was only because it represented for him a genuine and a sound explanation of certain irreducible facts. Faced with the obvious fact of man's operation of intellectual understanding, and with the equally evident fact of man's dependence upon the imagination for the source of his intellectual activity from the side of its specification and perfection, St. Thomas made no compromise on the unity of the nature or on the unity of the being which underlay both facts. Unity of nature (intellectual even in its materiality, for matter exists in a spiritual orbit and for a spiritual end), unity of act of existing (*esse est intelligere*), unity of being—these must all be accounted for. His explanation of man respects all of these unities. Wholly intellectual, man seems almost to be a creature of another world, and in a sense he is, for his source is there and his end; but since in his very intellectuality his soul is ordered toward matter, he is never totally a stranger in this world. To attain his ultimate perfection through the operations of intellect and will, that is, to fulfill his destiny as a being whose *esse* is an *intelligere,* man must use the material things of this earth on which he finds himself. That the humblest things of this world are here to serve all men in the attainment of their ultimate perfection as spiritual substances is a lesson of permanent value; that man is wholly spiritual even in his bodiliness is another lesson of special significance today. These are lessons which are written clearly and pointedly across the pages of the *Quaestiones De Anima* of St. Thomas Aquinas.

ဒ္ဓ The Evidence Grounding
Judgments of Existence

by Robert W. Schmidt, S.J.

☆ ☆ ☆ ☆ .☆ ☆ ☆ ☆ ☆ ☆ ☆ ☆ ☆ ☆

IN HIS LONG and fruitful career as a philosopher and teacher our esteemed jubilarian, Etienne Gilson, has illuminated many topics and shown others what paths to pursue. Among the points of doctrine that have received most attention and emphasis from him, four in particular furnish the guideposts for this paper. Two pertain to metaphysics and two are more directly epistemological. First, there is the central role in metaphysics played by the act of existing.[1] Then there is the dynamic character of this act.[2] From epistemology there is the doctrine that existence is attained explicitly only in judgment,[3] and then the doctrine that the knowledge of the existence of sensible things is immediate.[4]

[1] "Existence and Philosophy," *Proceedings of the American Catholic Philosophical Association*, XXI (1946), 4-16; *Being and Some Philosophers*, (2nd ed.; Toronto: Pontifical Institute of Mediaeval Studies, 1952), pp. 2-5, 160-89, 209, 212-15; *L'être et l'essence* (Paris: J. Vrin, 1948), pp. 10-11, 19-20, 117-20, chap. 10, and concl., esp. pp. 319-28; *The Christian Philosophy of St. Thomas Aquinas* (New York: Random House, 1956), chap. 1 and pp. 363-72; *God and Philosophy* (New Haven: Yale University Press, 1946), pp. 63-72, 138-44, esp. p. 67: "a decisive metaphysical progress or, rather, a true metaphysical revolution was achieved when someone began to translate all the problems concerning being from the language of essences into that of existences. . . . Metaphysics has regularly lost its very existence every time it has lost its existentiality."

[2] *Being and Some Philosophers*,[2] chap. 5 and pp. 5, 192-93, 200-203, and appendix, pp. 228-32; *L'être et l'essence*, chap. 3 and pp. 288-89; *The Christian Philosophy of St. Thomas Aquinas*, pp. 32-35, 41-45, 91-92, 368-71; *God and Philosophy*, chap. 2, esp. pp. 63-72; *Réalisme thomiste et critique de la connaissance* (Paris: J. Vrin, 1947), pp. 219-22.

[3] *Being and Some Philosophers*, chap. 6, esp. pp. 201-5, 209; *L'être et l'essence*, chap. 9 and pp. 286-89; *Réalisme thomiste*, chap. 8; *The Christian Philosophy of St. Thomas Aquinas*, pp. 40-42, 44, 232, 374.

[4] *Le réalisme méthodique* (Paris: Téqui, 1936), esp. chaps. 1, 2, and 4; *Réalisme*

Although the first of these points sets the stage for the present investigation, it will not enter directly into the discussion but will rather be taken for granted. The relationship of the other three points will be considered.

It is not the intention of this inquiry to demonstrate the truth of these points. That will rather be assumed as already established by Professor Gilson or by the philosopher whom he professes to be interpreting, St. Thomas Aquinas. Neither is it the intention to establish textually that Professor Gilson or St. Thomas held these doctrines. Historical questions will be pretermitted, and a philosophical study will be undertaken.

If we grant that existence is of primary importance in metaphysics, and, therefore, in all philosophy, then it is also of great importance to investigate our knowledge of existence. For philosophy is a science and, as such, must be not only knowledge but also reflective knowledge; that is, we must be aware of what we know, the fact that he know it, and how we know it.

If we admit that existence is known expressly only in judgment, since the judgment that something exists cannot be purely gratuitous but must be based upon evidence, it devolves upon us to inquire what that evidence is. It is not difficult to see that somehow this evidence must be found in sense knowledge because all of our knowledge begins in our senses. But it is neither necessary nor possible that the evidence should be exactly the same in all cases. Some of the objects of our knowledge will be directly presented in sensation; others will not, whether it is because they are by nature immaterial and non-sensible or because, though material and sensible, they are not actually perceived. For the existence of non-sensible beings, the evidence cannot be directly and immediatly sensible but yet must be reduced to the evidence of our senses. For beings sensible in themselves but actually not sensed, the case is similar since they are by supposition not perceived by the senses. For the existence of actually sensed beings, however, the evidence is sensible, not just mediately but immediately; their existence need not be reduced to that of something else but is known in itself directly and without discourse or reasoning. This immediate evi-

thomiste, chaps. 7 and 8, esp. pp. 187-90, 196-203, 210, 226-27; Being and Some Philosophers, pp. 206-7; L'être et l'essence, pp. 249-49, 305-6; The Christian Philosophy of St. Thomas Aquinas, pp. 215-17, 233.

dence of the existence of sensible things, then, is the primary evidence for judgments of existence.

Granted that the evidence for existence is found in sense knowledge, two further questions arise. If existence is a dynamic act, what must the sense evidence be to manifest existence under this guise? And exactly what is the evidence for existence which is, in fact, found in sense knowledge? These are the questions which this paper will most directly investigate and attempt to answer.

In regard to sensible things, once it has been acknowledged that their existence is self-evident and immediately known, does nothing further need be said on the matter? Are we thereby dispensed from any further inquiry into this evidence? By no means. Regarding the immediately known we may inquire in what the knowledge of it consists and on what it is based. And regarding its self-evidence we may still ask in just what the evidence consists and how it is presented to us. Philosophy is necessarily reflective. Epistemology undertakes the reflective examination and analysis of the motives for assent. In an epistemological investigation even immediate evidence must be pointed out, described, and detailed. Philosophy does not steer away from the "obvious" and the "elementary." Because it is concerned with basic causes, it must deal with the elementary; and because it is concerned with primary principles, it must concern itself with what is obvious. Nor does the obviousness of certain truths make their consideration otiose. The obvious is all too often overlooked and neglected. And if it is taken into account at all, there is always the danger that different observers will not see the obvious in exactly the same way and will, in fact, disagree in their conception of it. Then, when they take propositions that they consider obvious and make them the tacit assumptions of their discussions, if they do not make clear exactly what their assumptions are, confusion can easily result. The clarification of one's assumptions or of the supposed "obvious" requires reflection and analysis—reflective analysis or analytical reflection.

In the case of the self-evidence ascribed to the existence of sensible things, which is to be made the starting point and basis of all philosophy, there is particular need to examine it very carefully and point out exactly what the evidence is. There is, of course, no question of demonstrating the self-evident in the proper sense of demonstration. But there can and should be indication, description, and explication. If the evidence for an intellectual judgment of existence is to be found in sense perception, there must be attained in that perception something which the intellect recognizes or interprets as existence or as revealing existence. Just what is it? And if existence is to be interpreted as dynamic—the basic act or essential activity of a being—this dynamism and activity must somehow be manifested in sensation. Just what is manifested there, and how is it manifested?

Reflective analysis reveals that there are different levels of evidence in sense perception, all conducive to knowldge but not all equally indicative of existence, especially as dynamic.

The first level of evidence and the most widely recognized (for it is accepted by all philosophers except the most absolute sceptics) is formal determination, a definite suchness, or the presence of determinate sensible forms or "qualities." Our sensation is clearly determined by such characters as a definite color and shape, a sound of a certain pitch and intensity, a certain odor or flavor, relative hardness or softness, smoothness or roughness, heat or cold. These characters give specification to our sensing and constitute a definite object or definite objects of our knowledge. But if the evidence is restricted to this formal determination alone, there is not yet any proper evidence of existence. Determinateness is, to be sure, necessary for existence; but existence is something over and above this. It is, therefore, not manifested in pure determinateness. When we grasp such determinations, we grasp "objects" which are not properly things; we know determinations, but do not know them as beings or as belonging to beings. But there is as yet no revelation of what is characteristic of existence itself.

This level of sensible evidence, if taken exclusively, yields a doctrine of pure phenomenalism.[5] "Phenomena" are attained in

5 "The theory that all knowledge is limited to phenomena ... and that we cannot penetrate to reality in itself." J. M. Baldwin, (ed.), *Dictionary of Philosophy and Psychology* (New York: Macmillan Co., 1928), II, 288b; "A doctrine which holds that men can know only phenomena and not things in themselves," André Lalande, (ed.), *Vocabulaire technique et critique de la philosophie,* (5th ed.; Paris: Presses Universitaires de France, 1947), p. 745 b; and "phenomenon" is defined as "that which appears to consciousness, that which is perceived" or (in the Kantian sense) "anything that is an 'object of possible experience,' that is, everything that appears in time or in space," (*ibid.,* pp. 746-47). As Jules Lachelier puts it, "a phenomenon is ... the pure sensible given prior to any intervention of the self," (*ibid.,* p. 746). This is the equivalent of "content of consciousness" given under the second sense of "phenomenon" in Rudolf Eisler, (ed.), *"Handwörterbuch der Philosophie,* (2nd ed.; ed. by R. Müller-Freienfels, Berlin: Mittler, 1922), p. 479. Cf. A. J. Ayer, *Philosophical Essays* (London: Macmillan Co., 1954), chap. 6, "Phenomenalism," p. 162; G. F.

knowledge; that is, we grasp a definite formal content of knowledge, certain determinate characters or sets of characters. But since by supposition nothing further reveals itself to us, there is no indication in this formal content whether it has any status apart from our knowledge; it is neither distinguished from our cognitive activity and ourselves nor yet identified with them, because only a formal content is given and this does not include us or our cognitive activity. Thus, even the "objects" are not attained formally as objects because they are not known as opposed to the knower or "thrown up before" him.

. It might at first appear that from this phenomenalistic evidence at least the existence of our knowledge is known, even if no existence apart from this is evidenced. But if knowledge is taken to mean the activity of a knower, this would be quite beyond the evidence that is supposedly had; for the formal content of which we are aware is not the cognitive activity in which it is in fact found. Only if knowledge is taken to mean the content itself, can its existence be held in any sense to be manifested. But what could existence mean in that case? It could not in any way mean an independent status of the object of our knowledge apart from our awareness; it could not mean its status within our awareness, which is not itself known. It could at most mean the bare presence to awareness, the fact of being before our consideration, but with the awareness or consideration itself remaining out of consciousness.[6] Existence could thus be at best a pure presence or beforeness of a formal content or set of formal determinations.[7] At this level, accordingly,

Stout, "Phenomenalism," *Proceedings of the Aristotelian Society*, n.s. XXXIX (1938-39), 6; D. G. C. Macnabb, "Phenomenalism," *ibid.*, XLI (1940-41), 67-68.

[6] Berkeley's *esse est percipi* would seem to fall here. So too, J. S. Mill, *System of Logic*, (9th ed.; London: Longmans, Green, 1875), I, 113, n.; Shadworth Hodgson, *The Metaphysics of Experience* (London: Longmans, Green, 1898), I, 61 and 454; W. P. Montague, *The Ways of Knowing* (New York: Macmillan Co., 1948), p. 324. Cf. G. E. Moore, *Philosophical Studies* (London: Routledge & Kegan Paul, 1948), p. 72.

[7] This seems to be the meaning of Alexander Bain, "The Meaning of 'Existence' and Descartes' 'Cogito,'" in *Dissertations on Leading Philosophical Topics* (London: Longmans, Green, 1903), p. 4: "I contend . . . that, for the meaning of 'Existence,' we need always refer to some of the other attributes of things; that, as an independent attribute, it is devoid of all real standing." See F. W. Thomas, "Existence and Conventional Existence," *Proceedings of the Aristotelian Society*, n.s. XXVI (1925-26), 97-99: "There is a sense in which every presentation exists, namely as a presentation; and similarly every presented content exists as such. . . . It is not a fact that all presentations are accompanied by an I-consciousness. We constantly have experiences from which all duality of subject and object, all 'awareness,' seems to be absent. . . . For, if I am aware of something, I am not usually aware of that awareness."

there can scarcely be said to be any proper evidence for existence itself as such.

There is a second level of evidence in sense knowledge which is not entirely unlike the first but yet goes considerably beyond it. On this level the evidence is the presentedness of things. This is like the first-level evidence in that the evidence consists in presence in either case. But it differs from the first in several respects. First of all, what is present is not a mere formal content by itself, abstractly and absolutely given, but a thing or concrete subject of multiple determinations.[8] Secondly, it is an *object*, not just materially, as on the first level, but formally; that is, it not only happens to be an object of our knowledge but is known as an object.[9] Thirdly, this object is recognized to have a status in reality independent of our knowledge and in some sense external to the knower.[10] And fourthly, it is seen to have a definite situation in space and time.[11]

For this second level of sense evidence it is clear that more is required than the mere awareness of a formal determination or several different ones in isolation. For the concrete perception of an object as a "thing," various formal characters must be perceived together (whether directly grasped in their present togetherness, as color, shape, and expanse, or associated by means of memory and experience from the past, as a colored shape, hardness, and a sound) and referred to a single focal point or subject as the bearer of these characters. The proper sensibles are given as concretized in the

8 *Ibid.*, pp. 102-4, 107; G. E. Moore, *Some Main Problems of Philosophy* (London: Allen and Unwin, 1953), pp. 84-86, 300-301, 347-49, 375; *Philosophical Studies*, pp. 226-27; H. H. Price, *Perception*, (2nd ed.; London: Methuen, 1950), pp. 35, 38-39, 168-69, 176-77, 218-72 (where he speaks of"*families* of sense-data") 318-21; R. W. Sellars, *The Philosophy of Physical Realism* (New York: Macmillan Co., 1932), pp. 86-88, 209.

9 Thomas, *op. cit.*, pp. 102-3, 115; Moore, *Some Main Problems*, pp. 31-32, 49; *Philosophical Studies*, pp. 70-72; Price, *op. cit.*, pp. 49, 122-23; Montague, *op. cit.*, p. 392; Sellars, *op. cit.*, pp. 74-76, 92-93, 221.

10 *Ibid.*, pp. 76-78, esp. p. 77: "The thing . . . is external to the act and independent of it"; W. P. Montague, "Current Misconceptions of Realism," *Journal of Philosophy*, IV (1907), 100; *The Ways of Things* (New York: Prentice-Hall, 1940), pp. 236-40; *Ways of Knowing*, pp. 329-30, 374, 381, 392-394; Thomas, *op. cit.*, pp. 103-4; Moore, *Some Main Problems*, p. 300; Price, *op. cit.*, pp. 49, 122-23, 274-75, 321.

11 Montague, *Ways of Knowing*, pp. 110-11, 118, 294: "To be real, or to exist, is to have position in space and time"; Thomas, *op. cit.*, p. 101; Bain, *op. cit.*, p. 5; F. H. Bradley, *The Principles of Logic*, (2nd ed.; Oxford: Oxford University Press, 1922), I, 44; Moore, *Philosophical Studies*, p. 76; *Some Main Problems*, pp. 39, 128; Price, *op. cit.*, pp. 239-52, 271-72.

common sensibles; and these are similarly given as concrete, and, therefore, implicitly as in a subject. Thus a group of sense data are apprehended together as belonging to a single subject and as constituting with it a concrete whole. For the recognition of a content of knowledge as an object, we must have an awareness not only of the content but also of our knowing in order that the content may be seen as "thrown up before" our cognitive activity, opposed to it, and distinguished from it. This requires reflection upon our operation of knowing. And since there is question here of a sensible object and of sense knowledge, the reflection must take place on the sense level. From the opposition between the operation of knowing and its content or object, the independent status of the thing known is recognized. It is by that fact seen to be "outside" ourselves and thus in a general way situated spatially. It is implicitly situated temporally because it is given as contemporaneous with the activity of knowing. For a more definite situation in space and time the thing known must be seen in relation to surrounding things. The content of our knowledge must therefore be known, not just absolutely, but relatively also, that is, in relationship both to the knower and to other things known.

It must be understood, of course, that the knowledge of the sense object explicitly as a "thing" or a "subject of determinations," as an "object," as standing independently, and as related in space and time is not had in our senses themselves, but is the result of understanding or intellectual interpretation. But this interpretation by the intellect is grounded in the evidence presented by the senses, as has been pointed out.

Now what sort of notion of existence could be derived from this level of sense evidence? What could our intellect interpret existence to be? Existence or "to be" would have to mean "to be there" (like the etymological meaning of the German *Dasein*), that is, to be before us for our consideration, to be an object of knowing and at the same time independent of the knowing itself, to be situated in the "objective" or real world, and this in a determinate fashion relative to the other occupants of this world. It is a concrete determinate presence; it is the givenness of things. This is certainly more of a notion of existence than can be derived from the first level of sense evidence explained above, but it is still very inadequate. It is a purely static notion and has none of the dynamism that Professor Gilson has shown to belong to the act of existing. On such evidence, too, it would seem that a spectator theory of knowledge would be sufficient. Knowledge could be merely the confrontation of a thing known and a knower, with no activity on the part of the thing known and none or little on the part of the knower. Room might perhaps be left for the knower to engage in a little activity of arranging and organizing sense data into a single concrete whole, but that would be about all. Knowledge could scarcely be given any causal explanation, and the thing known could hardly be understood except in a formal or essentialistic way. At most its essential structure might be grasped, but its actuality would remain quite unattained. Existence would not be something to take into account in the constitution of things. It would have to be presupposed; but, once supposed, it would no longer need to be considered in philosophy, even in that part of philosophy which is expressly concerned with being, metaphysics.[12]

What further evidence would be required if existence is to be known as dynamic? The thing to be known must present itself dynamically and actively. It must not only be given or presented, but it must *present itself* and do so through its own activity, an activity which must have an influence upon the knower. The knower must get into the stream of the activity of the sensible object, be affected by it, and be in some sense passive in regard to it. This activity must be *action* in the strict sense, as it is understood in the special Aristotelian category of that name; it must be the exercise of efficient causality. Professor Gilson has pointed out the intimate relationship between efficient causality and existence.[13] And he has dropped a brief hint, without much development, of the role of efficient causality and of operation in our knowledge of existence.[14] Efficient causality not only brings about existence in the effect, but must proceed from the act of existing of the agent; for nothing can act except in so far as it actually exists; and its existence, being dynamic and an active energy, flows out into an operation that brings about existence in another being. Thus, efficient causality manifests the existence of the cause and does so in a dy-

12 Cf. Gilson, *Being and Some Philosophers,* p. 5.
13 *Ibid.,* pp. 168, 172; *The Christian Philosophy of St. Thomas Aquinas,* pp. 178-79, and esp. n. 14, p. 468; *God and Philosophy,* p. 131, n. 12; *The Spirit of Mediaeval Philosophy* (New York: Scribner's, 1940), pp. 94-95.
14 *The Christian Philosophy of St. Thomas Aquinas,* p. 468, n. 14; *Le thomisme,* (5th ed.; Paris: J. Vrin, 1947), p. 252, n. 2.

namic fashion.[15] A sensible being which acts upon our senses presents itself to us through its action and activity. From this dynamic self-presentation the sensible thing can be interpreted by the intellect as existing, and existence or "to be" can be interpreted as a dynamic act and the basic activity of a being as a being.

Such evidence is, in fact, had in sense knowledge, and this constitutes the third level of evidence. It is not properly a higher level of evidence; not something superadded to the other two levels; rather it is a more profound level which underlies the other two, grounding them. Things are presented or given because they actively present themselves. And there are definite formal determinations in sensation because sensible things present themselves through formally determinate activity. Thus, the first level of sensible evidence is more superficial than the second, and the second more than the third.

This third level of evidence must now be carefully examined and analyzed in order that we may see exactly what it comprises and what basis it gives us for our judgments of existence. Although evidence is properly objective and belongs to things and propositions, being the clarity with which objects of knowledge manifest themselves to a knower, yet it is essentially relative to the knower, since it is always evidence for someone and becomes evidence formally and actually only when the thing manifested is perceived. Evidence must, therefore, be viewed from the standpoint of the knower. We must ask how the thing manifests itself to him. In the present discussion the object of knowledge in question is not the sensible thing merely as a thing but its existence. The pertinent question, then, is how the existence of a sensible thing manifests itself to the one sensing. Naturally it is through his sensation or sense perception. It is accordingly necessary, if we are to understand how the existence of the thing manifests itself, to bear in mind the nature of sensing. When we sense, we "receive an impression" and "are affected by a stimulus" not only corporally but cognitively. The sensible thing acts upon a specially adapted organ, which is af-

[15] The connection between efficient causality and existence has been observed by Hodgson (*op. cit.*, p. 457: "the term [existence] has a fourth meaning: . . . This is reality in the fullest sense that we can conceive; reality in the sense of *efficiency*, as well as in that of simple existence"), by Bradley (*op. cit.*, pp. 44-45), by Moore, (*Some Main Problems*, p. 229), and by Thomas (*op. cit.*, p. 104: "it is likely that the idea of practical efficacy, causality, is also included in the concept of every physical existent"), but all have failed to arrive at the full notion of existence as a basic dynamic act.

fected and undergoes modification; and at the same time the soul, as informing and vivifying that organ and making it capable of receiving the impressions into its own vital activity, apprehends the thing affecting the organ; that is, the soul in conjunction with the organ undergoes a modification or "receives an impression" which is supercorporeal (and in this respect immaterial), and thus the knower becomes aware of the thing under the particular sensible aspect according to which the thing is affecting the organ and the sense power. Sensing is, therefore, essentially passive; it is a type of undergoing or being affected. The sensible being acts with efficient causality upon the sense organ (as by reflecting to the eye light of a definite wave length, by vibrating at a certain audible frequency and communicating this vibration to the air in the vicinity of the ear, or by heating the hand laid upon it). The sense organ is now physically modified under the action of the sensible thing (as the nerve ends in the retina are given an impulse of the wave length of the reflected light which falls upon the eye, or the tympanum and ossicles and auditory nerve are set vibrating in harmony with the air that strikes the ear, or the flesh of the hand is heated and the tactile nerves receive and pass along this agitation of molecules), and the soul itself undergoes a non-corporeal modification. Thus, the sense power (which is a composite of the soul and the sensory organ) is acted upon by the sensible thing in a supercorporeal way by reason of the corporeal modification and affection of the receptive organ. From the passion of the sense the action of the sensible thing and the import of the action is grasped. Thus the existence of the thing can be interpreted by the intellect.

But the mere fact that the sense power is modified and acted upon does not suffice for the evidence of the existence of the sensible being. Evidence is not formally evidence unless it is cognized. There must be, on the sense level, an awareness of this modification and undergoing. It is not enough that this undergoing take place, but it must also be known. The sentient power must get into the stream of the activity of the sensible thing not only physically but also cognitively and as a knower. And this does, in fact, occur. When we sense, we are conscious of sensing. Even though this consciousness is not had through the external sense which is directly affected but rather by an internal sense called the "central sense" or the "common sense," it nevertheless belongs to the complete act of sense knowledge and is had on the sense level. Thus by a natural reflective awareness we sense our sensing. And since sensing is essentially passive, a reception or undergoing, when we are conscious of sensing, we are by that fact conscious of undergoing and being acted upon. It is, of course, true that this is not an explicit and formal knowledge of undergoing and passion as such (which could be had only in intellectual knowledge), but it is knowledge of a concrete singlar instance of being impressed, receiving an impression, being affected, or being acted upon.

The evidence for the existence of sensible things requires both the fact of undergoing and the consciousness of this fact. Though this evidence is had through the senses, it is evidence for the intellect, is made use of by the intellect, and grounds the intellectual judgment of existence. Since it becomes the motive for assent, it must be recognized formally and reflexively as evidence by the intellect. There is no difficulty about sense evidence (that is, evidence derived from the senses) becoming intellectual evidence (that is, evidence for the intellect) unless we adopt Cartesian presuppositions of an abyss between "body" and "spirit," as if they were two complete and independent substances. If the substantial unity of man is recognized; if man is grasped as a composite of body and soul in which the soul is the substantial form of the body, informing, specifying, actuating, and vivifying it, operating in conjunction with it in some operations and surpassing it in others; if the human supposit is seen as the ultimate principle of all human operations, which, nevertheless, operates through a variety of operative powers arranged in a hierarchy and subordinated to one another; then the supposed problem is a pseudo-problem. That there can be intellectual knowledge of sense operations is obvious from the fact that there is such a science as sensitive psychology, in which the operations of sense powers are described and explained. The description and explanation are clearly intellectual, but they must be based on data supplied by the senses. These data are had not only through external observation (which takes place through the activity of the external and internal senses) but also through introspection, in which the observer has intellectual awareness of sensing and of making use of sense data in his intellectual acts. Where there is a hierarchy of cognitive powers, the higher can have consciousness of the activity of the lower.[16]

---

[16] Gilson, *Réalisme thomiste*, chap. 7, esp. pp. 187-88, 195-97, 202-11.

When the intellect is confronted with the sense consciousness that accompanies sensing, it performs in regard to it its own characteristic operation, which is understanding. The intellect interprets what it sees. It penetrates beyond the concrete singular fact to its underlying meaning, its significance, its nature, its implications, and its relationships. Confronted with the fact of undergoing or being acted upon which is reported by the central sense, the intellect understands not only the givenness or thereness of the object and its distinction from the subject, but also the correlative of undergoing or passion, which is action; for wherever there is passion there is action. Action and passion are but a single motion considered from opposite points of view. In the one case the motion is viewed from its source; in the other, from its termination. Since any determinate motion must have beginning and end, principle and terminus, source and termination, whoever understands either action or passion must understand, at least implicitly, the other. Thus, when passion is understood, action is understood. But when action is known, an agent is also known; for the action is given in the concrete determinations of a thing (expanse, shape, size, color, etc.) and as in an individual subject, and thus is known as the action of something which is acting. Action as we know it in our human experience is not subsistent but always the action of a subject or supposit from which the action proceeds. Action bears for the intellect, then, the significance or implication of an agent. And since nothing can act unless it is, the agent must be understood as an existent. When an existent is known, existence is also known; and when the action of this existent is known, its existence is known dynamically. In this way the intellect knows the existence of the sensible thing which is acting upon the knower.

The understanding of existence that is derived from this third level of sense evidence is much more than pure formal determinateness or mere givenness or even otherness and distinction from the knower. It is quite true that the sensible thing is present and given, that it is given as distinct, and that it is given in a determinate way with a definite set of formal determinations. But because the thing is given through its action, it is given actively. Its presence is not static but dynamic. The thing presents itself to the knower through its activity, and its existence is manifested through this activity. This activity, it is understood, is a particular activity, such as sounding or heating, with qualitative and quantitative aspects and in a

definite time and place. It is not that basic activity which is existence, but a secondary and superficial activity distinct from existence as such. Yet it is a particular manner in which the sensible
thing is existing. And if a thing is existing in a particular manner,
it is most certainly existing. In sense knowledge only the particular
manner in which it is existing is grasped, but in intellectual knowledge the existence as such is attained. The intellect grasps the truth
of the adage *agere sequitur esse,* whose primary and fundamental
meaning is that action presupposes existence and, presupposing it,
manifests it.

The action of a being is its act and its perfection; for while it
is acting the being is in a state of actuality which it does not have
when it is not acting, and it fulfills its potentialities, at least in
this respect. Thus the action is seen to be an act and a perfection of
the agent.[17] The action is what makes an agent to be an agent, and
thus is the perfection of the agent as such. From action or activity
the term "act" has been extended to perfection of any type, so that
in Aristotelian terminology any perfection is called an act.

Because the agent must actually *be* before he can be an agent,
there is an actuality or perfection or act more fundamental than
that of action. This is existence. It must underlie every other type
of actuality, whether formal or operative. Existence, then, is the
basic actuality and act of all. Existence, or the act of being, is that
which makes a being to be and to be a being, and so is the perfection of a being as such. Since the act of existing is manifested
through action and activity, and activity is a particular way of existing, the act of existing must contain eminently the perfection
that is contained in activity and be in some sense an activity itself.
It is not a superficial, adventitious, or accessory activity such as the
name "activity" ordinarily suggests to us and from which we come
to know the existence of a thing; rather, it is the underlying,
fundamental, and basic activity of any being as a being. It is the
activity which makes anything to be a being, just as action is that

---

[17] This is not to deny that *actio est in passo* or that *actio est perfectio patientis.*
Action is the act, and therefore the perfection, of both agent and patient, but in
different ways. It is the activity of the agent just as immanent operation is, and by
it the agent is actually an agent. But because it does not terminate in the agent but
affects something outside and there has its effect, action is considered as *from* the
agent but *in* the patient. That is, the activity and efficiency proceeds from the agent
and terminates in the patient. It is one activity which is determined by the form of
the agent and determines the form of the patient. It perfects the patient formally
and perfects the agent operatively and existentially.

which makes something to be an agent. Existing is not what some particular sort of being does under particular circumstances, but what any being does by the very fact of being a being. If the being is actual, it actually exercises the act of existing. If it is only potential or possible, it is nevertheless referred to the actual exercise of the act of existing and is regarded as a being because of this reference. From the dynamism of action and activity, then, existence is known and is known to be dynamic.

Although it is only in intellectual judgment that existence is expressly signified and explicitly known, it would be a serious mistake to suppose that this judgment is our first contact with existence and that existence enters into our cognition here for the first time. Such a mistake would render the act of judgment unintelligible. It would imply that existence is gratuitously added to the thing previously apprehended. Our intellect depends upon the sense presentation of what it undersands (or at least of that from which it understands), and it judges upon evidence which ultimately is sense evidence. When its judgments are immediate judgments, the evidence must be immediate evidence. Judgments about the existence of sensible things that are directly presented to us must be immediate judgments, and they must be immediately formed from sense evidence; for the existence of sensible beings, which are contingent, cannot be deduced a priori; neither can it be deduced in any way except from the immediately known existence of other things. It must be given in our sense experience and sense perception or at least known from these. This is why Professor Gilson says that "each 'it is' is either given in or related to a sensory perception. ... To perceive is to experience existence."[18] Our sense experience is a grasp of a particular concrete existent. For this reason it gives evidence of existence. But it remains true that existence as such is not directly and properly sensed. There is no special sense peculiarly adapted to be affected by bare existence, nor can a number of the senses together attain existence as such. It is, therefore, neither a proper nor a common sensible but must be regarded as, in some sense, an accidental sensible which is known only through what is directly and properly sensed.[19] It is attained through its accidental manifestations. While these sensible manifestations are

18 *Being and Some Philosophers*, p. 207.
19 Gilson, *Réalisme thomiste*, pp. 184-86, 205, 213-15.

being attained by the senses, the intellect attains the existence itself
and expresses it in a judgment.

It may at first appear that the analysis here given of the evidence
which grounds our judgments of existence involves the mediate
realism or illationism which Professor Gilson has so strongly attacked.[20] It may appear that what is intended in the explanation
is a rational discourse in which, from the evidence given in the
senses, the existence of the sensible being is deduced; or more specifically, from the consciousness of being acted upon there is deduced action; from action, an agent; from an agent, an existent; and
from an existent and from the action of the existent agent its existence is deduced. Were this the case, the doctrine would most
certainly be one of mediate realism. But this is by no means what
has been intended or expressed. It is true that in the analysis there
is a succession of steps, but it is not the analysis of a succession. The
analysis does not mean to detail a progression from an intellectual
state in which existence is not known to a knowledge of existence
caused by the knowledge of something else previously and better
known. It is not the advance in knowledge *from* one thing *to* another but the discovery or uncovering of one thing *in* another. It
is not the drawing of what is only potentially known out of something else actually known, but it is the passage from the implicit
to the explicit. What is implicit in knowledge is already contained
there actually though involved in something else that is being directly and explicitly attended to. To go from the implicit to the
explicit is not to reason or infer in the strict sense but rather to
penetrate and inspect. The different steps of the analysis do not
represent steps from the knowledge of one thing to that of another
but different levels of penetration, of insight, and of understanding
regarding one and the same thing. Thus action is not understood
from passion but is understood in understanding passion; for cor-
relatives are understood together. The agent is not understood
from the action, but is understood in understanding the action.
Similarly, existence is not grasped from the action but in the action
or under the action. The complexity of the evidence set forth,
therefore, in no way detracts from the immediacy of our knowledge of sensible existents or of their existence itself, nor does the
detailing of this evidence make the explanation one of mediate

[20] The whole of *Le réalisme méthodique* is on this topic. See especially pp. 18-32,
80, 82-86. See also *Réalisme thomiste*, pp. 226-27, 230.

realism or illationism, but it leaves it unequivocally one of immediate, direct, or "natural" realism.

Immediate realism does not imply, however, that the existence of anything which is not directly and immediately sensed is unknown to us. From the existence of what is immediately sensible we can reason by way of causality to what is not sensed. It makes little difference in this case whether the thing whose existence is concluded is in itself sensible or non-sensible. In either case its existence must be reduced in our knowledge to that of something that is immediately sensed. A geologist accepts the interior of the earth not because he sees it, but because he concludes that it must exist to explain the sensible phenomena. Yet it is assumed to be sensible in itself even though not actually sensed. Beings that are essentially non-sensible not only are not sensed but cannot be sensed. Of them, then, naturally speaking, there is not and cannot be immediate experience or immediate evidence. The evidence can be only mediate, and our judgments about their existence must be arrived at by a deduction from the existence of sensible things. In our knowledge their existence is reduced to that of beings that are sensible and actually sensed. Non-sensible beings are inferred to exist because they must exist as causes of the beings that are sensibly perceived. When a metaphysician affirms philosophically that God exists, he does this because he understands that God must exist as the cause of the sensible beings and events whose existence is immediately known to us.

Just as the nature of non-sensible, immaterial, and spiritual beings is known analogously from the nature of sensible beings, so too is their act of existing understood, affirmed, and predicated with a meaning analogous to that of the act of existing of sensible beings. The notion of existence had in the two cases is only analogically the same. The note of basic actuality, dynamism, act, and activity is kept, but without the temporal and spatial limitations with which the act of existing is found in sensible beings.

Every judgment of existence is accordingly seen to be based, either directly or indirectly, upon the immediate evidence of existence provided by our sense knowledge. This evidence includes determinateness and givenness, but these notes alone could never ground an adequate understanding of the act of existing. If our judgments of existence are to convey the dynamism that belongs to the act of existing, evidence of this dynamism must be found in sense knowledge. It is found there under the guise of the activity and action of sensible beings. And for this dynamism to enter our knowledge we must somehow enter into the stream of the activity of the sensible object, not only ontologically and physically but also cognitively and intentionally. This requires that we not only undergo the action of the sensible thing but also become conscious of undergoing it. In the dynamism manifested through the efficient causality of sensible things we can recognize and understand their act of existing. Our awareness of undergoing the efficient causality of sensible things is the natural evidence upon which all our judgments of existence are grounded.

ᗺᔔ Toward a Metaphysical Restoration of Natural Things

by Kenneth Schmitz

☆ ☆ ☆ ☆ ☆ ☆ ☆ ☆ ☆ ☆ ☆ ☆ ☆ ☆

I T IS COMMONPLACE to remark that technology is everywhere rapidly altering the face of our world. It is also changing an age-old pattern of man's relation with animate and inanimate physical things. The philosophical overtones of prevailing modern philosophies for the most part obscure certain transcendental conditions which must be present in a proper relation of man to things. Properly, man's mastery of nature is a conditional mastery, in which the natural thing loans its being to a sublimation and in which the master recognizes and respects its integrity. Man cannot justify his use of things solely in terms of his own being. His history has meaning in the measure to which it is understood as a movement of the whole people of God towards God and within God; but in his spiritual odyssey man carries along with him the world of physical things, elevating them to his own spiritual being by his knowledge, art, and love. As he elevates them he must respect their integrity. There is some danger today that an abuse of technology may pauperize physical things and thereby impoverish man's own spiritual being by obscuring the self-possessed value of natural things. We herewith sketch the intellectual history of natural things in order to discover the source of their value and the fullness that is in them.

The Philosophy of Object

Within the breakdown of the socio-cultural structure of the high middle ages a metaphysical reorientation took place which radically changed the intellectual perspective. The reordering was metaphysical because it was absolutely foundational. It was a half-understood decision to discover a new principle of metaphysical order. Whereas God had served as the *principium* of the mediaeval world-view, it was felt that the new center would be a better citadel from which to probe the new troubles and hopes that alternately yexed and buoyed the human spirit. The main deficit of seventeenth century philosophers was their failure to grasp how radical their decision was. There was not merely a changed order, a new learning, and a new man. There was also the loss of the primary value of the mediaeval world, the loss of the primacy of being. To dominant seventeenth century thinkers, being had no absolute value. Being as body, being as spirit, being as idea were values. But being as being was not a value. Many mediaeval theologians never arrived at a natural assent to the value of being as being. They read *Exodus* in which God declared His sacred name, *I am Who am,* and went back to their writing to describe God as *Dator Formarum,* and *Unica Forma.*[1] Nevertheless, even for these men, being was their absolute *principium.* They may have tried to pour the new wine of Judaeo-Christian being into the old skins of Greek form, but they were held to thinking within a universe whose *principium* was a creative God-being, whose absolute value was being as being, and whose order was grounded in the ontological relations of created beings to Uncreated Being.

The "modern" world arose with the search for a new order, around a new center, and with new values. The metaphysical *principium* of the new universal order was subjectivity *qua* human. Paradoxically, although the early modern thinkers were moved by the primacy of human subjectivity, they sought to avoid its results. There was, after all, too much of creaturely being and too little of the transcendental ego about human subjectivity as the seventeenth century thinkers saw it. The human subject had not yet appropriated certain attributes of divinity from an "extinct" God; it was still far too fallible, far too finite to bear the weight of the universal order. And so, many seventeenth century thinkers sought to measure all with the value of "objectivity." Nevertheless, the centrality of the human subject was indirectly expressed, theoretically in an

[1] For example, Robert Grosseteste, "De Unica Forma Omnium" in *Beiträge zur Geschichte der Philosophie des Mittelalters,* ed. L. Baur. The more general notion of *Dator formarum* has several sources. See St. Augustine *De Libero Arbitrio* II, 16.44-17.45, PL. 32, 1264-5. There were mediaeval currents which sought to reduce *being* to *essence,* but this was an interior ontological reduction. It minimized the integrity of natural things, but is quite different from the modern dissolution of things.

idealist theory of knowledge and practically in the purposive conquest of nature. In order to avoid the caprices and confusion of a
subjectivity still too human they sought a discipline which closed
off the knower from the more profound resources of the human
spirit. Yet in order to preserve their new metaphysical *principium*
they sought a discipline which was intrasubjective. They chose
mathematics, the science of idealized quantity. Inasmuch as the
quantity was idealized the primacy of subjectivity was assured; and
inasmuch as the ideas were patterned after quantitative relations
the safeguard of a standard non-subjective uniformity was maintained. Moreover, the knowables of mathematics are accidents of
a human knower; they have no independent being; they are merely
objects of the human mind. The universe became an order of "objects," disciplined and ready for the human subject. In Spinoza there
is an apparent return to a mediaeval vantage point, *sub specie
aeternitatis*, but the God of Spinoza bears the marks of mathema-
ticization, and behind him stands a rationalist human subject whose
image he bears. There is no materiality which is not idealized, and
spirituality is the shade of mathematicized quantity. With Hobbes,
true spirituality is meaningless and God is peripheral. In sum, the
reasonings of Spinoza and Hobbes issue from a common ground;
both proceed from a human subject which is their metaphysical
principle and whose instrument is mathematics.

The seventeenth century search for "objectivity" must not be
identified simply with an older search for scientific knowledge. The
search for communicable and certain knowledge is as old as philosophical endeavour itself. The insistence that science be of the universal is a necessary condition never to be given up. But metaphysics shows what becomes of science which is also wisdom. The
very foundations of science are both quickened and shaken by the
touch of metaphysics. The ordinary logic of demonstration gives
way to a logic of analogy. The character of universality itself is
radically changed. Universals are arrived at, not merely through
abstraction, but primarily through judgment. A universal term is
an indefinite prolongation of actual and possible judgments. The
metaphysical term is determined and determinable in the whole
range of being. Scientific truth must be of the universal, but metaphysical truth is of universals which are transabstractive. In the
measure that they are transabstractive, they are also transobjective.
They must include the subject, and not merely as another "object,"

but precisely as it *is, as subject.* The equation of universality with "objectivity," then, is somewhat recent. It began in the modern world with an innocent search for communicable and certain knowledge. But the outcome of that search was predetermined by two commitments: the first, to order all things in the light of human subjectivity; the second, to use mathematics to achieve an idealized, disciplined, "objective" order.

The reduction of universality to univocal "objectivity" is concomitant with a changed attitude toward the nature and role of evidence. Evidence becomes impermeable; its role is to be manipulable. It is simply what one begins with, and to which one perhaps returns for verification of his rational exercises. In neither empiricist nor rationalist is there any sense of the polyvalent nature of evidence; nor is there the insistence that one enters *within* the evidence to permeate his understanding with its permanent truthvalues. To mediaeval philosopher-theologians the Judaeo-Christian dogmas and the world of natural things were profoundly mysterious evidences. Such evidences were inexhaustibly penetrable because they led back to a Divine Abyss of intelligible being. The first immediate revelations of this evidence were sufficient only to lead one more deeply within its intelligible light and toward its ontological Source. But in the early modern world, natural things became mere "objects" and were therefore expected to yield their intelligibility promptly and entirely. Not even the laborious Baconian method is an unqualified exception. The method seeks above all to remove impediments from the knower, to tabulate our observations of natural phenomena, and to place man in control of nature. Whatever mystery surrounds natural things is to be found in the darkness of our faculties and in the relative lack of order in things.[2] Such a negative "mystery" withers in the face of increasing knowledge, whereas the positive mystery of the mediaeval thinkers waxed more brilliant as they grew in knowledge. Like his mathematical contemporaries, Bacon also sought an "objective" standard. It is not, however, an "objectivity" guaranteed by mathematics; but still less was it a conformity to real natural existents. Through the Universal Laws of physical processes he sought a practical subordination of things to man, and attempted to resist the in-

[2] "Novum Organum" I, Aphorisms xli, xlv in *The Physical and Metaphysical Works of Lord Bacon,* ed. Spedding, Ellis, and Heath (Boston: n. d.), 1, 251 and 253-55.

roads of subjectivity by a theoretical guarantee which was not mathematical and which instead rested in quasi-concrete "Forms of Simple Natures."[3] The integrity of individual beings is as absent from Bacon's non-mathematical thought as it is from Spinoza's.

It is a truism that seventeenth century philosophies were mathematical, but so were several ancient philosophies. However, mathematics was now called upon to play an entirely new rôle in the history of thought. Initially, among the ancient Pythagoreans and Atomists, mathematical entities had an undefined and somehow real existence; and, among ancient astronomers and mechanics, Euclidean geometry was thought to provide a faithful mirror of real things; thereby mathematical philosophers were open to an idealistic turn of thought. But idealism did not arise until mathematics was placed at the service of a metaphysics whose central perspective was human subjectivity. Ptolemy had remarked that mathematics is the most useful of sciences because the material nature of things is most surely revealed by their local motion.[4] And the Atomist philosophers had equated reality with its quantitative features. Nevertheless, the original Atomists had put forth their theory in answer to a problem raised by the Parmenidean notion of being; whereas, with somewhat less metaphysical sureness, early modern thinkers advanced the theory against the forms of scholastic philosophies of being and as an idealized disciplining of matter.[5] Their motive for equating the essential nature of physical things with their quantitative characters was the search for an evidence which does not escape the human reason. It was a search for an evidence which is clear and distinct, self-explanatory, determinate, vivid, known once-for-all. In the mediaeval universe, and in an incipient sense in the Greek universe, it was not scandalous to begin and remain with evidence which was inexhaustibly and positively mys-

---

[3] _Op cit._, II, v and vii (_ed. cit._, I, 346, 351).

[4] _Mathematike Syntaxis_ I proem. In the _Almagest_ translated and edited by M. Halma (Paris: Henri Grand, 1813), I, 4. Cf. Descartes' interesting comment on the perennial value of mathematics, _Regulae ad directionem ingenii_ in Oeuvres, ed. Charles Adam and Paul Tannery (Paris: Cerf, 1908), X, 374 ff.

[5] Instead of accepting a full atomism, it is more usual to speak of it favourably and to mention somewhat vaguely the motion of "parcels," "corpuscles," "minima," "particulas veras," or even "atoms" in the interest of a more general mechanism. For example, Bacon, _op. cit._, II, viii (_ed. cit._, I, 352); see also I, 1, lvii and lxxi (_ed. cit._, I, 258, 261 and 277). Also Hobbes, _De Corpore_ IV, 27, 1 and 29, 17 _Opera Philosophica Latine_, ed. Molesworth (London: Bohn, 1839), I, 364, 412. Cf. Descartes, _Principia Philosophiae_ III, 46-47 in _Oeuvres_, ed. Charles Adams and Paul Tannery (Paris: Cerf, 1905), VIII, pt. 1, 100-103.

terious, for it was a universe whose *principium* was the infinite, ineffable God-being, and whose absolute value was the non-abstractive being as being. But such an evidence fitted poorly with the early modern thinkers who, not being sceptics, were traditional enough to strive to render their evidence intelligible, yet, being rationalists, were novel enough to demand that it surrender all its intelligibility to them. The seventeenth century mechanistic systems display many features already found in ancient philosophies— the distinction between primary and secondary qualities, the externality of relations, the mechanism of causality, the lack of finality, and the appeal to myth in order to give a likely account of certain irrepressible phenomena. For, seeking the safe path of "objective" mathematical discipline, early modern thinkers had fashioned an evidence which was impervious and an external causality in place of the causality in being.[6] With the externality of elements there could be no finality ascribed to the compound things apparent to the "common sense" observer. Even Leibniz, with a new mathematics which helped him to subordinate extension to intensive qualitative units, succumbs to this fundamental mechanism. Nevertheless, the new systems declare their difference from all that has gone before. Having no positive mysteries, they are not philosophies of being; having a primacy of the human subject, they are not the ancient mathematical philosophies. Among these modern philosophers of "objectivity" there is a lingering suspicion that the "objective" truth of things leaves some value untapped, but this is usually relegated to the care of religion.[7] The suspicion is betrayed by a self-consciousness of the hypothetical character of metaphysical affirmations, and by a critical indirectness of approach. But the telling mark of their novelty is that they are *closed* systems.

The human subject, seeking its value in an absolute measure, adopted mathematics as its *modus cognoscendi*. The character of mathematical knowledge determined the connotations of seven-

---

[6] Its externality is recognized by Leibniz who banishes secondary efficient causality to the order of *phenomena bene fundata* and thereby removes it from metaphysical reality. See *New Essays* IV, 2, 14 trans. A. Langley (2d ed., Chicago: Open Court Publishing Co., 1916), pp. 419 ff. and "A New System" 13, 14, 17 in *Philosophical Papers and Letters*, trans. L. Loemker, (Chicago: 1956), II, 746-69. The mechanical nature of causality may be seen in Descartes' description of physical motion, *Principia* II, 36 and 41 (*ed. cit.*, VIII-1, 61 ff. and 65 ff.). Also Hobbes, *De Corpore* II, 9, 7 (*ed. cit.*, I, 110 ff.)

[7] Cf. Descartes, *Principia* I, 28 *ed. cit.*, VIII-1, 15-16 and Albert Balz, *Descartes and the Modern Mind*, (New Haven: Yale University Press, 1952), p. 19, n. 24.

teenth century "objectivity," universality, and science. Nevertheless it is not just to say that mathematics is the cause of the deliberately closed character of the seventeenth century systems. When
mathematics is in search of its principles, definitions, and original
data, it is abstractive but not deliberately closed. The systems of
the seventeenth century were *mechanical* because of the type of
mathematics employed. They were *externalized* because of the
philosophers' attempt to use mathematics to provide the light and
order of universal wisdom. But they were *closed* because of their
principium. What is meant by saying that they are closed is that
there is deliberately no development *in* the primary principles of
each system, but only the production of further conclusions and
refinements.[8] Similarly, any Thomists who seek to apply the supposedly fixed principles of their master to the solution of modern
problems are steeped in this modern viewpoint. For them, philosophy is a closed system, changing only in its problems and their
new conclusions. Their system grows by addition, not by impene-
tration. In a truly perennial philosophy, on the contrary, the immutability of principles is not a fixity. In a special sense, principles
do undergo change, and yet they retain their identity through a
host of varying realizations. Perennial principles are not static; they
are enduringly permanent. Only a philosophy of being such as that
of St. Thomas or a philosophy which is at least incipiently ontological such as Aristotle's can generously recognize the reality of
the potential and secure a permanence which is not static. This
original act of generosity makes a philosophy of being the home of
analogy. On the other hand, univocity invites closure, and mathematical philosophies are univocal. They therefore invite closure.
Why did the seventeenth century philosophers accept this invitation and realize the liability of mathematics to closure? We must
now anticipate our remarks on the philosophy of subject, in order
to mark off exactly the reason for the closed aspect of certain modern philosophies. Recently, among philosophies of subjectivity,
the independent originality of the given has been emphasized. Such
a philosophical system is not closed in the measure that the data
can impinge on our consciousness in the most surprising and hitherto unconceived ways. There is no mechanistic preconception of
the data. But it is closed in the measure that it demands that the

[8] Descartes, *Letter to the French translation of the Principia* (ed. cit., IX-2,
passim but especially p. 15); and Hobbes, *De Corpore* I, 1, 6 (ed. cit., I, 6).

given must appear within the "world-unity of possible experiences."[9] To insist that the given meet the "subjective conditions for
the possibility of experience" is to take one's stand decisively in a
subjective ground. And, what is more, he consolidates his subjective metaphysics who cries, "Nonsense!" to any intelligibility which
eminently escapes the human subject. Much of the modern respect for the subjective conditions of intelligibility, however fruitful, and the demand for an evidence which derives its meaning
from the matrix of possible experiences, are twin aspects of a determination to surrender to the human subject the order and value
of all experienced reality. This determination is the key to the
closure of certain modern systematic philosophies.

The seventeenth century metaphysical decision was to face
things toward the human subject. Yet, paradoxically, that subject
went out from itself in search for an order which bore its mathematical image but excluded the recognition of its own deepest
values. In so attempting to serve human subjectivity while limiting
it, the philosophy of object was forced to ignore the human spirit's
profound worth as the highest instance of experienced being. What
is even more surprising, however, is that the philosophy of object
impoverishes the understanding of natural things. It is a metaphysical failure even in the physical world. Afraid of its own resources, the human subject sought nevertheless to discipline things.
They became "objects" for the human subject, and to these sub-
ject-disciplined termini the human subject was then ready to submit. Truth became "objective fact"; the criterion became an "objective agreement" which sought to reduce things to a minimal
residue in order to avoid the ravages of a latent subjectivity. Not
a cause of being itself, human subjectivity could not establish an
order of natural things *as beings;* it had to order them to itself *as
instruments.* It bound them to itself *as objects;* it could not abide
them *as subjects.* For the human subject can never be a cause of
being; and so, while things can be *for-it,* they cannot *be* if they are
merely for-it. The human subject can appropriate to itself as subject a world of "objects," but it cannot create for itself a world of
beings with the integrity, dignity, and value that attaches to each
and every being. The peculiar meaning with which the words
"object" and "objectivity" are endowed even today is a result of

[9] For example, Edmund Husserl, "Ideen" III, ii, 76 and II, iii, 47-49 in *Gesam-
melte Werke,* (Louvain: 1950), III, pt. 1, 174-77 and 110-117.

the first shock of modern thinkers as they sought to order all things to the human subject by a norm of "objectivity" to which all might come once the arbitrary and isolationist additions of the subject were withdrawn. In its deepest strivings for "objectivity" the temper of the seventeenth and eighteenth centuries sought to fight its way out of certain idealist dilemmas which arose only because of a half-understood metaphysical decision. It is not until Kant, however, that the idealist *solution* presents itself: and that is to accept openly the foundational role of (human) subjectivity, and to reorder all in accordance with this decision.

After Christian Wolff had given an impressive formation to the philosophy of object, the manual writers among the scholastic authors turned more and more to the philosophy of object as a safeguard against the subjectivism which they feared in modern philosophy.[10] In the face of the stream of modern philosophy, they stoutly strove to reject subjectivity as the metaphysical principle; yet they took up its values, and for them things became "objects," and "objectivity" became the goal of human knowledge. Meanwhile, modern idealism and much of modern life had passed beyond the seventeenth century philosophies of object and was probing the depths of human subjectivity in the arts and sciences. Faced with the contemporary fascination for the subjective aspects of human existence, the scholastic manual writers of the nineteenth and twentieth centuries have often been incapable of rendering intelligible the major cultural achievements of their time. They have also been unable and unasked to give significant direction to their contemporaries. The study of St. Thomas has acted as a leaven. For, although St. Thomas knew nothing of subjective idealism, he knew just as little of objective idealism. He did not attempt to close off being from subjectivity. He did not approach beings as objects, and thereby inadvertently from the vantage point of subjectivity. He did not equate the values of being and knowledge of being with those of "object" and "objectivity." He knew the values of being absolutely;[11] and so we may fairly judge that he was ready to admit subjectivity within being, and to leave being open to subjectivity. Indeed, whereas "objectivity" has no place

10 See John Gurr, S.J., "Some Historical Origins of Rationalism in Catholic Philosophy Manuals," *Proceedings of the American Catholic Philosophical Association,* (1956), pp. 170-180.

11 For example, *Summa Theologiae* I, q. 44, aa 1, 2; q. 4, a. 1 *ad* 3m; also *Questiones disputatae: De potentia Dei* q. 7, a. 2, *ad* 9m.

at all as a metaphysical value, subjectivity, if properly understood, has a very important metaphysical rôle. St. Thomas' modern disciples do not have to interest themselves explicitly and especially in human subjectivity, but they must be open to it and ready to admit it and its characteristics into being and their study of being. They cannot approach being solely from the perspective of object.

The Philosophy of Subject

The philosophy of object which characterizes so much of seventeenth century thought is a half-conscious philosophy of subject. During the breakdown of the mediaeval intellectual structure the *subject* came to mean a subject of consciousness. Natural things came to be viewed as that which is thrown over against a subject, and their new rôle was to be objects.[12] With the growth of the empirico-mathematical experimental sciences in the seventeenth and eighteenth centuries, the subjective *principium* further disciplined natural things. The Kantian resolution converted them into true principiates by treating them as "facts." In Hegelian philosophy, subject does not have an absolute primacy over object. The subjectivity we are considering, however, is not that which functions *within* the Hegelian system. We are considering rather a philosophical attitude which lies prior to the *system* of Hegel, but upon which that system is grounded. For the Hegelian system contains only the principiates of an absolute subjectivity. Within the Hegelian system one cannot say, "Being is subject," without remaining one-sided and incomplete. But, prior to that system, there is a deeper root of subjectivity; and of this it can be said: "It is being; being is it. Being is subjectivity."[13]

The technological spirit is the cultural force which arose from the philosophies of object and finds full expression in some philosophies of subject. In the measure that natural things become objects, the technological spirit receives its theoretical and practical warranty. Reality becomes an arena in which an absolutized human spirit seeks an absolute conquest of the non-subjective world. Abso-

---

[12] Cf. C. Prantl, *Geschichte der Logik*, (Graz: Akodemische Druck, 1867), III, 208, n. 105. Also R. L. Nettleship, *Philosophical Lectures and Remains*, I, 193.

[13] Certain transcendental philosophers have disclaimed the possibility or relevancy of a metaphysics of real being; but still such a decision commits one to a basic *principle*, and in this sense we can speak of a "metaphysics" of subjectivity. Cf. *The Logic of Hegel* 24 trans. from the *Encyclopedia of the Philosophical Sciences* by William Wallace, (Oxford: Clarendon Press, 1874), p. 38.

lute mastery for an absolute spirit. All the marks of man's conditional mastery must be removed. The primary mark of his conditional mastery is that of his being caused. The principle of efficient
causality must therefore be cut out of the metaphysical fabric.
Moreover, it is ineffective in the new order of things. In the old
order, the human subject was finite and caused to be. But to be
caused is an unfitting status for the absolute *principium* of the
new metaphysical order. An absolute cannot be caused and thereby
be relative to another. In the old order, efficient causality had been
a chief mark of the God-principle. He alone was a creative efficient cause, making things to be. And his principiates, in the degree to which they participated in his creative causality, were efficient causes in being. The new *principium,* however, could not
appropriate such an attribute to itself. Kant and even Fichte refused to say that the Ego creates its objects in the sense that God
had created beings. Even Hegel's cosmic subject did not dare to
assert itself as a creative efficient cause. For this reason he relegated
causality to a subordinate level of explanation, and gave to the
ground-consequent relation a primacy of function.[14] And so too,
Husserl's strictures against efficient causality have a deeper cause
than that of a revolt from the genetic notion of causality which he
found among contemporary psychologists. They lie in a recognition that efficient causality has metaphysical meaning only in a universe at whose center is a creative God and whose principiates are
full-fledged beings. To admit this would have been to return (or
go on) to metaphysical realism. The non-causal phenomenological
method, so promising in a modified application, was born of the
unhappy situation in which a human subject reads a universe whose
principium is human subjectivity. Thomists and other metaphysical realists have experienced the basic difficulties which confront
them in rendering the proofs for the existence of God intelligible
to modern non-realists. For the latter think within a metaphysical
order which can find no basic meaning and metaphysical function

---

[14] I am not referring only to the precise category of "Ground," although see
"Wissenschaft der Logik" II, 1, iiiBb in *"Sämtliche Werke,* ed. Georg Lasson, (Leipzig:
F. Meiner, 1934), IV, pt. II, 85-86; trans. Johnson and Struthers, (New York: 1929),
II, 92. Cf. Geoffrey Mure, *A Study of Hegel's Logic,* (Oxford: Clarendon Press, 1950),
p. 107 ff. I am using it rather to describe the non-causal nature of the dialectical
movement, in distinction from "causing" which is "influence to *another in its being."*
See the comments on Aristotle in Mure, *op. cit.,* p. 148 ff. Also W. T. Stace, *The
Philosophy of Hegel,* (London: Macmillan and Co., 1924), p. 50 ff.

for efficient causality. Before the proofs can become intelligible one must remain open to the initial evidence and the final issue. Is the initial datum being? Or is it object? And is the final issue God or human subjectivity? Is causality to be discovered in the initial experience and retained? Or are its services to be dismissed as one moves on toward a metaphysical order whose *principium* is human subjectivity? It would be nonsense to say that the proofs will prove only if God's existence and His order are assumed at the beginning. But it is important to approach the evidence fully and without presuppositions. For presuppositions at the beginning always act as blinders. It is here, in the approach to the evidence, that a very careful use of a phenomenology may provide a reading and listening aid for cautious deontologized minds. But as long as human subjectivity remains the half-understood *principium* of the metaphysical order, the entry of a transcendent God is effectively excluded. In securing its character as *principium,* the philosophy of subject has rooted out the marks of its creaturehood and closed off access to its Creator. Our central problem is to determine the grounds of the integrity of natural things. We have, therefore, traced the abandonment of efficient causality among certain thinkers; and we have insisted that its recognition is an intelligibility that preserves natural things as beings and keeps them from becoming objects for and facts of an absolutized subject.

There are other important consequences which follow from the attempt to make the human subject bear the weight of the universal order. Since the human subject cannot take on an attribute of divinity such as creative causality, it gets along without it. Thereby it occupies a vague status as neither created nor creating. Uncreated and uncreating, it takes on the task of reconstructing the metaphysical order after its own manner. Such an order cannot admit a clear distinction between finite and infinite. For because it is, after all, only finite, there can be no true infinite in the order of which it is the principle. And because it refuses to function as a finite being, with other finite beings, there is not really any finitude therein either. Another not infrequent result is the relegation of the principle of identity (and its logical derivative, the principle of contradiction) to a subordinate and non-metaphysical rôle. The ambivalence of the human subject arises from the irreconcilable disparity between its truly finite ontological status and the rôle which it is called upon to play in a consistent philosophy of subject.

The integrity of natural things is bound to these intelligibilities. Things retain their identity only in a universe whose primary value is being and at whose source is Pure Being exercising an act of creative efficient causality. On the other hand, the philosophy of subject can preserve its own order and maintain the absolute principality of subject only by the emasculation of the principles of efficient causality and identity, by the dissolution of the distinction between finite and infinite, and by the appropriation of natural things as objects and facts.

The Philosophy of Spirit

The foregoing sketch has traced the emergence of two modern philosophical perspectives: being is object, and being is subject. We are not here seeking to schematize the manifold and conflicting patterns of modern thought, but to grasp the ground of its dominant movement. It would be sanguine to expect a total consistency; and, indeed, man is often saved by his inconsistencies, especially where they are a departure from his conceptions in order to answer the voice of being. Nevertheless, both the subjectivist and objectivist perspectives are situated within a more profound grounding in which a transcendental subjectivity dominates and accommodates both positions and from which they derive their order and sensibilities. The "object" is only a paupered thing, idealized by the human mind. Such a philosophy is indeed "objective," a science of "facts," a knowledge of reality ideally formalized by a mathematicized mind, a science of "mathematifacts." The disappearance of *res* or *thing* as a concept having scientific value and its displacement by the concept *fact* is a half-understood testimony to the "creative" and ordering temper of modern subjectivity. Even the philosophy of "objective" being is, then, underneath it all, a desperate attempt to reach being from the standpoint of subjectivity. The philosophy of subject, on the other hand, openly confesses the primacy of subjectivity and orders all from this standpoint. It is superior to a philosophy of object because it is conscious of its first principle, human subjectivity. Although it presses its principle to excess, even to suppressing the being of the other or compressing it into mere principiates nonetheless, it does not fail to discover deep resources peculiar to itself, and within these it can offer insights which are on the threshold of being. Whereas the philosophy of object strove to formalize being after the image of quantified reality,

the philosophy of subject rests its truest insights upon this irrefrag-
able claim: Spirit is prime, spirit alone is necessary. And, surely,
it is true that the only being which *must be* is spirit—the triune
God; or, to speak within philosophical range, the only Necessary
Being is the God Who is *Ipsum esse subsistens.* Furthermore, the
philosophy of subject better appreciates what a spirit is. In the
philosophy of object spirit appears as the spectre of quantified
being. In the philosophy of subject spirit reveals itself as fully real
especially in the developments from Hegel on. Herein, subjectivity
reveals itself as *somehow* capable of being the *principium* of the
true metaphysical order of being. Unfortunately, in the measure
that spirit is conceived as human subjectivity, it is incapable of
assuming this central rôle. On the contrary, the true metaphysical
import of this primacy of spirit should not be understood as a
withholding of the absolute value of being from non-spiritual reality. It is not correct to interpret an inequality between spiritual
and non-spiritual being as a lessening of the absolute possession
of being by non-spiritual realities. The philosophy of subjective
spirit is guilty of this restrictive niggardliness whenever it makes
some non-spiritual reality a mere principiate of human subjectivity.

If primacy in being must be given to spirit, primacy must be
given to subject also, for every spirit is a subject. We must go
further. In its primary metaphysical value, no being is an "object."
No being merely "is-for." Its possession of being is its fundamental
value, within which its "being-for" and "being-toward" derive their
value. Now, an "object" is something-for-a-subject." This cannot
be a primary metaphysical value. When "object" and "objectivity"
are transferred to a metaphysical plane they are necessarily abstractive, reductionist, and impoverishing. Things are de-ontologized.
The only restorative is to recognize that even non-spiritual realities
are primarily *subjects.* This quite removes us from the province
of idealism. The meaning of subject, then, can be twofold: subject
of consciousness, and subject of existing. Classical statements of
subjective idealism emphasized the cognitive values of the human
spirit; more recent statements have stressed its affective aspects.
In both, however, experience or consciousness remains the primary
mark of reality, and subjectivity remains the primary value. Under
this pressure, *existing* becomes submerged in experience or ig-
ored. Some recent statements of the philosophy of subject have

insisted upon the independent noetic character of objects and have insisted that the subject of consciousness does not make its objects, even in the sense that Kant's consciousness determined its objectivity. Nevertheless, the datum is still conceived as object-for-consciousness. Its ability to render truth-value may be original and independent of the subject within experience, but the value of the datum is determined within an order which is constituted by the demands of experience and whose *principium* is human subjectivity. When, on the contrary, one insists upon the primacy of subject *as existent,* the prime value is being. There can then be a subject whose existence is not conscious. Natural non-conscious things are then beings because they are existing principiates of a *principium* Who is Pure Being.

The Philosophy of Being

We have been insisting upon the proper description of the characters of experience. Our experience is of the being of things, and not merely of "objects." Experience is the community of subject with subject, in which at least one is a subject of consciousness. It may seem that such a description leads back to a philosophy of subject. For if being is subject, and if the human subject is the highest being known without demonstration, then can we not discover a metaphysics from a study of the human subject? Indeed, our generosity in indiscriminately claiming the transcendental value of being for all that is, and the vehemence with which we have rejected a philosophy of object seem to leave us defenseless before a philosophy of subjectivity. The reply, however, is twofold. First and briefly, the subject in the philosophy of subject is a subject-of-consciousness; the subject in the philosophy of being is a subject-of-being. Second, among philosophies which concentrate upon the human subject, there are philosophies which claim to be philosophies of being. However, they identify being with consciousness and thereby disinherit themselves. Such so-called philosophies of being are really philosophies of subject. For them, the identification of being with consciousness is inevitable. For we cannot study the human subject to the exclusion of natural beings, or (what is the same) by treating them merely as "objects." And the reason is that the human subject is not simply subject. It is a *subject-with;* its being is a being-with. We cannot, therefore, safely ignore the other subjects for which it is proportioned and intended to be-with through its knowledge and love. These other subjects are natural things, as well as persons. The human subject is not so much a person that its relationships are only to other persons. But it is so much a being that its relationships are always to other beings. When a metaphysician ignores natural beings by reducing them to "objects," he is unable to distinguish what is proper to the subject *as human* from what belongs to the subject *as being*. This inability is the crutch which is the support of rationalism. Metaphysics demands integrity. A subject which *is-with* can neither be nor be understood in its metaphysical fullness without considering that-with-which-it-is. With this reply we reach a point which demands precision. It is not enough to begin a metaphysics with the polarity of subject and object, and to retain the "whole" experience—subject-act-object. In the measure that the natural thing appears within experience only as an object, the value of being cannot be preserved; and such a subjective-objective "realism" loses itself in a philosophy of subject whose *principium* is the human subject and whose principiates are the various "objects" which receive their meaning and value within a metaphysical order established by "finite" human subjectivity. For a thoroughgoing metaphysical realism, it is not enough to underline the presence of "objects" in experience: we must be ready to receive the impact of natural things in the fullness of their being.[15]

Conclusion

What is the key to determining value and disvalue in man's relation to his physical world? What can restrain him from seizing an apparently absolute mastery which is not really his? Only the recognition of the transcendental value of being prevents things from becoming merely objects of man's knowledge and instruments for his well-being. The ontological integrity of natural things is not in opposition to the mastery of man, but is rather a necessary ingredient within man's proper conditional mastery. Only the providential God has absolute mastery over things, because He is the cause of their very being. And to this absolute Master, natural

[15] See Pierre Scheuer, S.J., "Notes on Metaphysics," *Cross Currents*, VII (Fall, 1957), pp. 337-46. On "being as an intelligible object," p. 337; on the Ego, p. 342b; and on ourselves as "the first principle of metaphysical explanation," p. 344b.

things are not "objects," for the being which He has given them is not a being-for-Him but a being-with-Him. *Being-with* is the mark of a subject of being. Since natural things are not merely "objects-for" but are *originally* subjects of being, and since man is not the cause of being, the being of things can never be dissolved in man's mastery. The deliberate and wanton destruction or deformation of natural things by man is a sin against human reason, but it is causally and originally a sin against the being of things which bear the trace of the ontological presence of the Divine Being. Whenever undue influence is given to technology, natural things dissolve into mere objects for consciousness and instruments for action. With the dissolution of natural things, the way is clear for the erection of a new hierarchy of values in accordance with a metaphysics grounded in human subjectivity.

The true metaphysical ground, however, must be absolute, unqualified, presuppositionless. It must be that value which presents itself as an absolute value within all our experience. Indeed, the supremacy of a metaphysical insight may be gauged by its ability to absorb within itself all other metaphysical insights. In its absorption, furthermore, the others ought to receive their proper intelligible location, realize their ontological identity, maintain their integrity, and be charged with a profundity which is not theirs alone.

One may then ask: Which of these philosophical perspectives meets these conditions? Is it the philosophy of object? Is it the philosophy of subject? Or is it the philosophy of spirit? The answer must be: the philosophy of being. For being is truly the transcendental value, whose acceptance is alone absolutely presuppositionless. The so-called naivety of non-critical philosophy is simple recognition. The sophistication of critical philosophy is merely a careful guarding of presuppositions. The critical methods do not bring into the open presuppositions in human knowledge, but rather carefully cloak one or another presupposition from the shock of a direct face-to-face meeting with being. They cautiously demand of being that it submit to their prephilosophical decision that being is something other than itself. For the presupposition of the philosophy of object is that being is object. The presupposition of the philosophy of subject is that being is subject. The presupposition of the philosophy of spirit is that being is spirit. But the philosophy of being has no presuppositions. It begins simply with this: that being is being.

The Sensibles and Metaphysics

by Gerard Smith, S.J.

☆ ☆ ☆ ☆ ☆ ☆ ☆ ☆ ☆ ☆ ☆ ☆ ☆ ☆

TO SEE UNITY in multiplicity is to see a cause of multiplicity. This is to possess a science.[1]

So far as can be ascertained no one ever successfully denied that scientific knowledge exists. There are, however, different interpretations of science, especially of the science of metaphysics. These different interpretations arise, naturally, from the different ways the data are interpreted and, consequently, from the way the causes of those data are interpreted. I shall endeavor to present St. Thomas Aquinas' version of the data of metaphysics and of their cause with a view to establishing the strictly scientific character of metaphysical knowledge as St. Thomas understood it.

The first move, it seems, should be to describe multiplicity, the data, the situation of the many. The many are passive potentials, related to their respective actuations. A passive potential is anything which exists in such wise that whatever it can be is consistent with non-being.[2] Let us run through the cases. First, what is possible in being man, e.g., a man *can* be white, is consistent with a man's *not* being white. Again, what is possible in being a living being, e.g., a living thing *can* die, is consistent with the fact that a living thing is *not* dead. In both cases the data (the many, consequents, multiplicity) stand in the following situation: the many exist, and in that existential situation of theirs whatever they, the existents, can be is in them non-being; but *they* are not non-being. They are beings, existents, existing in such wise that whatever they are in the order of existence is consistent with their *not* being whatever they *can* be.

[1] *Expositio super librum Boethii De Trinitate* q. 6, a. 1, *ad tertiam quaest*; *Summa Theologiae* I, q. 79, a. 8; *Quaestiones disputatae: De veritate* q. 10, a. 8.; ad 10m; q. 15, a. 1; *In duodecim libros Metaphysicorum expositio*, II, lect. 1, n. 278.

[2] *Sum. Theol.* I, q. 9, a. 2.

The insight is not the easiest in the world. We must have several go's at it. It is as *not* being white, but nonetheless as *being* a man, that a man *can* be white. It is as *not* being dead, but nonetheless as *being* alive, that a living thing *can* die. To be a white man is impossible unless there *be* a man. To be organically alive *is* impossible unless there *be* the dead. To put it again, it is not because passive potentials do *not* exist that they are ordered to their actuations. It is rather because they *do* exist. But they exist without being affected by the surplus of whatever they can be. And on *that* very score they are passive potentials. It is as an *existent* that a man is not but can be white. It is as an *existent* that a living thing is not but can be dead. Were passive potentials not in an already existential situation, they would not be at all, and so they would not be ordered or related to anything at all. The bare cupboard cannot be filled, even though there are things to fill it with, unless there is a cupboard.

Aristotle saw the point about passive potentials. None better: ἔτι τῶν πρός τι ἡ ὕλη[3] he says, and his description still holds. St. Thomas Aquinas also saw the point: *cum esse in potentia nihil aliud sit quam ordinari in actum.*[4] The operative word in St. Thomas' text seems to be *esse*: to *be* in potency is nothing else but to be ordered to act. St. Thomas further notes that "potency is a principle, not because it is the very relation which the word principle means but because it is that which *is* the principle."[5] In other words, potency as a principle is an existent which is not that which it can be. Potency does not exist. The potential exists, but it does not exist as being in the actuation to which it is related as to that which the potential is not but can be; nevertheless, the potential exists with its own actuation. In sum, to be in potency or to be a passive potential is to exist, but not with the perfection to which the potential is related as to its possible actuation.

There was something, however, which it seems Aristotle did not see: he did not see the relation of the passive potential in existence to its existence. Professor Eslick thinks, and with good reason, that for Aristotle sensibles in themselves simply cannot be non-being.[6] Surely the man who opposed Plato all his life cannot

---

[3] Aristotle, *Physics,* ii. 2, 194b9. Cf. *Quaestiones disputatae: De Anima* a. 12, c.

[4] *Quaestiones disputatae: De Malo* q. 1, a. 2, c.

[5] *Quaestiones disputatae: De potentia Dei* q. 1, a. 2, ad 3m.

[6] Leonard Eslick, "What is the Starting Point of Metaphysics?" *Modern Schoolman,* XXXIV (1957), 254.

have thought that! However, whatever Aristotle may have thought, St. Thomas Aquinas most certainly meant that sensibles in themselves are simply non-being, and this without the slightest surrender to Platonism. The point is essential, it seems, to the validation of metaphysics as a science.

In order to see that it is, let us recur to the notion of passive potential. The passive potential is that which exists in such wise that it is not whatever it can be, although the passive potential does exist. We must now run the crucial case. Any experienced existent in Christian metaphysics can quite well not exist at all, and so that which is possible in regard to an existent, viz., its complete non-being, must be consistent with the fact that it does exist. At this point we must ask on what grounds this could be true? Is it upon the score that *in* the existent there is the possibility of non-existence? Impossible. Here Aristotle seems to be dead right, and Plato dead wrong. It is unthinkable that a sensible, which exists but can also not exist, be able not to exist as though its existential act were affected by a coefficient of non-being when non-being means precisely not to exist at all. So to exist, viz., so as by not existing, is complete nonsense. True, a sensible's existential act *qua* sensible can be affected with a coefficient of relative non-being. For, the non-being of a sensible *qua* sensible is a non-being of this or that accidental or substantial way of being; it is not a non-being without qualification. Complete or unqualified non-being simply cannot reside in a being, though a qualified being, or, if you will, a qualified non-being, can exist in a sensible. Yet every sensible being which exists can also not exist at all. Where, then, are we to locate the sensible's possibility of not being at all? St. Thomas Aquinas answers: "in its Creator, in whose power lies both its being and non-being."[7] It would seem, then, that sensibles in themselves are non-being.

To resume the matter, all passive potentials are (1) in *some* existential situation, and (2) are ordered to an existential situation in either of two ways: (a) as to actuations which are as yet inexistent, be those actuations accidental, substantial, or existential; (b) as to actuations which are existent either in the causes of those actuations, or which are existent as effects of those causes. The crucial case is the sensible's actuation which is existential act *(esse)*. The crux is here: how can one say that a non-existent can exist, whereas

7 *Sum. Theol.* I, q. 9, a. 2, c.

there is no *esse* in it by which it can exist, and *esse* there must be, somehow, somewhere, if the non-existent can be? Or run the question this way: how can one say that an existent can not be, whereas there is no foothold in the existent for non-being? One cannot answer either question unless the being *(esse)* of the existent as well as its non-being lies in the power of God. Is this to destroy the *esse* of the sensible? On the contrary, this, it seems, is to establish the *esse* of the sensible. It is not in or of themselves that passive potentials exist. If they did, we should have an unexplained sensible world, a world without a cause. Sensibles themselves exist indeed, and this must be stated without any *arrière pensée* whatsoever, but they do not exist in or of themselves. In or of themselves they are nothing except in the *esse* of their divine cause, or in the *esse* which is their own but is not *from* them. In their divine cause, it may be added, they are not like pins in a pin cushion. In God, they are the power of God, that is, they are God. Outside of God they themselves exist, but they do not exist in or of themselves. *Non nostri sumus* each creature proclaims, and this proclamation of theirs is equivalent to each creature's proclamation that it is caused.

Having located the being and non-being of sensibles in the power of God, we have a science.

At this stage the point needs only elaboration. Sticks and stones are surely beings, and so is a straight stick and a hard stone. We have no difficulty about saying these things because there is no difficulty in there being these things. However, if we ask, how can a stick be straight, or a stone be hard? and if we desiderate an answer which is above the testing level of feeling and measuring the stick and the stone, above the level of physics and mathematics; if, in other words, we wish to answer the question in terms of metaphysics, then we must see that our question is precisely the one put by any Platonist. It is this: how can one distinct object of thought (stick) be another distinct object of thought (straight)? The question is not about the identity of a subject (stick) with a predicate (straight), not about the fact that this stick is straight. The question is rather about the nature of that identity, or if you will, about the meaning of the copula "is." Now, it is impossible to see how one can answer the question if a stick is allowed an *esse* in the stick's own right, or if "straight" is allowed an *esse* in "straight's" own right. For, if you allow that a stick is *esse* in its own right, you thereby confine a stick to being a stick, and by the same token you eliminate the possibility that a stick may be straight. Similarly for "straight": if "the straight" is nothing but straight, there could not be, e.g., a straight arm instead of a straight stick; for that matter nothing could be straight except "straight." Nonsense. No, it is only when two distinct objects of thought *are* one another than you can *say* that they are one another. And one cannot say that a stick is straight unless each distinct object of thought shares but is not by identity the nature of being. The *esse* of a stick lies in being a stick, and the *esse* of a straight stick lies also in being a stick. Further, precisely because neither stick nor straight are, of or in themselves, *esse*, yet both are in the same *esse;* therefore the *esse* of both is caused. To see this, namely, to see the effect in the cause, is to possess a science, and since we are here seeing the shared *esse* of God, we are within the science of metaphysics.[8]

There should be no illusion that the point made here is clear, or that it can be made very clear. One reason why the point cannot be made clear is because it cannot be made in physical or mathematical terms. Another, and the main reason is this: the predicate, "is caused to be," said of any sensible's being, is no clearer than the predicate "is," said of God, and for exactly the same reason. Both propositions are conclusions of *quia* demonstrations. We do not know what the predicate "is" said of God means when that predicate is viewed as in God. We know what that predicate means only in so far as it is involved in the truth of the proposition *God is.* Just so, we do not know what the predicate "is caused" means in so far as that predicate is in sensibles, but only in so far as that predicate is in the truth of the proposition, *the sensible is caused to be.* There is indeed a difference between the two propositions, *God is* and *a sensible is caused to be.* For a sensible to be caused to be is for a sensible to exist, and we can quite well know what it means for a sensible *qua* sensible to exist: it means that a sensible is hot, cold, man, fish, six feet tall, thin, and that sort of thing. On the other hand, we do not know what God is. Thus, we neither know what God's "is" may mean except in the sense that "is" is true of Him; nor do we know what the sensible's predicate, "is caused to be," may mean except in so far as that "is caused to be" is true of the sensible, and, of course, in so far as that sensible's "caused to be" is describable in sensuous terms. These sensuous

8 *De potentia Dei* q. 3, a. 5, c. ad 1m, ad 2m.

terms, however, are not the sensible's "is" at all. These considerations show that the science about sensibles is, because more familiar, easier to possess than the science about *esse*. Perhaps also it shows one source of our perennial difficulties about metaphysics: we should dearly love to know what "is" means, and we cannot, except in terms of nature; but the sensible's "is" is not a nature predicate at all.

We may see the same point in another way. We all love to make necessary propositions. Indeed, this is one of our deepest loves, the love of knowledge at knowledge's peak. These necessary propositions are in one way or another in the area of science. Now, the only absolutely necessary proposition we can make about sensibles in terms of their *esse* is that they are caused to be, and the propositions derivative therefrom. Should we make a necessary proposition about sensibles in terms of their nature which is involved in their *esse,* or in terms of their *esse* which is involved in their nature, we are not talking about the sensible's *esse qua esse.* In order to talk about the sensible's *esse* as existential act, we must first see that its *esse* is accidental to it in the sense that "accidental" means non-necessary. Next, we must see that this non-necessary *esse* of sensibles, which is the source of their necessity and their contingency, would be an impossible accident if sensibles had either perforce to be, or if, once in *esse,* they did not have perforce to be what they are. The only way, it seems, to understand the sensible's *esse* as at once necessary and contingent is to understand it as being caused by that which is only *esse.* The "only-*esse*-cause," being alone *esse,* is a free cause. Thus the sensible has no "must be" or "must be caused" about it at all. It has only a "must be caused to be" predicate, and that predicate is proved by the acknowledgement that the sensible exists and that its existence is accidental to it. One may submit that rational animals do not like this situation one bit. They would much prefer, as the history of philosophy shows, to reduce the accidental *esse* of sensibles to some nature predicate, and make that nature predicate accidental, as in modern existentialism; or else they would much prefer to make the nature predicate absolutely necessary (something in itself) as in some variety of Platonism. Doubtless the reason for this is because we should like to have a God whom we can handle. We cannot handle the God of Abraham, Isaac, and Jacob. We might as well get used to our similar philosophical inability to handle the One who is.

If faith seeks intellect, which, if faith found, would no longer be intellect but the beatific vision, then intellect must seek faith, which, if intellect found, would no longer be faith but a kind of syllogizing of ourselves into heaven.[9] There is, it seems, an intellectual prostration before *esse*, just as there is a faith prostration before God the Father, and nobody likes to prostrate himself before anything.

Again (we are still at the business of trying to make a point clear which really cannot be made clear in mathematical or physical terms), knowledge of *esse* always involves some knowledge of essence and vice versa. At first glance that proposition looks to be untrue, because, after all, we do seem to know what things are, without involving ourselves in knowing that they are; and we do seem to know that things are, without involving ourselves in knowing what they are. This is not so. If I read St. Thomas Aquinas rightly, we never know what things are, without knowing that they are, and we never know that they are, without in some sense knowing what they are.

Let us see if that last proposition can be somewhat clarified. Let us take the case of absolute nature, which is precised form (e.g., the number six) or formed matter (e.g., the six which is six sensibly uncharacterized bits of substantial or intelligible stuff). Assume we know that number. Now, the number need not be *known* in order to be itself, nor need it *exist* in order that it may be itself. The number is itself, whether it be *known* or not, whether it *exist* or not. Nevertheless, that number, which does not depend upon knowledge or upon things in order that it be itself, cannot *exist* except in knowledge. How "exist"? Obviously it does so in a state of being, as in an intentional or cognitive way of being. The number's self is a *cognitive* self, an *intentional* self. It peers at us clothed in the drapes of *esse*, namely, its intentional *esse;* yet it does not peer at us through those drapes as something which, if it didn't stick its head through the drapes of intentional *esse,* would be behind them nonetheless. Nor indeed does the number peer at us through the curtain of six existent things as if there were a six in *esse* which is not six things. The number is an intentional number, just as six things are natural *esse's.*[10] The situation then is this:

[9] Cr. Bernard J. F. Lonergan, S.J., *Insight* (New York: Longmans Green and Co., 1957), *Introduction,* p. xxix and *Epilogue,* pp. 743-744.
[10] *Quaestiones de Quolibet VIII,* q. 1, a. 1, c.

the number can be *abstracted* from all *esse,* real or intentional: it cannot be *separated* from its *esse,* whether real or intentional; rather, the number's *esse,* intentional or, as in six things, real, can be *separated* from the number or from six things. The number's intentional *esse,* however, cannot be abstracted from it; nor can the natural *esse* of six things be abstracted from them. To make the point this way: if the number's *esse* in the intellect could be abstracted from that intentional *esse* which it has in the intellect, and if six things' *esse* could be abstracted from them; if, furthermore, abstractive knowledge is the only knowledge we have, then *esse* would come loose with a mighty plop—from itself! Thus, our knowledge of the number, or our knowledge of six things, would be knowledge of nothing. But abstractive knowledge is not the only knowledge we have. We also know things according as they are in *esse,* intentional or real, and we cannot abstract from either *esse,* though we may separate either *esse* from its intentional or real mode of being. We may now assist at the experiment of separating *esse:* since it is not *because* existents are six that they exist (else there would be only six existents), physical or natural *esse,* therefore, is not necessarily involved in being six things; again, since it is not *because* the number is *known* as six that six is six (else nothing would be known but six), intentional *esse,* therefore, is not necessarily involved in knowing only that number. Thus, *esse,* real or intentional, is separated from both six existents and from its intentional *mode* of intentional *esse* (a knowing-six mode instead of a knowing-seven mode). And so essence is abstractively or quidditatively known without knowing its *esse;* but essence is never known as separate from its *esse,* real or intentional, else it would not be essence nor would it be known as such. *Esse* is separated from essence, but not the other way about: essence is not known separately from knowing *esse,* real or intentional. Thus, we never know *what* things are without getting ourselves involved in knowing *that* they are, and vice versa: we never know *that* things are without having been involved in knowing *what* they are.[11]

This being so, the intellect knows separated *esse,* not as having tagging along with that knowledge the knowledge of precised

[11] St. Thomas Aquinas, *De Ente Et Essentia* ch. 3: natura hominis absolute considerata abstrahit a quolibet esse, ita tamen quod non fiat praecisio alicuius eorum. Cf. *De potentia Dei* q. 5, a. 9, ad 16m; *Sum. Theol.* I, q. 44, a. 1, ad 1m.

form, or of form and form's appropriate matter, as though the intellect's knowledge of separated *esse abstracted* from precised form or from formed matter. Rather, the intellect's knowledge of separated *esse* does separate *esse* from the knowledge of precised form and from the knowledge of formed matter. (Formed matter abstracts from inappropriate matter, and precised form from individuals.) Thus, the intellect's knowledge of separated *esse* is not necessarily involved in knowing form, nor is it not involved. This, of course, means that the intellect, in knowing separated *esse,* is getting the hang *(ratio)* of *esse (entis),* not the hang *(ratio)* of material quiddities. And that means, since the intellect always, overtly or covertly, gets the hang of being, *(ratio entis),* that the intellect is open to knowing the cause of *esse* without which separated *esse* wouldn't have any hang to it at all.

Where does all this leave us? It leaves us facing a situation which is at once a knowledge situation and a situation in being. I shall now redescribe both situations simultaneously.

The human intellect is so structured that in any judgment which it proffers, it knows, explicitly or implicitly, an *esse* which is not identically its *knowing* of the essence, or identically the *essence* of that esse. A marvelous resource of spirit, this: or better, a marvelous resource, this, which is a spirit: to be all set, prepared, and readied to know what it means to exist in its very first encounter with existential act! For, the intellect in that first encounter with *esse* knows that its knowing that *x exists* is not a knowing of an "exists" which expires in being x. "More, more," a spirit ever cries. More of what? More of that *esse* which doesn't expire in being x, of course. But there isn't any more if *esse* expires in being x when x represents the totality of physical and mathematical predicates. This, a spirit cannot admit. Such an admission kills spirit. True, a spirit can develop its quidditative knowledge of x, from the bottom of the top of any Porphyrian tree, but reflection will reveal to it that such additions to knowledge are knowable and known only because they are known to be, actually or possibly. Just as quiddities in *esse* exist only because of their *esse,* so quiddities in knowledge are there only because they are known to exist, intentionally or really. And so, although the quest for quiddities is a great and laudable venture, the spirit would die from refusing the food upon which it lives if it refused quiddities in *esse.* For, if quiddities are not in *esse,* real or intentional, there aren't any quiddities at all.

Let us assist at the last gasp of an intellect's life which refuses quiddities in *esse.* Absolute nature or the knowledge of form (precised or a *totum*) exists only by an intentional *esse* whose content or intelligible structure is nonetheless not that intentional *esse.* The knowledge of separated *esse* also exists only by an intentional *esse* whose content is—what? It is the very structure of intellect itself, a knowing-separated-*esse*-structure, and this knowing is implicit in its every judgment. Deny that and you deny spirit, kill it, that is. Thus, spirit simply must move on by a necessity of its nature to know more than the separated esse which is involved in quiddities but which transcends them. That "more" is, of course, more quiddities in *esse,* and the knowledge that God exists. Should the knowledge that God exists be not enough to satisfy spirit (God's existence is known as in the truth of the proposition *God exists;* and this truth is not the truth which He is), this would mean that a spirit cannot be satisfied without seeing God, although philosophy cannot tell us how a spirit is to see God. A spirit's knowledge of God is here and now a knowledge of something like God, viz., knowledge of separated *esse;* furthermore, it is knowledge that God exists as a cause of that separated *esse,* both in knowledge and in things.[12]

Here is where the shoe pinches. Just as we might like to be God instead of being like Him, so we might like here and now to know God instead of knowing something like Him. Both situations show up in our knowledge of sensibles: Just as we might prefer sensibles, including ourselves, to be in themselves, so we might like to know them in themselves. The trouble is they are *not in* themselves, nor can they be known in themselves *qua esse* if their *esse* is accidental, and if in order to explain that accidental *esse* of theirs, and so have science about it, we must know that they are caused.

It may be noted in conclusion that the difference between the two propositions, *sensibles exist in or of themselves* and *sensibles themselves exist,* may be only verbal. If it is, there is no point in being finicky about using either one. Apart, however, from the rhetoric of the propositions which describe Greek and Christian metaphysics there is a vast difference between those two philosophies, and one way of locating that difference is in the way each

---

[12] *De potentia Dei* q. 3, a. 5, ad 1m.

relates the passive potential to *esse*. St. Thomas Aquinas did not like to hear people go around saying that essence "has of itself a potency to *esse*," because, he thought, there was no essence apart from its *esse*. He suggests that we say rather, "essence does not of itself have *esse*."[13] Clearly, he thought, essence is always related to *esse*, either to its own, which is from God, or else it is related to God's *esse* in which lies being and non-being, finally, it is related to an intentional *esse*, which is created by as much as God creates the operations of a created intellect.

13 *In octo libros Physicorum expositio* VIII, lect. 21, 5; Cf. *Summa Contra Gentiles* II, 53.

ᏊᏍ Doctrine of Creation in

Liber De Causis   *by Leo Sweeney, S.J.*

☆ ☆ ☆ ☆ ☆ ☆ ☆ ☆ ☆ ☆ ☆ ☆ ☆ ☆

T HE *Liber de Causis* has had an influence completely out of
proportion, to its size. Although this anonymous booklet
amounts to little more than twenty-five pages in any modern edition, it has influenced most if not all philosophers and
theologians throughout the Middle Ages and even later.[1] Accordingly, investigating any important doctrine in the *Liber* will
not only acquaint us with the *Liber* itself but will also furnish
the necessary background for understanding fully that same topic
in authors throughout subsequent centuries. One such problem
is creation, which is vitally important in itself and which holds,
as we shall see, a prominent place in the *Liber* as well as in most
later writers.

The present paper is, then, an attempt to discover what creation means in the *Liber de Causis*.

In this attempt, however, certain restrictions must be made.
Although the identity of its author is still an open question, the
Liber de Causis seems to have originally been written in Arabic.[2]
At the end of the nineteenth century Otto Bardenhewer published
the Arabic text, based upon a Leiden Ms. (cod. Gol. 209).[3] No

---

[1] See E. R. Dodds, *Proclus: Elements of Theology* (Oxford: Clarendon Press,
1933) [hereafter referred to as Dodds], p. xxix ff.; E. Gilson, *History of Christian
Philosophy in the Middle Ages* (New York: Random House, 1955), "Index of
Authors," see *Liber de Causis*, p. 811. Among the references there furnished, especially see pp. 181 ff., 211, 236 ff., 436.

[2] See H. D. Saffrey, *Sancti Thomae de Aquino Super Librum de Causis Expositio* [hereafter referred to as Saffrey] (Fribourg: Société Philosophique Louvain;
Éditions E. Nauwelaerts, 1954), p. xv.

For a survey of positions on its authorship up to 1938, see H. Bédoret, "L'auteur
et la traducteur du *Liber de Causis*," *Revue néoscolastique de Philosophie*, XLI
(1938), 519-533. For a survey up to 1954, see Saffrey, pp. xv-xxv.

[3] Otto Bardenhewer, *Die pseudo-aristotelische Schrift Ueber das reine Gute*

Arabic scholar, however, has yet studied creation within Bardenhewer's edition in any detail. Consequently, I shall confine my
efforts mainly to the *Liber de Causis* as translated into Latin by
Gerard of Cremona (d. 1187). This translation was so widely
diffused throughout mediaeval Europe as still to exist in nearly
150 extant Mss.[4] as well as in the modern editions of Bardenhewer[5] and of Robert Steele.[6] True enough, research in the Arabic
text must eventually complement the present study. Nevertheless, investigating the Latin treatise apart from the Arabic is profitable and even necessary in view of the fact that Western mediaeval
scholastics were acquainted with (and thereby influenced by) the
Liber almost solely in its Latin version. Accordingly, the Latin
version is the basis for the present inquiry.[7]

Secondary Sources

As was just mentioned, apparently no one has yet investigated
that topic in the Arabic text with any thoroughness. Has any one
done so in the Latin translation? The answer again is almost entirely negative. Satisfactory doctrinal studies on theological and
philosophical aspects of creation are at hand.[8] So too, rather
numerous historical inquiries into other authors exist. For instance, A.-M. Goichon in her *La distinction de l'essence et de
l'existence d'après Ibn Sina* has several sections on Avicenna's

---

bekannt unter dem Namen Liber de Causis (Freiburg im Breisgau: Herder, 1882),
pp. 58-118.

   [4] Saffrey, p. xv.   [5] Bardenhewer, *op. cit.*, pp. 163-191.

   [6] Robert Steele, "Liber de Causis," in *Opera hactenus inedita Rogeri Baconi*
(Oxford: Clarendon Press, 1935), XII, pp. 161-187. Another edition has recently
been published but is hard to obtain—"Neoplatonici apud Arabes," ed. Abdurrah-
man Badawi, in *Islamica*, XIX (Cairo: 1955).

   [7] The text used is that edited by R. Steele (see note 6), "IV, 164, 11" means:
Steele's edition, Proposition IV, p. 164, line 11. Bardenhewer's Latin text, as well
as his German translation of the Arabic text, will also be constantly consulted and
will complement Steele's edition wherever necessary or helpful. A reference to
Bardenhewer's Latin is this: "B (Lt), IV, 167, 2." Read: Bardenhewer's Latin
edition, Proposition IV, p. 167, line 2. References to his German translation will be
similarly made, except that (G) replaces (Lt).

   In an important section, "Charakteristik und Kritik der lateinischen Uebersel-
zung" (pp. 192-203), Bardenhewer discusses mistakes in Gerard of Cremona's translation when compared with the Arabic text. These Bardenhewer has rectified in his
German translation and will be taken into acount in the present study.

   [8] For example, A.-D. Sertillanges, O.P., *L'idée de création et ses retentissements
en philosophie* (Paris: Aubier, 1945).

theory of creation.[9] J. M. Parent, O.P., has written a volume on
the twelfth century school of Chartres.[10] As the result of the long
controversy on whether or not Aristotle was genuinely aware of
creation, abundant literature has arisen with reference to Aristotle, both in himself and in relation to thirteenth century authors.[11] No separate exploration, however, has been conducted
on the *Liber.* It is, in fact, silently by-passed even in historical
surveys of the problem. For example, in his lengthy and otherwise valuable article on "Création" in the *Dictionnaire de Théologie Catholique,* H. Pinard devotes the entire second section
to an "Aperçu Historique," wherein he aims at tracing the odyssey
of the notion of creation from the Scriptures through the Latin
and Greek Fathers and ecclesiastical writers up to the mediaeval
and renaissance scholastics and, thence, from Descartes on to the
twentieth century.[12] He fails, however, to take into account our
anonymous treatise.

Neglect of the *Liber* would be universal were it not for inci-
dental statements which authors sometimes make and many of
which, actually, tend to challenge the authentic meaning of creation in the *Liber.* For instance, Heinrich Barth in his *Philosophie der Erscheinung: Eine Problemgeschichte* notes that the
Arabian word translated by "creatio" in the *Liber* is not the same
as the word used in the Koran.[13] In the introduction to his critical edition of St. Thomas' commentary on the *Liber de Causis,*
H. D. Saffrey, O.P., lists the essential differences which separate

[9] A.-M. Goichon, *La distinction de l'essence et de l'existence d'après Ibn Sina*
(Paris: Desclée de Brouwer, 1937), Livre II, Chap. 2: "La dépendance de l'essence: la
création," pp. 201-334.

[10] J. M. Parent, O.P., *La doctrine de la création dans l'école de Chartres* (Paris:
J. Vrin; Ottawa: Inst. d'Études Médiévales, 1938).

[11] For bibliographies and a survey of the centuries-long discussion, see Faustinus
Prezioso, O.F.M., *De Aristotelis Creationismo Secundum S. Bonaventuram et Secundum S. Thomam* (Romae: Officium Libri Catholici, 1942), pp. 11-26; J. F. Sagués,
S.J., *De Deo Creante et Elevante* (in *Sacrae Theologiae Summa*), (Matriti: Biblio-
teca de Autores Cristianos, 1955), II, pp. 487-88.

[12] H. Pinard, "Création," *Dictionnaire de Théologie Catholique,* (Paris:
Librairie Letouzey et Ané, 1938), III, ii, 2042-2100. The entire article runs from col.
2034 to 2201. For a list of pertinent literature up to and including the first decade
of the twentieth century, see cols. 2199-2201; for more recent literature, see Sagués,
op. cit., passim.

[13] Hans Barth, *Philosophie der Erscheinung: Eine Problemgeschichte* (Basel:
Benno Schwabe & Co., 1947), p. 282, n. 3. On creation in the Koran, see Goichon,
op. cit., p. 202, n. 1; Arthur J. Arberry, *The Koran Interpreted* (New York: Macmillan,
1956), II, 364.

the *Liber* from Proclus' *Elements of Theology*. The second of
these is what Father Saffrey calls, "la transposition du système
néoplatonicien des 'processions'. en celui d'une véritable création."[14] That same transposition has even more recently been
described by M.-D. Chenu, O.P., as the reason why twelfth century theologians so readily assimilated traditional neoplatonism.[15]
But, as is easily intelligible in view of the specific aims of their
treatises, neither author investigates that doctrine in the *Liber*
and is content, within the single paragraph each devotes to the
topic, merely to question whether the author of the *Liber* was
really aware of creation in its strict sense.[16]

Data From the Liber *Itself*

In view of such almost universal silence, then, little help can
be expected from secondary sources[17] and we must concentrate
our attention solely upon the Latin treatise itself. What pertinent
data does the *Liber* contain?[18]

[14] Saffrey, p. xxxi.

[15] M.-D. Chenu, O.P., *La théologie au douzième siècle* (Paris: J. Vrin, 1957),
p. 137.

[16] Especially see Saffrey, p. xxxi. According to J. Doresse, creation is one factor
in which the *Liber* differs from Proclus: "Le verbe créer s'introduit dans le *Liber*
et y est entendu au sens de la création chrétienne" ("Les sources du *Liber de Causis*,"
Revue de l'Histoire des Religions, cxxxi [1956], p. 235). He makes no detailed
investigation of creation itself, though, nor does Pierre Duhem, *Le système du monde*
(Paris: A. Hermann, 1916), IV, 333 ff.

[17] At least three thirteenth century studies of the *Liber* exist in easily available
editions—that of Roger Bacon, of Albert the Great, and of Aquinas. These three
theologians all discuss creation in connection with the *Liber*, but their discussions
must, obviously, be reserved for future articles.

[18] One should be forewarned that understanding creation (or, for that matter,
any doctrine) in the *Liber* will be difficult for at least three reasons. First of all, its
author constantly uses Proclus' *Elements of Theology* yet in such an independent and
complex manner as almost to conceal whether and to what extent his thought actually
is Procline. Secondly, relevant information on creation is not abundant because he
attempts too much in too little space. In Steele's edition the *Liber* runs only to
twenty-six pages, yet within that relatively small area an entire and complex universe
is unfolded. At its summit is the First Cause, at its base is the sensible universe, and
on the two intervening levels are souls and intelligences. Each level of creatures is
again sub-divided hierarchically. Moreover, within those same few pages our author
also aims at disclosing the mutual relationships between its various levels and, even,
between various items within one and the same level. Significantly for our problem,
such disclosures reveal the deep layer of neo-platonism underlying the *Liber*. Finally,
our author frequently is inconsistent and this on matters touching causality and
creation.

For a discussion of these three points, see Leo Sweeney, S.J., "Research difficulties
in *Liber de Causis*," *The Modern Schoolman*, XXXVI, (January, 1959), 108-115.

First of all, the word *creare,* in some form or other, occurs at least forty-five times in Gerard of Cremona's translation and those occurrences are rather evenly distributed from beginning to end of the book—twice in Proposition III, seven times in IV, once in V, twice in VII, four times in IX, ten times in XVI, twice in XVIII, once in XX, twice in XXII and in XXIII, once in XXIV and in XXIX, eight times in XXX and, finally, twice in XXXII.[19]

Secondly, the common theme throughout these occurrences is that the First Principle of the universe is a creator and that His creative causality extends to absolutely everything—immediately to the First Intelligence and through this latter to all else. The First Cause, we are told, is above intelligences, souls, and the sensible universe precisely because He is a creator *(Et causa quidem prima . . . est supra intelligentiam et animam et naturam, quoniam est creans omnes res),*[20] and what He, the First Creative Being *(ens primum creans),*[21] has first and immediately created is the First Created Being *seu* the First Intelligence, which also is prior to other creatures in eminence, in power, in simplicity, and unity.[22] Through this Intelligence He created the being of the Soul, in virtue of which origin the Soul itself exercises even divine activity, and, after thus creating the being of the Soul, He placed it under the operational influence of the Intelligence so that the Soul might thereby be capable also of intellectual operations.

> Quod est quia causa prima creavit esse anime mediante intelligentia, et propter illud facta est anima efficiens opera-

---

[19] In Bardenhewer's translation, the word *erschaffen,* occurs forty-two times: twice in III, eight times in IV (which also includes V in Steele's text, since IV in the Arabic text is divided into IV and V by many Mss. of the Latin translation), once in VI, ten times in XV, four times in XVII, once in XIX, twice in XXI and in XXII, once in XXIII, twice in XXVIII, seven times in XXIX, and twice in XXXI. The term, *Urheber,* occurs four times in VIII.

Consequently, if we may judge by Bardenhewer's version, a term signifying creation occurs, by and large, as frequently in the Arabic original as in the Latin translation and in the same propositions.

[20] IX, 169, 27 ff. See XXIII, 179, 22: "creator intelligentie"; XXIV, 180, 30 ff.: "causam primam creantem"; XXXII, 187, 8 ff.: "unum verum primum est creans unitates."

[21] XVI, 174, 14 ff., where the phrase, *ens primum creans,* occurs three times.

[22] IX, 169, 31 ff.: "Et causa quidem prima . . . est creans intelligentiam absque medio." VII, 167, 25 ff.: "Et intelligentia . . . est primum creatum." XVI, 174, 19 ff.: "Ens autem creatum primum, scilicet intelligentia." XXIII, 179, 12: "et intelligentia est primum creatum." On its pre-eminence in power and the rest, see IV, 164, 1 ff.; X, 170, 21 ff.; etc.

tionem divinam. Postquam ergo creavit causa prima esse
anime, posuit eam sicut stramentum intelligentie in quod
efficiat operationes suas. Propter illud ergo anima intelligibilis efficit operationem intelligibilem.[23]

In fact, all eternal and self-subsistent entities have come from His
creative hand,[24] as well as all temporal items (i.e., the heavenly
bodies and all material things) and even Time itself:

> Omnis substantia creata in tempore aut est semper in tempore
> et tempus non superfluit ab ea quoniam est creata et tempus
> aequaliter, aut superfluit super tempus et tempus superfluit
> ab eo quoniam est creata in quibusdam horis temporis.[25]

In a word, absolutely every intelligible and sensible being takes
its origin from creation, and the First Being thereby is rightfully
described as their measure and creator.[26]

A Definition of Creation

Moreover, our anonymous author even furnishes what seems
a definition of creation. This shows up in the contrast set up in
Proposition XVIII between the creative causality attributed solely to the First Cause and the "formative" kind predicated of all
else. Absolutely all things, he begins, are beings because of the
First Being, whereas living things alone have self-motion through
the First Life and only intellective things have knowledge from
the First Intelligence.[27] Why that gradation in the extent and kind
of causal influence? Because every cause makes a unique and
characteristic contribution to its effects *(omnis causa dat causato
suo aliquid)*. Hence, First Being gives being to every being, First

[23] III, 163, 17 ff. See IX, 169, 32 ff.: [The First Cause is] creans animam et
naturam et reliquas res mediante intelligentia."
[24] XXIX, 183, 9 ff.: "Omnis substantia simplex est stans per seipsam . . . Nam
ipsa est creata sine tempore." B (G), XXVIII, 109, 14 also repeats the notion of
creation at the end of the Proposition: "Jedes Wesen, welches durch seine Wesenheit
subsistirt, ausser der Zeit erschaffen ist."
[25] XXX, 183, 19 ff.
[26] XVI, 174, 22 ff.: "Ens ergo primum est mensura entium primorum intelligi-
bilium et entium secundorum sensibilium, scilicet quia ipsum est quod creavit entia
et mensuravit ea." IX, 169, 28 ff.: "Et causa prima . . . est creans omnes res." See
also XXII, 178, 30 ff.; XXXII, 187, 6 ff.
[27] XVIII, 175, 20 ff.: "Res omnes sunt entia propter ens primum. Etc." B (Lt),
XVII, 179, 19 has "Res omnes habent essentiam" as the first four words. B (G),
XVII, 92, 2 has: "Alle Dinge haben das Sein durch das erste Sein."

Life gives life to self-movers, First Intelligence gives knowledge to knowers.[28] By way of summary, he concludes in the crucial lines of the passage, let us say that the First Being is the cause of causes and, if it confers being on absolutely every thing, it does so through creation. On the other hand, both First Life and Intelligence confer, respectively, life and knowledge on their resultants not through creation but only after the manner of a form.

> Redeamus autem et dicamus quod ens primum est quietum et est causa causarum, et si ipsum dat rebus omnibus ens, tunc ipsum dat eis per modum creationis. Vita autem prima dat eis que sunt sub ea vitam, non per modum creationis, immo per modum forme. Et similiter intelligentia non dat eis que sunt sub ea de scientia et reliquis rebus nisi per modum forme.[29]

Creatio, then, is here contrasted with *formatio,* the type of causality proper to creatures, and is restricted entirely to the First Being, which is the cause of causes and the extent of whose efficacy is maximal. But even more importantly, a definition is provided—creation is the bestowal of being upon all *(dare rebus omnibus ens).*[30]

More precisely, though, what is the meaning and the value of that definition? In describing it as a causality which is proper only to God and by which He establishes the very being of creatures, is our author accurately conceiving creation in its strict sense? In order to answer, we must return to the *Liber.*

The first Cause, we there are frequently told, exercises three functions in the universe, of which the first is creation.[31] The second is His outpouring of perfections *(influere bonitates)* upon

---

[28] *Ibid.,* lines 25-32.

[29] XVIII, 175, 32-176, 7. See B (G), XVII, 92, 15 ff. There the definition is translated as follows: "Wenn es allen Dingen das Sein mittheilt, so theilt es dasselbe in der Weise eines Erschaffung mit" *(ibid.,* 93, 1 ff.).

Dare per modum formae is, as we shall see, linked with a creature's completing or *forming* itself (XXV, 181, 12 ff.: "est ipsa causa formationis sue et sui complementi"), as well as with its ontological structure as a composite of *esse et forma* (IX, 170, 5 ff.).

[30] Throughout the treatise, *ens, esse* and *essentia* all seem to be synonyms. See Duhem, *op. cit.,* p. 342. Hence, *dare esse* or *dare essentiam* might as easily have been used as *dare ens.*

[31] See texts cited *supra,* notes 20, 21 and 26.

every creature,[32] while the third is the typically divine activity of directing and governing the world *(regere res creatas)*.[33] This last, however, is immediately consequent upon or even identical with the second, for God directs the world by imparting various perfections within it.[34] Consequently, the Supreme Cause has, basically, two activities—creation and, secondly, His outpouring of perfections.

As we have already discovered, the former is the bestowal of being upon absolutely every thing. The latter consists in the divine communication of life, light, power and the like—in fact, seemingly of every perfection except being. If *creare* is *dare ens*, then *influere* is *dare omnes alias bonitates*, which God imparts to the First Intelligence and, thence, to all else.[35]

Corresponding to those two divine activities is a two-fold receptivity on the part of creatures, of which the first is that by which a creature receives being and, thereby, is. The other is that by which it receives more determinate perfections and, thereby, is such and such.[36] In the case of intelligences (and, most likely, also of intellectual souls), this latter reception, actually, is achieved through its own activity of knowledge and, in this sense, such a creature is suitably termed "self-constituted," "self-forming," "self-causing," and the like.[37] Take, for instance, the First Intelligence. Through creation God causes that Intelligence to be, which thereupon receives all other perfections by turning toward its Source in knowledge.[38] As created by God it has *esse*,

[32] For example, XX, 177, 10 ff.: "Prima enim bonitas influit bonitates super res omnes influxione una. . . ." See B (G), XIX, 95, 11 ff.: "Das erste Gute lässt . . . ausströmen." See, among others, XXII, 178, 31 ff.; XXIII, 179, 14 ff.

[33] For instance, XX, 177, 1 ff.: "Causa prima regit res creatas preter quod commisceatur cum eis." B (G), XIX, 95, 2 ff.: "Die erste Ursache lenkt und leitet alle Dinge . . ."

[34] This concomitance or identity seems textually clear. For instance, in XX, 177, 7 ff.: "Et ipsa [causa prima] *regit* res creatas omnes et *influit* super eas virtutem vitae et bonitates . . ." [italics added]. XXIII, 179, 14 ff.: "Et sicut Deus . . . *influit* bonitatem super res . . . et *regit* res regimine sublimiori . . ."

[35] Concerning life, light and the like as *bonitates*, see, for example, XVI, 174, 29; XX, 177, 8 ff.; etc. *Ens* seems never to have been so listed. For the divine outpouring through Intelligence, see IV, 164, 33 ff.

[36] See among others: XIX, 176, 8 ff. and 25 ff.; XX, 177, 10 ff.; XXII, 179, 1 ff.

[37] See XXIV, 180, 5 ff. and especially, l. 29: "secundum modum quo cognoscit res causam primam creantem, secundum quantitatem illam recipit ex ea." This Proposition is analyzed below, p. 286. On "self-constitution," see XXV, 181, 12 ff.; XXVI, 181, 30 and 182, 8.

[38] This position concerning the First Intelligence is an application of XXIV, 180, 29 ff., quoted in the preceding note, as well as a legitimate inference from X,

yet through this act of contemplation it forms itself and, in fact, becomes a plenitude of forms *(plena est formis)*.[39] It is, then, a composite of being-forms *(intelligentia est habens helyatin quoniam est esse et forma)*,[40] of one-many,[41] of unity-powers, and of finitude-infinity.[42]

Through that Intelligence God then gives being to lower intellects and to souls by creation, each of which then constitutes and forms itself by similarly contemplating what precedes.[43] Thereby each mediately receives its additional perfections and becomes a combination of being-forms, of one-many and so on.[44] This mediate creation and consequent transmission of other perfections continue, through the influence of the World Soul, even throughout the sensible universe, where, however, the reception of *bonitates* is not through knowledge but only through motion and through generation.[45]

Such, then, is the two-fold activity and corresponding receptivity which the *Liber de Causis* attributes, respectively, to God and to creatures and which will perhaps be more readily intelligible if the Latin treatise is seen against Plotinus' *Enneads* and Proclus' *Elements of Theology*.

Plotinus and Proclus

According to Plotinus, the production of an item involves two atemporal moments—the *over-flowing* of the cause and, secondly, the *self-completion* of that which has overflown by turning back to its source. Consider, for example, the genesis of the Intelligence. Because of its super-abundant perfection, the One overflows and produces that which is other than Itself (ὃν γὰρ τέλειον . . . οἷον ὑπερερρύη καὶ τὸ ὑπερπλῆρες αὐτοῦ πεποίηκεν ἄλλο). This otherness then turns back to contemplate its Cause and, thereby, achieves full entitative status and perfection as an Intelligence full of forms, as a one-many, as an All, as a combination of entitative determination

171, 1 ff.: "Quapropter fit quod intelligentie secunde proiciunt visus suos super formam universalem que est in intelligentiis universalibus . . ." If lower intelligences receive perfections by contemplating what precedes them, *a pari* the First Intelligence by contemplating the First Cause does also.

[39] X, 170, 12 ff.
[40] IX, 170, 4 ff. On the meaning of *helyatin*, see Bardenhewer, p. 194.
[41] IV, 164, 9 ff.; V, 165, 23 ff.; VII, 167, 21 ff.   [42] IV, 164, 13 ff.
[43] See XXIV, 180, 29 ff. and X, 171, 1 ff., quoted above, notes 37 and 38.
[44] See IX, 170, 5-6; V, 165, 5-10; *ibid.*, lines 25-27; XIV, 172, 25 ff.
[45] V, 165, 16, 22; XXX, 184, 5-19; *ibid.*, 185, 8-15; XXXII, 186, 8 ff.; III, 163, 23-31.

and infinite powers.[46] The Intelligence, in turn, overflows and
produces the Soul, which thereupon looks back at its source and,
likewise, completes itself by becoming, in its own way, a plenitude
of forms, and powers, an All, a one-many, a combination of limit-
infinity.[47] Finally, also the Soul overflows and produces the sensible
universe.[48] Because of its inability to contemplate, however, this
product does not *complete itself* but, rather, *is completed.* It does
not fill itself with forms but instead, through movement communicated by the Soul and eventually translated into generation, it
is filled with forms or, more accurately, with reflections and images
of that plenitude of forms which abide immutably in the Soul and
Intelligence.[49]

Plotinus, then, divides the genesis of the universe into two
moments—over-flowing of the cause, and, next, the effect's completing itself by turning back to its source. What the author of
the *Liber* has done seems quite obvious: retaining Plotinus'
second moment in all important essentials, he has simply substituted creation for the first moment. The First Cause no longer
produces by over-flowing: He *creates,* He *gives being* to the Intelligence (or whatever the item may be). That Intelligence then proceeds to develop itself by receiving through contemplation the
additional perfections God pours upon it.[50]

What of Proclus? Although nearly smothered by his excessive
multiplication of first principles and almost unrecognizable because of his manner of proceeding *more geometrico,* still Proclus'
explanation of how the universe is produced does not basically
differ from that of Plotinus[51] and the author of the *Liber* perhaps
derived his knowledge of the two moments in that production
directly from the *Elements* rather than from the *Enneads.* However that may be, certainly our author uses two expressions which
only Proclus contributed since Plotinus seldom or never spoke

46 V, 2, 1, 7-13. For additional texts, as well as an interpretation, see Leo Sweeney,
S.J., "Infinity in Plotinus," *Gregorianum,* XXXVIII (1957), 531-35.
47 V, 2, 1, 14-18. See Sweeney, *ibid.,* 724-29.
48 V, 2, 1, 18-28. See Sweeney, *ibid.,* 729-30.
49 Texts are furnished in Sweeney, *ibid.,* pp. 715-16, 729-30.
50 See above, pp. 280-82.
51 Evidence for this similarity can be gained from Proclus' Propositions on
"Procession and Reversion" (Props. 24-39), from his theory concerning *auth-
hypostata* (Props. 40-51), etc. Also see Dodds, p. xxi: "The greater part of the
treatise agrees with Plotinus in substance if not in form." See the entire section,
pp. xviii-xxvi.

that way. The first is *substantia stans per seipsam*,[52] which is equivalent to Proclus' αὐθυπόστατον[53] and which now is applied to any intelligence or soul as capable of constituting, developing, and forming itself by contemplating its source and, thereby, receiving perfections.[54]

The other expression is *influere bonitates*, which, as we have recently seen, describes the second divine function within the universe and which obviously corresponds to τὸ τῶν ἀγαθῶν μεταδιδόναι of Proposition 120 in the *Elements*. In that section of his treatise, Proclus is discussing the nature and function of the gods *seu* henads, which transcend being and intelligence and by which the One carries out its causality throughout the universe.[55] In Proposition 119 ·he stresses that every god by its very nature is pure, supra-entitative goodness (ἡ ὑπερούσιος ἀγαθότης).[56] In the process of concluding within the next Proposition that every god by nature exercises a function-which-is-prior-to-intellection (τὸ προνοεῖν),[57] he locates that function precisely in its bestowal of goodness (τὸ τῶν ἀγαθῶν μεταδιδόναι) upon all else.[58] Intelligence has as the function proper to it a bestowal of knowledge upon all lower intelligences; Being in its characteristic activity confers form upon all subsequents. Since the One, together with the henads, transcends Intelligence and Being, His proper causality must be an activity which is prior to intellection and to formation and which touches

[52] See XXVI, 181, 19 ff.; XXVIII, 182, 18 ff.; XXIX, 183, 9 ff.   Bardenhewer's translation of the word in Arabic is: "Jedes Wesen, welches durch sich selbst subsistirt" (B [G], XXV, 105, 9).

[53] Dodds, Proposition 40, p. 42 to Proposition 51, p. 50. The term itself seems not to have been used prior to Jamblichus (Dodds, p. 224). William of Moerbeke, who translated the *Elements* into Latin in 1268, handles the term by a transliteration and gloss: "authypostaton, id est per se subsistentem" (see C. Vansteenkiste, O.P., "Procli Elementatio Thelogica Translata a Guilielmo de Moerbeke [Textus Ineditus], "*Tijdschrift voor Philosophie*, XIII [1951], 281).

[54] See above, p. 281. With Proclus, too, the word is restricted to intelligences and souls since the One transcends causality, whereas material things are caused rather than self-causing (Dodds, p. 224).

[55] See Dodds, pp. 257-60.   [56] Dodds, Proposition 119, p. 104, 1. 16 ff.

[57] Dodds translates this Greek expression as "providence," which, however, is misleading because of its connotations. "Providence" has come to be linked with a *knowledge* of events before they happen, whereas what the Greek phrase means is an activity which is prior to knowledge itself. Moerbeke's translation is similar to Dodds': "CXX: Omnis deus in sua existentia providere totis habet et primitus providere in diis" (Vansteenkiste, "Procli Elementatio," *op. cit.*, p. 498).

[58] Dodds, Proposition 120, p. 104, 1. 35. Proclus expresses that bestowal by various Greek verbs—e.g., πληροῦντες (Prop. 120, p. 106, 1. 9) ἐπιλαμπόντων (Prop. 122, p. 108, 1. 9), χορηγοῦσιν (*ibid.*, 1.11), διδόντων (*ibid.*, 1. 13).

even prime matter. It is, namely, the bestowal of goodness and unity upon absolutely every item.[59]

Here, then, is the second expression which our anonymous author took over from the *Elements* and which he easily fitted within his *Weltanschauung*. His is a First Cause which confers both being and other perfections. The first conferring he called creation; but what was he to name the second? In Proclus' phrase he found the answer—a description which signifies a divine communication of perfections which are other than being because prior to being. Merely change "prior" to "posterior" and the expression would fit: if *dare esse* is *creare*, then *dare omnes alias* [*et posteriores*] *perfectiones* is *influere bonitates.*[60]

When seen against the *Enneads* and the *Elements*, then, our treatise readily reveals that its basic *Weltanschauung* is typically neoplatonic with, however, the one important exception of its doctrine of creation. The First Cause no longer produces by over-flowing but by *creating*, by *giving being*. The very fact, though, that this doctrine is so neatly woven into a neoplatonist fabric makes its genuinity all the more suspect and we are once more confronted with the crucial question: in stating that creation is the bestowal of being upon all *(dare rebus omnibus ens),*[61] is our author accurately defining strict creation?

What Does "Being" Mean?

The crux of the matter is the word, "being." What does it mean?

When applied to creatures, the term can be used in at least three different ways.[62] At times it is equivalent to "inanimate" or some such term. Such is its meaning in Proposition I. Remove rationality from a man, our author there explains, and you still have a sentient, living being. Remove life, and *being* still remains —namely, the various inanimate and mineral composites which

---

[59] On the causal functions exercised by Intelligence, Being, and the One, see Dodds, Proposition 56, p. 54; Proposition 57, especially, p. 56, l. 4 ff.; Proposition 59, p. 56; Propositions 70-72, pp. 66-68; Proposition 134, p. 118; Proposition 138, p. 122.

[60] See texts cited above, note 35.

[61] XVIII, 176, 2 ff., analyzed above, p. 261. On neoplatonic elements in the *Liber,* see Leo Sweeney, S.J., "Research Difficulties in *Liber de Causis,*" pp. 111-114.

[62] As we have remarked earlier (note 30), "being" can be expressed by *ens,* by *esse,* or, even, by *essentia* without any notable change in meaning.

went to make up his body.[63] Obviously, this meaning is not intended by our author in his definition of creation, since there "being" signifies a perfection which God gives also to strictly immaterial beings.

In other contexts, "being" can be synonymous with knowledge. What determines, he asks in Proposition XXIV, how many and what sort of perfections a thing receives from God? The degree of its closeness to Him, he answers, together with the kind of power and of being it has. And by "being," he continues, I mean *knowledge,* for a thing receives in proportion to the manner and extent in which it knows.

> Quod est quia non recipit res ex causa prima et delectatur in ea nisi per modum esse sui. Et non intelligo per esse nisi cognitionem, nam secundum modum quo cognoscit res causam primam creantem, secundum quantitatem illam recipit ex ea et delectatur in ea.[64]

Manifestly, though, by "being" in his definition of creation he does not mean "knowledge," for does not God create also noncognitive existents, and even in cognitive ones is not "being" the divine gift which precedes knowledge? Moreover, in the original setting of the definition (Prop. XVIII), "being" is explicitly contrasted with "knowledge."[65]

Finally, the word can designate the absolutely first stage in the genesis of a thing. Consider Proposition III, where our author is recounting the various activities which a more perfect type of soul can carry out. Because God Himself has created its being, he explains, such a soul has divine operations. After having created its being, God then so placed it under Intelligence that this latter can effect its own operations within it and, thus, a soul has intellection. Thereafter it proceeds to accomplish its own sort of activity by communicating motion to the visible universe.

> Quod est quia causa prima creavit esse anime mediante intelligentia, et propter illud facta est anima efficiens operationem divinam. Postquam ergo creavit causa prima esse anime, po-

[63] I, 161, 23-30: "Quando removes virtutem rationalem ab homine, . . . remanet vivum spirans sensibile. Et quando removes ab eo vivum, . . . remanet esse. . . . Cum ergo non est individuum homo, est animal, et si non est animal, est esse tantum." See B (G) I, 59, 13 ff., especially *ibid.,* 60, 4 ff.: "Ist also ein Einzelding nicht Mensch, so ist es lebendes Wesen; ist es nicht lebendes Wesen, so ist es nur Seiendes."
[64] XXIV, 180, 24-32. See B (G), XXIII, 103, 9 ff.   [65] XVIII, 175, 20 ff.

suit eam sicut instrumentum intelligentie in quod efficiat operationes suas. Propter illud ergo anima intelligibilis efficit operationem intelligibilem et quia anima suscipit inpressionem intelligentie, facta est inferioris operationis quam ipsa in inpressione sua in id quod est sub ipsa. Quod est quia ipsa non imprimit in res nisi per motum, scilicet quia non recipit quod est sub ea operationem ejus, nisi ipsa moveat ipsum. Propter hanc ergo causam fit quod anima moveat corpora.[66]

Here, then, "being" expresses the absolutely first moment in the constitution of a soul. Subsequently it will receive intellection, motion and other perfections, but at the initial moment of coming from the creative hand of God, all that one can apparently say of it is that it has *being,* that it *is,* that it *exists.*[67]

This, I submit, is the meaning which the word has in our author's definition. When God gives *being* to any thing, He causes that to be which before was not. Later perfections will cause it to be *such and such,* but *being* causes it simply *to be.*

But how does His causality differ from that of Proclus' One? The difference is that the function of the One is to instill unity and a hunger for goodness in all its products. [68] These then become "beings" by receiving forms under the influence of the Being, which holds only second place in the line-up of causes.[69] The Greek author, then, accounts for how an item becomes united and informed but seemingly takes its actual existence for granted. In the *Liber,* however, the first Cause is *Being,* and the being which it bestows upon a creature comes *before* the reception of forms, knowledge or any other perfection and results, apparently, in the very existence of the creature

Conclusions

The crucial question throughout this study has been whether

66 III, 163, 17-29.

67 See B (G), VIII, 76, 2: "Jede Intelligenz hat ihre Existenz und Subsistenz durch das reine Gute." Gerard's translation (IX, 169, 1) has, "Omnis intelligentie fixio et essentia ejus etc." On "Existenz" as a translation of "fixio," see Bardenhewer, p. 193-94.

68 For example, Proposition 115, p. 100, 1. 36 ff.; Proposition 134, p. 118, 1. 28 ff.; Proposition 138, p. 122, 1. 12 ff.; Proposition 129, p. 114, 1. 30 ff.

69 Besides the texts cited in the preceding note, see Proposition 72, p. 68, 1. 24 ff.; Proposition 57, p. 56, 1. 8 ff.

the causal function of the First Principle in the *Liber de Causis* is a genuine creation.

When understood in its strict sense, creation necessarily involves three factors. First, the producer himself must undergo no change in the act of producing, neither losing nor acquiring any perfection, and the implication is that he is both all-perfect and entirely free. Next, what is produced must be really distinct from the producer and, finally, must be *wholly* produced.[70] For the causality ascribed by an author to his First Principle to be authentically creationist, it must include all those factors. Obviously, that inclusion need only be implicit, provided the writer somehow indicates his mind. For example, one can be sure that the product is *wholly* produced if the author states that God made it from nothing or that He produced even its prime matter or that He does not cause the item merely to be such and such but actually to exist. Obviously, too, the clear presence of one factor can imply another. For instance, if divine causality makes something actually exist which before was not, one can infer that such an effect is really distinct from its cause.

If we view creation in the *Liber* under the light of those necessary factors, what do we see? At first sight, there is a rather disconcerting absence of information. Consider the first factor. Although in the *Liber* God is described as all-perfect (literally, as more-than-perfect)[71] and, most likely, as immobile,[72] still our author seems completely silent on divine freedom.

Next, take up the second. Perhaps he comes closest to affirming that God and things are really distinct when he depicts the First Cause as totally transcending all else.[73] Yet transcendency is not automatically equivalent to real distinction, since even Proclus makes his One-Good completely transcendent and nonetheless holds that every effect is distinct from and yet *identified with its cause.*[74]

[70] This conception of creation is based upon statements from the Fourth Lateran Council (H. Denzinger, *Enchiridion Symbolorum* [29th edition; Friburgi Brisg.: Herder, 1953], no. 428) and the Vatican Council (*ibid.,* nos. 1782 ff. and 1901 ff.). For an analysis of these statements, see Pinard, *op. cit.,* 2081 and 2181-2195. Also see Sagués, *op. cit.,* pp. 468-95.

[71] XXII, 178, 30.

[72] For example, see VI, 166, 27 ff., where God is implied to be immutable because He transcends corporeal and even intellectual existents.

[73] See VI, 166, 27 ff.; IX, 169, 28 ff.

[74] Dodds, Proposition 30, p. 34, 1. 12 ff.

Finally, reflect upon the third. Is the product *wholly* produced? Our author neither speaks of creation as *ex nihilo* nor mentions prime matter. Does he at least state that God causes reality to actually exist? Although our author would have to be much more generous with relevant data to enable us to answer affirmatively with complete certainty, nevertheless our reply is *yes*. It seems highly probable that his First Cause not only causes every thing to be such and such but also and primarily *to be simply*. What else does "being" here designate but an existent immediately after it has felt the creative touch of God and directly before it receives other perfections?[75]

If this interpretation is accurate, then, the impact of divine relevation upon our author has been strong enough to break through an otherwise rather rigid neoplatonism and his Supreme Cause becomes the "First Creative *Being*." Whereas Proclus' One causes all things to be *unified*,[76] the *Esse Creans* of the *Liber de Causis* makes every thing simply *to be* by an act of genuine creation.[77]

[75] See III, 163, 17-29, analyzed above, p. 286.

[76] See texts cited in note 68. Occasionally, though, Proclus speaks in such a way as to suggest that even more should be abscribed to the causality of his First Principle. See Proposition 72, p. 68, 1. 26: "Matter, which is the substrate of all, has come forth from the cause of all [i.e., the One]." Also see Proposition 59, p. 56, 1. 36 ff.; *In Platonis Timaeum*, (Diehl edition) I, p. 384, 1. 30 ff.

[77] This interpretation is confirmed by Father Anawati's brief survey of creation in the Arabic text, which we obtained only after completing the present study. See G. C. Anawati, O.P., "Prolégomènes à une nouvelle édition du *De Causis* arabe," *Mélanges L. Massignon* (Paris: A. Maissoneuve, 1957), p. 93: "L'intention de l'auteur est nettement d'affirmer une 'création' au sens monothéiste du mot. L'expression employée est *abda'a* (64,2) que les Latins ont traduit par *creans*, avec ses dérivés: mubdi' (78.4), *al-mubtada'at* (65,11), *al-mubtadi'* (65.4). Le mot *halaga* ne s'y trouve pas mais l'emploi du mot Dieu avec *abda'a* ne laisse aucun doute sur l'intention de l'auteur."

For an account of positions on the authorship of the *Liber*, see *ibid.*, pp. 73-85.

࿐ The Universal in an Anti-Ockhamist Text *by Edward A. Synan*

☆ ☆ ☆ ☆ ☆ ☆ ☆ ☆ ☆ ☆ ☆ ☆ ☆ ☆

" Certain deluded moderns wish to save everything through concepts . . . they stand in need both of rebuke and of sense." They "bring to naught all philosophy as well as many a particular science." What is worse, "they would like to be addressed as 'rabbi,' and have every one believe what they say on no motive whatever . . . as if they were making pronouncements on articles of faith." Their philosophical principles, on their own showing, break down when applied to theology. Surely there is room, in the presence of such a threat to the rationality of Christian wisdom, for some one "to treat briefly of certain points necessary in logic and in theology for the benefit of beginners."[1]

Thus did the doctrine of Ockham's *Summa Logicae* appear to the author of a manuscript *Logica* preserved in the Library of the University of Bologna.[2] The Ockhamist scandal had already moved John Lutterell to delate William to the papal curia on a charge of heresy and what he had to say on universals was not the least of his

[1] *Logica, v. infra,* note 2, fol. 43v: . . . quidam moderni decepti qui salvare volunt omnia per conceptus. Fol. 41v: . . . aliqui moderni . . . indigent poena et sensu. Fol. 76r: . . . est negare totam philosophiam et multas scientias particulares . . . Fol. 64v: . . . videtur enim quod velint vocari 'rabbi' et quod quilibet credat dictis eorum sine quocumque motivo. Fol. 9r: . . . volunt quod in talibus ita eis credatur sicut si de articulis fidei loquerentur. Fol. 29v: . . . breviter de quibusdam necessariis in logica et theologia ad utilitatem simplicium pertractare. The reader will not miss in this line an echo of Ockham, *Summa Logicae,* I, 9; ed. Boehner, (St. Bonaventure, N. Y.: Franciscan Institute, 1951), p. 33, 20.

[2] Ms. Bologna, number 2653, Library of the University of Bologna, *Logica Campsale Anglici valde utilis ét realis contra Ocham;* for a description of this text and an edition of the chapters on the universal and supposition, v. E. A. Synan, "The Universal and Supposition in a *Logica* Attributed to Richard of Campsall," J. R. O'Donnell, C.S.B., ed., *Nine Mediaeval Thinkers: A Collection of Hitherto Unedited Texts,* (Toronto: Pontifical Institute of Mediaeval Studies, 1955), pp. 183-232; references to edited material are by page number of this edition, to unedited portions by folio as above, note 1.

offenses.[3] The author of this *Logica* reacted in another way: he
undertook to re-write Ockham's *Summa* from a "realist" point of
view and the single extant manuscript provides us with the chapters
which parallel the *pars prima* of that work. This text gives evidence of having been written by an Oxford man, in England, not
long after the publication of the *Summa Logicae*. Both in the
heading: "The Logic of Campsall the Englishman, very useful and
realist against Ockham," and in one line of the text itself, our author's name is "Campsall,"[4] but whether he can be identified with
the Richard of Campsall who died a Fellow of Merton, perhaps
shortly after the time of Ockham's death, is far from certain.[5]

Whatever his name, the *Logica* tells us more than a little about
this author. Duns Scotus above all others has inspired his thought;[6]
we shall not be unfaithful to this inspiration if we call the work,
valde utilis et realis as it is, "The Real Logic." Although he considers Aristotle by no means infallible, still the Philosopher is a
man to be respected[7] and this realist logician is no less disposed
than is Ockham himself to search the Aristotelian scriptures for

[3] Cf. F. Hoffmann, *Die erste Kritik des Ockhamismus durch den Oxforder Kanzler Johannes Lutterell*, (Breslau, 1941), p. 29: Der grosse Streitpunkt, um den der Kampf zur Zeit Lutterells ging, ist die Universalienfrage; for treatment of universals, *v.* pp. 29-39; for the related problem of supposition, *v.* pp. 22-29.

[4] *Logica*, fol. 21v: Et ego Kamsal, auribus meis, audivi unum doctorem solemnem Oxoniae qui ista determinatione publica dixit: hoc verum esse et quod sine periculo potest dici.

[5] *Cf.* E. A. Synan, "Richard of Campsall, an English Theologian of the Four-teenth Century," *Mediaeval Studies*, XIV (1952), 1-8, for a discussion of this figure and of the authenticity of the *Logica*.

[6] The author of the *Logica* is notable for a certain independence with respect to the "authors" and "doctors," including Duns Scotus himself, but there is an air of respect for the Subtle Doctor even when he permits himself to disagree: *ibid.*, fol. 70v: Sed licet illud [an opinion of Scotus] sit bene dictum, posset tamen dici aliter . . . Fol. 79r: Cui placet ista solutio, teneat eam; mihi tamen non placet; non enim videtur mihi quod sine magna necessitate, ut puta, si fides compelleret, sit negandum omne ens creatum infra x praedicamenta contineri . . . Fol. 79v: De sexto articulo, requiritur in Doctore Subtili, libro 2°, distinctione 2ª, quaestione quinta; et modus suus dicendi ibi non placet mihi . . . The deference of our author toward Duns is the more sig-nificant when compared with his acerbity toward other theologians: fol. 70r: . . . istius opinionis fuit Herkole [Henry of Harclay] quidam cancellarius Oxonii . . . illud est contra rationem et contra Philosophum . . . Fol. 66r: . . . et arguit Henricus de Gandavo . . . utrum autem illud argumentum valeat aut non, ingeniosus discutiat. Fol. 69v: . . . opinio Porretani in libello *Sex Principiorum*, qui fuit rudis logicus . . .

[7] *Ibid.*, fol. 20r: Non est enim aliquis ita insanus qui umquam dubitet istam propositionem esse veram ex quo praedicatum et subjectum stant pro eodem et, per consequens, Philosophus docuisset facere quaestionem inutilem et irrationalem—quod non est sibi imponendum.

the truth about logic. He is much concerned with the fruitful use of "authorities"[8] and it is one of his grievances against the Venerable Inceptor that he so often fails to determine the "intention" — always valuable — of each traditional formula:

> . . . therefore, a man of understanding should not find support in 'authorities' adduced improperly and at variance with the mind of the Philosopher. Rather should he seek out the trail of truth and the intention of the Philosopher, and — granted that the Philosopher's words might express the opposite — still, if right reason judge even this, with effective development, to be true, then he ought to explain the 'authority' of the Philosopher and give his words the meaning that was intended.[9]

On the crucial matter of the universal, this author has had a happy inspiration: he lets Ockham speak for himself. Two chapters of the *Summa Logicae* (I, 15 and 16) are quoted verbatim, without significant omissions, and the standards of a mediaeval professor required that our author weigh and refute each syllogism, reinterpret each authoritative text. We consequently assist at a kind of dialogue on universals and, if Ockham is a party to that dialogue only by courtesy of his opponent, the thought of the Venerable Inceptor is expressed in no words but his own. Whatever the doctrinal value of the arguments our author has been able to marshal against Ockhamism, the historical interest is incontrovertible: it is the response of a contemporary who has already perceived the seed of those developments — disasters, he has judged them — implicit in the "modern way" in logic.

II

Ockham has told us that the universal will be understood only if we grasp "its opposite, the singular."[10] In one sense of the term,

---

[8] *Ibid.*, fol. 20v: . . . nec debent auctoritates tortuose, praeterquam sonant, exponi nisi manifesta necessitas appareat . . . Fol. 85r: . . . abusio est negare tales propositiones concessas a philosophis et doctoribus et dicere quod falsae sint "de virtute sermonis"; dando expositiones extortas per actum exercitatum et significatum. Nam, eadem facilitate qua dicetur mihi de una auctoritate Philosophi, vel de una propositione, quod est falsa "de virtute sermonis," eadem ratione dicam ego de quacumque, et peribit locus ab auctoritate, et non erit amplius nisi quod quilibet sequatur miserias et fallacias suas.

[9] *Ibid.*, fol. 31v: . . . non ergo debet aliquis intelligens inniti talibus auctoritatibus male allegatis et non ad mentem Philosophi, sed debet veritatem et intentionem Philosophi investigare et, dato quod verba Philosophi sonarent oppositum, adhuc si ratio recta judicaret et hoc cum bona probatione esse verum, debet auctoritatem Philosophi exponere et dare intentum verbis suis.

[10] *Summa Logicae*, I, 14; *ed. cit.*, pp. 43-45.

a singular for Ockham is what is one in itself and of such a nature
that it cannot function as the sign of many. In another sense, there
is a singular, one in itself to be sure, but by nature ordained to
signify many. This is the "universal" of interest to the logician.
As an intention of the soul, it is an irreducible psychological unit,
but, because it signifies many, this intention is aptly termed "universal." Nor does Ockham lay claim to any originality here: Avicenna has said as much in his *Metaphysics*.[11] According to this
analysis it is permissible to say that the universal is a "singular."
Ockham thinks this striking statement should not disturb us: the
sun, as a thing in itself, is one; yet, inasmuch as the sun is the cause
of everything subject to generation and corruption, the single sun
is correctly termed a "universal" cause.

A further precision is that the universal at issue here is the very
concept which by nature signifies many, not the common term
which does, indeed, signify many, but only because men have arbitrarily agreed to assign it this function.

The *Real Logic*, too, provides us with a preliminary sketch of
singulars as a pedagogical device to help us with universals.[12] A
reality may be singular either "both according to being and according to meaning," or "according to being only." The first is the
concrete singular: Plato, this lion, this relation. It is any created
thing, not the sign of something else, taken in terms of the last
formal notion of which it is the ground. Such is the complete singular; such also the accident which borrows existence from its subject; such even the matter and the substantial form for each of which
"to be" is "to be in essential composition" with its correlate.

But the singular "according to being only" is stated of many
in one of two ways. Some singulars of this class are asserted of
many, one of which can exist without another — man, animal, lion,
stone are instances. Whether taken as words or as concepts, each
is singular according to being and each is, in itself, one in number;
yet, because each can be stated of many, none is restricted to singu-
larity "according to meaning."

What are these words and concepts, singular in their own being,
universal in their application, but the common terms and universal
intentions of Ockham? The apparent harmony is an illusion. True
enough, the *Real Logic* acknowledges that some terms are common

11 *Metaphysica*, V, 1; ed. Venice, 1508, fol. 87r, E.
12 *Logica, ed. cit.*, pp. 185-87.

and that some concepts are predicable of many. But neither term
nor concept is the universal defended by our author and his first
mention of supposition will dispel any impression that he and
Ockham are saying the same thing.

As for those singulars asserted of many which cannot exist independently of each other, the *Real Logic* is insistent on still another subdivision. All created relations are predicated of many
which can in no way be one in number, but the uncreated relations
of the Trinity are predicated of a plurality which is an infinitely
simple reality, one in number and unique. Hence no univocal
description of the created and uncreated singular can be given:
the attempt would shipwreck on equivocation. The created singulars, however, do fall under one definition, a formula which assumes that in every singular, no matter how simple its structure,
there are many formalities other than that which renders it "singular." For such a real individual to be possessed by many is, of
course, in contradiction to that ultimate and complete formal
notion by which it is *this*. Thus our author will not be uneasy
about his own position when Ockham undertakes to refute a
realism which would make some entity, one in number and a substance, present at once in many singulars.

A matter of the first importance, introduced by the *Real Logic*
before launching into the debate with Ockham, is the doctrine
of "supposition." It is not precise to say that "what is predicated
of many" is the universal; the true universal is rather an underlying
reality for which a term in proposition has the mysterious power
of standing as surrogate. Not the word, not even the concept, but
a thing (*res*) for which both stand, this is the genuine universal.

> Before this proposition, 'Socrates is a man,' is formed in the
> mind, it truly exists in reality (*in re*); not that these terms
> or these spoken words come first in reality, but a correspond-
> ing proposition does. For, just as a proposition in the mind
> corresponds to a proposition in spoken words (not that these
> propositions come first in the mind but a proposition which
> has the same meaning, true of the same items as is the vocal
> proposition, does come first and, to this extent, it is said that
> the proposition formed of spoken words is first formed in the
> mind), so a proposition in reality corresponds to and comes
> before a proposition in the mind. And, although it exists in
> truth, this proposition nevertheless lies hidden from us, nor

does it become known except through the mental or vocal propositions.[13]

Hence, in human speech, words are predicated of other words in vocal propositions; one concept, in intellectual discourse, is predicated of another. But to these propositions, verbal and mental, there corresponds a "proposition in reality," the same in meaning—if our thought and speech are accurate—and in this basic proposition alone are the true universals to be found. Thus early does the author of the *Real Logic* warn us that, for him, as for Ockham, no doctrine on universals is complete without a discussion of supposition.

With these preliminaries completed, it is easier to see how we ought to define the universal. It is that which can belong to many without contradiction of its formal notion. In the spirit of Duns Scotus, to whom he refers us for "all the other arguments which can be contrived for this conclusion," the author of the *Real Logic* offers three proofs that this definition meets the case:

First, lest his readers miss the point, no one intends the absurdity that something one in act should also exist in many. What those who "speak correctly" say is that, of itself, the human nature of Socrates could just as well be that of Plato. That a given instance of human nature be *this* nature is not owing to nature as such. For if it were, then human nature could not, as it does, belong to many. Of themselves natures are indifferent and common with respect to any and all individuals.

Second, what is expressed by a definition, "rational, mortal, animal," for instance, is something through which Socrates either is distinguished from Plato or something through which Socrates agrees with Plato. The first alternative is impossible: if it were the source of their distinction, it could not be found in both.

Third, what is defined is not in contradiction with Socrates, yet it does belong to Plato—hence indifferent to each and common to both.

III

When Ockham had completed his sketch of the universal, he proceeded to give both reasons and authorities in favor of his analysis. In this connection, his first attack is against a realism so

---

[13] *Ibid., ed. cit.,* pp. 186-87; Ante enim quam ista . . .

extreme as to make a substance of the universal.[14] Did the Venerable Inceptor have in mind a concrete opponent in this attack? It
is hard to believe that he did. I should judge that his procedure
is dictated by motives in the order of method: he is clearing the
ground by sweeping away the "pure position" to which, if he is
right, any form of realism must consistently be reduced. If the
object of attack is a caricature, it has the virtue of every reduction
to absurdity: clear and pungent, it will be disturbing to those who
see in it, however distorted, some reflection of their own explanations.

   Thus in the *Real Logic* it is Ockham who opens the exchange
with a piece of close-knit reasoning intended to establish the conventional Aristotelian position that "no universal is a singular substance, one in number," or, more briefly, that "no substance is a
universal." If the terms be taken formally, precisely in the meaning
they express, these propositions are conceded by the *Real Logic*.
But for all that, Ockham has gone too far: his facile inference of the
disjunction: "every substance is either one thing and not many, or
it is many things" is not valid. Of itself, a common nature is neither
one nor many. And the reason Ockham has not seen this, our author thinks, is that he makes of every distinction a real distinction,
of every unity a real unity. Blind to the formal distinction and to
its correlate, the less than numerical unity, he has missed the subtle
structuring of the concrete singular. One white thing is "like" another and "unlike" all that is not white: the formal notion of white,
therefore, is surely indifferent to similarity and to dissimilarity; yet,
in the concrete, there is no real distinction between that in virtue
of which a thing is white and that in virtue of which it is like other
white things. No more is there a real distinction between that in
virtue of which a being is "of some nature" and that in virtue of
which it is this "one" being. And the author of the *Real Logic* here
makes use of a technique characteristic of his opponent: what is
possible to the divine omnipotence? "Even if God could separate
likeness from whiteness," could a colorless subject truly be like or
unlike another in color? The like and the unlike bespeak a relation,
and relation has been excluded in the posing of the problem—hence
contradiction, a wound not even omnipotence can heal.

---

[14] *Summa Logicae*, I, 15, *ed. cit.*, pp. 45-49; this material is to be found reported
in the text of the *Logica, ed. cit.*, pp. 188-90.

Such an appeal to what lies under the power of God is, in fact, the basis for Ockham's second gambit: if the universal were distinct from the singulars in which it is found, then, since God can make anything by nature prior to another exist without that other, God could make it exist apart from all singulars. This is a conclusion no more acceptable to the *Real Logic* than to Ockham himself. But, so the defense against this assertion goes, God can make to exist apart only those things which are really distinct, not those which are divided only by a formal non-identity. It is not without interest that in making this defense, the author of the *Real Logic* explicitly adopts the position of Duns that matter and form might, by the divine power, exist apart;[15] matter, he agrees, "coincides with no form through real identity."

Ockham's next indictment of the real universal is that, in a world of common natures, given the existence of even one individual, creation and annihilation alike are rendered impossible. If one individual, enshrines even one common nature, how could a second be produced from absolute nothing? Would not the second to some point derive from the first? And if so much as one individual should be guaranteed survival, how could any other be reduced to absolute nothing? Would not the common nature of the individual destroyed in some way perdure in that which remained? Yet no Christian theologian can admit a First Cause powerless to create and to annihilate. For the *Real Logic*, this ingenious reasoning is "frivolous." The argument has no validity against the theory of common natures because that theory does not assert that there is something one and the same in two individuals, but rather that there is in one "something of the same nature as that which is in another." This formal identity is perfectly compatible with a real distinction between the two beings and consequently with their independent coming to be and ceasing to be.

Is the singular, in which, the realists allege, a common nature and individual difference ground universal predication, a composite of universals itself better termed a "universal" than a "singular"? If Ockham is right in saying so, then consistency obliges him to admit a real composition wherever formally distinct items are found to constitute a true unity. In one context, Ockham has admitted formally distinct relations, and the author of the *Real Logic* knows

15 *Logica, ed. cit.*, p. 192; *v. ibid.*, n. 28 for references to this opinion in the *Opus Oxoniense.*

it. He and his have conceded a formal distinction between the
divine essence and the divine relations.[16] Does he wish to say that
God, the Absolute, the One, is a composite? If not, then let him
confine himself to terming "composite" only what is a construct
of really distinct principles, for the exposition he has given in the
Summa Logicae would lead him into the absurdity that there is
as much, and indeed more, composition in God than in creatures.

The last of Ockham's five introductory arguments is dramatic
but, alas, no more than a restatement of the theme he has presented
in his second. He warns us that if we grant the theory of common
natures, something of Christ is damned in Judas. If human nature
is something truly one and common, how can the total Judas, universal nature and individual difference, not involve in his fall the
Christ who is man (if we are to believe the realist logicians) thanks
only to that same universal nature and different from Judas thanks
only to His individual difference?

Once more, and a modern reader may be forgiven if he wearies
of the exhaustive application of principle that ran in the fourteenth
century, Ockham is insisting that there are no unities save real unities, no distinctions but real distinctions. With equal doggedness,
the *Real Logic* answers, under the sign of the formal distinction and
the less than numerical unity, that there is no impropriety in admitting that something present in Judas the damned is "of the same
ratio" as something in Christ: the fact that the human nature of
Judas would never belong to Christ does not compromise its intrinsic indifference to redeemer or to betrayer. And the defense
concludes by remarking bluntly that the arguments of the Venerable Inceptor reveal "insanity rather than efficacy."

The author of the *Real Logic* meets the "authorities" which
Ockham adduces from Aristotle in a way which might well mislead
us. He asserts that they bear only upon the position of Plato "who
posited one man who would be of the essence of individuals" and
that "no universal such as Plato posited is a substance because none
such exists" and finally, "if something such as Plato posited be asserted, it is impossible that this thing should be a substance." Taken
at face value, these remarks invite us to think that the *Real Logic*
shares Aristotle's critical views of Plato's one beside the many, but
a later chapter will serve to correct this impression. When our author there has occasion to cite, as instances of "antonomastic" sup-

[16] *Ibid*, p. 192, n. 30 for references to this effect.

position, expressions which make Aristotle or Plato the greatest of
philosophers, he states his own preferences unequivocally: "But I
believe Plato more excellent than Aristotle, for he never thought
of those abuses with which Aristotle burdens him, as, dealing with
the third book of the *Physics,* I have made clear at greater length
in the chapter on The Infinite."[17] Hence we must conclude that
for our author it is against the Aristotelian Plato that Ockham's
strictures have some force: but this "Plato" was a creature of Aristotle before he was a victim of Ockham.

The point has been made[18] that when Ockham surveyed the
"authors" in support of his position on the universal, he chose without exception their metaphysics rather than their logic for his
source. And so it is that he can quote Aristotle, Averroes, and even
Avicenna himself to the effect that it is impossible for any universal
to be a substance. Here the *Real Logic* does more than point out
that Aristotle, at war with Platonic ideas as the Philosopher understood them, is opposing a doctrine which is far from identical with
that of common natures. Our author insists that the common nature, formally but not really distinct from individual difference,
is fully universal only when considered with its reference to that
individual difference. Thus it is that Aristotle's remarks on the
universal are clouded by a certain ambiguity. At times he means
the common nature as substrate of a reference to singulars; at others,
he means that very reference itself. How else shall we understand
his saying at times that universals are the same as the essence and
quiddity of their inferiors, whereas at other times he asserts that
universals are not substances? What other explanation for the term
"second substance," so conspicuous in the fifth chapter of the *Categories?* Yet Ockham's partisans have done more to distort that authoritative source than they did to mask the intention of the Philosopher in the text from the *Metaphysics* which has been cited in the
present context of Ockham.

The theme of the *Real Logic* in dealing with Ockham's authorities, however, is primarily to distinguish "this way"—the theory
of common natures—from the more extreme realism which Ockham is explicitly attacking. This is particularly clear in the view

17 *Ibid.,* p. 231.
18 Gilson, *History of Christian Philosophy in the Middle Ages,* (New York:
Random House, 1955), p. 786, n. 14.

our author takes of the text borrowed from Avicenna.[19] The term
"universal" is a fluid one with more meanings than Ockham likes
to give it. Avicenna is no opponent of the theory of common nature
and his remark is rather in support of "this way." True, like the
Ockhamists after him, he calls the universals "intentions," but when
he says that there is a universal "in act" he gives us to understand
that there is something which actually exists under the reference
that terminated in the genus "action." Avicenna's universal "in
potency" is that very reality without such reference and, to that
point, it fails of universality: it could be, but is not, an actual universal.

IV

Now must the *Real Logic* face Ockham's explicit attack on the
formal distinction, the open assertion of the Venerable Inceptor
that, in creatures, there is no distinction but the real distinction
and his syllogistic proof of that position.[20] Here our author returns
to a point he has made before: even Ockhamists concede a formal
distinction between the divine essence and the divine relations.[21]
No mere *tu quoque* this: to deny the distinction in creatures on
the ground that it would ruin their unity, yet to admit it in the
most simple Being of all, the Being most self-identical, the Being
where, nevertheless, the most thoroughgoing distinctions are to be
found, is an absurdity. If the reasoning Ockham suggests in the
name of infinitely deficient created unity were applied to God, the
conclusion would be heretical. But if there is no defect in the
reasoning, how can the antecedent stand?

The fact of the matter is, our author will have it, Ockham has
stumbled like a tyro in logic. To go from "this difference is not this
nature" to "this difference is formally distinct from this nature" is
to argue by negation from the higher to the lower; such an inference
will hold. But William has reversed this consequence: from the
weaker, he has tried to infer the stronger:

> this nature is not formally distinct from that nature; this indi-
> vidual difference is formally distinct from this nature; therefore,
> this individual difference is not this nature.

---

[19] *Meta.*, V, 1; *ed. cit.*, fol. 86v, A.

[20] *Summa Logicae*, I, 16, *ed. cit.*, pp. 49-52; this material is to be found reported
in the text of the *Logica, ed. cit.*, pp. 194-96.

[21] *V. Supra*, note 16.

All he needed to know what that an adverbial determination in the premises demands the same qualification in the conclusion. Individual difference is indeed distinct formally from the nature it contracts but this is not to say that the difference is really distinct from that nature.

When the proponents of a real universal say that the nature is common and the difference proper, is this not to assert opposites of the same thing? Do they not ruin the unity of the singular? But there is no contradiction, the *Real Logic* insists; community and difference do pertain to the same individual, but because of formally different *rationes*.

To the assertion that in the theory of common natures there is no true community because there would be as many natures as individuals (really distinct for all their alleged "formal" identity), our logician retorts that William has again blundered into a fallacy: he starts in the category of substance when he speaks of "the same," but he finishes in the category of discrete quantity with his "as many as" in the conclusion.

Furthermore, he is wrong in the way he handles a disjunctive syllogism, adding to a disjunctive major a minor which has no connection with either member of that premise. It is invalidly, then, that he posits one member as the conclusion. In any case, his minor is false. The "same" and the "diverse" pertain, not to natures, but to complete substances: Avicenna's *equinitas*, which is eternally *equinitas tantum*, is no more neutral than our author's *humanitas*: neither "like" nor "unlike": it is just humanity.

Ockham is not only guilty of omitting from his conclusions qualifications necessary for the truth of his premises; when it suits him, he introduces a qualification unjustified by the premises in his conclusion:

> in the opinion of Aristotle—what differ in species differ in number; the nature of man and the nature of ass are, of themselves, distinguished in species: therefore, each, of itself, is one in number.

This argument, too, is a paralogism: the qualification "of itself" is missing from the major and so not justified in the conclusion.

"Through no power" (and it is of the divine power that Ockham is thinking) can a nature really one with its difference belong to many; consequently, it cannot be predicated of many. What

does he mean by "belong to many"? Does he mean that what cannot "belong to many through real identity" cannot be predicated
of many? If he does, the *Real Logic* retorts, then he contradicts his
own theory of universal concept and common term, predicable of
many to which, because concepts and terms are singulars, they cannot belong by real identity. And if he means that what cannot
belong to many "through predication" ought not be predicated of
many, then this is true, but the minor of his argument is false: "a
nature really one with its difference, can through no power belong
to many because it can in no way belong to another individual":
that nature, precisely as such, can be predicated of many.

The following argument allows our author to add a precision
to his theory of common natures. Ockham has held that

> the distinction between difference and nature is either greater
> or less than that between two individuals; not greater, because
> they do not differ really and individuals do; nor is it less, for
> then they would be of the same *ratio* and consequently, if one
> were of itself one in number, the other would be of itself one
> in number.

Individual differences and specific natures differ less, the *Real Logic*
answers, than do two individuals; yet it does not follow that "if they
differ less, then they are of the same *ratio*." White differs less from
black than from stone, but it does not follow that black and white
are of the same *ratio*.

The last exchange turns on whether the adverb "really" is one
which limits a verb or not. For Ockham, it does not. If in any sense
one item is not another, then it "really" is not that other. Hence,
if individual difference is not the same as nature, then individual
difference is not "really" the same as nature—a formula which appears innocuous until we realize it would mean that a composite of
nature and difference would then not be a true unity. Contrariwise,
he suggests, one might argue: individual difference is "really" nature—thus unity is saved; therefore, individual difference is nature—
and Ockhamism is saved with it.

Now our author's virtuosity in seeing distinctions will not permit this easy assimilation of "is" to "really is." True, he concedes,
"really" is not always a limiting term: like the expression "as to his
head," this adverb sometimes limits and sometimes does not. "He
is white as to his head"; it does not follow that we can infer: "there-

fore, he is white." But, "He is curly as to his head," then we can infer: "therefore, he is curly." So, too, does "really" play different roles in different contexts: "he really runs"; then it is right to say: "therefore, he runs." But this is not the case when "really" qualifies "the same": real identity is compatible with a certain non-identity, that is, with formal distinction. Thus two invalid inferences may be cited: "what is the same by the lesser identity is therefore the same by the greater identity"; "what is really the same is therefore formally the same." In both instances the consequent is stronger than the antecedent, and thus there is in each a pseudo-consequence.

Such is the last exchange, but it is a particularity of our text that Ockham is represented by yet another argument, which, to compound the oddity, is ignored in the series of answers.[22] Perhaps a second manuscript would resolve the puzzle; as it is, we can do no more than note a last thrust by the Venerable Inceptor against the realist logicians.

In a context of formal distinctions, he says, the intellect can perceive the nature of Socrates without perceiving his individual difference. So also might the intellect perceive the nature of Plato apart from the perception of his difference. Seeing the two natures, the intellect cannot but know that one is not the other, and this is seen without reference to individual difference. Thus does an individual difference, formally distinct from substance, fall victim of that razor, which Ockham, although he did not invent it, wielded with enthusiasm.

V

Our author's anti-Ockhamist and realist view of the universal is not without bearing on the tract on suppositions[23] which completes his work. We have seen the *Real Logic* allude to this function of the term in proposition where it takes the place of the reality (*res*) which alone can justify either concept or word because it is their ground. What then are the implications?

---

[22] The *Logica* reports this tenth argument in the series (*ed. cit.*, p. 191) but answers the ninth argument under the heading "Ad ultimum" (p. 196); this last argument is also missing from the Boehner edition of the *Summa Logicae* where the chapter at issue ends with a summary statement of Ockham's denial of the formal distinction in creatures—an item missing from the *Logica* text.

[23] For the propriety of regarding the series of chapters on Supposition in the *Logica* as a unified tract, *cf.* the usage of the author himself, *ed. cit.*, p. 223, n. 84; p. 231, n. 93; p. 232, n. 97

In Ockham's world of homogeneous singulars,[24] universal terms can signify only individual things. If such a term stands for an intention of the mind, or, perhaps, for itself, this is only because words and concepts are themselves true signs of those individuals. Hence it is a world in which science is "of propositions,"[25] a world in which propositions are regulated by a logic that systematically denudes the universal of any role other than to designate the singular.

The *Real Logic* breathes another air. Here the singular is not homogeneous: under analysis, this structured entity will yield a whole series of formalities, irreducible to each other, no one of them a substance, but each of them real, each a *res*, all conspiring to constitute one single real thing. And science, for this author too, will be formulated in propositions; indeed, he could hardly deny that science is "of propositions." Has he not assured us that beneath the proposition expressed in words there lies a proposition composed of concepts and that to them both there corresponds what he does not balk at calling a "proposition *in re*"? Thus will two doctrines of supposition complete the two logics of the universal.

"Simple" supposition, for the *Real Logic,* is the substitution of a term for one of two items. It may be for that concept which another concept naturally signifies (we have, after all, a concept of our own concept of "man"), hence in the statement "man is a concept of the mind," the subject substitutes for the concept it naturally signifies. The other possibility is that a term stand for a conceived reality precisely "as conceived," and here, in agreement with Ockham, the subject of the proposition "man is a species" is described as exercising simple supposition. But for Ockham, the term stands for no more than the concept: for our realist, the term stands for the true reality which is conceived in the concept "man."

---

[24] The term "homogeneous" has been applied to the Ockhamist singular to emphasize its freedom from every internal division; the archformalist, Francis of Mayronis, has used "heterogeneous" to describe the opposite (Ms. Vat. Lat., 891, fol. 177v, *II Sent.*, d. 16): Hic incipit d. 16ª circa quam quaero: Utrum in corpore hominis organico sint plures formae substantiales? Et videtur quod non: per unam enim omnia salvari possunt.· Contra: ubi est etherogenitas, ibi est necessario distinctio specifica . . . Dico ergo quod omnes partes etherogenes partialiter differunt specie.

[25] *I Sent.*, d. 2, q. 4; ed. Lyon, 1495: M Ad secundum principale dico quod scientia realis non est semper de rebus tanquam de illis quae immediate sciuntur, sed de aliis pro rebus tamen supponentibus . . . scientia quaelibet sive sit realis sive rationalis est tantum de propositionibus tanquam de illis quae sciuntur, quia solae propositiones sciuntur . . .

The "formal" supposition of the *Real Logic* has no analogue in Ockham's exposition. It is that exercised by a term for its primary significate, whether common and communicable or singular and incommunicable. For, indeed, any formality, grounded in the structure of any thing, can be the object of this type of supposition: hence there can be just so many formal suppositions with respect to one thing as there are formalities in that thing.

"Personal" supposition is that of a term for an individual, or for several individuals, not (as Ockham would have it) for the significates of a term. For Ockham, this is the only supposition which is also significative: it is the most basic and, so to say, the norm against which his simple and material suppositions are measurred and found to be deficient. For what after all do they convey but concepts, intentions of the soul, and words contrived to serve our knowledge of things?

"Material" supposition, in Ockham's view the least impressive of all, is the role of a word that stands for nothing but itself: " 'Man' is a noun," for instance, or: " 'Man' is a written expression." And he points out that since words are either spoken or written, we would be authorized in subdividing this supposition, "if names had been imposed," to designate each type.

Not a word of Ockham on material supposition is unacceptable to the *Real Logic,* not even the detail that only our "poverty of terms" prevents a special terminology for the material supposition which has regard to the spoken word and for that which looks to the written word. But the unwonted harmony is marred by the insistence of the *Real Logic* that the traditional formulation *positio pro alio,* accepted by Ockham, is inadequate both for material supposition and for any instance in which a concept "naturally" signifying another concept exercises simple supposition; it ought to be: *pro alio vel pro se positio.*

Nor is this by any means the most serious defect our author finds in Ockham's tract on suppositions. If supposition invokes the world of reality which underlies the universe of discourse, then the realist logician is bound to think Ockham's world sadly impoverished. For if Ockham has seen the whole truth, for what realities can words stand? First, for the spoken or written significant term: if for this, then such non-significative use of a term for itself is "material" supposition. Second, for those intentions of the soul in which scientific knowledge achieves expression; these are brought into play whenever the supposition of a term is the non-significative "simple" supposition: "Man is a species"—and here it is that Ockham has located the universals. Third, there is the world of things, of substances. Each a unity of itself, each impervious to inner division, each secure against so thin a wedge as the formal distinction, such are the sole objects of the signification of words. If it is for these that words substitute, the supposition is "personal." And so it ends: the universe is one of words, concepts, things; no natures, no differences, no common and indifferent realities.

The world of the *Real Logic* contains, to be sure, terms which are but arbitrary signs, concepts which are natural signs—sometimes of other concepts, sometimes of things. But things are much more than they appear to an impercipient observer, be that observer the Venerable Inceptor himself. Only the true metaphysician, equipped with the virtualities of the logician, sees them in all their structured density. For there is in each singular a galaxy-like system of formalities, delicately balanced and never confused, so neatly fitted, one into the other, that the composite is "really" a unit. In the austere nomenclature of mathematics, each composite thing is but one, for all its manifold inner wealth.

VI

Both authors agree that ignorance of logic has serious consequences for theology. The *Real Logic* has concluded that the *Summa* of Ockham is, in fact, vitiated by an opinionated and puerile insolence which makes itself ridiculous in the accusations it levels against realist doctrine.[26] Concerned with theology, not only for its own sake, but also as a kind of testing-ground for logic, our author does not hesitate to make capital from what is, at best, only remotely "theological." His exposition of the category "action," for instance, finds support in the experience of the three young men in the fiery furnace[27] and he thinks that, before committing himself on whether weight inheres in quantity, a logician will do well to consider what the ordinary *Gloss* on the *Decretals*

---

[26] *Logica*, fol. 50v: . . . quando dicunt quod ad istam poistionem sequitur haeresis in anima, dico quod hoc est simpliciter falsum et sine dubio valde derisorium est quod tales homines velint alios reputare haereticos propter sophisticationes pueriles.

[27] *Ibid.*, fol. 71v: . . . potest Deus, de potentia sua absoluta, producere calorem aeque intensum et ejusdem rationis cum calore qui posset produci ab igne approximato illi ligno; quo facto, est planum quod ista propositio esset falsa: 'hic ignis agit in hoc lignum.' Et hoc probatur per exemplum trium puerorum in camino ignis.

has to offer the priest who has dropped a consecrated host.[28] Ockham, author of a eucharistic treatise by no means innocent of philosophical assumptions, is here countered by an opponent who cites ecclesiastical decisions on transubstantiation to clarify the rational analysis of material things.[29]

In the end, the fault Ockham has had to find with a realism of universal natures has been that such a doctrine involves irrational, because self-contradictory, conceptions: unities which are less than numerical, distinctions less than real. In Ockham's world, the sovereignly free divine power is bound by no natures. Limited only by the nothing which lurks under contradiction, this power does not extend to formally distinct entities. Hence the creator does not find among the possible terminations of omnipotence creatures split by formal distinctions, natures at once one and in many. Yet the faith may force us to allow such distinction: indeed, the doctrine of the Trinity requires that we explain the unity of nature and the plurality of Persons by what reason has condemned. How can the *Real Logic* avoid concluding that Ockhamist theology, served by so capricious a handmaid, is radically unintelligible?

Can it be said, finally, that the *Real Logic,* careful to guard the validity of universal predication, has been guilty of substituting the exigencies of thought for the constitution of things? Has this author reified the universal and made a pseudo-metaphysics of what is but an over-formalized logic? As early as his *Commentary on the Sentences* Ockham has said of all his predecessors that, to some degree, they have made "things" of what he is sure are no more than thoughts.[30] If our logician, dazzled by thought, has distorted things,

---

[28] *Ibid.,* fol. 53r: . . . si quantitas esset subjectum illarum qualitatum, ista quantitas vero esset ponderosa et sapida et colorata; consequens est contra *Glossam Decreti, de Consecrationibus,* super illud capitulum: "si per negligentiam," ubi dicit *Glossa* quod ponderositas remanet ibi cum aliis accidentibus, et tamen nihil est ibi ponderosum . . . (*cf. Corpus Juris Canonici,* t. ii, p. 1323, c. 27, D. ii, de cons.).

[29] *Ibid.,* fol. 67r: . . . illud patet in Sacramento altaris, nam sicut tenemus per fidem quod qualitas separatur ibi a proprio et propinquo subjecto, ita habemus consequenter dicere quod Deus posset albedinem a quantitae separare . . . Fol. 67v: . . . qualitati non repugnat esse sine subjecto, sicut patet in Sacramento altaris, ergo, etc. Et si dicas quod in Sacramento altaris remanet aliqua substantia panis, illud dicere est simpliciter contra determinationem Romanae Ecclesiae . . .

[30] *I Sent.,* d. 2, q. 7, B; ed. Lyon, 1495: In conclusione istius quaestionis omnes quos vidi concordant dicentes quod natura quae est aliquo modo universalis, saltem in potentia et incomplete, est realiter in individuo; quamvis aliqui dicant quod distinguitur realiter, aliqui quod tantum formaliter, aliqui quod nullo modo ex natura rei, sed tantum secundum rationem vel per considerationem intellectus.

he has blundered in spite of himself; he is persuaded and once at least has told us explicitly that, for him, reality regulates thought:

> A thing is not judged to be this way or that from the fact that predication is this way or that, but rather the contrary. For it is from the fact that a thing is or is not that discourse is pronounced true or false.[31]

Thus has the battle we have witnessed been joined on a common ground so narrowly fenced that the struggle was bound to be bitter. Agreeing that when a logician explains the universal, the fate of science, and particularly the fate of scientific theology, is at stake, both authors think that Aristotle has a logic worth completing and hence worth using. But how different the use of identical materials! Yet these two gleaners of his texts would have been classified easily by the Philosopher: because they belong in the same genus, it was possible for them to be opposites.

[31] *Logica*, fol. 43r: . . . ex hoc quod praedicatio est talis vel talis non judicatur res esse talis vel talis, sed magis e contrario, cum ab eo quod res est vel non est dicitur oratio vera vel falsa.

৯৶ Presuppositions and Realism

by Linus J. Thro, S.J.

☆　☆　☆　☆　☆　☆　☆　☆　☆　☆　☆　☆　☆　☆

HERE is no need to insist upon the crucial importance of the matter of presuppositions in the starting point of philosophy. A philosophy, as rational explanation, stands or falls with the adequacy of its point of departure. If, in fact, it rests upon unexamined or surreptitious premises, it disqualifies itself at the outset. Mere harmony of its conclusions with common sense or with a faith or a theology can at best be only a superficial recommendation of a philosophy; the same is true of agreement with the results of experimental science, or of ready adaptability to the needs of practical action. Such extrinsic criteria as these might lead to pragmatic acceptance of a philosophy, but not to its validation or verification. As rational inquiry, a philosophy is in need of a rationally acceptable foundation. Moreover, the strong development given in the last half-century to mathematical logic, emphasizing as it has the rigorous dependence of deductive systems upon initial axioms and rules, has pointed up for every organically reasoned philosophy as well the urgency of formulating explicitly whatever presuppositions may lie concealed in its starting point.

In fact, when the question of presuppositions is discussed, the pretension of any philosophy to operate without presuppositions is naturally challenged. The critical challenge is leveled in a special way against metaphysical realism — which makes an attractive target. Its doctrinal claims are considerable and very positive; if its claim to be presuppositionless is shown to be illusory, its pretended hold on objective truth will by that much be weakened or destroyed.

I

In taking up the challenge to realism, I should like to dwell briefly on a series of instructive views on the beginning of philo-

309

sophy which furnish some of the background for a contemporary approach to the problem. Hegel, it will be remembered, was convinced not only that his predecessors had failed to found an adequate philosophical system, but that an absolute beginning for philosophy is both necessary and feasible. In his *Science and Logic* his long preliminary chapter "With What Must the Science Begin?" opens with a remark on the contemporary discussions of the problem of the beginning of philosophy. He inveighs against those who settle for a merely objective concept or content as the beginning and those especially who, like Schelling, "begin with explosive abruptness from their inner revelation, faith, intellectual intuition, and so forth, and desire to dispense with Method and Logic."[1] Farther on he rejects the view that philosophy can begin from a hypothetical or problematical truth, so that at first it must be a mere seeking; moreover, the Self taken as an Absolute, as by Fichte, remains inevitably confused with the empirical self, is concrete and objective and, hence, not a suitable beginning.[2]

The beginning, Hegel asserts, must be "made within the sphere of Thought existing freely for itself, in other words, in pure knowledge."[3] This is the beginning of philosophy as absolute system, the pure science of Logic, wherein method and content, form and principle are blended: the Idea has become certainty of truth and "pure knowledge taken as shrunk into this unity, has transcended all reference to an Other and to mediation; . . . nothing is there but simple immediacy." This, he makes clear, is the purely abstract knowing of Pure Being, Being in general without further determination, exhausted of all particular or specific content. "That which constitutes the beginning," he repeats, "must be taken in its simple immediacy without content, as something not admitting analysis, hence as pure vacuity, as Being."[4]

What is this paradox of the immediate that arises from mediation, the absolute beginning in a "pure knowledge that is the result of finite knowledge, of consciousness"?[5] Hegel refers us to the *Phenomenology of Mind*, which he says is the Science of Con-

---

[1] *Hegel's Science of Logic*, trans. by W. H. Johnston and L. D. Struthers (London: Allen and Unwin, 1951), I, 79.

[2] *Ibid.*, pp. 82, 87-90.

[3] *Ibid.*, p. 80.

[4] *Ibid.*, p. 87.

[5] *Ibid.*, p. 81. Compare on "dialectical immediacy," Otis Lee, *Existence and Inquiry* (Chicago: University of Chicago Press, 1949), pp. 136-140.

sciousness demonstrating dialectically that consciousness results in
pure knowledge: immediate consciousness (i.e., in the *Phenomenology*, sensory perception) is "the first and immediate element in
the science, and therefore the presupposition." Whereas "in the
Logic, that is presupposition which appeared as the result of those
reflections, namely the Idea as pure knowledge."[6] "Nothing is
there except the decision (which might appear arbitrary) to consider Thought as such. The beginning must be an absolute . . .
it must presuppose nothing, must be mediated by nothing, must
have no foundation: itself is to be the foundation of the whole
science." The apparent loose end of a presupposition to the genesis
of the absolute System is taken care of, Hegel is confident, within
the system itself. "What is essential for the Science is not so much
that a pure immediate is the beginning, but that itself in its totality
forms a cycle returning upon itself, wherein the first is also last,
and the last first."[7]

Philosophers have questioned the legitimacy of locating an absolute beginning at a transcendent level of discourse which needs
first to be dialectically established. Julius Loewenberg, for example, in a paper entitled "The Comedy of Immediacy in Hegel's
Phenomenology," makes the point that the contradictions of immediate sensory experience which Hegel succeeds in proving are
really only its failure to measure up to the categories of Hegel's
absolute system.[8] He cites the boutade of the gentleman who was
told of the decapitated St. Dennis walking through the streets of
Paris: "C'est le premier pas qui coûte" — the only difficult thing
about the performance is the first step; he adds: "Hegel's dialectical

[6] *Ibid.*, pp. 80-81.
[7] *Ibid.*, pp. 82, 83. Cf.: "It is by the free act of thought that it (philosophy) occupies
a point of view, in which it is for its own self, and thus gives itself an object of its own
production. Nor is this all. The very point of view, which originally is taken on its
own evidence only, must in the course of the science be converted to a result,—the
ultimate result in which philosophy returns into itself and reaches the point with
which it began. In this manner philosophy exhibits the appearance of a circle which
closes with itself, and has no beginning in the same way as the other sciences have.
To speak of a beginning of philosophy has a meaning only in relation to a person who
proposes to commence the study, and not in relation to the science as science." (*The
Logic of Hegel*, translated from *The Encyclopedia of the Philosophical Sciences* by
William Wallace. [2nd edition revised and augmented; Oxford: Clarendon Press,
1892], n.17, pp. 26-27).
[8] *Mind* XXXXIV (1935) 21-38; cf. on the same issue, James Collins, *A History of
Modern European Philosophy*, (Milwaukee: Bruce Publishing Co., 1954), pp. 618, 636.

march is equally plausible if we offer no resistance to the manner in which he takes *his* first step."[9]

Much nearer to Hegel's own time, Søren Kierkegaard took issue vigorously with the pretensions of "absolute beginning."[10] In fact, Kierkegaard made a lengthy effort to show that the Hegelian system and the world of existential fact and Christian responsibility are mutually exclusive."[11] Above all, he uses against Hegel the dialectic of the unconditioned beginning: "This, that the beginning is, and again is not, just because it is the beginning — this true dialectical remark has long enough served as a sort of game played in good Hegelian society."[12] First to be attacked is the pretense of the System to begin without presuppositions and hence absolutely on the ground that it begins with the immediate: "How does the System begin with the immediate? . . . does it begin with it immediately?" This is impossible, says Kierkegaard: if the system is presumed to come after existence, then it is *ex post facto* and cannot begin immediately with the immediacy proper to existence, but must reach its beginning *mediately* through a process of reflection. Now, reflection of itself is endless — it cannot halt itself. "But if a resolution of the will is required to end the preliminary process of reflection, the presuppositionless character of the System is renounced."[13] The beginning made thus arbitrarily by breaking off the process of reflection cannot be absolute.

The Hegelian logicians, Kierkegaard acknowledges, insist that the "immediate" has not its usual meaning, since it is a beginning arrived at by a preliminary reflection. They define it as "the most abstract content remaining after an exhaustive reflection." But, says he, this definition says indirectly that there *is no* absolute beginning, for "with what do I begin, now that I have abstracted from everything? . . . with nothing!"[14]

Dismissing all this as perverse nonsense, Kierkegaard expresses in a word his distrust of the philosophic System and his burning concern to set about the creaturely task of being a Christian: "What if, instead of talking or dreaming about an absolute beginning we

[9] *Art. cit.,* 38.

[10] On the historical circumstances of Kierkegaard's reaction to Hegelianism, see J. Collins, *The Mind of Kierkegaard* (Chicago: Regnery, 1953), pp. 99-102.

[11] *Concluding Unscientific Postscript,* trans. by David F. Swenson (Princeton: Princeton University Press, 1941), pp. 99-133.

[12] *Ibid.,* p. 101; cf. p. 104.

[13] *Ibid.,* pp. 101-103.

[14] *Ibid.,* pp. 103-104; on the whole issue see also a comprehensive footnote, p. 134.

talked about a LEAP!" Kierkegaard's consistent respect for Aristotelian realism has been noted, as also the implicit realism of
many of the positions he takes up with respect to the existential
subjectivity of the individual and the moral and religious life.[15]
But as far as the availability of existent things to philosophical understanding is concerned, Kierkegaard has no confidence in philosophy. With the exception of the challenge it offers to personal
freedom, existence remains opaque, a surd.

In several of these respects, as is well known, Kierkegaard has
exercised a considerable influence upon at least some of the existen-
tialist thinkers. M. Merleau-Ponty, for example, states clearly what
he means by reality in such fashion as to locate himself among the
philosophers of existence. Primitive consciousness, he says, not
only is orientated toward human intentions rather than objects in
nature, but it grasps them as experienced realities rather than as
true objects.[16] In thus interpreting the real as that which exists for
the subject or the "humanly significant," he cites as evidence studies
in infant psychology, where, as might be expected, appetitive responses do predominate. He makes the further point, however, that
transcendental reflection will confirm what psychology has established with certainty about the priority of knowledge of other persons over knowledge of objects as considered in the sciences of
nature; but it will complete psychology. What transcendental reflection uncovers in particular, Merleau-Ponty asserts, is the pre-
objective sensible field which is prior both to perception of other
persons and to knowledge of objects. His later work on perception
attends throughout, implicitly or explicitly, to the presuppositions
of experience. Reflection, perpetually renewed reflection upon the
subjective life, is the very center of philosophy. But this procedure
can be gone through only at the cost of continual displacement of
the object, because the reflection bears upon the dynamically reflecting self. Unable to work from the simpler suppositions of a
creative absolute consciousness or of a transcendental self as pure
object, philosophy in fact can become transcendental only when it
focuses upon philosophic reason itself as its problem. The ultimate
problem for philosophy is that reason, conditioned as it, presumes to embark upon universal philosophical explanation. Mer-

15 Cf. Collins, *The Mind of Kierkegaard,* pp. 130f, 179, 246ff; and John Wild,
"Kierkegaard and Classic Philosophy," *The Philosophical Review,* XL (1949), 536-551.
16 Cf. *La Structure du comportement* (2nd ed; Paris: Presses Universitaires, 1949),
pp. 180-182.

leau-Ponty thus justifies his insertion of clinical psychology into the crucial point of departure of philosophy: without what psychology reveals of personal involvement in perception, we might have moved into an already established transcendental dimension of systematic idealism and missed the genuine problem, namely, that of the constitution of the transcendental out of the experiential.[17] With this orientation Merleau-Ponty describes the initial realism of lived experience as a continuous field wherein self, body, and others-and-things are neither confused nor distinguished. And in this perspective "the human order of consciousness appears not as a third order superimposed upon [those of the living organism and the physical realm], but as the condition of their possibility and their foundation."[18] In other words, by reason of my being thus radically and inescapably situated, every truth I express is only truth *for me* about *my* world, every evidence I appeal to is at once irresistible and yet rejectable.[19]

Now, by way of gingerly criticism, this picture of the conditions of human experience seems, even leaving aside the Hegelian elements, to be a reconstruction — in fact, a reconstruction resulting from the predominant control of psychological preoccupations in what should be a reflective description of what is given in experience. If this is correct, it is not surprising that this account fails to reveal the distinctness of experienced existent from experiencing subject which most experiencing subjects seem to find in their experience.

Ironically, excessive psychologizing might seem to be the least likely fault to impute to Merleau-Ponty, especially in view of his critical demolition of psychologism among the neo-behaviorists. *La Structure du comportement* accomplishes this so effectively that the presuppositional aspects of the behaviorist position can be passed by without other comment than one slight reference to a recent and readable proponent. The neuro-biologist, R. Z. Young,

[17] See *Phénoménologie de la perception* (Paris: Gallimard, 1945), pp. 75-77. On the problem of the radicality of beginning with Doubt-and-Cogito or *Epoché*-and-*Cogito*, compare Pierre Thévenaz, "La question du point de départ radical chez Descartes et Husserl," in *Problèmes actuels de la phénoménologie*, ed. H. L. van Breda, O. F. M. (Paris: Desclée de Brouwer, 1952), pp. 9-30.

[18] *La Structure du comportement*, pp. 204, 218. The kinship of this phenomenology of lived experience with the Hegelian *Phenomenology of Mind* has been noted by A. de Waelhens, *Une philosophie de l'ambiguité* (Louvain: Institut Supérieur 1951), p. 9.

[19] Cf. *Phénoménologie de la Perception*, pp. 453-455.

admits in a few places that the approach *via* nerves and brain has
not yet succeeded in solving all the problems of human knowledge.
Amid fluent uses of analogy — from nervous reaction in an octopus
to electronic computers, to human responses to stimuli — he acknowledges that the "most difficult part for us to understand is the
selection of the right response" even in octopuses; farther on it is
admitted that more information is needed for the problems of
generalization to be manageable.[20]

Perhaps one last contemporary treatment of presuppositions in
philosophy can be singled out for special attention. Ernest Nagel
in his American Philosophical Association presidential address two
years ago defended naturalism against the charge of resting, in its
commitment to scientific method, upon an indemonstrable faith.
In his refutation Mr. Nagel interprets this imputation of a presupposition to naturalism as though it were an attack upon the
methods of science. That is to say, he takes the point of the objection to be the reliance of science upon the uniformity of nature
(which is assumed and not justified empirically). His answer is
(a) that a wholesale justification for knowledge and its methods is
an unreasonable demand; and (b) that the warrant for any proposition in science or in naturalism derives exclusively from the specific evidence for that proposition, and additionally from the contingent historical fact that the method has been generally effective
in yielding reliable knowledge.[21] If I may be allowed a brief re-
buttal: this refutation is seen to be specious and ineffective when it
is realized that the assumption objected to in naturalism is rather
different. It is that a method capable of handling only data trimmed
to the empiricist pattern of sensorily verifiable evidence can ever
afford an adequate explanation of human experience and the world
of human experience. It was really the basic assumption of radical
empiricism that was in question.

II

This sampling of a variety of views about philosophical presuppositions is meant to be illustrative and suggestive rather than
exhaustive. Hegel, who maintains that his beginning in the Absolute System is presuppositionless, is nearly alone in believing this
is so. The failure of his absolute beginning was not in his having

20 *Doubt and Certainty in Science, a Biologist's Reflections on the Brain,* (The
B.B.C. Reith Lectures 1950 [Oxford: The Clarendon Press, 1951]), pp. 32, 86-87.
21 Cf. "Naturalism Reconsidered," *Proceedings and Addresses of the American
Philosophical Association,* (1954-1955), 14-15.

begun in Mind but in his not being able to do this without dependence upon a prior stage of finite consciousness. Hegel's real
weakness, as Kierkegaard suggests, was that he was not, in fact, God.

Professor Nagel, in speaking for pragmatic naturalism, fails, in
my opinion, to clear this sort of philosophy of the charge that it
begins with a massive, unjustified presupposition. Knowledge is
knowledge, says he, and there is only one valid sort: sensibly verifiable knowledge. For systematic naturalism to develop, this must
be presupposed.

Hence, to claim a presuppositionless beginning in philosophy
and actually to begin without a presupposition are not the same
thing. On the other hand, Kierkegaard was very sure that Hegel's
attempt was a pretentious hoax, and that at least one thing wrong
with it was that it systematically ignored the existential status of
human living. Kierkegaard may not have been equally sure that
no philosophy could give a reasoned account of existence but he
seems to have thought that he at any rate knew of none.

Merleau-Ponty's thought, from one point of view, centers upon
the impossibility of presuppositionless knowledge, science, and philosophy. It was intimated above that the chief relativizing condition he discovers in experience is perhaps one he has himself forced
upon experience as a result of his approach to it through psychology.[22]

In his *Logic and the Nature of Reality*, Louis Katsoff expresses
impatience with all the talk of commitments and presuppositions,
as though philosophy were a matter of persuasion and not a project
of reasoning men. Yet he volunteers a noteworthy distinction.
"Commitment," says Katsoff, generally connotes dedication to a
cause, and ordinarily not one's basic acceptances which are disclosed for explication or critical analysis. By contrast, inquiry is
undertaken into basic presuppositions in order to see what justification is possible. In this sense "assumption" would be the usual
word.[23]

A philosophy controlled by a commitment in the sense of dedication to a cause would, of course, destroy itself as philosophy.
Katsoff makes this point with respect to dialectical materialism in

[22] For another thoroughgoing reduction of experience to subjective interpretation by reason of the inescapable conditioning of the knower, see Angus Sinclair, *The
Conditions of Knowing* (London: Routledge, Kegan Paul, 1950).

[23] Louis O. Katsoff, *Logic and the Nature of Reality* (The Hague: Martinus Nijhoff, 1956), pp. 234-239.

the Communist orbit of intellectual influence. Personal and emotional involvement are determinants in the practical order, not in the speculative, which is our present concern. Perhaps we can exclude "commitments" from our discussion of "presuppositions." Along with them, we may put aside prephilosophical influences, attitudes, or orientations (cultural, temperamental, and so on) such, for example, as Plato's being born at the height of the Age of Sophists. Such influences and predispositions need not affect the substance of a vigorous thinker's philosophy.

What we need is an acceptable definition of philosophical presupposition. Here is one proposed by Arthur Smullyan: "By the presuppositions of a particular inquiry I refer to the assumptions, unquestioned in that inquiry, which control the progress or development of that inquiry," so that ". . . the result of the inquiry would be different if those assumptions had not been made . . ."[24]

According to this statement, a philosophical presupposition (or assumption) must not only control the result of the philosophical inquiry by serving as ground for at least some of its conclusions, but it must be unquestioned and unjustified within the inquiry. That is to say, it must be unquestioned, *yet questionable.* But questioning is strictly possible and desirable only when the full and luminous answer is not given. Now, to get to the point, if the prototype and fundamental source of intelligibility is given in experience, if it is given with such evidence as to render questioning it mere "paper doubt" (in Peirce's phrase), then we are not dealing with a presupposition or assumption.[25]

My contention is that this is the case with realism.[26] I mean to maintain that *realism does not assume, presuppose, or dogmatically assert* that there are knowable things existent and available to knowledge, and that man operating normally has true knowledge about them. On the contrary, I contend that both are discovered in ordinary human experience, and that realism, in reflective evalu-

---

[24] "Some Implications of Critical Common-sensism," in *Studies in the Philosophy of Charles Sanders Peirce,* ed. by Philip P. Wiener and Frederic H. Young (Cambridge: Harvard University Press, 1952), p. 111.

[25] The phrase, "paper doubts," is Peirce's (cf. text cited in the Smullyan article, cited above in note 24, from Vol. V, paragraph 416, of the *Collected Papers*) in his plea for intellectual honesty with the Cartesian type of doubt; his "indubitables," however, remain presuppositions, not evidences.

[26] Hence, the notion of Stephan Körner, in *Conceptual Thinking* (Cambridge: The University Press, 1955), p. 268, that all metaphysical propositions are beliefs resulting from "a choice between alternative possibilities" I regard as a mistake.

ation of the self-evidence of these insights into the real, stands upon
them as its basic principle. The evidence is accepted because it is
understood to be unquestionable. Hence, realism, I maintain, is
founded, not upon an unexamined and unjustified presupposition
of a harmony between the "subjective *logos*" and the "objective
logos"[27] but upon the discovery in experience of the intelligibility
of being and upon the development of its own directive principle
as realism through reflection upon the evidentiality of being.

III

One can, of course, settle the case for our knowledge of reality
with simplicity and speed by the dogmatic assertion the British analysts used: "No existential proposition can be logically necessary;
only analytic propositions are necessary and these carry no information about existence."[28] It is quite another thing to show, as positivistic analysis has not shown, that there is no philosophically acceptable evidence of existence or that no criteria of evidence may
reasonably be applied except those dictated by classical rationalism
or empiricism.

Customarily, presentations of the availability of being to knowledge, or of the evidentiality of existence, have been made in terms of
the union of knower and known, or the transparency of representative media, or non-physical intentional being in the knowing subject, or still others. These approaches all betray ontological and
psychological preoccupations that tend to obscure the central point
in realism, which is the cognitive immediacy of the evidence of existence. Now I would suggest that each act of the awareness of being,
every knowledge, in other words, is a new actuality in the order of
intelligibility. Hence, as cognition, it is neither explained by the
operation of ontological causation or physical and psychological
mediation, nor is it explained away if unanswered difficulties crop
up in these areas.

Let me attempt an illustration: There is a "blip" on the radar
screen, the observer reacts forthwith, taking a penciled note, speaking with urgency into his mouthpiece, perhaps showing signs of

---

[27] Paul Tillich, *Fundamental Theology*, (Chicago: Chicago University Press,
1951), I, pp. 23, 75-77.

[28] Raphael Demos, "The Meaningfulness of Religious Language," *Philosophy
and Phenomenological Research* XVIII (1957), 97, in a critique of *New Essays in Philosophical Theology*, ed. by Anthony Flew and Alastair Macintyre (New York: Macmillan, 1955). In the volume under criticism see pp. 47-75, especially the contribu-
tions of J. N. Findlay.

extreme concern — but he reacts, and because of the new state of affairs transmitted to him through this slight flicker of light. The significance for him of the manifestation on his instrument is without question a matter of "learned experience." The observer after long and arduous training knows how to interpret this occurrence against a background of specialized experience. But suppose we ignore the sign-value and fasten upon the sudden light-flash itself. This is mere brute fact, fresh existential event. However many times the observer may have seen flashes on this screen, this one now is another one, a new one not merging into the others, demanding on its own to be acknowledged and accepted as part of the real order. As this presently occurring event, it owes nothing of its evanescent but new reality to the observer's past experience. And before the observer can in sophisticated fashion make his interpretation of its meaning, he sees it as this something that is now taking place. This is evidence of an existence — and it is not shrugged away.

Perhaps another sort of example will help further along the same line. We may take a fairly typical instance of the experimental situation in contemporary science. In a recent study on the genesis of alcoholic behavior[29] the injection of alcohol is found consistently to reduce an "anxiety-state" in cats. We may consider two phases of the experimental procedure. First, the cat must be brought artificially to a state of "anxiety." A behavior pattern is established of taking food at one corner of the cage. Then over a period of ten days an electric shock is administered each time the cat picks up his food. Before the end of the week the cat stands hesitant at its feeding-place anticipating the shock, snarling, clawing, hissing before it touches the food. This pattern of "approach avoidance," as the psychologist calls it, represents the "anxiety-state" which is to be reduced in the second phase of the experiment. The procedure now is simply to inject a small quantity of alcohol into the cat before the usual feeding routine. The experimenter discovers that the cat does not arch its back, snarl or hiss at the food before taking it, but goes straight for it, heedless of the shock. The "approach avoidance" has been eliminated, an "anxiety reduction" has been

---

[29] A number of clinical studies are referred to and instances of work of this kind are reported by J. Conger, "Re-inforcement Theory and the Dynamics of Alcoholism," in *Quarterly Journal of Studies on Alcohol* XVII (1956), 269-305.

achieved by the use of alcohol, and the scientist draws his analogy to human habituation to alcohol.

Allow me to indicate briefly some of the features of this situation which are to my point. The experimenter's purpose is to correlate the results of a series of experiments and so formulate in terms of stimulus-and-response coordinates the consistency of reaction within a definite controlled situation. To have any scientific value the experiment must be reproducible, testable by others. No one will ever, for example, reproduce the single concrete approach of experimental cat number seven to a given portion of food, in a given past and completed experiment. That approach was an existential occurrence which will never happen again, which could not be anticipated except in general (statistically, with high probability). But it is the kind of thing, which, when it happens, brings new knowledge to the experimenter. It might be thought trivial, but this recognition of a cat's singular activity here and now is available to this scientist alone; and if he is to make an original contribution to his science, a vast complex of personally acquired bits of similar factual knowledge will constitute the solid ground of experimental evidence which he presents to his colleagues. *Then* they check it, yes; but it has to be known to him before he can present it to others. If they are concerned to check his results and conclusions, it will be up to them to reproduce the conditions of his experimentation and achieve verification in new factual knowledge like his. Not that their knowledge will be identical with his, because experimental results in their *existential newness* — at the point when one can say: "Yes, look, it comes out so!" — are the experimental results of the experimenter who gets them.[30] Rather, even in its distinctness this new bit of knowledge carries with it intelligible elements which make it part of a connected series of factual dealings with, say, the experiment in feline anxiety and alcoholism. These common intelligible elements, moreover, make these experimental findings communicable to others, comparable to their findings, and open to verification by the scientific community. In a somewhat similar vein it is said, in answer to the canard that every experience is strictly private and incommunic-

---

[30] Witness the care with which the scientist guards his findings until he has been able to publish them as his own and has been duly credited with them; for on such achievements of new knowledge as these, as well as on the heuristic fertility of his interpretation of them, depend his prestige and success as a scientist.

able, that, although the experiencing is by definition private, *what-is-experienced* can well be common and communicable.[31]

It needs especially to be emphasized here that even in the private experiencing of the newly here-and-now-known there is given and known a *common* structural character over and above, or rather underlying and supporting, the quantitative, qualitative, and relational features in which it compares and contrasts with other known things. I mean the not obscure fact that this newly-known reality is above all comparable with all other experienced realities in its being something, so that it presents itself existentially in experience as something-that-is. The singular existent, insofar as it exists, proves *not* to be opaque to understanding, however indeterminate other characteristics of it may be. Thus, reflection upon each newly presented reality leads one to the conclusion that there is available to knowledge the common intelligibility of "what actually exists." When by further reflective consideration this has been duly purified, the conception of being serves as the principle which founds and guides a realistic metaphysics. Such a metaphysics ties in each newly experienced being with other beings; it focuses the speculative intelligence upon what constitutes these as being. It always requires uninterrupted contact w i t h existent things in its pursuit of deeper understanding. As for the realism of the correlative theory-of-knowledge, the availability to awareness of every newly experienced existent has been likewise given in each experience. In sum, realism may be said to grow, under the light of reflective consideration, out of the twin roots of the given existence of material beings and the evidential manifestation of them in knowledge.[32]

Perhaps a third effort will help to catch in the concrete this almost, but not quite, ineffable intelligibility of being. From the point of view of the sympathetic outsider, scientists today seem to have developed a pronounced group-consciousness. They tend to resent the attempts of philosophers of science to categorize them and methodologize their work. In rebelling, they will emphasize, on the part of the scientist, the imaginative, the creative, the personal, the human character of each man's contribution to scientific

[31] Cf. Stephen Körner, *Conceptual Thinking* (Cambridge: The Harvard University Press, 1956), pp. 172-179.

[32] That this knowledge cannot either be credited exclusively to the organic sensory apparatus nor achieved entirely without it is a corollary of this thesis. I will not enter this issue. It is treated in Fr. Henle's paper; see pp. 76-81.

knowledge and its dissemination and application. At the same
time they will insist that the physical things they investigate are
not the pale abstractions of the philosopher of science, but each a
fresh *existential* challenge, that the problems they must face are
not ivory tower conundrums they have dreamed up but each an
urgent demand for more adequate explanation of the data they
are working with, each a new drain upon the scientist's resourceful-
ness and ingenuity. There is a certain irreducible uniqueness,
they will tell you, in every thing they deal with. Every time even an
established distillation process is gone through, every stage must
be watched alertly, because laboratory supplies are pestiferously
individual. Every sounding they take in a wartime experiment in
jungle acoustics is a fresh shock to their settled preconceptions.
Their instruments turn out to be insufficiently sensitive to record
the extremely variable behavior of sound amid rapidly changing
temperatures.

The experimental scientist operates in a highly existential context, accepting as real the same things the ordinary normal layman
takes as real. He has no choice: these are the things he must deal
with in his work if he is to make any progress in understanding
the physical order. The demands of their vocation make all experimental scientists existential realists in practice, no matter what philosophical view of the world their theoretical conceptualizations
may lead them to adopt. Basically, the reason seems to be that in
all experimental work, although there is much that is familiar and
common, there is always the existential situation of data that are
refractory and challenging, results that are disappointing or puzzling or startling, so much that is here and now newly given, demanding recognition and new understanding as nothing before
it had.

At the same time, it is these data, these instrumental readings,
this set of revised correlations, which bring fresh information about
perduring characteristics of the existent things which are their constant concern. The continuing intelligibility of such characteristic
structures is, of course, requisite to the scientist if he is to remain
on the same research project for even one day. However, when we
undertake to assess this situation philosophically, certain observations must be made. Let us note, then, the uniqueness of each individual thing with which the scientist deals as well as the uniqueness of his experimental data. In addition we note the obtrusive,

existential novelty with which the data present themselves in experimental results. We note also the structural intelligibilities that we find among these data as we found them before. Here again we will have the evidence giving the realist a direct grasp (and not an irrationally founded postulation) of the world of beings and inviting him to pursue ultimate questions about the nature and causes of reality.

There is some concern among scientists over the dangers of distortive metaphysical presuppositions in science and the necessity of clearing them away. Probably some would disagree substantially with Whitehead's conviction that science is an enterprise in which reason is based on a faith, rather than faith on reason, that science "is essentially an anti-rationalist movement, based upon an instinctive conviction and a naive faith," and that "this faith cannot be justified by an inductive generalization. It springs from direct inspection of the nature of things as disclosed in our own immediate present experience," and "is impervious to the demand for a consistent rationality."[33]

There seems no reason to doubt that at least some metaphysical intrusions into science are harmful and, like many of Galileo's and Newton's assumptions, are mere outworn baggage. Some, on the other hand, seem to underlie all scientific inquiry. The conviction, for instance, that the behavior of nature is not entirely arbitrary or, more generally, that some kind of order prevails in nature, seems without question to be the driving force in experimental research. The experimentalist approaches his work, not with mere inquisitiveness or the eagerness of a child for novelty, but with intelligent expectation. When he is on the track of what promises to be a new phenomenon, "it does not occur to him to wonder whether it follows any law"; he expects it to be orderly in its behavior; "he only wonders *which* law" or laws it will follow, and his experimentation is shrewdly planned toward the discovery of its orderliness in detail.[34]

---

[33] *Science and the Modern World* (New York: Macmillan, 1926), pp. 23, 27, 6.

[34] E. F. Caldin, *The Power and Limits of Science* (London: Chapman and Hall, 1949), p. 60, who adds: "Whitehead remarks that science depends upon 'the inexpugnable belief that every detailed occurrence can be correlated with its antecedents in a perfectly definite manner, exemplifying general principles. Without this belief the incredible labours of scientists would be without hope. It is this instinctive conviction, vividly poised before the imagination, which is the motive power of research: that there is a secret, a secret that can be unveiled.'"

With respect to convictions such as these, i.e., about the orderliness of natural phenomena and their openness to understanding, several remarks seem appropriate. First, instead of being written off as relics of an era of magic and superstition or as inspired by the "mediaeval insistence on the rationality of God,"[35] or as based on belief in the Christian Creator-God,[36] their origin in ordinary human experience might much more reasonably be acknowledged. After all, the tides as well as the seasons *do* recur with clock-like regularity. There are specific types of things as common as water and coal which are knowable as such along with their reliable properties. One could extend such a list. The conviction that the universe over-all makes sense, and that with persistence he can uncover more of it — this seems simply to be part of the natural realism of ordinary men engaged all their lives in existential contact with the world about them.

Secondly, such convictions are not strictly within the experimental procedure of the science but are extra-scientific assumptions. They are "presuppositions" in the full sense of the term. But, it should be noted, there is nothing illegitimate or unreasonable about their being accepted. Apart from his career in science and by prior title, the scientist is an intelligent human being with long experience of existing things and their behavior.

Thirdly, the same convictions, since they arise out of the evidence of being and assured experience of being, are *not presuppositions to realism*. Within the realist metaphysics the intelligibility of being functions as an evidential principle rather than an assumption or presupposition. In that context the obtrusive demand of being to be acknowledged and studied in relation to all its manifestations leads in due course to the discussion of the problems of order in the cosmos.

To sum up, realism, as I understand it, rests its case for a sound starting-point upon the twin elements which reflection finds in ordinary knowledge. There is the givenness of the subjective experiencing, but only simultaneously with the inescapable givenness of what is experienced; the experiencing is not a detached phenomenon any more than the experien*ced*; neither is accounted for in terms of impressions, ideas, representations, or sense-data, wheth-

[35] Whitehead, *op. cit.*, p. 18.

[36] Cf. Arthur F. Smethurst, *Modern Science and Christian Belief*, (New York: Abingdon Press, 1955), pp. 12-31.

er atomic or contextual. What is experienced may be a remembered event, or a present pain, or, as the realist will insist is the most usual situation, some other reality apart from the experiencer *but acting in some way upon him.* This is real prior to the experience and independently of it. Presumably, it is real following upon the experience as well. The realist points in support of his thesis to the massive evidence of existence and activity of things in the world about him, the same world in which his critic finds himself.

If this actually is the case in human knowledge, then realism cannot be charged with resting upon the unjustified assumption that beings exist and are understood in experience. On the contrary, these are not presuppositions but are the fundamental insights in human experience upon which all human knowledge, action, and aspiration depend. Rather than remaining outside realism as a philosophical discipline, they are taken up as its basic principle whose evidence is confirmed anew at each new step within the discipline, applied again to every successive issue, and exploited throughout with complete openness to fresh experience.

Now, if the things I have been attempting to express about the evidentiality of existence and the correlative discovery of the first principle of realism seem to have degenerated into "triviality," as A. J. Ayer would describe the fate of any proposition about existence,[37] I can only suggest that most of the largest philosophical issues cannot fit into a positivistic idiom. Or if my argument for the presuppositionless character of realism has seemed to bog down in persuasive rhetoric, that is unfortunate, but not surprising. If my analysis of the situation of being and knowledge is correct, the realist can do little more on a difference in principles than try to lift veils, point in inadequate fashion to what he sees and understands, and invite all others to take another look.[38]

---

[37] *The Problem of Knowing* (London: Macmillan, 1951), p. 52.
[38] See Louis O. Katsoff, *Logic and the Nature of Reality* (The Hague: Martinus Nijhoff, 1956), pp. 119-124, on sensory and eidetic intuition and the ways in which the veridicality of intuition must be established, if it is to be established at all.

Concept Formation in Certain Empiricist Thinkers in America

by William M. Walton

☆ ☆ ☆ ☆ ☆ ☆ ☆ ☆ ☆ ☆ ☆ ☆ ☆ ☆

THE THEORY of concept formation has always been considered to be of major importance among the traditional followers of St. Thomas Aquinas and of Aristotle. In recent years much attention has been devoted to the equivalent of concept formation by empiricist philosophers in America. The writer believes that a confrontation of some of their views with the traditionally accepted Thomistic analysis as he understands it might throw additional light on the theory of knowledge with reference to this problem.

Since the logical empiricists are devoting considerable time to this area of research one of their number has been included. Members of this group use *concept* rather loosely, however, to include the act of judging and the proposition. For some, moreover, abstraction is simply that formalization which is exclusively concerned with language, an example being the change of a statement into sentential function by the substitution of variables for referential constants. Analysis of their position has been restricted, therefore, to consideration of the *ex-professo* treatment of the problem found in Carl G. Hempel's *Fundamentals of Concept Formation in Empirical Science.*[1] Attention is then turned to the theory of F. S. C. Northrop as presented in *The Logic of the Sciences And the Humanities.*[2] Here, again, we have a serious—though, in many respects, quite different—attempt to delineate an acceptable theory

[1] Carl G. Hempel, *Fundamentals of Concept Formation in Empirical Science* (Vol. II, No. 7 of the International Encyclopedia of Unified Science) (Chicago: University of Chicago Press, 1952). Hereafter referred to as Hempel.
[2] F. S. C. Northrop, *The Logic of the Sciences And the Humanities,* (New York: Macmillan, 1947). Hereafter referred to as Northrop.

of concept formation. Finally, consideration is given to the views presented by the late Alfred Korzybski in his *Science and Sanity*.[3] In this work we find an altogether different, in that it is a much more psychological, approach to the problem. The process of abstracting is discussed in great detail and in terms of diagrams. No representative of the pragmatic school of thought has been included since these philosophers are chiefly concerned with the grounds for and consequences of our beliefs in generalizations and far less interested in how we attain them. The three thinkers considered have given much serious thought to the discussion and have presented their findings in detail. As implied above, the writer would like to make the analysis of their writings contribute to our common understanding of this question by comparing their views with the Thomist position.

For Professor Hempel the notion of essential nature is so obscure and so vague as to render it useless for the purposes of rigorous inquiry.[4] For him, no examination of a given object could establish any of its characteristics as essential.[5] In other words, there is no abstraction and no essential definition in the Thomist sense. Instead, there must be a search either for an empirical explanation of some phenomenon or for a meaning analysis of some statement. *Experiential* data are those obtainable by direct experience and which serve to test scientific theories or hypotheses; such are sensations or the simple physical phenomena which are accessible to direct observation, as, for example, the coincidence of the pointer of an instrument with a numbered mark on a dial or the clicking of an amplifier connected with a Geiger counter.[6]

Hempel accepts the modification of the earlier positivist insistence that each statement of empirical science must be verifiable or falsifiable by means of observational evidence. This change was brought about by the recognition that a scientific hypothesis cannot, as a rule, be tested in isolation but only in combination with other statements. In other words, the criterion of testability has to be applied to comprehensive systems of hypotheses rather than to

3 Alfred Korzybski, *Science and Sanity*, (3rd ed.; Lakeville, Conn.: The International Non-Aristotelian Library Publishing Co., 1948). Hereafter referred to as Korzybski. As indicated, the approach of Korzybski is much more "psychologistic" than that of Hempel or Northrop. There is no intention of linking their names together as though they represented a single school or position within empiricism. The differences between the three men are quite marked.
4 Hempel, p. 6.   5 Hempel, p. 52.   6 Hempel, p. 21.

single statements. The rigid standard of complete verifiability or falsifiability has been replaced, moreover, by the more liberal requirement that a system of hypotheses must be capable of being more or less highly confirmed by observational evidence.[7]

Thus a hypothetico-deductive-observational procedure is followed in the more advanced branches of empirical science. Guided by his knowledge of observational data, the scientist has to invent a set of theoretical constructs, lacking immediate experiential significance, a system of hypotheses couched in terms of them, and an interpretation for the resulting theoretical network; and all this in a manner which will establish explanatory and predictive connections between the data of direct observation. The term *point*, for example, as used in theoretical physics is a construct and does not denote any objects that are accessible to direct observation.[8] Theoretical constructs, which are often highly abstract terms used in the advanced stages of scientific theory formation, such as *mass point* in classical mechanics, *absolute temperature* in classical thermodynamics, and *electron* in quantum mechanics, are not introduced by definitions or even reduction chains b a s e d on observables. Rather they are introduced jointly by setting up a theoretical system formulated in terms of them and by giving the system an experiential interpretation, which in turn confers empirical meaning on the theoretical constructs.[9] It is these *fictitious* concepts, moreover, rather than those fully definable by observables which enable science to interpret and organize the data of direct observation by means of a coherent and comprehensive system which permits explanation and prediction.[10]

Of interest to the Thomist here is the recognition that for this strictly *deontologized* knowledge, i.e., scientific knowledge in its pure form, the signs and symbols he elaborates can be grasped and manipulated by the scientist only in the form of *entia rationis* that he or his fellow scientists have created and which they believe are in some way verifiable in terms of reality. Hempel does not recognize, as the Thomist does, that by the activity of the intellect itself there can be drawn from the data of the senses universal intelligible natures seen by the human mind in and through the concepts it engenders by illuminating the phantasms. The search is no longer for essences, but for necessary laws, which in actual fact presuppose essences as their ultimate ground. Thus a concept loses its

[7] Hempel, p. 43.   [8] Hempel, p. 37.   [9] Hempel, p. 32.   [10] Hempel, p. 31.

meaning in any field which excludes *a priori* any possibility, whether direct or indirect, of verifying its application. Knowledge is obviously a completely univocal notion, only realized in the sciences of phenomena.

For Professor Northrop human knowledge is not entirely encompassed in and limited to the impressions received by the senses and the imagination. In his discussion of ideas in Aristotle, for example, he claims that Aristotle has smuggled into the transitory data of sense awareness an immortal persistence which they do not possess. In other words, a slight element of postulation has been introduced in the sense that the thinker postulates for the intuitively given meanings of the concepts by intuition a logical status and resultant immortal persistence beyond the brief spans during which they are actually sensed. In short, to the immediately apprehended content which is transitory and sensed, there is added by postulation, merely an immortal logical status and subsistence. For Northrop, morever, it is precisely this slight element of postulation added to pure concepts by intuition that distinguishes obviously metaphysical theories like Aristotle's from positivism.[11]

Theories of any kind whatever, even metaphysical and religious ones, can be brought down to the earth of empirical fact and can be tested with respect to their truth and falsity. This test is made by relating the propositions of one's deductive theory to empirically given, directly inspectable data.[12]

There are two distinct types of concepts, namely concepts by intuition and concepts by postulation. A concept is simply a term to which a meaning has been assigned. There are two major ways in which this assignment can be made. The otherwise meaningless term may be associated denotatively with some datum or set of data which is given immediately and then it becomes a concept by intuition, or it may have its meaning proposed for it theoretically by the postulates of the deductive theory in which it occurs and then it becomes a concept by postulation. *Blue* as the sensed color is a concept by intuition. Intuition denotes what is directly apprehended purely inductively so that a concept by intuition is one which denotes, and the complete meaning of which is given by, something which is immediately apprehended. On the other hand *blue* as the number of a wave length in electromagnetic theory is a concept by postulation; a concept by postulation being one the

11 Northrop, pp. 89-90.   12 Northrop, p. 114.

meaning of which in whole or in part is designated by the postulates of the deductive theory in which it occurs.[13] Following the terminology of C. I. Lewis, Northrop refers to those concepts by intuition that are concepts by sensation or introspection as concepts by inspection. *Blue,* in the sense of an immediately sensed color, is a concept by sensation.[14] An immediately felt pain is a concept by inspection which is a concept by introspection.[15]

Mere observation and experimentation do not provide a trustworthy criterion of the verification of a scientific theory, since observation and experiment alone give only concepts by intuition whereas what is present in a scientific theory are concepts by postulation. What is required in addition is some unambiguous relation or *epistemic correlation* joining the one to the other. Ordinary empirical correlations, for example, that between pressure and volume in physics, hold between concepts of the same type. They join either a concept by inspection to another concept by inspection or a concept by postulation to another concept by postulation. The distinguishing characteristic of an epistemic correlation is that it joins a concept by posulation to its corresponding concept by inspection, or conversely, thereby making empirical verification referring to unobservable postulated entities possible.[16] Empirically given operations become a criterion of objectivity in science by way of the epistemic correlations which join them to the objective entities and relations designed by concepts by postulation. Conversely, verification of one postulated theory of the invariant or objective rather than another, depends upon concepts by intuition, epistemic correlations, and operational definitions.[17]

According to Northrop, positivism is the thesis that there are only concepts by intution. Positivism in the occident has tended, moreover, to maintain that all concepts by intuition are definable in terms of or reducible to concepts by sensation or concepts by introspection. For him, a metaphysical theory is one that holds that there are also concepts by postulation.[18] If such metaphysical theories are to be scientific, however, the philosopher must specify his metaphysical postulates unambiguously and set up epistemic correlations between the entities of his metaphysical theory and di-

[13] Northrop, pp. 82-83. For a more detailed analysis (though from a somewhat different point of view) see Joseph B. McAllister, "Northrop's Concepts by Intuition and Concepts by Postulation," *The New Scholasticism,* XXIV, 2 (1950), 115-135.

[14] Northrop, p. 98.   [15] Northrop, p. 103.   [16] Northrop, pp. 192-194.
[17] Northrop, p. 131.   [18] Northrop, p. 99.

rectly inspected data, thereby permitting verification. There is no justification, however, for supposing that it is necessary to reduce every concept in one's deductively formulated scientific theory to the type of meaning which only those "who think merely with their hands" can understand. As a rule, only some of the theoretical concepts by postulation of a scientific theory have operational meanings and denotatively given epistemic correlates.[19]

It is abundantly clear that for Professor Northrop there is but one type of genuine knowledge; he clings to the notion that the only object capable of giving rise to an exact and demonstrable knowledge is that which can be subjected to methods of experimental and mathematical analysis.

Alfred Korzybski frankly admits that he has decided to accept as his structural metaphysics that which is given exclusively by science.[20] In science, he finds, we observe silently and then record verbally. From a neurological point of view we abstract whatever we and the instruments can, then we summarize, and finally we generalize, which simply means the process of abstracting carried further. From a series of differing individual men, for example, by a process of abstracting the characteristics, we segregate the individuals by size or color; then, by concentrating on one characteristic and disregarding the others, we could build classes or higher abstractions, such as *whites*. Abstracting again, with rejection of the color difference, we would finally reach the term *man*.[21] Abstracting implies selecting, picking out, separating, summarizing, deducting, removing, omitting, disengaging, taking away, stripping and implies structurally and semantically the activities characteristic of the nervous system, and so serves as an excellent functional physiological term. On the neurological level, what the nervous system does is abstracting, of which the summarization, integration and so on, are only special aspects. In short, the term *abstracting* is the fundamental one.[22]

. Since the structure of the nervous system is in ordered levels, moreover, and all levels go through the process of abstracting from the other levels it is comparatively easy to accept the term *abstractions of different orders*. The term thus implies a general activity, not only of the nervous system as-a-whole, but even of all living protoplasm. Those characteristic activities of the nervous system,

[19] Northrop, pp. 123-124.   [20] Korzybski, p. 381.   [21] Korzybski, p. 377.
[22] Korzybski, p. 379.

such as summarizing, integrating and the like, are also included by implication. If we unite all the abstractions our nervous system performs under the one term and distinguish between different abstractions by their order we can abandon the older division of physiological abstractions, implying body, and mental abstractions, implying mind. We simply postulate abstractions of different orders.[23]

Abstraction so considered includes not merely the evidence of sense impressions, i.e., changes in nervous tissues, but also the assistance of extra-neural means and higher order abstractions. Our gross macroscopic experience is only a nervous abstraction of some definite order.[24]

The abstractions from events which we call objects are not the same when abstracted by different human beings. For instance, that form of color blindness known as Daltonism implies that an object which appears green to most persons appears red to those who suffer from this disease. Thus Korzybski concludes that the nervous abstractions of all organisms are *individual*, not only in the case of this individual in contrast to another individual man, but at different times for the same individual. Nervous abstractions differ also for these higher groups (abstractions) which we call species. Thus objects for Fido, the dog, are not the same as they are for Smith, the man. Animals have no speech, in the human sense. If we call the verbal labelling of the object *second order abstraction* we may say that animals do not abstract in higher orders.[25] The term *abstractions of higher orders* does not eliminate body or senses although it corresponds roughly to mental processes. The term *first order abstractions* or, what is the same, abstractions of lower order, roughly corresponds to senses or immediate feelings but it does not distinguish between body and mind hence, by implication it does not eliminate mind.[26] To the abstractions of the simplest living cell we ascribe the term *first order*.[27] Only to man do we ascribe abstractions of the higher order. Fido can never be conscious of abstracting, as his nervous system is incapable of being extended by extra-neural means, and this extension is, for Korzybski, a necessary condition for the acquiring of consciousness of abstracting.[28]

[23] Korzybski, p. 380.   [24] Korzybski, pp. 382-383.   [25] Korzybski, pp. 390-392.
[26] Korzybski, p. 380.   [27] Korzybski, p. 391.   [28] Korzybski, p. 409.

Smith can always say something about a statement on record. Neurologically considered, this second statement is the nervous response to the first one which he has seen or heard or even produced by himself. This new statement about the former statement is a new abstraction, which, for Korzybski, is an abstraction of a higher order. This process has no definite limits, for, whenever statements of any order are made, we can always make a statement about them, and so produce an abstraction of still higher order. Here is a fundamental difference between Smith and Fido. Fido's power of abstraction stops somewhere. Not so with Smith; his power of abstraction has no known limits. Thus there is, for Korzybski, a sharp distinction between man and animal. The number of orders of abstraction an animal can produce is limited while the number of orders of abstractions a man can produce is, in principle, unlimited.[29] Fido has no science; for him the object is not an abstraction of some order. Smith not only abstracts in indefinite numbers of different orders, and does it automatically and habitually, but if he inquires he may also become conscious of abstracting.[30]

What should be of interest to the Thomist here is that Korzybski stumbled upon an important differentiation which could have led him to a genuine metaphysics of knowledge. The intellect, as St. Thomas teaches, is spiritual and, thus, distinct in essence from the senses. It was his great achievement (as Professor Gilson has made clear) in that area of metaphysics which we now call *epistemology* to show and insist that, because the human person is an ontologically perfect agent, fully equipped to perform his natural operation of knowing, he has within himself an agent intellect as a constituent part of his nature. This agent intellect permeates the phantasms and actuates the potential intelligibility which is contained in them. The possible intellect, having been impregnated or fecundated by a *species impressa,* vitally produces the concept in and by means of which the content drawn from the phantasm becomes actually an object of intellectual vision.

> The name *intellectus* implies an intimate knowledge; for we say *intelligere* (to understand) as if *intus legere* (to read within). This is abundantly clear to any who consider the difference between intellect and sense, for sense knowledge is concerned

---

[29] Korzybski, pp. 392-394.   [30] Korzybski, p. 409.

with external sensible qualities, whereas intellectual knowledge penetrates to the essence of the thing.[31]

Essences are much more worth knowing than such accidents as the external sensible qualities of a thing but this knowledge must be sought by supra-empirical or meta-empirical means.

All three of the empiricists discussed in this paper belong in the tradition which sets aside the Thomist idea of the generic diversity of the demonstrative sciences, each with its own special degree of intelligibility and abstraction, manifesting the domination of the object over the human mind. Really to know through a demonstrative science is to possess the intellectual virtue which constitutes this demonstrative knowledge in the soul, and the latter then has a superadded perfection which makes it better in a given sphere. Virtues become so much a part of the intellect that they are rightly called second nature, as such, superior in quality to the capacity of the intellect considered in its undeveloped nature. "As a result of the habit of science there inheres an aptness for considering as from the proximate principle of that action."[32] The scientist or the philosopher in possession of the speculative intellectual habit in question finds that this habit creates a proportion between intellect and object. "For the intelligible object and the intellect must be proportioned and belong to one genus, since the intellect and the intelligible objects are on in act."[33]

As Professor Gilson has brought out very clearly in *The Unity of Philosophical Experience,* in the history of human knowledge we find first one, then another of the intellectual virtues, the typical ways of human knowing, endeavoring to prescribe, as it were, its rules and its methods to the whole universe of knowledge. Since Kant there has prevailed the sort of scientific imperialism we find in Hempel, Northrop, and Korzybski. In effect these thinkers are striving for the type of unity of science which would make science completely one with its parts distinguished only as we would distinguish the members of a single organism. They extend a single type of intellection to the whole realm of knowledge. All the disciplines of the human mind are put on the same level of intelligibility and all branches are seeking the same kind of certainty. Scientific

---

[31] *Summa Theologiae* II-II, q. 8, a. 1, c.   [32] *Summa Contra Gentiles* II, 73.

[33] *In duodecim libros Metaphysicorum expositio. Prooemium.* See also *In decem libros Ethicorum expositio* VII, lect. 3, (Pirotta 1344) where St. Thomas speaks of the objects of a demonstrative science becoming, as it were, connatural with the mind of the knower (*fiant ei quasi connaturalia*).

method is to be essentially the same—though varied somewhat in its applications—in all the sciences and it alone is to possess genuine methodological value.

Paradoxically, this effort bothered John Dewey in his later life.. In 1949 he wrote: "What is needed is not the carrying over of procedures that have approved themselves in physical science, but *new* methods as adapted to *human* issues and problems, as methods already in scientific use have shown themselves to be in physical subject matter."[34]

Centuries before, St. Thomas had warned against this mistake of making science generically one by telescoping together its three distinct and hierarchized orders: "They are in error who try to proceed in the same way in these three parts of speculative science."[35] For there is not a common level of abstraction and intelligibility for all the demonstrative sciences but three generic and hierarchically ordered levels: *physical,* mathematical, and metaphysical (each of which is irreducible to any other) grounded on the typical ways in which the abstractive operation of the human mind penetrates beyond appearances enabling it to perceive the inner nature of reality.

Besides these generic orders, grounded on the distinct ways in which the human intellect grasps reality, there are also diversities among sciences within one generic order of abstraction. As a result, a distinctive science has its own principles and uses specific methods of rational procedure which are appropriate to its object but not proportionate to the object of any other specific type of

[34] "Philosophy's Future in Our Scientific Age," *Commentary* VIII (1949), 388-94 note p. 393; italics are Dewey's.

[35] *Expositio super librum Boethii De Trinitate* q. 6, a. 2, c. The translation is from Armand Maurer, C.S.B., *St. Thomas Aquinas: The Division and Methods of the Sciences* (Toronto: Pontifical Institute of Mediaeval Studies, 1953), p. 65. Cf. *Sum. Theol.* I-II, q. 57, a. 6, ad 3m.; "In speculative matters for all matters of inquiry here is but one dialectical science (*dialectica inquisitiva*) whereas demonstrative sciences which pronounce judgment differ according to their different objects." In the works I have studied in this paper there is no specific distinction between the stage (or stages) of inquiry and that of critical judgment of conclusions reached. This, too, is in sharp contrast to the procedure of St. Thomas. True, Professor Northrop distinguishes three stages of inquiry and his epistemic correlation introduces no new element of knowledge: mathematics and formal logic are already there in the third, or deductively formulated theory, state of inquiry. See Northrop, p. 123, ". . . the basic meanings of the concepts constituting the deductively formulated theory . . . are derived from the basic concepts of mathematics and mathematical logic and from the images of the imagination—even the most speculative metaphysical imagination.".

scientific inquiry and critical evaluation. Furthermore each distinct science has its own proper procedure in the sense that it uses its own particular mode of defining. Since, moreover, these specific ways and principles of definition cannot be equal with reference to the degree of certainty they yield, each distinct science can have only that certainty which properly corresponds to the necessities of its proper object.

> As Aristotle says in the *Third Book* of *De Anima,* as things are separable from matter so also as they related to the intellect. For anything is intelligible, inasmuch as it is separable from matter. From this it follows that those things that are by their very nature separate from matter are actually intelligible of themselves: while those things that are abstracted by us from material conditions become actually intelligible through the light of our agent intellect. And since the habits of any power are distinguished in species according to a difference of that which is of itself (*per se*) an object of the power, it necessarily follows that the habits of the sciences, by which the intellect is perfected, are also distinguished according to a difference of separation from matter; and that is why in the *Sixth Book* of the *Metaphysics* Aristotle distinguishes genera of sciences according to diverse mode of separation from matter. For those things which are separate from matter both according to their act of existing (*esse*) and their intelligible constitution (*rationem*) belong to the field of the metaphysician, while those things that are separate according to their constitutive intelligibility but not according to their act of existing belong to the province of the mathematician and those things which involve (*concernunt*) sensible matter in their intelligible constitution belong to the realm of the natural scientist.
>
> And just as the different genera of sciences are distinguished according as things are diversely separable from matter, so also in the case of the single sciences, and especially in the realm of natural science, the parts of the science in question are distinguished according to the differing manner of separation and concretion.[36]

It is manifest that for all three of these empiricists human knowledge includes not merely the evidence of direct sense impres-

---

[36] *In librum De sensu et sensato expositio,* lect. 1 (Pirotta 1-2). See Aristotle, *On the Soul,* iii. 4. 429b21; *Metaphysics* vi. 1. 1026a18. In St. Thomas' day the term *natural scientist* would include natural philosopher.

sions but also involves that evidence provided by sense readings of all those impersonal recording devices. They are, moreover, as concerned with the order and structure of relations between different "kinds" of data as they are with the data from any single source. We might attempt to generalize their approach in the following manner: their approach is one that uses the data derived from sense impressions and physical operations of measurement, corrected by any standard hypothetico-deductive-observational procedure, so that both observations and calculations can be accurately repeated by any competent investigator. It remains true, however, that the conditions of observation and measurement of the object play an essential and necessary part in regard to the very definition of things and the explanation proceeds by means of laws or regularities linking together entities which have meaning only with respect to the determined methods through which the phenomena are observed and measured. Concepts and definitions are resolved into the observable and measurable as such, that is, in the last analysis, in sense readings of measuring instruments upon which a system of signs and symbols (especially mathematical entities) is to be built. The explanatory value of the system thus depends upon the verification of (or at least some of) its conclusions in experience. Any statement has meaning only to the extent that it refers to sense observation and expresses the experimental ways through which it can be verified.[37]

This is somewhat paradoxical since both Northrop and Korzybski lay great stress on the fact that sensed qualities vary from person to person.[38] Korzybski gives the old example of the three pails of water to indicate that, for him, the language of the senses is not very reliable and that we cannot depend on it for general purposes of evalution. Let us, he says, take three pails of water; the first contains water at ten degrees, the second water at thirty degrees and the third one water at fifty degrees centigrade. Let us, then, put our left hand in the first pail and our right hand in the third. If we remove the left hand from the first pail and put it in the second we find the water there reasonably warm. If we withdrew the right hand from

---

[37] See, in this connection, the discussion "Science, Materialism and the Human Spirit" between J. Seelye Bixler, Walter Stace, Jacques Maritain, and Percy Bridgman, under the chairmanship of Dean Everett Baker, in *Mid-Century, The Social Implications of Scientific Progress*, (New York: John Wiley and Sons, 1950), pp. 196-251.

[38] Northrop, pp. 130-131.

the third pail and place it in the second, however, we notice how cold the water is.[39] The paradox lies in the fact that for an empiricist like Northrop, who initially distrusts his senses, reality insofar as it appears to his senses or to instruments that are read with the help of the senses, is the ultimate basis upon which a hypothetico-deductive system of explanatory constructs rests for verification. For Northrop or Hempel a fact is a datum of experience which is verified by specified methods of observation and/or measurement and which is conceptualizable with regard to its use in a coherent explanatory system of observable and/or measurable phenomena. As we noted earlier, any concept would lose its meaning in a field which excludes *a priori* any possibility of verifying its application, that is, of finding out whether such things exist or not, or whether such events occur or not. In the last analysis, then, there is no ontological knowledge in the Thomist sense in which concepts are defined in terms of intelligible being, which, though perceived by the intellect of the philosopher through experiential data, does not depend on any methods of sense verification: "in divine science we should go neither to the imagination nor to the sense."[40]

[39] Korzybski, pp. 372-373.
[40] St. Thomas, *In Boeth. De Trin.* q. 6, a. 2, c. The translation is from Maurer, *op. cit.,* p. 64; for the force of "go to" cf. *ibid.,* p. 60, note 1.

Amicus Amicis *by Etienne Gilson*

☆ ☆ ☆ ☆ ☆ ☆ ☆ ☆ ☆ ☆ ☆ ☆ ☆ ☆

IT IS EMBARRASSING to find oneself thanked by those to whom one feels heavily indebted. At the end of a long career, a professor cannot help but wonder how he ever dared to enter a classroom and to announce his intention to teach philosophy. His best excuse for such youthful audacity was a burning love for wisdom and a fervent desire to impart it to others. And now, after so many years, his memory is crowded with so many nameless faces and faceless names. It is fortunately true that he has been mercifully granted the privilege of turning many a student into a lifelong friend; but there are also not a few whose faces and names have been rubbed away by the passing years. Surprisingly enough, some of these students still survive, in the teacher's memory, under the anonymous form of unanswered, or unanswerable, questions. All in all, whatever justification the professor of philosophy may invoke for his daring, he cannot fail to realize that, without the good will and active co-operation of so many students, his own life would not have been possible. To each and to every one of them, he feels deeply indebted for helping him to become the very man he has been—the man who is still filled with his old question.

What right has any man to teach wisdom, of which he himself has so little? To be sure, philosophy is not wisdom itself, it is only the love of wisdom; but, even so, there is some difficulty in imparting to others the love of something one cannot clearly define for the good reason that one does not possess it. This is an old problem with which St. Augustine already was well acquainted and to which he repeatedly suggested the answer. The first form under which wisdom is accessible to us is quite probably our early love for it. So long as we succeed in keeping this love alive within us, we have something to teach. It is all the more important to know this as, when all is said and done, there always remains in wisdom a residue that cannot properly be taught and the love of which it yet remains the teacher's noblest business to impart to his students. As he himself makes some measure of progress in his own search, the philosopher grows acutely aware of the shortcomings of the *verbum exterius* as an adequate expression of the *verbum interius* in matters of metaphysics. The teacher of wisdom then finds himself with a divided mind. Along with a growing personal longing for silent contemplation, he still experiences an urge to talk in order to lead others to this same state of learned unlearning in which the greatest philosophers have situated the apex of wisdom.

There are other difficulties, not all of which can be blamed on the nature of philosophy. One of them is tied up with the very condition of those whose function in society is to teach philosophy. One may well wonder whether, among the professors of philosophy, a large proportion first felt attracted to this learned profession by an overwhelming desire to teach logic, ethics and metaphysics. What usually happens is that, themselves drawn by the love of wisdom, young men and women make up their minds to devote their whole lives to its study. But *primum vivere, deinde philosophari*. Since they cannot hope to be paid for devoting themselves to the pursuit and contemplation of truth, they fall back on what seems to them to be the best alternative, namely, to make a living by teaching philosophy. Now, to teach philosophy may well be the next best available alternative to the pursuit of wisdom; still, it is not the same thing. The young teacher of philosophy sincerely believes that he has chosen to live the life of a philosopher, whereas, in fact, he soon finds himself living the life of a professor of philosophy. It will not take him many years to realize that one of the main obstacles on the path to philosophy a professor has to overcome is his self-imposed commitment to teach it.

The plight of a modern teacher of philosophy has little in common with what used to be the life of a Greek master of wisdom. In history, we find Socrates, Plato, Aristotle, and their successors surrounded by a small number of disciples, usually free to study philosophy for a great many years under some illustrious master, and usually qualified for this pursuit. With such hearers, a philosopher could indeed content himself with thinking aloud. The master would go first; it was up to his disciples to follow after him as best they could, to learn from him at last the art of finding their own way themselves. Socrates, Plato, and Aristotle never found themselves

at grips with the task of teaching philosophy at the rate of twelve
to twenty hours a week, following an examination program set up
by someone else and about whose questions they themselves had
little or nothing to say.

This is a fundamental difficulty inherent in the modern notion
of a philosophical education. The job of a philosopher is to think,
that of a professor is to teach. To be sure, Thomas Aquinas has
elegantly reconciled these two noble tasks by saying that, as an
action, teaching was but the overflowing of contemplation. But
before it overflows, water must first accumulate. What too often
happens is that, because there is a drought of contemplated truth,
there is an overflowing of words, and, while he is busy keeping the
stream of words flowing, the teacher makes it impossible for more
wisdom to accumulate.

The difficulty is rendered all the greater by the fact that the
teaching of philosophy is now part and parcel of a system of education that is everywhere tending, directly or indirectly, to become
a public service. To put the point more bluntly. Today, the teaching of philosophy is included in the curriculum of countless arts
colleges and universities with the inevitable result that teachers no
longer have the opportunity to introduce a small number of genuinely eager disciples to the mysteries of philosophy; they must push
ever growing numbers of students, with assorted talents, through
the compulsory study of great philosophical questions and do so
in a very short time. The philosophy teacher finds himself reduced
to the condition of an employee hired by a certain institution and
salaried by it to do a certain job.

Such institutions are of many kinds, from the best ones down
to those wherein every one, including the student himself, either
is engaged in some form of business or else is preparing himself
for a future business career. Even in the best ones, a young teacher
of philosophy will have to consider his freely assumed function as
a job to do and, naturally enough, he will want to do it well. Various incentives will invite him to become a successful teacher. In
order to achieve this result our young man or woman will feel
tempted to concentrate less upon philosophy itself than upon the
best way to present it to his students. The guiding thread of his
teaching cannot be this: what is true? Rather it must be this: can
I convey to them some little truth? If I can, *how* can I do this?
Thus arises that constant fear in every professor who really

cares about what he does, of leading his students to believe that
they understand philosophy; although this is a sure way to prevent
them from ever understanding it. Still, there are many times when
he can do little else. For when it is a question of pedagogy versus
philosophy, the philosophy students of a professionally successful
teacher stand a good chance of passing their examinations successfully., Hence, for each of us, the temptation to reduce the stream
of philosophical wisdom to a tiny rivulet. It is our professional
duty to do so, since we have no other choice, and it is to be feared
that, step by step, we shall find it harder and harder to distinguish
wisdom itself from what we have had to make it in order to make
it teachable. And while, admittedly, this is not very good for the
teacher, it is not even in the best interests of his students.

Very few professors of philosophy rebel against the situation.
In the first place, most of them cannot afford to do so, but, even
worse, their very love of wisdom should advise them against rebellion. Should any one of them feel tempted to give up hope, he
would find good advice in the wise words of Emerson: "It is hand-
somer to remain in the establishment, and conduct that in the best
manner, than to make a sally against evil by some single improve-
ment, without supporting it by a total regeneration. Do not be
fain of your one objection. Do you think there is only one?" Emerson was right. At any rate, to regenerate a whole system of education completely is not a philosopher's job. Even if he limited
his effort to the field of philosophical education, the task before him
would still remain concerned with action rather than with contemplation. The only philosophical way to carry a social reforma-
tion is to write a utopia. Plato wrote a good one, but the Aristotelian virtue of prudence advises against any attempt to turn it
into a social reality.

There is, therefore, a great deal to be said in favour of Emerson's
advice, but this does not entail the consequence that there is no
problem. Even if we leave aside the grave question of knowing
how and to whom philosophy can profitably be taught, we still find
ourselves confronted with an urgent personal problem to be solved.
It is: how to be and to remain, *in* the establishment taken exactly
such as it is, *better than* the establishment?

In a remarkable passage of the *Republic*, after investigating the
causes of the disorder then obtaining in the field of philosophical
studies, Plato fell to wondering whether the minds of many men

under thirty were not being corrupted by the teaching of the Sophists. Whereupon he suggested, as a suitable remedy, that if we wish to keep some men fit for the study of the highest parts of philosophy, an important precaution to take is to prevent them from tasting dialectic while they are young (*Republic,* vii. 539ab). Plato here calls dialectic what we now call metaphysics. If there be any truth in his remark, then, since we all have to teach metaphysics to our students, we should do every thing in our power not to teach it in a way that will render them metaphysical cripples for the rest of their lives. Sophistic cleverness is the triumph of reason; metaphysical wisdom is the supreme achievement of intellection. Would it be hard, in introducing students to philosophy, to lay as much stress on the education of the intellect as we usually do on the training of reason? This would go a long way to give the best students a foretaste of what philosophical wisdom truly is and, at the very least, to prevent them from mistaking it for something that apes it but is not it.

There are reasons why a teacher of philosophy should feel tempted to appeal to the reasoning power of his students rather than to their power of intellection. Thomas Aquinas has expressedly maintained that, in man, reason and intellect are the same power. Whether we call it intellect, intelligence, mind, or reason, we are talking about the same thing, namely, the cognitive power of the human soul considered under several different aspects, or as exercising different functions. As intellect, this cognitive power apprehends truth absolutely (*intelligere enim est simpliciter veritatem intelligibilem apprehendere*); as reason, the same power proceeds from one intellection to another (*ratiocinari autem est procedere de uno intellecto ad aliud*). These two operations are necessarily required for human knowledge but they are not equal in dignity and perfection. Angels are such perfect intellectual substances they apprehend intelligible truth directly, without resorting to the discursiveness of what we call reason. In other words, angels are much too intelligent to be rational. Not so with man, whom we call a *rational* animal, precisely because, owing to the imperfection of his cognitive power, he must proceed slowly from one understood truth to another in order to increase his knowledge.

Obviously, these two functions of the same cognitive power are unequal in dignity. Reasoning is motion, intellection is rest; the one is acquisition, the other is possession; more precisely, to reason

consists in proceeding from the immovable understanding of the
first principles, which is its starting point, to the understanding of
the same principles in which it sees the truth of its newly acquired
conclusions. It is enough to reread *Summa Theologiae* I, q. 79, a. 8,
in order to make sure that, in the mind of Thomas Aquinas himself, the discursive use of our cognitive power is typical of the human soul precisely because, of its own nature, it is an inferior kind
of intellect.

There would be no point in attempting to transcend our human condition. Pascal has told us what happens to man when he
pretends to play the angel. Nor would it be good for us to pretend,
that, in its capacity as an intellect, our cognitive power enjoys the
intuition of any pure intelligible. Even our intuition of the first
principles is that of abstract conceptions drawn by the intellect
from sense knowledge. No meditation on the first principles, however deep and protracted it may be, will ever succeed in turning
our abstractive knowledge of them into an intuitive apprehension
of their objects. Such is the justification for our insistence on the
early training of the reasoning power of our students. In man,
reason is the driving power in the acquisition of knowledge. The
human mind must learn how to reason in much the same way as
the human body must learn how to walk.

Still, anybody reading the same article of the *Summa* will likewise observe that the doctrine from which Thomas Aquinas is there
drawing his inspiration comes from Dionysius and Boethius, who
"compared the intellect to eternity, and reason to time." Human
reason draws from sense perception the content of all its concepts,
but it knows them all in the light of the first principles of the intellect, from which reasoning takes its start and to which it returns.
In short, the motion of reason takes place entirely within the light
of intellection. Science busies itself with the concepts of material
things and their ordering according to the exigencies of intellectual
light. The truly prodigious adventure of Einstein's discovery clearly
shows what revolutions in our interpretation of reality the human
reason can achieve simply by reconsidering acquired knowledge
in the light of principles. Metaphysics busies itself with the consideration of the first principles themselves, and of the first causes.
In forming them, the human intellect achieves no intellectual intuition of their content, but it goes straight to that which, in material
reality, participates in the nature of the first causes. Since he is but

a man, even the metaphysician is bound to use the power of reasoning in order to progress in knowledge of his own object; but instead of reasoning from the first principles to the first principles about the nature of things, he reasons from the first principles to the first principles about the first principles, that is ultimately, about being.

The solemn warning issued by Plato, reissued by Aristotle, by Thomas Aquinas, and even by Descartes, essentially means that, unless he applies his mind to this highest of all objects, no man can consider himself as engaged in philosophical speculation at its best. It also means that a truly philosophical formation should not consist in training young minds in the art of running away from principles in order to see how they apply to reality, but, first and foremost, in training young minds to investigate, from the reality known by science, the intelligible content of the first principles. Thirdly, the same warning implies that there is great danger in overstressing the necessary training of reason at the expense of a patient and slow introduction to the practice of intellectual meditation and contemplation. By so doing, we simply substitute in the minds of our students food for talk for food for thought. This wrong training, at the beginning of what should be their first philosophical formation, threatens to make them permanent philosophical cripples. This is what Plato gives us to understand, and to refuse to take his warning seriously is to assume a serious pedagogical responsibility.

As I have more than once said and written, it is not the job of a professor of philosophy to reform the system of education in which he has freely chosen to engage. Moreover, even if something had to be done about it, no one man would be qualified to perform the task, the more so as there probably are many different ways of doing it well. Still, given the present programs of philosophy in use in many colleges and universities, and accepting them such as they are, it should not appear impossible to inculcate into our students a proper feeling for the respective importance of intellectual insight and of rational virtuosity. In dealing with our students, and still more in rating them, let us remember that there once was a student whose nickname was the "dumb ox." Better ones will never be easy to find.

As concerns the teacher himself, the safest protection against the invasion of pedagogical rust is to remember constantly why, and in what spirit, he first resolved to become a teacher of philosophy.

At that time, what he actually wanted was the opportunity to remain permanently in close contact with what he then rightly considered the noblest and most honorable of the purely human call-
ings. Not only for our own sake, but for the sake of our students
as well, we must strive to keep alive within us the true lovers of
wisdom we must have been at the time when we first undertook to
lead other men toward it. This is best achieved by never allowing
our teaching activity to become a complete substitute for our philosophical speculation. It is a good thing to think in view of knowing
what one is going to teach; but there is something still better. The
true philosopher, says Plato, is a man that seeks after truth with all
his might and in all possible ways, τοῦ γνῶναι χάριν: for the sake
of knowing it (*Republic*, vi. 499a).

Unless he reserves in himself at least a small corner for purely
disinterested speculation, a professor of philosophy will soon cease
to be a philosopher. He even will cease to be truly a professor of
philosophy, since there will be left in him no philosophy that he
can teach. What then remains is what Socrates and Plato used to
call a sophist. For, indeed, it is most natural that lovers of wisdom
should sometimes speak or write, but, on the whole, the true life
of philosophy is a silent one. Its stream flows for a long time before
it overflows. The true dignity of those whose social function is to
teach philosophy is measured exactly by their success in keeping
alive within themselves the love of sapiential truth pursued for its
own sake. This, according to Plato, is philosophy itself.

Thus actively and creatively to perpetuate sapiential truth is a
function that every teacher of philosophy necessarily assumes in
his own country. But those among us who have been privileged to
share in the life of American institutions of learning are well aware
of the great honor that has been ours. Whatever else we may have
done, or failed to do, men such as ourselves have been in a position
to take part, however modestly, in a collective undertaking whose
outcome is of decisive importance for the future of the western
world.

No man knows what this future will be, but one may safely assert that the destiny of western civilization has today become the
common business of both Europe and America. The fall of ancient
Greece and ancient Rome should suffice to warn Europeans against
the illusion that the destiny of philosophical wisdom is necessarily
tied up with the survival of the social bodies and of the political

entities within which such wisdom arose. The realization that it is not so must have entered into the motives that impelled some European teachers to carry on their activities beyond the frontiers of their own countries. If the common good of the city is better than that of any private citizen, the common good of many nations should likewise be considered more noble than that of any nation, however noble and worthy of love this particular nation may happen to be. This is still more true of the wisdom of the Church which is not merely the good of any single nation, nor of any particular family of nations, but of all the nations of the earth.

The truly heroic courage of so many young men and women, who, year after year, freely decide to dedicate themselves to the pursuit and teaching of sapiential truth on the very continent where, for the good of mankind, it is most urgent that the survival of wisdom should be insured, is an inspiring example for those who have witnessed it. As for those to whom it has been given to share in this most noble undertaking, they cannot fail to realize that this opportunity has been the greatest honor of their lives. After so often expressing to them his sympathy and his affection, how could an old teacher not avail himself of this unique opportunity to extend to those who once were his students and are now his colleagues, his heartfelt wishes for a happy continuation of their journey to the land of their heart's desire? *Adsit Dominus supplicationibus nostris: et viam famulorum suorum in salutis suae prosperitate disponat; ut inter omnes vitae hujus varietates suo semper protegantur auxilio.*

DATE DUE

THREE DAY		
DEC 4 '65		
DEC 10 '65		
DEC 13 '65		
FE17 '66		
MY7 '66		
MY9 '66		
MY12 '66		
MY20 '66		
JA20 '67		
SE19 '68		
GAYLORD		PRINTED IN U.S.A.

CPSIA information can be obtained
at www.ICGtesting.com
Printed in the USA
BVHW052316130223
658471BV00002B/82